The Soviet Economic Experiment

The Soviet
Economic Experiment

JAMES R. MILLAR

Edited and with an Introduction by
SUSAN J. LINZ

UNIVERSITY OF ILLINOIS PRESS
Urbana and Chicago

Library of Congress Cataloging-in-Publication Data

Millar, James R., 1936-
    The Soviet economic experiment / James R. Millar ; edited and with
an introduction by Susan J. Linz.
        p.   cm.
    Includes index.
        ISBN 0-252-01657-2 (cloth : alk. paper).   ISBN 0-252-06088-1 (paper :
alk. paper).
        1. Soviet Union—Economic conditions—1918- 2. Soviet Union—
Economic policy—1917- I. Linz, Susan J.   II. Title.
HC335.M495   1990
330.947'084—dc20   89-31777
                                                                         CIP

In memory of Leo S. Millar

Contents

Introduction

Since the inception of the Soviet economic experiment in central planning over a half-century ago, the USSR has recorded impressive economic achievements. Most notable has been the speed with which the relatively backward, predominantly agricultural economy has been transformed into an industrialized economy. By devoting a large share of resources to defense, the Soviets also have been able to achieve military parity (in some areas, superiority) with the United States and Western Europe, and they did so utilizing an economic base that even now is only approximately half that of the United States.

After more than two decades of steady progress, however, the Soviet economic experiment has entered an era of increasingly difficult challenges: the exhaustion of accessible and easily exploitable deposits of raw materials and, hence, growing recovery costs and transportation hauls; the inconvenient location of available labor supplies; a growing defense burden; high investment outlays without corresponding increases in output, especially in agriculture, the anticipated decline of oil available for export to hard-currency nations and the concomitant effect on Soviet trade with Western nations; the disincentive effect of persistent shortages of consumer goods; and a slowdown in the growth of a quality work force, as measured by years of education.

Each of these factors has contributed to an abatement in output growth in the USSR. Three bad harvests, rising costs of obtaining and using natural resources, and declining capital and labor productivity in the 1970s combined to cause the output growth rate to fall to its lowest peacetime level (less than 1 percent in 1979). The ability of Soviet leaders to redesign the experiment in order to reverse this trend has been constrained by a number of factors, including poor agricultural performance, rising consumer demands, a mismatch of energy supply and demand, labor shortages, barriers to technological advance, a rising defense burden, and foreign trade deficits.

These same factors no doubt will continue to constrain Mikhail Gorbachev's efforts to offset declining growth in the near future.

The essays collected in this volume examine many of these factors and are, in large part, a consequence of the effort to better understand how the Soviet economic bureaucracy works and how individuals work the Soviet economic bureacracy. Written as many as two decades ago, they are reprinted here to bring a broader perspective to the nature and scope of the issues that confront Soviet leaders than one might gain from volumes that focus exclusively on current domestic or foreign policy issues or on recent reform efforts. Largely nontechnical in nature, these essays present an interdisciplinary and multidisciplinary view of the Soviet economic experiment.

Part 1 focuses on the role of agriculture in the Soviet economic experiment. Agriculture has been called the Achilles' heel of the Soviet economy because of the relatively unfavorable and highly variable climate but also because of the backward social and inefficient economic organization of the rural sector. Soviet leaders know that bad weather alone is not responsible for the poor performance of agriculture. In past decades, for example, they emphasized regional self-sufficiency over regional specialization by setting plan targets that necessitated the production of a wide assortment of farm products regardless of climate, thus effectively reducing the efficiency of farm production. The predominance of unskilled farm labor, the lack of fertilizer, pesticides, and other inputs, and waste arising from transport and storage difficulties (which, Soviet sources estimate, annually claim over 25 percent of the harvest) also contribute to poor performance.

Despite such knowledge, this aspect of the Soviet economic experiment has remained unchanged for over five decades. So far the official response to agricultural problems has been limited to minor administrative and policy changes aimed at improving production while keeping management centralized. Why? The essays in part 1 go a long way toward explaining how and why agriculture has been consistently exploited during Soviet development. Specifically, chapter 1 lays the foundation for an appreciation of the nature and scope of decision making by Russian peasants, an appreciation apparently not shared by Bolsheviks in the 1920s and 1930s. Based on empirical data from post-1861 European Russia, A. V. Chayanov formulated a theoretical model to account for what he believed to be irreconcilable discrepancies between the observed behavior of the bulk of peasant farms and profit-maximizing behavior. The most significant discrepancy is found in the greater work effort and marketings under deteriorating price conditions. In Chayanov's view, increasing work effort during bad times and decreasing work effort during good times was not consistent with profit-maximizing behavior. James Millar reevaluates the characteristics of peasant farms to demonstrate why such behavior is rational. Had Soviet leaders not been "city boys," had they better understood the peasantry, policies adopted in the late 1920s and early 1930s to exploit agriculture by forcibly extracting the "surplus" would no doubt have been drastically different.

In chapter 2 Millar analyzes parallels in the theoretical concepts underlying the transformation from feudalism to capitalism and from capitalism to socialism. For Marx, primitive capitalist accumulation was a means to establish the institutions, or relations of production, necessary for the existence of capitalism. Primitive capitalist accumulation forced peasants into labor contracts and created a "surplus" in the form of unpaid wages that went to the capitalists. Preobrazhensky's concept of primitive socialist accumulation provided the theoretical basis for establishing the necessary conditions to ensure socialist institutions. Primitive socialist accumulation meant that the socialist state could intercept *both* the surplus created in the private sector that would otherwise go to the capitalist (through "nonequivalent exchange" policies that imposed a tax on the peasantry) and the surplus arising from the self-exploitation of workers in the industrial sector. Under this scenario, the socialist sector would grow faster than the capitalist sector, although Preobrazhensky did not present the concept of primitive socialist accumulation in the context of unbalanced growth.

One of the most compelling questions addressed in part 1 is where the resources came from for the Soviet rapid industrialization drive in the 1930s. In chapter 3 Millar addresses two issues that provide the key to understanding the economic development process in the USSR. The first involves the notion of an "agricultural surplus" and the extent to which it can be uniquely identified—by technological or biological limits, or by geographical boundaries or census definitions. The second involves the role of agriculture in the Soviet development campaign and the extent to which the agricultural sector contributed resources during the early stages of the industrialization process. This chapter more fully develops the theme introduced in chapter 1, that Soviet agricultural policy in support of rapid industrialization was founded on an incorrect analysis of peasant economic behavior, and suggests that mass collectivization of agriculture was introduced for noneconomic reasons or as a consequence of inappropriate statistical information. Thus it begins to lay the foundation for understanding the Soviet economic experiment. Had this foundation been understood in the 1940s, 1950s, or even 1960s, it may not only have altered policies adopted in the USSR after Stalin's death but also efforts to introduce the Soviet economic experiment in other countries.

Chapter 4 uses official Soviet sources to demonstrate unequivocally that agriculture was a *net recipient* of resources between 1928 and 1932. In this chapter Millar first summarizes the standard story of the Soviet rapid development drive: the "extraction" of a surplus from agriculture, which permitted rapid industrialization, and the collectivization of agriculture, which permitted a greater contribution of agricultural output than would have been possible under voluntary arrangements. Using Barsov's data he constructs several alternative measures of the contribution of agriculture during the First Five-Year Plan. Each of the measures substantiates Barsov's conclusion that the contribution of agriculture to rapid industrialization between 1928 and 1932 was overstated. Reasons for overstating the role of collectivized agriculture and the centralized agricultural procurement system as components of Soviet development strategy are evaluated, and for the first time in either Soviet or Western literature the mass collectivization of Soviet agriculture is shown to be an unmitigated economic policy disaster.

Mass collectivization, emerging as an official policy in 1929 in response to a grain procurement crisis in 1928, was essentially complete by 1934. During this time agricultural output stagnated both quantitatively and qualitatively. Millar's analysis examines the basic economic and political questions and issues raised by the New Economic Policy (NEP) in the 1920s and, more important, how these issues were conceived by Stalin and others. What were the links between rapid industrialization, the decision to abandon the NEP, and the collectivization of agriculture? To what extent was collectivization a component of Stalin's bid for power? Was mass collectivization a conscious policy?

Whether collectivization was really necessary is the topic of the debate with Alec Nove that is presented in chapter 5. Both participants provide persuasive arguments regarding the role of collectivized agriculture in the Soviet rapid industrialization drive. The final chapter of part 1 then examines Soviet agriculture from a historical and world perspective.

With the recent campaign for *glasnost'*, or "openness" in discussions of conflicts or problems in contemporary Soviet society, agriculture in general and the mass collectivization of agriculture in particular have been prominent in literary works and newspaper articles. Although no official research has yet disputed the Stalinist concept of collectivization, frank descriptions of the excesses of "dekulakization," the negative effects of collectivization on agriculture, and the demoralization of the peasantry during collectivization (which Aleksandr Solzhenitsyn suggests is responsible for the collaboration of some peasants with German invaders in 1941) have been published in recent years. The horrors of Stalin's collectivization drive are recalled, for example, in the poet Evegnii Evtushenko's address to the Sixth Congress of Writers of the RSFSR, even though the Soviet press's version of the speech omitted some of the more pointed remarks. Vladimir Shubkin writes in *Znamya* that collectivization can be viewed as direct violence to crush the peasantry. By all accounts the dramatic experiment to reorganize Soviet agriculture failed: one-third of the capital stock in agriculture was destroyed, agricultural output fell, and the cost of obtaining agricultural output rose. Collectivization was also "successful" at putting an end to peasant private enterprise, reducing the role of money in economic transactions, and underscoring the emphasis by Soviet leaders on heavy industry. These legacies continue to hamper agricultural performance to this day.

Whereas part 1 focuses on where the real resources came from to permit the continuation of the Soviet economic experiment, part 2 deals with the financial resources. The role of bonds as a device for raising funds from the Soviet population during the rapid industrialization drive, World War II, and the period of postwar reconstruction is highlighted in chapter 7, which provides the foundation for further analysis of the use of mass subscription and state lottery bonds in the USSR and the reasons underlying a preference for lottery bonds. Chapter 8 uses the state budget to analyze how the Soviets financed the Great Patriotic War, tracing not only the impact of the war cost but the structural changes in the economy that World War II necessitated. The fundamental ambivalence of Soviet financial policy is highlighted in chapter 9, wherein the preference of Soviet authorities to minimize and control the discretionary dimensions of money is underscored. Such financial conservatism has inhibited development of the Soviet economic experiment, especially in agriculture and despite numerous reform efforts.

Soviet history is replete with abrupt, traumatic changes in social and economic conditions: revolution, civil war, collectivization, purges, rapid industrialization, World War II, postwar reconstruction, economic reforms, and bureaucratic reorganization. Yet the Soviet economic experiment has remained largely unchanged. Why? Part 3 focuses on central management and the emergence of acquisitive socialism in the USSR. Chapter 10 offers an economic overview that traces the principal strucural and performance changes that have taken place in the Soviet economy since Stalin's death in 1953. As such it highlights factors that promote and factors that constrain change in the Soviet economic experiment. Millar also spells out the economic alternatives facing Soviet leaders in the 1980s and the extent to which they are shaped by a growing defense burden, labor shortages, trade deficits, barriers to technological advance, rising energy costs, and increasingly costly relationships with East European countries, Afghanistan, and China. Countering these domestic and international challenges is the size and overall strength of the Soviet economy, the skills of the Soviet population, the richness of natural resources, and the demonstrated ability of the Soviet leadership to establish the priorities that generate desired outcomes: a victory in World War II, military parity with the United States, doubling the standard of living in the USSR, and continued economic growth, albeit slower than desired. This is the environment with which Gorbachev must deal when he proposes a radical restructuring of Soviet society.

How receptive will the Soviet people be to efforts to redesign the economic experiment? Part 3 includes essays that were the first in a now growing wave of essays that examine the Soviet economic experiment from the household's rather than the leadership's perspective. In chapter 11 Millar investigates the consequences of persistent shortages of consumer goods on the quantity and quality of labor, a pressing issue for Soviet leaders for the past two decades. In chapters 12 and 13 he describes in some detail one of the more salient features of Soviet society: *nalevo* transactions and the reciprocity system as a means for organizing economic activity. (*Nalevo* activities are those occurring "on the left," or beyond the realm of legality. Reciprocity systems are founded on a network of mutual exchange, although without any contractual or legally negotiable claims.) These two chapters show how the structure and functioning of the Soviet economic experiment, which generates persistent shortages of consumer goods and endless queuing, reinforce the benefits of *nalevo* activities and the reciprocity system.

Chapter 14 reports the results of a mass survey of recent emigrants, highlighting the degree of relative satisfaction of contemporary Soviet consumers. Three-hour interviews with some 3,000 former Soviet citizens provide a wealth of data on the quantity and quality of housing, the availability of consumer goods, occupational prestige, health care facilities, differential earnings of men and women, and a whole range of other economic, political, and social variables. With data from this living archive, propects for the reform of Soviet society can be evaluated from the perspective of how willing the Soviet people will be to go along with proposed changes in the economic experiment.

The Soviet economic experiment has been under close scrutiny for over seven decades. Despite periodic efforts at redesign, much of the original experiment has remained intact. Soviet leaders are once again attempting to redesign the experiment, perhaps on a grander scale than ever before, and it appears that the current efforts are, for the first time, addressing the very foundations of the experiment itself. While it may seem rather presumptuous to collect the work of such a young scholar in the field of Soviet studies, these timely essays penetrate the basic issues underlying the Soviet economic experiment. That they address the same issues Soviet scholars are addressing now that they have, under the policy of *glasnost'*, more discretion in selecting (and publishing) their research attests to the durability of Millar's work.

The essays collected in this volume span the major theoretical and policy issues that have confronted all Soviet leaders. That they have withstood the test of time comes as much from the fact that each offers either a unique analytic framework or unique data which has proven crucial for advancing our understanding of Soviet society. Although the focus is primarily economic, political and social dimensions are explored in nearly every chapter. Consequently, the reader profits from the breadth and depth of knowledge of an established scholar of the Soviet economic experiment.

—SUSAN J. LINZ

Acknowledgments

I would like to thank Mark Swords for his yeoman assistance both in preparing the manuscript and in compiling the index. Special thanks also go to Sheila Roberts and Christine Esckilsen for handling many of the final details, and to Theresa Sears for her care in shepherding the manuscript through the production process.

PART 1

Development as Exploitation:
The Case of Soviet Agriculture

1

A Reformulation of A. V. Chayanov's Theory of the Peasant Economy

1

This essay suggests an alternative theoretical vehicle for the data and generalizations presented by A. V. Chayanov in his recently translated *Peasant Farm Organization* (1925):[1] a reformation which nevertheless retains the spirit of Chayanov's efforts.

Students of economic development, economic anthropology, and the economic history of Russia and the Soviet Union will find Chayanov's careful, systematic description of peasant economic behavior, synthesizing as it does a wealth of empirical data drawn largely from post-Emancipation European Russia, excitingly relevant to a number of contemporary concerns and problems. However, his attempt to formulate a unique theoretical model to account for what he believed were irreconcilable discrepancies between the observed behavior of the bulk of peasant farms and the profit-maximizing canons of either Marxist or neoclassical doctrines is much less successfully executed and of dubious merit.

2

Chayanov's analysis of the peasant economy is founded upon four major empirical findings. First, investigation showed that the bulk of peasant farms were strictly (extended) family operations. In Chayanov's terminology, the "family labor farm," which employed no, or very occasionally, nonfamily labor, was the typical form of peasant enterprise. Second, the intensity of family labor application (i.e., working days per year per family member) was found to be directly related to the ratio of consumers to workers in the family (measured in adult male equivalents) and, within broad limits, in-

From *Economic Development and Cultural Change* 18, no. 2 (January 1970):219–29. Reprinted by permission, with minor editorial changes.

versely related to real hourly earnings. Third, economic differentiation among the peasantry, particularly by farm size, was more a measure of relative family size and composition than of differential economic success, that is, farm size tended to follow a cycle coincident with the peasant family life cycle, increasing as family members matured into workers and declining as the family aged and disintegrated with the formation of new families. Economic stratification due to these causes Chayanov called "demographic differentiation," to distinguish it from differentiation attributable to a persistent and cumulative process of petty capitalist accumulation with which it was usually confounded by Marxists and neoclassicists alike. Fourth, the evidence indicated that the family labor farm could survive, and in some cases prevail, in competition with commercial farm enterprises.

In Chayanov's view these four characteristics were inconsistent with the hypothesis that peasants manage their farms so as to maximize profits, that is, as rational petty capitalists. He thought that he had found the theoretical key to the peculiarities of peasant economic activity in the fact that the family labor farm did not contract wage payments with its own members. Instead, the family as a whole was a residual claimant to the farm's proceeds. Since wages were indeterminant, he argued, so too must be profits and economic rent (where the family worked its own land). On the premise that the family could not maximize what it could not measure, Chayanov reasoned that the absence of these capitalist categories precluded profit as the motivation and guide to peasant economic behavior. Unlike capitalist enterprise, the peasant family worked for a living, not for profit. The spur to peasant economic activity was "the motivation of the worker on a peculiar piece-rate system which allows him alone to determine the time and intensity of his work" (p. 42).[2] Chayanov's theory of the peasant economy is simply the formal expression of this conception in what are essentially neoclassical terms: equilibrium of the family labor farm is depicted as the outcome of a subjective balancing of a marginal increment in family consumption against a marginal change in the "drudgery" of family labor application. The degree of "self-exploitation" of family labor was determined, therefore, not by capitalist criteria but by a hedonic calculus.

In Soviet Russia of the 1920s, Chayanov's theory presented a direct challenge to and an unmistakable contradiction of the accepted Marxist conception of the peasantry, and it raised a doctrinal dispute with immediate policy consequences. If, as Chayanov alleged, the mass of peasant farms were not incipient capitalist enterprises, then the peasant economy could not be fitted into Marx's general evolutionary scheme as an antecedent stage of capitalist development. On the contrary, Chayanov's theory lent support to the worst kind of heresy: that the peasantry might have both social justification and the economic capability to coexist with socialism as it had done with capitalism. If so, the peasantry formed an economic category in and of itself. That Soviet Marxists found Chayanov's theory of the peasant economy static, apologetic, and subjective is no surprise.

However, if Chayanov was not an orthodox Marxist, neither was he a consistent neoclassicist. First, the premise supporting his deductive case against profit maximization as a peasant motive — that the peasant family could not maximize what it could not measure — is meaningless on neoclassical grounds. The absence of the wage contract and the residual determination of wages may preclude wages and profits as social categories in the Marxian sense, but they do not rule out profit-maximizing behavior in the neoclassical conception. As long as each separate exercise of economic discretion is guided by a rational comparison of the differential gain and cost attributable to the particular unit of business at stake, the enterprise will attain maximum profits (minimum losses) regardless of whether total period profits (losses) are actually computed or even computable. Accounting procedures certainly may improve the accuracy and consistency of enterprise decisions, but they are not logically necessary for profit maximization to occur. Chayanov's theoretical, or deductive, case against profit maximization as a possible determinant of peasant behavior is, therefore, insubstantial. Second, the alternative theory that Chayanov proposes, if modernized by substituting for the disutility-of-labor approach the conception of family leisure as a want-satisfying alternative output of the farm, may readily be incorporated under the contemporary theory of household behavior. However, it is not true, as Chayanov apparently presumed, that utility and profits necessarily represent alternative and mutually incompatible guides to the exercise of economic discretion. The doctrinal controversy, in which Chayanov was engaged essentially as a partisan of the peasantry, made it desirable to distinguish unambiguously the peasant and the capitalist farmer. Unfortunately, Chayanov's theoretical attempt to do so resulted in the translation of the whole of his empirical findings into purely subjective terms — utility-disutility comparisons — and his explanations of peasant decisions, whether regarding investment, land purchase or work intensity became, consequently, little more than rationalizations with no predictive power whatever.

There are two kinds of discrepancy, and thus two standards of comparison, implicit in Chayanov's argument differentiating the peasant economy from the capitalist. First, Chayanov is certainly correct in asserting that the observed behavior of the family labor farm was inconsistent with the tenets of the neoclassical (or Marxist) theory of the firm, and in this context one of the main discrepancies was most certainly that the family labor farm did not maximize profits in the sense of pushing output to the point at which marginal cost was equated with marginal revenue. The question involved in this comparison has to do with the appropriateness of the theoretical model to the facts in hand. The second kind of discrepancy, however, has to do with differences between the observed behavior of the family labor farm and the actual behavior of commercial farm enterprises. Chayanov apparently assumed that this second kind of discrepancy was a consequence of the first, but this is probably wrong and certainly unnecessary. It is in this context, however, that his emphasis upon the presence or absence of the wage contract and his division of agricultural enterprises into those employing hired labor and those that did not are crucial; for, to the one, labor costs are variable and avoidable, while, to the family, labor represents an unavoidable overhead cost. Thus, quite apart from the doctrinal dispute in which he was engaged, Chayanov's emphasis upon the presence or absence of the profit motive was misplaced, for he assumed that the prescriptive standard of the neoclassical model could be taken as a reasonably accurate description of commercial farm behavior, that is, one that was comparable with his description of peasant farm behavior.

It will be maintained in the argument that follows that the peculiar features distinguishing the family labor farm from the commercial farm do not turn on the question of profit maximization but, instead, stem from differences in the shape and behavior of their respective costs. Most, if not all, of the peculiarities of peasant economic behavior may be derived from the fact that its labor force was, according to Chayanov's evidence, fixed (i.e., determined by exogenous, noneconomic factors) and its labor bill, consequently, both unavoidable and predominantly invariant to changes in the level and composition of the farm's output.[3]

3

If we grant the indivisible integrity of the family labor farm as a consumption and labor unit, as Chayanov suggests, then it will be seen that the peculiar characteristics of peasant farm organization largely result from the fact that labor presents itself as an overhead rather than as a variable cost. That decision concerning the proportions of inputs, the level and assortment of output, sideline activities, and so on, would differ substantially from those taken by an enterprise for which labor is predominantly a variable cost is quite obvious and proper, even if both seek to maximize profits. Furthermore, since the peasant family could not avoid these costs even by shutting down the farm altogether, the tenacity of the family labor farm in competition with commercial establishments employing hired labor is explicable, provided that the family had no competing alternative outlets for its labor, or that these alternatives were either physically or culturally remote.

Treating the family's labor cost as predominantly overhead also makes understandable the discovery that peasants were prepared and able to outbid capitalists for land and that, frequently, the poorer the peasant family, the higher the purchase or rental price it would pay. An increment in sown area, permitting a more optimal utilization of the family's fixed stock of labor, would be worth more to the peasant family than to an enterprise that must include the additional labor costs for working it in the total differential cost of the projected expansion. Given the remoteness of alternative employments, the more land-poor the peasant family, the greater the land cost it would be able to absorb.

The particularities of capital investment decisions of peasant families, as described by Chayanov, are largely related to the fact that field work poses a "peak load" problem. Given the size of the family's own labor resources, labor requirements of the peak season determine the maximum feasible size of the farm as a production unit. It follows that, although receptive to capital innovations that reduced peak season labor requirements, the family labor farm would show little interest in the saving of labor during off-peak periods of the year, unless the labor so economized could readily find alternative employment. We have in this approach a simple and straightforward explanation to substitute for Chayanov's almost unintelligible, inconsistent, and subjective interpretation of capital investment decisions on the family labor farm (chap. 5). Chayanov cites, as cases peculiar to the family labor farm, the difficulties that were encountered in attempting to introduce threshing machines "in areas where there are no crafts and trades in winter and, apart from threshing, nothing else with which the population can occupy itself. . . . Since these hands can find no other work to do, this does not increase peasant family income by a kopek. The cost of the thresher, though, is a considerable deduction from the meager peasant budget" (pp. 211–12). The converse is seen in the case involving small farms in the southeast of Russia (pp. 212–13), which introduced harvesting machines to compensate for a short harvest season that did not permit the family to reap as much as it could sow and cultivate, even though the effect was to reduce the return per unit of family labor time expended. However, the increased intensity of labor application, spread more evenly over the year, yielded a larger total family net income than was otherwise possible because the harvester expanded the sown area one family could work. These two cases are fully consistent with our approach.

Chayanov demonstrated that the intensity of family labor application, for example, working days per year per family member, was a function of the ratio of consumers to workers ($c : w$) in the peasant family (in adult male equivalents). Other things being equal, the higher the ratio, the greater the labor expenditure per family worker and, conversely, regardless of the fact that the real wage per unit of labor expenditure ordinarily moved inversely with labor intensity. Thus, changes in family composition may be classed as favorable or unfavorable much in the same fashion as changes in the family's economic environment, for example, a change in the terms of trade. Chayanov considered it peculiar that the family generally reacted to unfavorable changes with an increased expenditure of family labor and to favorable changes with decreases in family labor expenditure. It is quite clear that such behavior is inconsistent with strict profit maximization, on the one hand, and with the behavior that might be expected of a farm enterprise that relied predominantly upon hired labor, on the other; and the behavior of labor costs provides an important insight into both of these discrepancies.

Where the alternative is involuntary idleness, the differential cost (opportunity cost) of labor is negligible, whether one works for another or is self-employed. The same proposition holds for a family enterprise, such as the family labor farm, given the integrity of the family, that is, given that economic support is not contingent upon, or a function of, labor effort. Thus, for the family labor farm, the only costs that varied significantly with the expenditure of family labor were the alternative costs of other employments available to family members. Therefore, if alternative income opportunities were nonexistent or remote, whether for reasons of low remuneration, costs connected with their location and exploitation, or because of cultural and legal bars, the only cost that might have varied with family labor application would have been the cost of giving up leisure (within the limits of permanent physiological damage).

As Chayanov somewhat dimly perceived, it was only by assigning a cost to family labor expenditure per se, for example, disutility, that the family's responses to either adverse or favorable changes in its economic environment might be accounted for in rational terms. For the fact that the family could respond to an adverse change with an increase in labor intensity is proof that, prior to the change, the family had foregone a utilization of family labor that would have more than paid its own way *in pecuniary terms,* that is, that there had existed idle family work capacity. From the standpoint of overhead costs, the elastic character of the family's work capacity makes it impossible to assign, or trace, the added costs of additional family effort. The fundamental problem is that the family has unused productive capacity, the utilization of which "costs" only the alternative "nonproductive" activities that must be foregone, and these are costs for which it is often extremely difficult or impossible to assign pecuniary evaluations.[4]

Unlike the family labor farm, a commercial farm enterprise relying upon hired, nonfamily labor can respond to an adverse change in its nonlabor costs and/or its product prices by laying off workers. By reducing its output, such an enterprise can avoid a portion of its labor costs. This is the analytic significance of the wage contract and hired labor: the conversion of what are overhead costs for the worker into direct, avoidable costs to the employer. The family labor farm could have obtained no such cost reduction by decreasing output. And, if the differential cost of family labor was negligible, then it is not at all unlikely that its response to an adverse change would be an increase in the intensity of family labor application, especially if there existed any conventional notion of a minimum acceptable standard of living, or if the previous level of living exerted any continuing influence.[5]

Responses of the family labor farm to changes in its economic environment had important policy implications in the Soviet Union at the time Chayanov published his monograph, and they have quite general significance today in the many fields concerned with economic development in predominantly peasant economies. From the analysis above, it is clear that the response of the family labor farm to a general deterioration in its terms of trade is likely to be, as Chayanov indeed found it to be, an increase in the intensity of family labor application, for there are virtually no costs that might be avoided by acting otherwise.

It has sometimes been assumed that the peasantry might respond to a general deterioration in its terms of trade with other sectors by reverting to "subsistence," thereby avoiding some portion of the impact of this adverse change in circumstances. However, Chayanov's careful examination of peasant budgets makes clear why this is not likely to be the case, for the assumption predicates two misconceptions about the peasant farm. First the budget studies (see especially pp. 118–26) show that "subsistence" did not mean the same thing as complete self-sufficiency, at least in European Russia. The subsistence farm family budget contains necessary expenditure items for which the production of substitutes on the family labor farm would be impossible or highly unlikely, for example, salt, condiments, sugar, milling services, spiritual needs. Moreover, it would be virtually impossible for a single family farm to produce in the necessary quantities a sufficiently diversified output even of those items in which self-sufficiency is technically feasible, and especially to do so year in and year out. According to Chayanov, even in the "most obscure, nonmonetary corners of the country," money disbursements, in 1910, averaged 22 percent of total family consumption expenditures (pp. 121–23). Even more interesting perhaps, these budget studies reveal that the subsistence farm entered the market for as many or more separate items and sold a much more diversified output on the market than the more monetized farm. The principal difference in the market behavior of subsistence and monetized farms is to be found not in the number of market transactions in which they engaged but in the total volume of products transacted. Reverting to subsistence would not mean, therefore, leaving the market altogether but simply a diminution in the volume of marketings.

Second, Chayanov shows that as the family labor farm moves away from subsistence and enters the market in greater volume it simplifies its production plan by eliminating from production those items that are less advantageous to produce, and "only that which *either gives a high labor payment or is an irreplaceable production element for technical reasons* remains in the organizational plan" (p. 126). Therefore, although an adverse change in relative market prices could be avoided or minimized by resuming production for own use those products affected, reversion to subsistence does not provide a means by which the monetized farm could evade a *general* deterioration in its terms of trade.

Thus, withdrawing from the market was not a feasible course of action for the subsistence farm, and reverting to subsistence did not provide a costless alternative to the monetized farm in the face of a general adverse change in the terms of trade. The response to be expected for both types of farm is, in the absence of alternative employment opportunities, an increase in the intensity of family labor application. It is reasonable to suppose a similar response to the imposition of a quit-rent, poll tax, redemption payment, or other general and unavoidable charge on the peasant household. It is important to note in this connection that the family labor farm's response to an adverse change, whether in family composition, fixed money charges, or the terms of trade, did frequently occasion a change in the assortment of farm output toward more labor-intensive, higher-value products in the face of constant relative prices, as the family attempted to compensate with an increased labor effort.

In this light, it is not difficult to understand how the family labor farm might prevail in competition with "capitalist" commercial farms during hard times. At best, the commercial farmer could close out his farm altogether in favor of an alternative line of endeavor, while, at worst, he could simply lay off his hired workers and convert his enterprise into a family labor farm. The survival value of the family labor farm in hard times, then, rests on the family having no alternative but to stick it out to the end.

The implication is what one might expect: that it takes a combination of hard times and relatively lucrative alternative (e.g., industrial) employment possibilities to destroy the peasant economy. Neither by itself is sufficient. Of course, what is immediately destroyed thereby is not the integrity of the peasant family—as remittances to the village in Russia verify—but its sole or predominant reliance upon agricultural and other home industries, although geographical separation may eventually undermine the unity of the peasant family as well.

If the survival value of the family labor farm under conditions of prolonged adversity can be readily explained in terms of the behavior of costs, Chayanov's data permit only a highly tentative explanation of the persistence of demographic, as opposed to economic, differentiation in more prosperous times. There are two questions involving the use of hired labor. First why was permanent or year-round hired labor so rare? Second, was temporary or seasonal labor employment infrequent—and, if so, why?

With regard to permanent or long-term employment of non-family labor, a number of explanations are possible. The most simple, perhaps, is that times of general prosperity were sufficiently infrequent and short-lived to preclude significant economic differentiation in European Russia during the period subjected to study. It is likely that this was a significant factor, and the small relative size of Russia's industrial sector, and thus of alternative industrial employment, would support this argument. Moreover, the diminishing but still potent influence of the repartitional commune and of other legal bars to differentiation would also have pushed in this direction.

Two additional considerations are worth mentioning. First, the employment of permanent hired workers would have exacerbated the ordinary family's problem of finding adequate off-season employment for its labor supply. Second, population pressure would have tended, by driving up the purchase prices and rents of land, to restrict the size of farm enterprises. On the one side, land-hungry peasants would be led to make the highest bids for available land, and, on the other, families with land in excess of their own labor capacity might very well have found it more advantageous to rent or sell the surplus at the advantageous rates so established rather than to assume the risk and costs of working it with hired labor.

There are, then, a number of factors that would have operated to limit hiring of year-round nonfamily labor, but the same cannot be said for the hiring of seasonal labor. What is more, Chayanov shows that peasant families were prepared to invest in equipment and other innovations that served to economize family labor requirements in peak seasons; and it would be curious if the same families failed to employ seasonal labor for the same purpose, unless it was somehow culturally anathema, which is not suggested by Chayanov.

One factor is that seasonal labor may not have been available in peak seasons either because of the geographical distribution of surplus labor or because of the flexibility of family demand for its own members' labor. There may also have been some advantage to crafts and trades activity as an alternative family labor application as opposed to seasonal farm work. Another possibility is that the small farm enterprise found it easier to finance capital investment expenditures than wages for temporary workers, since capital equipment provides its own security to the lending institution and since payments can be scheduled to coincide more nearly with the time shape of farm receipts than can wage payments to seasonal workers.

4

The alternative theoretical interpretation of Chayanov's findings that has been presented above focuses upon the integrity of the peasant family, not principally upon the question of profit maximization or of the profit motive, for it is the integrity of the peasant family that causes its labor costs to behave as overhead rather than as variable and avoidable costs of production. The integrity of the peasant family in times of relative adversity is easy enough to explain and, with it, the main outlines of peasant economic behavior. However, the preservation of the integrity of the peasant family, given prolonged prosperity, seems highly doubtful on the basis of the evidence Chayanov presents. The question comes down to this: Did the peasant family refuse to take on hired labor, permanent or seasonal, that would have paid more than its own way? If so, it would be worthwhile attempting to ascertain the factors underlying such behavior.

Whatever may be the case regarding the design of an alternative theoretical explanation of Chayanov's data, it is obvious that his careful and detailed description of the Russian peasant economy is important in its own right and that it has significant implications for a number of subjects of contemporary interest. Most directly affected, perhaps, is the analysis of Soviet economic development. The commonly accepted interpretations of the 1924 "scissors crisis" assume that the response of the peasantry to a general adverse change in the terms of trade would be a diminution in the volume of agricultural marketings.[6] This assumption does not square with Chayanov's findings, which, as we have seen, would lead us to expect just the contrary. If so, then the so-called industrialization debates of the late 1920s also rested on a false premise, that is, that an increased volume of voluntary agricultural marketings would require an improvement in the terms of peasant trade. Chayanov's description of peasant economic behavior suggests the discriminatory price and tax policies might have been more effective instruments than is (and was) generally credited in forcing up the volume of Soviet agricultural procurements through market channels. Thus, disregarding political considerations, collectivization may not have been as appropriate, or as "necessary," to the Soviet industrialization drive as it has generally been considered.[7] Ultimately, the appropriateness or desirability of the "Soviet model" of economic development depends upon the realism and the accuracy of assumptions made about the economic behavior of the peasant sector.[8]

It will be obvious to students of economic development that Chayanov's concept of self-exploitation of family labor has an important bearing on the notion of disguised unemployment in agriculturally backward economies, and it helps to explain the difficulties that are encountered in its operational specification. Similarly, demographic differentiation and the survival value of the peasant farm are highly relevant to development policy. Finally, the family labor farm is merely one member species of a genus of family-owned and -operated enterprises. Such enterprises can be expected to have in common the fact that a large proportion of their labor costs behave as overhead rather than variable cost. It would seem to follow that such enterprises would also share many of the behavioral traits of the family labor farm. The significance of Chayanov's pioneering study of the family labor farm, therefore, may have broad implications for the formulation of development policy.

NOTES

1. Daniel Thorner, Basile Kerblay, and R. E. F. Smith (eds.), *A. V. Chayanov on the Theory of Peasant Economy* (Homewood, Ill.: Richard D. Irwin, Inc., published for the American Economics Association, 1966), pp. 29–269. Unfortunately, the translation from the Russian by R. E. F. Smith is rather clumsy, and the editors have done only a half-hearted job in the elimination of errors in the original text (e.g., figs. 3-4, 4-5, 4-12, 4-18; and tables 4-1, 4-42). It is also a shame that the editors did not see fit to clarify and modernize the presentation of Chayanov's numerous tables and figures.

2. Page references in parentheses refer to the Thorner et al. edition.

3. Most neoclassical models are designed to minimize or avoid overhead cost problems, a fact that helps to account for Chayanov's conclusion that the failure to maximize profits lay at the root of the discrepancies he found. The reference for the analysis that follows is another neglected classic: J. M. Clark, *Studies in the Economics of Overhead Costs* (Chicago: University of Chicago Press, 1923).

4. Chayanov, in subscribing to the utility-disutility analysis, assumes that a cost is always attached to the surrender of leisure (i.e., the disutility of work). This is highly unrealistic. It is quite clear that there exists for any individual or family a level of real income below which leisure is not a meaningful alternative, otherwise there could be no such thing as involuntary idleness. Furthermore, the term "leisure," as utilized in contemporary neoclassical analysis, encompasses a variety of activities, most of which—e.g., education, travel, hobbies, religion, drinking, unlike general laziness—require an income to be enjoyed. To this extent leisure and income are complements, not substitutes. Hence, potential working time is not the only cost of enjoying leisure. It follows that, over some range, the cost of giving up leisure increases with the level of income, not conversely.

5. Chayanov shows this was generally the case (see pp. 105–6).

6. See, e.g., Maurice Dobb, *Soviet Economic Development since 1917* (New York: International Publishers, 1948), chap. 7; Alexander Erlich, *The Soviet Industrialization Debate, 1924–1928* (Cambridge, Mass.: Harvard University Press, 1960), esp. pp. 21–23, 32–36, 50–52, 117–21, 175–80; Nicolas Spulber, *Soviet Strategy for Economic Growth* (Bloomington: Indiana University Press, 1964), esp. pp. 56–70; A. N. Malafeev, *Istoriia tsenoobrazovaniia v SSSR, 1917–1963* (A history of price formation in the USSR, 1917–1963) (Moscow: Izdalel'stvo "Mysl'," 1964), chap. 1, secs. 4 and 5.

7. See, for example, Alec Nove, "Was Stalin Really Necessary?" in *Was Stalin Really Necessary?* (London: Allen & Unwin, 1964).

8. It is interesting to note in this connection a recent article by Jerzy Karcz in which it is demonstrated that the so-called grain problem of 1926/27–1927/28 was a "magnificent Stalinist hoax." Karcz shows that, contrary to what we had been led to believe, gross agricultural output and marketings

were rising substantially during the later part of the 1920s and that, to the extent grain marketings presented a problem, it was a problem created by state price policy which discriminated against grain and in favor of products for which grain was a farm input ("Thoughts on the Grain Problem," *Soviet Studies* 18, no. 4 [April 1967]: 399–434).

2

A Note on Primitive Accumulation in Marx and Preobrazhensky

Alexander Erlich's article in 1950[1] was without doubt the most important single factor in popularizing the concept of "primitive socialist accumulation." With the help of this concept Erlich's article offered what has become the standard conception of Soviet industrialization: as a process dependent upon the extraction of a surplus from the peasant-agricultural sector.

It is true that Maurice Dobb, as early as 1928,[2] had explained what Preobrazhensky meant by the term "primitive socialist accumulation." But it was Erlich who posed the Great Industrialization Debate in terms of "Preobrazhensky's dilemma,"[3] and who argued that this dilemma was resolved by Stalin with the decision to collectivize. Propagation of the standard story was doubtless aided by its presentation as a drama of tragic irony. According to Erlich,[4] "no other viewpoint [than Preobrazhensky's] developed during these years [of the debate] was so violently repudiated at the beginning only to be implemented ultimately on a scale surpassing anything its author had ever thought possible." Alec Nove has retold this story with even greater effect by quoting Preobrazhensky's recantation of his theory at the Seventeenth Party Congress.[5] Nove goes on to say: "Preobrazhensky was surely expecting at least some of his audience to see the point. Stalin had 'exploited the peasants by accumulating the resources of the peasant economy in the hands of the state.' Of course he had! But Preobrazhensky had not seen *forced* collectivization as a way out."

I have criticized this standard story of the actual role of Soviet agriculture during rapid industrialization elsewhere on both theoretical and empirical grounds,[6] and it is not my intention tŏ press the matter further here. My purpose is to reexamine primitive socialist and primitive capitalist accumulation as theoretical concepts and, in

From *Soviet Studies* 30, no. 3 (July 1978):384–93. Reprinted by permission, with minor editorial changes.

particular, to contrast Preobrazhensky's and Marx's conceptions. Most discussions of the Great Industrialization Debate show little awareness of Marx's original use of the notion of primitive accumulation,[7] and several misconceptions have arisen in consequence. For example, it has come to be generally believed that Preobrazhensky, in the formulation of his concept of primitive socialist accumulation, was primarily concerned about the absolute (as opposed to the relative) tempo of economic growth of the main sectors of the Soviet economy and that the issue was primarily, if not exclusively, one of the accumulation of capital stock in physical terms.

I shall argue in what follows that both Preobrazhensky's and Marx's concepts are much richer analytically than has been generally presumed. By implication, I shall also argue that Alexander Erlich's famous article[8] infused more consistency and contemporary economic meaning into Preobrazhensky's theoretics than were there in the first place. Erlich essentially admits that this is so in the opening pages of his article. Moreover, careful examination of Erlich's use of sources (see his footnotes throughout) suggests that later works of Preobrazhensky were utilized heavily in the interpretation of earlier works. The result has been a distorted view of Preobrazhensky's conception of primitive accumulation and thus of the theoretical underpinning of the Great Debate.

Primitive Capitalist Accumulation

It is important to note that, for the most part, Marx treats the concept of primitive capitalist accumulation with contemptuous irony.[9] He does so because this and analogous terminology had been and continued to be utilized to defend private property and thus to justify property income. Indeed, part 8 of *Capital* is entitled "The So-Called Primitive Accumulation," and the second paragraph of the first chapter reads in part:

> This primitive accumulation plays in Political Economy about the same part as original sin in theology. . . . Its origin is supposed to be explained when it is told as an anecdote of the past. In times long gone by there were two sorts of people; one, the diligent, intelligent and, above all, frugal elite; the other, lazy rascals, spending their substance, and more in riotous living. . . . Thus it came to pass that the former sort accumulated wealth, and the latter sort had at last nothing to sell except their own skins. . . . Such insipid childishness is every day preached to us in the defence of property. (pp. 784–85)

Marx however, used the term to refer to the process of expropriation of the many by the few in the formation of capitalist relations of production.

Primitive capitalist accumulation is, in its fullest and richest sense, not an accumulation of previously created capital stock (although some accumulation is required for labor to be divided) but a process by which capitalist institutions are established: "The so-called primitive accumulation, therefore, is nothing else than the historical process of divorcing the producer from the means of production" (p. 786).

Reformulation of the traditional concept of previous, or primitive,[10] accumulation in this fashion, as a concept comprehending the historical transition from feudalism to capitalism, served Marx as an introduction to a survey of the creation of capitalist institutions (mainly in England) via the enclosure movement. For comparison with Preobrazhensky, Marx's sardonic description of the process ought to be noted as well:

> The spoliation of the church's property, the fraudulent alienation of the State domains, the robbery of the common lands, the usurpation of feudal and clan property, and its transformation into modern private property under circumstances of reckless terrorism, were just so many idyllic methods of primitive accumulation. They conquered the field for capitalistic agriculture, made the soil part and parcel of capital, and created for the town industries the necessary supply of a "free" and outlawed proletariat. (p. 805)

The expropriation of the agricultural population not only created a potential urban labor force but also set free their former subsistence for exchange with urban areas, for Marx assumed that the process was accompanied by an increase in the productivity of agriculture owing to technological change and to a larger and more efficient scale of production. Thus the process increased agricultural output, provided a labor force, and created a "home market" (pp. 817, 819).

Marx also considered the role of the state in the process of primitive capitalist accumulation. The "power of State, the concentrated and organized force of society, [was utilized] to hasten, hothouse fashion, the process of transformation of the feudal mode of production into the capitalist mode, and to shorten the transition . . ." (pp. 823–24). The state assisted the process not only by not protecting the population from expropriation but also by the acquisition of colonies and by the creation of the public debt and of the modern system of taxation (pp. 827–29).

In summary, then, insofar as Marx was prepared to treat the concept of primitive capitalist accumulation seriously, he used it as a shorthand reference for the process by which capitalist relations of production replaced feudal relations of production.[11] This transformation, of course, created a system by which capitalists could extract resources in the form of unpaid labor from the productive process. In a sense, then, the concept of primitive capitalist accumulation does comprehend accumulation proper (i.e., the question of where the resources come from to support industrialization). But the "stage of development" is not really critical, nor is any true "prior accumulation," for the efficacy of capitalist relations of production does not depend upon what may have been previously accumulated but upon the efficiency with which the system promotes capital accumulation in the present. Conceived as a product of the abstinence of the capitalist, primitive capitalist accumulation is little more than a bad joke to Marx. On the contrary, primitive capitalist accumulation, if it meant anything at all, meant the forced abstinence of the laborer.

Primitive Socialist Accumulation

This term has, I think, come to mean something much narrower and much less rich than Preobrazhensky intended when he first developed the concept. In one sense, the concept has also, I believe, come to mean something other than what Preobrazhensky intended (at least when he first formulated the concept), and that is with respect to the question of the tempo of industrialization. But I shall take this issue up in the next section. My purpose here, however, is to attempt to discover what primitive socialist accumulation *really* meant.

It is important to note at the outset that Preobrazhensky was, in *The New Economics*,[12] seeking to analyze the economic system of the early NEP (New Economic Policy) in terms of pure theory. The NEP represented a novel form of economic life for the contemporary Soviet Marxist, and Preobrazhensky was attempting to reorient his thinking from the position he and Bukharin had assumed earlier (during the Civil War) in their *ABC of Communism*.[13] Although Bukharin apparently did not deign to recognize the fact in their ensuing dispute, Preobrazhensky went to considerable lengths to make it clear that he was abstracting from considerations other than the purely theoretical (e.g., from political feasibility): "I devote myself to the modest task of first abstracting from the actual economic policy of the State, which is the resultant of the *struggle* between two systems of economy, and the corresponding classes, so as to investigate in its pure form the movement towards the optimum of primitive socialist accumulation . . ." (p. 63).

In essence, the problem with which Preobrazhensky was grappling is exceedingly simple. If the Bolshevik regime was to survive and socialism eventually to predominate in Soviet Russia, then two conditions had to be realized. First, an absolute increase in total output (and thus the capital stock) had to be achieved each year in order that relative plenty might eventually be attained. Second, the state (socialized) sector had to grow more rapidly than the private sector. The fact that the second condition is stated in relative rather than in absolute terms is crucial, for nowhere does Preobrazhensky argue in this important work that a particularly high *absolute* rate of growth is essential for the state sector.

It is clear that Preobrazhensky *accepted* the existence of the NEP setting. But he saw it, as did all good Bolsheviks, as a transitory state of affairs and one that could go either way in the absence of enlightened state policy. Should the private sector (which included as a predominant share agricultural producers) grow more rapidly, then Soviet Russia would revert to capitalism. Overcoming the actual state of economic dualism in favor of the public sector was for Preobrazhensky synonymous with primitive socialist accumulation. In fact, Preobrazhensky recommended: "Instead of 'new economic policy' it would be more correct and appropriate to say now: policy of socialist accumulation, period of socialist accumulation" (p. 129, n.1).

Like Marx, Preobrazhensky viewed primitive accumulation as a process of expropriation, and, indeed, it was perhaps as much his use of terms such as "expropriation" and "exploitation" that brought the wrath of Bukharin and others down upon his head. Alec Nove has suggested that:[14] "It may well be that some [of Preobrazhensky's opponents] reasoned privately thus: 'Of course we will have to exploit the peasants in due time, but for goodness' sake let us keep quiet about it now.' "

Also in keeping with Marx, Preobrazhensky did not differentiate between the gathering in of material resources via expropriation and the accompanying process of social change and class displacement. According to Preobrazhensky, socialism "can begin only after the conquest of power by the proletariat. The nationalization of large-scale industry is also the first act of socialist accumulation" (p. 80). But in a relatively backward economy it was not possible to proceed on the basis of true socialist accumulation exclusively:

> *Primitive socialist* accumulation . . . means accumulation in the hands of the state of material resources mainly or partly from sources lying outside the complex of state economy. This accumulation must play an extremely important part in a back-

ward peasant country, hastening to a very great extent the arrival of the moment when the technical and scientific reconstruction of the state economy begins and when this economy at last achieves purely economic [as opposed to political] superiority over capitalism. (p. 84)

This statement of the task follows directly from the initial problem of economic dualism, and clearly the issue is equally one of relative rather than absolute rates of growth of the two sectors. Consequently, in his reply to Bukharin, Preobrazhensky is quite correct when he asserts:

It is the same [respect to] Comrade Bukharin's idea that I propose to kill the goose that lays the golden eggs for our state industry, that is, that I propose to hinder the development of peasant economy; this is in crying contradiction with the actual text of my work. And it is necessary to say further that my article gives no numerical analysis of the economy. . . . (p. 255)

Preobrazhensky's feeling of a need for haste was a result of his estimate of the relative weakness of the state sector:

Fighting for the existence of the state economy means at the present stage hastening as fast as possible through that dangerous period of its life when it is both economically and technically weaker than capitalist economy. This process of extending and consolidating the state economy can proceed both at the expense of its own forces and resources, that is, the surplus product of the workers in the state industry, and at the expense of private, including peasant (itself including middle-peasant) economy. Can it be otherwise? (p. 226)

It is difficult at this remove to see how it could have been conceived differently, and it is indeed unfortunate that Bukharin did not ever present a well worked out alternative theoretical solution.[15]

Having analyzed the dual economy, Preobrazhensky turns to an examination of the main methods by which primitive socialist accumulation might take place, and he compares these with the methods of primitive capitalist accumulation. (Interestingly, Preobrazhensky at no point indicates a recognition of Marx's sardonic use of the latter phrase.) The fundamental underlying character of primitive capitalist accumulation is force, whether applied directly by capitalists or indirectly by the state for the benefit of capitalists. According to Preobrazhensky, the role of the state in primitive socialist accumulation is even more important than in the capitalist.

The state under premature socialist conditions is, according to Preobrazhensky, to implement primitive socialist accumulation through tax, price, and financial policies. The two critical differences between primitive capitalist and primitive socialist accumulation are found:

> First, in the fact that socialist accumulation has to take place at the expense not only of the surplus product of petty production but also of the surplus value of capitalist economic forms. Secondly, the difference . . . is conditioned by the fact that the state economy of the proletariat arises historically on the back of monopoly capitalism and therefore has at its disposal means of regulating the whole economy and of redistributing the national income economically which were not available to capitalism at the dawn of its history. (p. 95)

There is no need, I think, for us to explore in detail the particular policies Preobrazhensky recommended or considered as means for ensuring that there would be no leakage of surplus product from the state sector and for ensuring a net inflow of surplus value from the private sector, except to note that it was the proposal of nonequivalent exchange with the private peasant economy that raised most of the dust with his opponents in the ensuing debate. In this connection, Preobrazhensky's defense of nonequivalent exchange sounds very modern: "Accumulation by appropriate price policy has advantages over other forms of direct and indirect taxation of petty economy. The most important of these is the extreme facility of collection, not a single kopek being needed for any special taxation apparatus" (p. 111).

However that may be, Preobrazhensky envisaged self-exploitation by the workers in the public sector during the period of primitive socialist accumulation.[16] Somehow this aspect of Preobrazhensky's program has been lost track of, despite its obvious significance. Primitive socialist accumulation was to be accompanied by the "self-denial" of the workers in the public (largely industrial) sector which would provide "socialist accumulation" to match primitive accumulation in the private (mainly agricultural) sector.

The fundamental problem with which Preobrazhensky was struggling may be broken down into several component parts. First, the initial "socialist" revolution had occurred in a relatively backward and primarily agrarian economy. Second, revolution elsewhere was no longer expected in the near future (at least not on a large scale), which meant that Soviet Russia would have to help itself or backslide into capitalism. Third, socialism was weak and likely to remain weak relative to the main, advanced capitalist countries for the foreseeable future, both militarily and from the perspective of economic development. Consideration of these aspects and of the fact of the NEP, which in and of itself signaled a revision of Marxists' hopes, led Preobrazhensky to attempt a modification of Marxism that would provide the analytic basis for state policy. In this Preobrazhensky was a realist as well as a theorist.

Primitive Accumulation: Marx and Preobrazhensky

Most scholars who have confronted Preobrazhensky's concept of primitive socialist accumulation have done so exclusively in the context of his debate with Bukharin. Erlich, who has defined the contemporary framework for this analysis, presents Preobrazhensky's argument in terms of the *rate of industrialization* and the notion of unbalanced growth. However, if one considers Preobrazhensky's initial presentation of the concept, what is striking is that there is nothing to be found of either unbalanced growth or rapid industrialization. Indeed, Preobrazhensky merely urged that the rate of growth of the socialized sector must exceed that of the capitalist, and this was *not* specifically an argument for the more rapid growth of industry. It was, of course, true that the socialized sector was primarily industrial. In this connection, compare Maurice Dobb's first description of Preobrazhensky's concept of primitive socialist accumulation with that in the revised edition of 1966, where suddenly in the latter it is the "scale" of exploitation required to maintain the rate of growth allegedly envisaged by Preobrazhensky, rather than the very fact of exploitation itself, that is objectionable. Dobb was particularly concerned in the early edition with the danger that the workers might become accustomed to exploiting the peasants.[17]

The concept of primitive socialist accumulation is very closely related to Marx's notion of primitive capitalist accumulation, even though it is based on an exception in which the socialist revolution occurred first in a backward, underdevloped capitalist system. Given the legitimacy of revising Marx, Preobrazhensky seems to have applied the concept properly, although without the contempt Marx exhibited for the capitalist parallel. Like Marx, Preobrazhensky views the concept as one in which two questions need not be differentiated. The first question is: where did (or must) the resources come from to support accumulation during the transition period? The second question is: how did (or must) the relations of production develop such that capitalism (socialism) might be established on a self-sustaining basis? Consequently, both Marx and Preobrazhensky speak at times as though primitive accumulation refers to the accumulation (expropriation) of material resources. Primarily and fundamentally, however, the concept refers to institutional change.

It was clear to Preobrazhensky that there was a need to extend socialist relations of production into the private sector and that socialism was endangered precisely to the extent that capital remained in the hands of petty capitalists. He was also clearly aware that the line between public and private ran mainly between industry and agriculture and that this division raised delicate political issues.

The question remains: why did Bukharin (and others) react so violently to Preobrazhensky's concept? Was it, as Nove suggested, a matter of impolitic terminology? Why, also, has Preobrazhensky's concept come down to us in so distorted a form—both stripped of richness and positively twisted? Is it because the Great Industrialization Debate was presented to the profession initially under the misconception that collectivization actually led to a successful net extraction of resources from the private, agricultural sector? Preobrazhensky certainly thought this would be necessary, and this view is clearly compatible with his Marxist conception of the economy. In formulating the concept of primitive socialist accumulation Preobrazhensky *was* a revisionist, but he was a careful Marxist theoretician as well, and one quite sensitive to the pragmatic concerns of the new Soviet regime. There is considerable empirical evidence today that suggests that Preobrazhensky's policy proposals, while not "necessary" as he thought, were at least feasible.[18] If so, they would certainly have been superior to what has come to be thought of as Stalin's "solution" to the Bolsheviks' development "dilemma."

NOTES

1. Alexander Erlich, "Preobrazhenski and the Economics of Soviet Industrialization," *Quarterly Journal of Economics* 64, no. 1 (February 1950): 57–88.

2. Maurice Dobb, *Russian Economic Development since the Revolution* (New York, 1929).

3. Erlich, p. 81.

4. Ibid., p. 58.

5. Alec Nove, *An Economic History of the USSR* (London, 1969), p. 220. For a similar view, see E. H. Carr, *1917: Before and After* (London, 1969), p. 156.

6. James R. Millar, "Soviet Rapid Development and the Agricultural Surplus Hypothesis," *Soviet Studies* 22, no. 1 (July 1970):77–93, and "Mass Collectivization and the Contribution of Soviet Agriculture to the First Five-Year Plan," *Slavic Review* 33, no. 4 (December 1974):750–66. See also Michael Ellman, "Did the Agricultural Surplus Provide the Resources for the Increase in Investment in the USSR during the First Five-Year Plan?" *Economic Journal* 85 (December 1975):844–63.

7. An exception is Vaclav Holesovsky, "Revision of the Taxonomy of 'Socialism': A Radical Proposal," *Association for Comparative Economic Studies Bulletin* 16, no. 3 (Winter 1974):19–40.

8. This was later expanded into a book: Alexander Erlich, *The Soviet Industrialization Debate, 1921–1928* (Cambridge, Mass., 1960).

9. Karl Marx, *Capital,* vol. 1 (New York, 1906).

10. It would be more accurate to call the concept one of "original" accumulation, for reasons that this essay addresses. However, "primitive" has become accepted professional terminology.

11. This is the aspect that Karl Polanyi developed in *The Great Transformation* (New York, 1944).

12. E. Preobrazhensky, *Novaya ekonomika* (Moscow, 1926). All quotations are taken from the translation of Brian Pearce, *The New Economics* (Oxford, 1965).

13. N. Bukharin and E. Preobrazhenski, *The ABC of Communism* (Ann Arbor, Mich., 1966).

14. Nove, p. 126.

15. Stephen F. Cohen's excellent intellectual biography, *Bukharin and the Bolshevik Revolution* (New York, 1973), does not do so either.

16. "The law of wages is subordinated to the law of socialist accumulation which is expressed in conscious self restraint by the working class" (Preobrazhensky, *The New Economics,* p. 123).

17. Compare Maurice Dobb, *Soviet Economic Development since 1917* (rev. ed., New York, 1966), pp. 185–86, and Dobb, *Russian Economic Development since the Revolution,* pp. 260–68.

18. See n.6.

3

Soviet Rapid Development and the Agricultural Surplus Hypothesis

Students of Soviet development during the 1930s generally agree (1) that industrial growth was quite rapid, although there is still some disagreement concerning the precise rate of growth, and (2) that the peasantry was badly, even brutally, used by the Soviet regime. These two undisputed aspects of the Soviet experience are commonly held to illustrate two fundamental theoretical propositions regarding the requirements for rapid economic growth in backward economies: that the agricultural sector must make a substantial net contribution to the development and growth of the industrial sector; and that a rapid rate of industrialization may require coercion. Consequently, few have resisted the temptation to insert a "therefore" between observations 1 and 2 above, although this link has not yet been empirically verified. Others have gone even further to assert that Soviet agricultural policies were peculiarly appropriate, even necessary, to a program of rapid industrialization.

The principal aim of the first two sections of this essay is to demonstrate that the commonly accepted formulations of the role of agriculture in Soviet rapid development predicate a confusion of description and appraisal which has been obscured by analytically ambiguous concepts of an agricultural surplus. Although specifically directed to the Soviet case, the criticism of the concept of an agricultural surplus that is presented in sections 1 and 2 is pertinent to a number of general models of economic development, particularly many two-sector models. Sections 3 and 4 develop an alternative framework for description and appraisal of the role of agriculture in Soviet rapid development and suggest that future research along these lines may show that the role of agriculture in Soviet development has been generally misconceived. If so, our appraisal of Soviet ag-

From *Soviet Studies* 22, no. 1 (July 1970):77–93. Reprinted by permission, with minor editorial changes.

ricultural policies and of their general applicability as a guide to development strategy will have to be revised radically.

1. *The Agricultural Surplus Hypothesis*

Everyone seems to know what the "Soviet model" for economic development is, but it is impossible to find precise specifications in the literature. The characteristic nucleus of the model may be identified, however, by the critical significance that is attributed to the extraction of a sizable agricultural surplus of some sort in support of rapid industrialization.[1] A test of the agricultural surplus hypothesis requires that the concept be formulated so as to lend itself to empirical measurement. The protean guises of the concept of an agricultural surplus may be classified simply and generally according to the criteria utilized (1) to distinguish between what is surplus and what is not, and (2) to draw sector boundaries between agriculture and nonagriculture.

The word "surplus" refers to a remainder in excess of some specified need or use. The identification of a surplus requires therefore the erection of a standard of need or use. Specification of an economic surplus ordinarily involves a definition of need or use that runs in terms of the maintenance of some given economic condition. Although not exhaustive, two conceptually distinct approaches to the formulation of necessity standards are widely used. One seeks to ground the standard of need in technological relationships which may be expressed in physical magnitudes, as in a production function. An economic surplus defined with reference to a technological standard measures the physical volume of resources (or output) actually or potentially available in excess of those technically (including physiologically) necessary to maintain the given level of economic activity.[2]

The other approach has been to formulate the standard in behavioral terms. Functional relationships among economic actors or sectors are conceived as stimulus-response linkages. An economic surplus defined behaviorally measures a discrepancy between some given stimulus and that just necessary to cross the response threshold of a discretionary transactor. Economic rent in the neoclassical tradition, for example, refers to the difference between actual factor remuneration and that just necessary to maintain the factor's given self-allocation.[3] These two approaches to the definition of an economic surplus are fundamentally distinct, and a surplus defined behaviorally will not ordinarily correspond to one defined by a technological standard.[4] However, the failure to distinguish between these two conceptions of the economic surplus is a principal cause of the confusion that is found in discussions of the role of agriculture in Soviet development. It has contributed to the apparent agreement among analysts with quite different economic philosophies on the critical significance of the agricultural surplus, for each means something quite different by the phrase. Moreover, in conjunction with sectoring ambiguities, it has led to a revival of one of the main tenets of the ancient Physiocratic school of thought: the primacy of the agricultural sector.

Given the generic distinction between technological and behavioral concepts of the economic surplus, let us turn now to a consideration of the problems associated with the attribution of a surplus to a particular sector of the economy, for the operational meaning of an agricultural surplus obviously depends upon the way in which the economy has been sectored. There are, of course, a multitude of ways in which the economy may be sectored, one as valid as another so long as it is consistently followed. Despite the apparent simplicity of the task, ambiguity and inconsistency in sectoring criteria has tended to obscure the main obstacle confronting an attempt to attribute a surplus to a particular sector of the economy: sector interdependence.

Alexander Erlich, one of the foremost students of Soviet industrialization strategy, distinguishes the Soviet economy of the 1920s in the following terms[5]:

> In a modern industrialized economy the interdependence of its various parts is a two-way affair. However broadly or narrowly an "industry" is defined, the scale of operation will always depend on the supplies from the rest of the economy at least as much as the scale of operations of the rest of the economy will depend on the supplies from this particular "industry." The situation is very different whenever modern manufacturing and mining exist side by side with a backward and overpopulated peasant agriculture. While the first cannot function at all without a certain minimum of supplies from the second, the latter can, although at a price of a more or less considerable drop in output, remain in operation without supplies from the first. . . .
>
> In times of critical shortages of manufactured goods such a state of things could have definite advantages for the industrial segment of the economy. A determined policy of confiscating the agricultural surplus with practically no counterflow of goods from the cities need not under such conditions lead purely mechanically, i.e., by sheer lack of necessary factor inputs, to an immediate collapse of agricultural production.

Erlich's standard of need is obviously technological in character: it is not defined in terms of the behavioral response of the peasant sector to changes in intersector flows. What is ambiguous, however, is the way in which sector boundaries have been drawn. At first blush it would appear that the distinction is geographical: the countryside and the industrial-urban area; but in order to draw the line distinctly between "industry" and "peasant agriculture" considerable gerrymandering would be necessary, which ipso facto demonstrates that another more fundamental criterion is implicit. On the other hand, a strict type-of-product distinction between agricultural products and manufactures would make his assertion of a one-way technical dependency untenable, for the peasant sector could not dispense with all nonagricultural products (e.g., timber, iron, milling and blacksmith services, salt, sugar, woven cloth, fuel oil).

The most satisfactory explanation of the distinction Erlich seeks to make would appear to be a census criterion.[6] Given, for example, a census classification of the peasant household, the economy may be divided into peasant and nonpeasant enterprises. So defined, however, the Soviet peasant sector could not be uniquely identified with agricultural production, although it doubtless accounted for the greater share of it in the late 1920s. Whether or not the peasant sector, defined in some such fashion, was technically self-sufficient in the degree asserted by Erlich would seem to require empirical substantiation. As I have shown elsewhere,[7] A. V. Chayanov's examination of the Russian peasant economy implies the contrary. Erlich's description of the Soviet peasant economy also slights the extent to which specialization in production had taken place within the agricultural sector in response to the demand of nonpeasant sectors for agricultural products.[8]

Whatever the case, the agricultural surplus as conceived by Erlich must be the volume of peasant agricultural output produced in excess of the sector's own (minimal) needs. What is important in this connection is the fact that the self-sufficiency assumption permits one to conceive of the agricultural surplus in terms of physical-volume measures such as bushels, tons, and head of stock. The one-way dependency between the two sectors obviates the need to establish an appropriate system of relative prices with which to net intersector acquisitions from intersector deliveries in the determination of the magnitude of the peasant sector's surplus.

However, unless the power to create a surplus is attributed to a single sector (or factor) of the economy (e.g., the peasant sector or labor), measurement of the surplus produced by the other sectors (factors) will require a system of relative prices. Thus, determination of the relative significance of the peasant sector's surplus to Soviet industrialization will necessarily be sensitive to the price weights selected for its measurement. The tendency of investigators to slight the net contributions of other sectors of the Soviet economy to growth, coupled with the emphasis that is commonly placed upon the extraction of an agricultural surplus, as illustrated by Alexander Erlich's presentation of the case, has led to what I shall call a "neo-physiocratic bias" in explanations of Soviet rapid development. In its extreme form this bias is revealed by those who argue that development and industrialization require a preexisting agricultural (or food) surplus and thereby reduce the concept of the division of labor to a form of industrial parasitism. Unless the agricultural sector is assumed to be technologically self-sufficient, the surplus of agricultural output over the sector's own consumption cannot be attributed solely to the productive powers of agriculture. Given sector specialization and mutual interdependence, the existence of an agricultural surplus defined in this way is not "a precondition for industrial development" but a mere tautology.[9]

There is a marked similarity between an approach that attributes the power to create an absolute surplus to the agricultural sector and one that attributes this power to a particular factor type (e.g., labor). Hence the apparent agreement between the Marxist (Soviet or otherwise) and the unwitting neophysiocrat regarding the controlling significance of an economic surplus in development. However, unless the analyst is prepared to follow such a model to the bitter end, a preexisting surplus is otiose. But, if one does follow the model through, and this is the Achilles' heel of models of this sort, then economic growth and development must be explained solely in terms of those factors which determine the rate of growth of the surplus. Few contemporary model builders have been prepared to do so, and in this respect their models are logically inconsistent.[10]

2. Measuring the Agricultural Surplus

If we abandon the dubious quest for a self-sufficient sector with an exploitable absolute surplus, the measurement of any sector's actual or potential surplus, whether defined in terms of a technological or a behavioral standard, will involve finding a suitable common denominator for making the necessary intersector comparisons. For the net contribution of any sector to growth and development will depend as much upon the particular set of price weights utilized in its measurement as upon the physical-volume of intersector flows.

Given a system of interdependent sectors, how useful is the

concept of an agricultural surplus to an understanding of Soviet rapid development? Consider an economy divided in such a way that one sector produces agricultural products strictly defined to include, at most, semiprocessed fruits of the soil and of animal husbandry. The nonagricultural sector comprehends all nonagricultural production activities, including manufacturing, transport, communications, and other service industries. The labor force and the capital stock, including land, may be identified with one or the other sector, but this will not necessarily define unique collections of inputs since individuals, plant and equipment, and land may serve either or both sectors. Let us also identify intersector product flows by sector of origin and destination as well as by end use. This approach makes it possible to specify net or gross investment by sector of origin, and it therefore corresponds closely with the way in which the agricultural sector's contribution to Soviet growth has been conceived in the literature.

A portion of gross agricultural production will be consumed or used up in current production activities in each of the two sectors, and the remainder will be devoted to net capital formation in one or both sectors. Gross output of nonagriculture will also be distributed between the two sectors and between consumption and investment with each.[11] We may define the *unconsumed surplus* of the agricultural sector, therefore, as that volume of current gross agricultural output which is not consumed, used up in current production, or otherwise destroyed within the sector during the current year. The unconsumed surplus measures, therefore, that portion of agriculture's current production that has been marketed and/or delivered to nonagriculture plus any amount that has been retained within agriculture and devoted to nonconsumption purposes. Let us specify the *marketed surplus* of agriculture as the volume of goods and services the sector has provided in intersector transactions during the current period.

The marketed surplus may therefore be greater than, less than, or equal to the unconsumed surplus in any given period, for it differs from the unconsumed surplus by the algebraic sum of the change in agricultural inventories and the volume of net fixed agricultural investment attributable solely to the agricultural sector's use of its own output. However, the difference between the marketed and the unconsumed surpluses will measure the agricultural sector's actual (potential) net investment expenditures only on the unpromising assumption that capital account acquisitions from nonagriculture are (or could be reduced to) nil. Otherwise these two measures do not appear to have any significant analytic value for a determination of the role of agriculture in development.

However, if we net the value of current-account inputs, acquired by agriculture in intersector trade, from the sector's unconsumed surplus, we obtain what may be called the *net surplus* of agriculture. In any given period the net surplus may be positive, negative, or zero. Given appropriate price weights, the net surplus measures the sector's net contribution to net investment in the economy as a whole. It is really simply a measure of net investment by sector of origin, which may be seen if we *consolidate* net surplus accounts for our two sectors. All intersector final consumption, replacement, and intermediate product and service transactions cancel, leaving us with aggregate net investment.

Only if it could be shown that current-account intersector acquisitions of agriculture were in fact, or potentially, zero may the unconsumed surplus be uniquely attributed to the agricultural sector. Similarly, the marketed surplus may serve as a measure of the net contribution of agriculture to nonagriculture only if both capital and current-account acquisitions from nonagriculture prove actually or potentially zero. In this case the difference between the unconsumed and the marketed surplus would measure net investment or disinvestment in agriculture. Thus, although these two measures have been popular and widely used in discussions of Soviet rapid development, the analytic merit of either depends upon the validity of the assumption that agriculture was in fact, or potentially, self-sufficient. Otherwise, the contribution of agriculture to development will be sensitive to the price weights utilized in its measurement.

The net surplus is the appropriate concept for any model that assumes mutual dependency among the various sectors of the economy, whether conceived in technological or behavioral terms. Given any system of relative prices and the level of aggregate net investment, the larger a sector's net surplus, the larger its contribution to aggregate net investment. Similarly, given a sector's gross output, the smaller its acquisitions on current and capital account, the greater its net contribution to other sectors. It follows, therefore, that for any specified level of gross agricultural production, steps taken which (1) increase agriculture's unconsumed surplus and (2) restrain or decrease its intersector acquisitions for current consumption and productive use together serve to increase the net surplus of the agricultural sector. Moreover, other things equal, steps taken either (3) to increase the portion of the unconsumed surplus that is marketed and/or (4) to restrict or curtail capital-account acquisitions and uses by the agricultural sector serve to shift the real output available for net investment to nonagriculture.

Most discussions of Soviet industrialization imply that one or both of these paired steps were successfully implemented by collectivization and subsequent agricultural procurement policy, but this has not been demonstrated empirically, particularly with respect to steps 1 and 4. However, most investigators have not in any case been content with so relativistic a statement concerning the contribution of agriculture. As was pointed out above, the nucleus of the Soviet model for rapid development, as it has been quite generally conceived, implies that agriculture's contribution was relatively large and therefore a significant explanatory variable for Soviet rapid industrialization. But, since the relative size of agricluture's contribution depends upon the prices used in its measurement, any attempt to trace and measure its share unambiguously must first establish the uniqueness of the price weights utilized for this purpose.

As has already been shown, defining the agricultural surplus in terms of a technological standard avoids this problem only on the assumption of sector self-sufficiency.[12] Discussions of the process of Soviet industrialization in what are essentially neoclassical terms represent an alternative and incommensurable approach to the specification of the agricultural sector's contribution. This approach has tended to emphasize the "forced saving" of the peasant sector, which is attributed to collectivization and the predatory agricultural procurement system.[13] What investigators have argued with respect to the Soviet case is that the rate of real saving imposed upon the agricultural sector and the distribution of the economy's net product that obtained in the Soviet Union during the period of rapid industrialization were other than would have prevailed had Soviet leaders relied upon the preferences and free market behavior of the agricultural community. The discrepancy in this instance measures forced saving of agriculture. This portion of saving is forced, presumably, because the terms of trade that obtained in fact would not have been sufficient to have called it forth as voluntary behavior. Insofar as the underlying behavioral standard is normative rather than empirical, forced saving derives from an evaluation of Soviet development couched in terms of distributive justice. The prescriptive standard thus provides the necessary unique set of relative prices.

On the other hand, if the behavioral assumptions underlying the standard accurately reflect peasant market behavior in the Soviet Union at that time, it follows that nonmarket policy instruments (e.g., collectivization, obligatory procurement quotas, coercion) were necessary to enforce the net contribution realized in the agricultural sector. This appears to be what Alec Nove has in mind when he asserts that Stalin's agricultural policies were "objectively necessary."[14] But, as an empirical proposition, the necessity for collectivization has by no means been established. There is, indeed, evidence to suggest that the response of the peasantry to an adverse change in its terms of trade and/or to increased money taxation might well have been to increase both output and marketings.[15] Moreover, new research on collectivization suggests that a full-scale reappraisal is overdue.[16]

At the outset of this essay I suggested that most Western discussions of Soviet rapid industrialization are characterized by a failure to distinguish clearly between description and appraisal. What I had in mind is the attempt to explain the attainment of a high rate of industrial growth in terms of the exploitation or mobilization of an economic surplus of one sort or another. Western confidence in a necessary link between a high rate of industrial growth, on the one hand, and collectivization and a predatory, coercive agricultural procurement system, on the other, rests more on the normative preconceptions of Western analysts than upon an empirical, dispassionate examination of the process. The economic surplus and forced saving, as applied to the Soviet case, have been defined in terms of distributive justice rather than empirically. As such these concepts have no explanatory power. Surplus value in the Marxian scheme, an agricultural surplus in the neophysiocratic view, and forced saving in the neoclassical conception are derived from nonempirical standards of appraisal. The first two refer to the value of product that may be extracted from the rightful claimants to economic output. Forced saving refers to a discrepancy between the terms of trade that in fact obtained and what it is believed these terms ought to have been. So long as discussions of Soviet economic development predicate putative property rights or just price they cannot purport to explain in what way the agricultural sector served industrialization.[17]

Finally, the attempt to trace uniquely and unambiguously sector contributions to economic growth appears to be a futile exercise, at least as an empirical proposition where the sectors stand in a relation of mutual dependency to one another.[18] This suggests that we ought to treat the question of who ultimately paid the costs and/or reaped the benefits of Soviet development as an important but separable issue, one upon which general agreement has not and will not readily be obtained since it is value-loaded. Distinguishing the task of description and the problem of appraisal in this way makes it clear that the first step toward appraisal is a good description.

3. *Measuring Agriculture's Role in Soviet Rapid Development*

In what follows I shall formulate and elaborate four measurable aspects of the part an agricultural sector may play in the process of economic growth and development for application to the Soviet case in subsequent research. Since the research task suggested by the resulting framework is a substantial one, and only just now underway, I shall confine myself to certain speculations regarding Soviet agriculture's contributions to rapid development according to these measures.

Recognizing the inherent element of ambiguity in the assignment of contributions to member sectors of an interdependent economic system, let us follow the advice Professor Simon Kuznets has offered elsewhere and conceive any one sector's role "as the result of the activities of the economy whose particular *locus* is the given sector—rather than as a contribution of the given sector fully creditable to it as if it were outside the economy and offering something to the latter."[19]

A sector *participates in growth* if its own deflated gross or net output grows. Similarly, if the sector's product per worker grows, this is evidence of *participation in development*.[20] Defining the agricultural sector by type of product, it is clear that the process of industrialization implies a secular relative decline in agriculture's participation in the growth of the economy's GNP. But there is no necessary reason to expect that the agricultural sector's participation in development should differ from that of the more rapidly growing nonagricultural sectors. This will depend upon the sector's access to the sources as well as the fruits of modernization. However, agricultural production units, especially where peasant agriculture prevails, may be more resistant to change than is the case for other sectors. Also, given a more rapid growth of nonagriculture, the movement of labor out of agriculture may cause deterioration in the average quality of the agricultural labor force to the extent that it is the young and the ambitious who move. The focus of state development efforts will also affect the degree to which the agricultural sector participates in development.

The apparently small degree to which Soviet agriculture participated in development during the period of rapid industrialization (and after) seems to represent only a difference in degree rather than in kind by comparison with the early patterns of growth of other industrializing economies. What is striking about Soviet agricultural performance during the 1930s is the well-documented failure to participate in growth. Agricultural production stagnated during the period of rapid industrialization and the composition of agricultural output deteriorated by comparison with the more usual pattern of a developing agricultural sector.[21]

The question is, then, whether agriculture's other contirbutions were of a volume and nature so as to preclude the sector's participation in growth and development. Consider again the two-sector model presented in section 2 in which the economy is divided into agricultural and nonagricultural sectors according to a strict type-of-product criterion. Let us designate agriculture as sector 1 and non-agriculture as sector 2. Let M_1 and M_2 stand for the deflated vlaues of intersector marketings (and/or deliveries) by agriculture and non-agriculture respectively. We may determine the value of the net flow of products and services from or to agriculture:

$$P_1 = M_1 - M_2. \tag{1}$$

As we have seen, the conventional view holds that P_1, the *net product contribution* of agriculture, was positive, increased as a result of collectivization, and represented a significant provenance of resources to nonagriculture in support of rapid industrialization.[22] But this is by no means an established fact of the Soviet experience. In fact, when due account is rendered for the destruction of the capital stock of the agricultural sector in consequence of the peasants' resistance to collectivization, for investment in Machine Tractor Stations (MTS) by the state and their operating expenses, for the administrative costs of the system of state procurement agencies, and for the direct intersector purchases of agricultural enterprises, including counterpart sales,[23] on current and capital account, a significantly large or expanding net flow out of the agricultural sector cannot be assumed with any confidence. If private consumption of industrial products decreased, as seems likely, capital consumption (including destruction), capital acquisitions, and productive consumption of industrial output surely increased.

In the end, of course, the question must be resolved by empirical investigation. Unfortunately, reliance upon concepts of the economic surplus or forced saving has led to an attempt to resolve this question with partial data (e.g., grain marketings and deliveries). However, if we must await empirical investigation for a final answer, it is possible to examine certain implications of the hypothesis that P_1 was growing and significantly large in the 1930s.

Measured in current, rather than in constant, prices, product account 1 represents an abbreviated sources and uses of funds statement for the agricultural sector. Denoting current price magnitudes with small letters, we have:

$$m_2 + p_1 = m_1, \tag{2}$$

where m_2 represents uses of funds by agriculture in the acquisition of products and services from nonagriculture, m_1 is the revenue from sales to nonagriculture, and p_1 measures the net flow of funds through transfer and financial channels from or to agriculture. As the balancing item in the account, p_1 may be either a net source or a net use of funds for agriculture. If p_1 is negative, for example, the right-hand, or sources, side of account 2 would be: $(m_1 - p_1)$.

Let us assume that the net flow of funds through financial and transfer channels between agriculture and nonagriculture (p_1) is positive, and thus we may treat it throughout as a net use of funds by the agricultural sector. It is composed of two types of pecuniary flows: (a) net funds obtained or advanced and returned through financial channels (f_1), and (b) net transfers of funds paid out or received by agriculture (t_1). Obviously, a net use of funds for agriculture is a net source of funds for nonagriculture, and thus $p_1 = -p_2$; $f_1 = -f_2$; $t_1 = -t_2$. Substituting for p_1 in account 2 yields:

$$m_2 + (f_1 + t_1) = m_1, \tag{3}$$

which is a statement of sources and uses of funds for the agricultural sector on intersector trading account.

Now, if $p_1 = 0$, agriculture's product and service purchases (m_2) serve precisely to finance m_1, nonagriculture's purchases from agriculture. Thus, by purchasing the output of nonagriculture, the agricultural sector serves to finance nonagriculture's purchases of agricultural products. Let us label this the *market contribution* of agriculture, for to the extent that m_1 and m_2 grow simultaneously and commensurately the expansion of output and specialization of production for the two sectors is self-financing.[24]

Ordinarily, of course, m_1 and m_2 will not precisely offset one another for any sector, and f_1 and/or t_1 will usually be nonzero. The algebraic sum of net transfer payments and net financial flows (p_1) serves, therefore, to finance the difference between m_1 and m_2. However, since we want to relate the value of the net product flow (P_1) and the net flow of funds (p_1) for the two sectors, it is also necessary to consider the net change in the terms of intersector trade for the agricultural sector. For an understanding of how the various sectors have financed their intersector transactions, a Laspeyres price index seems the most appropriate deflator of current price magnitudes. Let us define for each sector the "gain from inflation" on intersector sales of its own products as the difference between its sales valued in current-period prices and in prices of the previous period. The gain from inflation for agriculture is, then,

$$g_1 = m_1 - M_1. \tag{4a}$$

For nonagriculture the gain from inflation is:

$$g_2 = m_2 - M_2. \tag{4b}$$

Substituting in account 3 for m_1 and m_2, according to 4a and 4b, we obtain:

$$M_2 + g_2 + (f_1 + t_1) = M_1 + g_1, \text{ which reduces to:} \tag{5}$$
$$P_1 = (f_1 + t_1) + (g_2 - g_1).$$

In plain words, account 5 states that the value of the net intersector product flow (P_1) is financed by the algebraic sum of the net flow of funds through financial channels (f_1), the net flow of intersector transfer payments (t_1), and the net change in intersector terms of trade ($g_2 - g_1$).

It follows, therefore, that if P_1 is positive, the algebraic sum of $(g_2 - g_1)$, f_1, and t_1 must also be positive. Which means that the sector providing a net value flow of products and services to other sectors must also help to finance that net flow in one or some combination of the three ways specified. These flows provide an alternative way of measuring and thinking about the net product contribution of a sector in development. Let us call this a *finance contribution*.[25]

Again, it is not possible on the basis of the data thus far put together to do more than speculate about the extent to which the agricultural sector helped to finance the development of nonagriculture in this sense. It is clear that the terms of trade did turn against the agricultural sector during the 1930s, but the degree to which this happened varied considerably for the various subsectors of agriculture. Producers of technical crops received better terms than did those of food products.[26] But the net change was, doubtless, adverse. With respect to transfer payment flows, the situation is considerably more complex, for the budgetary grants which financed the MTS system, as well as interest-free capital grants to state farms, must be treated as transfer payments to agriculture. Given that state investment in agriculture far exceeded plan and expectation,[27] it is not clear that the net transfer flow out of agriculture was large or even positive. Finally, it does not seem likely that the agricultural sector advanced and returned net funds through financial channels during the 1930s. The contrary seems much more probable, especially since collective farms had access to long-term borrowing.[28] On balance, therefore, one cannot assume with confidence that the net flow of products and services (P_1) and the net pecuniary flow ($f_1 + t_1$) + ($g_2 - g_1$) were large during the period of rapid industrialization.

Given that the agricultural sector did not participate significantly in either growth or development, that its market contribution was clearly negligible if not negative, and that a significantly large finance contribution appears dubious, we must, pending fuller examination of the facts of the case, leave open the possibility that agriculture played a very modest economic role in Soviet rapid industrialization. Indeed, the Soviet model for economic development, as usually formulated, may not be applicable to the Soviet experience in this respect.

4. *Appraising Soviet Agricultural Policy*

Once the job of description has been completed it will be possible to appraise the merits of Soviet agricultural policy, specifically, collectivization and the agricultural procurement system. Should it prove true that agriculture's economic role was a modest one, the appropriateness of Soviet agricultural policies is clearly questionable, if only because the long-term consequences of these policies have been so devastatingly deleterious to the agricultural sector and so difficult to reverse.[29]

The question we must seek to answer in appraising Soviet agricultural policy is not whether or not collectivization and a predatory procurement system were necessary or in accord with some standard of distributive justice, for an answer to the one flirts with the doctrine of historical inevitability and the other requires for most outside observers no sophisticated analysis. What we need to know is whether or not Soviet policy was appropriate to a program of rapid economic development, that is, whether or not it approached the optimal policy.

One possible approach to an objective standard of appraisal is to be found in the comparison of Soviet policies with those practiced in support of successful industrialization elsewhere (e.g., Japan). An alternative approach is possible in terms of the studies that are available dealing with peasant economic behavior in Russia prior to the decision to collectivize. These studies make possible the formulation of peasant behavior patterns as responses to different types of state policy (e.g., changes in the terms of trade, money taxes).

There is reason to believe that Soviet agricultural policy in support of rapid industrialization was founded on an incorrect analysis of peasant economic behavior, specifically, the official Soviet interpretation of the "scissors crisis."[30] Moreover, the decision to collectivize may have been taken on the basis of inappropriate statistical information or, perhaps, for completely noneconomic reasons.[31] Given the models underlying the famous industrialization debate preceding the decision to collectivize, it is clear that many Soviet economists, planners, and leaders intended to exploit agriculture in furtherance of industrialization,[32] but these models display a strong neophysiocratic bias.

It is possible, therefore, that we shall ultimately discover that Soviet agricultural policy was far from optimal with respect to a program of rapid industrialization. Let me suggest as a possible fruitful approach that we ought to give separate consideration to collectivization and the agricultural procurement system, for it may be that the latter served merely to offset the economic costs of the former. In any event, we may discover that the Soviet Union achieved growth and development not because the peasantry was exploited and agriculture neglected but despite it. If such a finding would make the fate of the Soviet peasant all the more tragic, it would also provide a somewhat more optimistic outlook for those countries currently hesitating between adoption of a Soviet model that works, with its attendant necessary evils, and the certain misery of indefinite stagnation.

NOTES

I am indebted to Morris A. Copeland, Walter C. Neale, Lenard Kirsch, and Judith Thornton for helpful comments on an earlier draft of this essay. They are not, of course, responsible for any remaining errors of commission or omission.

1. Bruce F. Johnston and John W. Mellor, "The Role of Agriculture in Economic Development," *American Economic Review* 51, no. 4 (September 1961):579: "If communist countries have an advantage in securing rapid economic growth, it would seem to lie chiefly in their ability to ride roughshod over political opposition and divert a maximum amount of current output into capital formation. And agriculture has been a prime target in squeezing out a maximum amount of surplus for investment." Or consider Paul Baran, *The Political Economy of Growth* (New York, 1962), p. 268: "If there were no other powerful reasons for the desirability of collectivization of agriculture, the vital need for the mobilization of the economic surplus generated in agriculture would in itself render collectivization finally indispensable. . . . Collectivization destroys the basis for the peasants' resistance to the 'siphoning off' of the economic surplus." And see William H. Nicholls, "The Place of Agriculture in Economic Development," in Carl

K. Eicher and Lawrence W. Witt (eds.), *Agriculture in Economic Development* (New York, 1964), p. 38: "When economic planning in the Soviet Union got under way there was already a sizable agricultural surplus, and the task facing the planners was the diversion of this to the towns and industrial centres. . . ." For additional examples, see Alexander Erlich, "Stalin's Views on Economic Development," in Ernest Simmons (ed.), *Continuity and Change in Russian and Soviet Thought* (Cambridge, Mass., 1955), p. 94; Alec Nove, "Was Stalin Really Necessary?" in *Economic Rationality and Soviet Politics* (New York, 1964), p. 22; Clair Wilcox, W. D. Weatherford, and Holland Hunter, *Economies of the World Today* (New York, 1962), p. 37; Abram Bergson, *The Economics of Soviet Planning* (New Haven, Conn., 1964), p. 237; Alexander Gerschenkron, *Economic Backwardness in Historical Perspective* (New York, 1962), pp. 146–48.

2. See, for example, Joan Robinson, *Economic Philosophy* (London, 1966), p. 108: "There is . . . a limit to the amount of investment that can be carried out by any given labour force (counting exports used to pay for imported equipment as part of investment). The limit is set by the surplus per man employed in producing the mere necessities of consumption over his own consumption. The ratio of the surplus to consumption per man governs the maximum proportion of the labour force that can be allocated to investment."

3. Kenneth E. Boulding, *Economic Analysis* (3d ed., New York, 1955), pp. 211–14; H. H. Liebhafsky, *The Nature of Price Theory* (Homewood, Ill., 1963), pp. 357–58.

4. Compare, for instance, the neoclassical and the Marxian conceptions of land rent as a "surplus" in the aggregate. However, it should be noted that Marx vacillated somewhat between a technological and a behavioral formulation of the economic surplus. So have many neoclassicists. Technological criteria are frequently utilized to specify the upper limit of the potential surplus, with behavioral criteria serving to explain the realized surplus.

5. Alexander Erlich, *The Soviet Industrialization Debate, 1924–1928* (Cambridge, Mass., 1960), pp. 119–20.

6. This criterion was suggested to me by Walter C. Neale.

7. James R. Millar, "A Reformulation of A. V. Chayanov's Theory of the Peasant Economy," *Economic Development and Cultural Change* 18, no. 2 (January 1970):219–29.

8. Daniel Thorner, Basile Kerblay, R. E. F. Smith (eds.), *A. V. Chayanov on the Theory of Peasant Economy* (Homewood, Ill., 1966). See especially chaps. 4 and 7 of "Peasant Farm Organization."

9. Nicholls has urged the necessity for a preexisting agricultural surplus ("The Place of Agriculture in Economic Development," p. 25). In a supporting theoretical argument he has defined the agricultural surplus as "the physical amount by which, in a given country, total food production exceeds the total food consumption of the agricultural population" ("An 'Agricultural Surplus' as a Factor in Economic Development," *Journal of Political Economy* 71, no. 1 [February 1963]:1). But unless his agricultural sector is

actually or potentially self-sufficient, Nicholls's argument reduces to a simple tautology.

Consider two self-sufficient peasant households, A and B, which are identical in all respects. Assume that, by mutual agreement, A takes over cultivation and husbandry for both farms and henceforward produces only food products, while B subsequently concentrates solely upon the nonagricultural tasks previously undertaken separately by each household (e.g., collecting firewood, processing field and animal husbandry products, weaving, maintenance and replacement of farm plant and equipment). Even if no increase in productivity accompanies specialization of production between the two households, a "food surplus" as defined by Nicholls is evident under the new division of labor. To which household is this surplus to be attributed? Of course, the "food surplus" did not arise out of thin air, as is obvious if a type-of-product distinction is applied both before as well as after the specialization agreement is concluded between the two households. And it would exist even if both are suffering severe malnutrition.

10. Gustave Ranis and John C. H. Fei present an example of this kind of inconsistency in the model associated with their names ("A Theory of Economic Development," *American Economic Review* 51, no. 4 (September 1961):533–65). Somewhere between phase 1 and phase 3 of the model they offer the basis of sectoring shifts from agricultural self-sufficiency to one of mutual dependence between industry and agriculture. What they have done is to convert a neophysiocratic model into a neoclassical model. They apparently realized that the Lewis labor-surplus model, upon which they based their phase 1 model, would run out of gas as soon as the agricultural surplus (i.e., the volume of "agricultural resources released to the market through the reallocation of agricultural workers") was exhausted. Otherwise, "sustained growth" would require a sustained growth of the agricultural surplus. So they introduce technological change in *both* sectors during phase 3 to perpetuate the "take off" provided by the phase 1 "agricultural surplus."

11. The discussion and definitions given in the text are based upon the following system of sector accounts: Let gross output of the agricultural sector and its distribution be

$$A_1 = C_{11} + C_{12} + I_{11} + I_{12};$$

where A_1 is the gross output of agriculture, C represents output used up or consumed in current production, I measures output devoted to fixed and inventory investment, the first subscript indicates sector of origin, and the second the sector of destination. C_{12} indicates, for example, a flow of agricultural products to nonagriculture for consumption uses. Gross output of nonagriculture and its distribution is given similarly by

$$A_2 = C_{22} + C_{21} + I_{21} + I_{22}.$$

For agriculture, the *unconsumed surplus, U,* may be defined as

$$U_1 = A_1 - C_{11}, \text{ or}$$
$$= C_{12} + I_{12} + I_{11}.$$

The *marketed surplus, M,* is

$$M_1 = C_{12} + I_{12}, \text{ or}$$
$$= U_1 - I_{11}.$$

The *net surplus, N,* is then

$$N_1 = U_1 - C_{21},$$

and it measures, given appropriate price weights, the agricultural sector's net contribution to net investment in the economy as a whole. This is made clear if we *consolidate* net surplus accounts for the two sectors:

$N_1 + N_2 = (U_1 - C_{21}) + (U_2 - C_{12})$, and substituting for U_1 and U_2,
$= I_{11} + I_{12} + I_{22} + I_{21}.$

12. The neophysiocratic bias alluded to above is a direct result of the attempt to substitute a technological standard for a price system.

13. Technically speaking, "forced saving" is the obverse of an economic surplus. If a surplus measures an amount in excess of some standard of need, forced saving measures the deficit between the behavioral standard and realized saving.

14. Nove, "Was Stalin Really Necessary?"

15. Millar, "A Reformulation of A. V. Chayanov's Theory of the Peasant Economy."

16. See, for example, Jerzy F. Karcz, "Thoughts on the Grain Problem," *Soviet Studies* 18, no. 4 (April 1967); M. Lewin, "The Immediate Background of Collectivization," ibid. 17, no. 2 (October 1965); M. Lewin, *Russian Peasants and Soviet Power: A Study of Collectivization,* trans. Irene Nove with the assistance of John Biggart (London and Evanston, Ill., 1968); Z. M. Fallenbuchl, "Collectivization and Economic Development," *Canadian Journal of Economics and Political Science* 33, no. 1 (February 1967):1–15.

17. It would serve clarity to avoid altogether the analytic use of the term "surplus" especially since alternative terms with precise operational meanings are available as substitutes. Or, at the very least, it would seem incumbent for authors to specify explicitly both the sectoring criteria and the standard of need being utilized to define the surplus.

18. The problem is illustrated by the question: does the bee depend upon the surplus product of the flower, or the flower upon the surplus labor of the bee?

19. Simon Kuznets, "Economic Growth and the Contribution of Agriculture: Some Notes on Measurements," in Eicher and Witt, *Agriculture in Economic Development,* pp. 104–5.

20. Kuznets treats these two aspects as a single type of contribution, which he calls the "product contribution" of agriculture (ibid., p. 114).

21. This is clear from Soviet official data, not to mention the somewhat more severe Western estimates. Gross product of agriculture exceeded the 1928 level only in 1937 and 1940, according to Soviet statistical handbooks (e.g., *Narodnoe khozyaistvo SSSR v 1958 godu* (Moscow, 1959), p. 350. For

a Western appraisal, see Arcadius Kahan, "Soviet Statistics of Agricultural Output," in Roy D. Laird (ed.), *Soviet Agricultural and Peasant Affairs* (Lawrence, Kans., 1963), pp. 134–60.

22. In terms of the "net surplus" defined in section 2, P_1 equals the difference between the net surplus of agriculture and agricultural net investment, that is, $P_1 = N_1 - (I_{11} + I_{21})$.

23. "Counterpart sales" provided preferential access and prices for industrial and processed products to producers of technical agricultural products (e.g., cotton, sugar beet, hemp).

24. This, I take it, is what Kuznets means also by the "market contribution of agriculture" ("Economic Growth and the Contribution of Agriculture," pp. 109–14).

25. Kuznets (ibid., p. 114) comes up with what he calls a "factor contribution," which would seem to correspond to our net product or finance contribution. However, he apparently had a geographical criterion in mind since he treats the flow of labor from agriculture to nonagriculture as a possible factor contribution. In our system of sectoring, a flow of labor from agriculture to nonagriculture may be viewed as an aspect of the agricultural sector's participation in growth, if gross agricultural product is constant or rising. Otherwise, it would show up in a declining gross product of agriculture.

There is, of course, nothing inherently wrong with a geographical criterion. But it should be noted that sectoring in this way tends to merge the question of the contribution of a particular sector such as the agricultural with the larger question of the emergence of the industrialized economy from the preindustrialized. And in a close economy the modern can only emerge from the older.

26. A. N. Malafeev, *Istoriya tsenoobrazovaniya v SSSR (1917–1963 gg.)* (Moscow, 1964), pp. 266–71.

27. Ya. I. Golev, *Sel'skokhozyaistvennyi kredit v SSSR* (Moscow, 1958), p. 19.

28. Ibid., pp. 20–25.

29. Joseph W. Willett gives a good survey of the results of the various programs instituted during the first decade after Stalin designed to help agriculture "to catch up" ("The Recent Record in Agricultural Production," in Joint Economic Committee, Congress of the United States, *Dimensions of Soviet Economic Power* (Washington, D.C., 1962), pp. 91–136; also Jerzy F. Karcz, "Seven Years on the Farm: Retrospect and Prospects," in Joint Economic Committee, Congress of the United States, *New Directions in the Soviet Economy* (Washington, D.C., 1966), Pt. 2-B, pp. 383–450.

30. Millar, "A Reformulation of A. V. Chayanov's Theory of the Peasant Economy."

31. Karcz, "Thoughts on the Grain Problem" pp. 399–434.

32. Erlich, *The Soviet Industrialization Debate,* pp. 119–20.

4

Mass Collectivization and the Contribution of Soviet Agriculture to the First Five-Year Plan: A Review Article

Explanations of the success of Soviet rapid industrialization during the 1930s, whether put forward by Western or Soviet scholars, have generally presupposed the "extraction" of a substantial net contribution from the agricultural sector. According to this view the rapid pace of industrialization, especially during the early years of the campaign, demanded an agricultural contribution well in excess of what might have been obtained by relying on the voluntary acquiescence of the peasantry. Forced mass collectivization, by replacing private (peasant) discretion over the amount, composition, and marketed share of agricultural output with centralized administrative coercion, has been supposed to have ensured the necessary increased flow of agricultural products to industry and urban centers and to have severed the potentially constraining link between the pace of industrialization and peasant willingness to expand output and, particularly, marketings in the face of increasingly adverse terms of exchange.[1]

This conception of the developmental role of Soviet agriculture and the economic rationale it has afforded the policy of mass collectivization have been challenged in recent years in the Western literature on both theoretical and empirical grounds.[2] However, an empirical test of the standard hypothesis has not previously been feasible because of the paucity of data on the relevant intersector flows of goods and services. It is indeed fortunate, therefore, that a Soviet historian, A. A. Barsov, has now joined the controversy with an attempt to measure directly the net material contribution of Soviet agriculture during the period 1928–32 (inclusive) based upon much

From *Slavic Review* 33, no. 4 (December 1974):750–66. Reprinted by permission, with minor editorial changes.

previously inaccessible archival data.[3] Barsov addresses himself to
three specific questions (Barsov 1969, pp. 8–10). First, to what extent
did the "surplus product" of agriculture serve as a source of socialist
accumulation for industrialization of the country? As Barsov notes,
earlier attempts by Soviet historians to answer this question have
relied either on data only tangentially related to the question (e.g.,
current-ruble as opposed to constant-ruble measures) or on purely
speculative considerations (Barsov 1969, p. 9, n.1). The same can
be said for most Western studies, but Barsov is somewhat less generous
in his criticism of the Western literature on this issue (Barsov 1969,
chap. 5). Second, given the direction and the size of the net flow of
material products between agriculture and nonagriculture, what was
the role of each trade (or transfer) channel between the two sectors?
Barsov's findings in this area represent a signal empirical contribution
to our understanding of both the process and the consequences of
mass collectivization. Third, how did the aggregate net flow of resources between agriculture and nonagriculture during the First Five-
Year Plan compare with that of the last year of the NEP (New
Economic Policy)? An answer to this last question is vital to any
appraisal of the success of collectivization.

In the course of his analysis Barsov has much of interest to say
about the appropriateness of state agricultural policy during the latter
part of the NEP and about collectivization itself, but the novelty
derives mainly from the fact that it is being said with such candor
by a Soviet scholar. His truly original contribution is an empirical
demonstration that Soviet agriculture's net material contribution to
industrialization was, at most, exceedingly modest. Unfortunately,
the particular measure Barsov presents is not likely to persuade the
Western non-Marxist economist, for he has recast the data in terms
of a labor theory of value approximation. In other words, Barsov
winds up measuring the extent to which income created in agriculture
and nonagriculture was allocated to the "rightful" claimants.[4] Thus,
the likelihood is that Barsov's findings may be ignored or misun-
derstood in the West. However, it is testimony to his careful scholarship that Barsov has made available his principal physical-volume
and price-time series, accompanied by extensive explanatory notes
on their construction. This has made it possible to construct several
alternative measures of the net contribution of Soviet agriculture
during the First Five-Year Plan. Interestingly enough, Barsov's main
findings are not invalidated by the alternative measures developed
here, for they suggest that, if anything, Barsov has overstated the
contribution of agriculture.

The main purpose of this review article is to render Barsov's data series accessible to the Western reader and to indicate their potential significance. The first two sections below are devoted to the development and assessment of alternative measures of the net contribution of Soviet agriculture for the period 1928 through 1932. The third section seeks to explain why most Western and Soviet students were led to overstate the development role of Soviet agriculture. The fourth undertakes a reevaluation of mass collectivization and of the centralized agricultural procurement system as components of Soviet development strategy.

1

There can, of course, be no unique and completely unambiguous empirical measure of the net contribution of any given sector of an economy to growth and development. The fundamental reason for this is that the net contribution of any sector will necessarily be sensitive to the price weights used to net intersector transactions, for a case can ordinarily be made for several alternative sets of price weights. That is, some set of prices must be used to compare the quantities flowing to and from the agricultural sector, and different sets of prices, drawn, for example, from different years, will usually yield different answers.[5] A second reason is that the given sector's net contribution also depends on the investigator's conception of the relevant intersector flows. A Marxist, for example, is likely to ignore nonmaterial flows. Third, the contribution measured depends on the criteria that have been used to sector the economy. The net contribution of, for example, a "rural sector," defined geographically, will necessarily differ from that of the "peasant sector," defined according to some kind of census criterion. An "agricultural sector," specified by type-of-product, will yield still a third result. Although this is not an unavoidable source of ambiguity in the measurement of sector contributions, widespread failure to specify sectoring criteria explicitly and consistently has produced a great deal of confusion in the literature on the developmental role of agriculture.

Barsov defines the "agricultural sector" by type-of-product produced, and it includes agricultural production units together with the population engaged in, or dependent upon, agricultural occupations proper. His measure is of the *net material trade surplus* of agriculture so defined, and thus the net flow of direct services to and from the sector is not considered. The nonrural sector is similarly defined to include industrial production units, governmental agencies, and ("nonproductive") service establishments, together with the population engaged in these occupations and their dependents (Barsov 1969, pp. 5–6, 52–55). Transactions with a third (and exhaustive) sector, composed of rural nonagricultural employments and population, are excluded from the trade accounts of both the agricultural and the nonrural (industrial) sectors because of data deficiencies. At a later stage we shall have to consider the significance of the omission of transactions in services and in trade with the rural nonagricultural sector.

Barsov has adjusted his price weights to reflect the "labor content" of the various intersector product flows (Barsov 1969, pp. 40–44). Any such adjustment must, of course, be regarded skeptically, but it has fortunately proved possible to recast Barsov's time series in terms of unadjusted price weights.

Four measures of the net material trade surplus of Soviet agriculture for 1928–32 are presented in table 1 (rows M, N, O, and P). Measures I and II (rows M and N) use 1928 price weights, and both agree that the net material trade surplus of agriculture was negative in each year covered, and substantially so. According to either of these measures, then, agriculture was a net recipient of material resources (measured in constant 1928 prices) both immediately before and during the First Five-Year Plan. Moreover, mass collectivization was accompanied by *increased net inflow*. The differences in magnitude between measures I and II reflect, mainly, the fact that measure II is the more comprehensive. Also, a difference in the reporting period for "market output" of agriculture is reflected for 1929 particularly (see rows A and B for 1929 and the notes to table 1). Because it is both more modest and more comprehensive, measure II is here adopted as the best available and used for the various computations that follow.

The price weights for measure III (row O) are 1913 world market prices. Barsov computed measure III as an aid in the construction of his adjusted labor content weights. It is of some interest because it shows the net material trade surplus of agriculture to have been positive in each year of the period and thus contrasts rather sharply with measures I and II. The difference reflects the fact that world industrial prices in 1913 were much lower relative to world agricultural prices than was the case within the Soviet Union in 1928. There are, however, two reasons why measure III should not be regarded as a validation of the standard view of the role of Soviet agriculture. First, there are some very substantial reasons for avoiding as a weight-base year one that is so very far removed in time from the years being compared by the index. There is, for instance, little reason to suppose that 1913 world market prices had any relevance to relative scarcities in the Soviet Union during 1928–32, especially considering the turbulent nature of the intervening historical period and the small number of domestic commodities that were actually traded in world markets. Second, even if we agree to accept 1913 world market prices, the positive trade surplus so obtained does not support the emphasis that has been placed on the "mobilization" of resources from the agricultural sector. Net material agricultural exports to the nonrural sector, in 1913 world market prices, do indeed increase between 1928 and 1931, but much more gradually than the increase in nonrural (industrial-urban) accumulation, measured comparably (see table 2, especially rows E and F). The "explanatory power" of the agricultural trade surplus diminishes sharply at the outset as well as during the course of the First Five-Year Plan.

The current-ruble volume of net material product exchange between agriculture and the nonrural sector is given by measure IV (table 1, row P). It cannot, of course, reveal anything about the flow of real resources, but it is important for other purposes. With this series it is possible to estimate the net gain (or loss) of the agricultural sector in material product trade resulting from the relative inflation of agricultural and industrial product prices. As may be seen in row Q, the agricultural sector did experience a net gain, because its prices rose faster than those of the goods it acquired from the nonagricultural sector. The terms of trade changed, on balance, in favor of the agricultural sector during the First Five-Year Plan. This is a very surprising finding, for it has been universally assumed that the reverse was the case.

2

As we have seen, by the best available measure (II), agriculture was a net importer of material products throughout 1928–32. The question remains, however, whether consideration of the net flow of services and of transactions with the rural nonagricultural sector might not change the outcome significantly. In 1928 (the only year for which data are available) agriculture, in its exchanges with the nonagricultural rural sector, received 330 million rubles worth of goods more than it gave up (Barsov 1969, table 3, pp. 60–61). Given the magnitude of the negative balance for 1928, and the relatively small and declining size of the rural nonagricultural sector during these years, there seems little reason to think that this net receipt of goods from the rural nonagricultural sector could have been reversed to create an outflow of resources that would have offset the large inflow which Barsov shows agriculture was receiving from the nonrural sector. We may be confident, therefore, that agriculture was a

Table 1. Trade Balance of Agriculture with the Nonrural Sector, 1928–32[a]

	1928	1929	1930	1931	1932	Operation
Market output[b] of agricultural sector						
A. Physical-volume index I (1928 prices)[c]	100.0	109.5	127.9	131.6	101.9	
B. Physical-volume index II (1928 prices)[d]	100.0	123.5	129.7	131.6	101.9	
			(millions of rubles)			
C. Value of marketings I (1928 prices)[e]	3,167	3,468	4,049	4,167	3,217	
D. Value of marketings II (1928 prices)[f]	3,876	4,687	5,027	5,101	3,949	
E. Value of marketings III (1913 world market prices)[g]	3,313	3,727	4,237	4,360	3,376	
F. Value of marketings IV (current prices)[h]	3,876	5,493	9,049	10,948	12,380	
Industrial goods purchases of agriculture[i]						
G. Physical-volume index I (1928 prices)[j]	100.0	122.2	134.7	130.4	120.7	
H. Physical-volume index II (1928 prices)[k]	100.0	112.2	128.4	130.4	120.7	
			(millions of rubles)			
I. Value of purchases I (1928 prices)[l]	3,951	4,805	5,322	5,153	4,768	
J. Value of purchases II (1928 prices)[m]	4,492	5,040	5,768	5,858	5,422	
K. Value of purchases III (1913 world market prices)[n]	1,463	1,787	1,971	1,908	1,767	
L. Value of purchases IV (current prices)[o]	4,492	5,065	6,316	9,829	13,062	
Trade balance of agriculture						
M. Export surplus I (1928 prices)	− 784	−1,337	−1,273	− 986	− 1,551	(C − I)
N. Export surplus II (1928 prices)	− 616	− 353	− 741	− 757	− 1,473	(D − J)
O. Export surplus III (1913 world market prices)	1,850	1,940	2,266	2,452	1,609	(E − K)
P. Export surplus IV (current prices)	− 616	428	2,733	1,119	− 682	(F − L)
Q. Net gain from inflation[p]	0	781	3,474	1,876	791	(P − N)

Notes and Sources for Table 1

ᵃ The agricultural sector is defined to include agricultural production units plus the population engaged in or dependent on agricultural pursuits. The nonrural (industrial) sector is similarly defined. Transactions with the third sector, rural nonagriculture, are excluded from the trade figures presented for the other two. See A. A. Barsov, *Balans stoimostnykh obmenov mezhdu gorodom i derevnei* (Moscow, 1969), pp. 52–55.

ᵇ Market output (i.e., "commodity production") of grain is computed net of the repurchase of grain products by the agricultural sector. All other products are reported as gross flows. Barsov (1969), pp. 100, 103.

ᶜ Barsov (1969), table 10, p. 113. The index is constructed from data on eighteen commodity groups (i.e., grains, sunflower seed, flax seed, hemp seed, raw cotton, flax fiber, hemp fiber, sugar beets, tobacco, makhorka, potatoes, vegetables, meat, milk, eggs, small and large animal hides, and wool), which accounted for 95 percent of market output in 1928 (p. 102).

ᵈ Barsov (1969), table 12, pp. 130–31. Market output of agriculture for 1928–30 (inclusive) is derived from the intersector accounts (*po mezhotraslevomu balansu*) adjusted to exclude repurchases of grain products by the agricultural sector. Index II is therefore more comprehensive for these years than index I. The relatives for 1931 and 1932 are, however, merely taken from index I. The substantial difference to be noted between the two indices for 1929 is explained by the fact that index I measures output from the harvest of that year while index II measures the volume of output marketed during 1929. Since the procurement campaign begun in 1928 developed slowly and became increasingly effective throughout 1929, the greater part of the harvest of 1928 as well as that of 1929 was procured during 1929. Thus index II indicates a larger increase in market output than index I does for this year.

ᵉ Barsov (1969), table 10, p. 113.

ᶠ The 1928 value figure is derived from the intersector balance given in table 3, Barsov (1969), pp. 60–61, adjusted to correspond to the definition of "market output" given in note d above. Values for the remaining years are derived by means of physical-volume index II (row B of this table).

ᵍ A. A. Barsov, "Sel'skoe khoziaistvo i istochniki sotsialisticheskogo nakopleniia v gody pervoi piatiletki (1928–1933)," *Istoriia SSSR*, no. 3 (1968):78.

ʰ Determined as the product of the constant-ruble value series II (row D) and the weighted, all-trade price index for agricultural marketings given in Barsov (1969), p. 123.

ⁱ Includes acquisitions of industrial commodities by the agricultural population as well as by productive units, on capital and current account, through all channels (Barsov [1969], pp. 118–19), exclusive of agricultural repurchases of grain products.

ʲ Barsov (1969), table 11, pp. 118–19. The reconstruction of the component time series is explained by Barsov on pp. 109–20.

ᵏ Barsov (1969), table 12, pp. 130–31. The relatives for 1928–30 are determined by means of the intersector accounts available for these years (only). Relatives for 1931 and 1932 are merely taken from physical-volume index I (row G of this table).

ˡ Barsov (1969), table 11, pp. 118–19.

ᵐ The 1928 value is derived from the intersector balance given in Barsov (1969), table 3, pp. 60–61, adjusted to exclude agricultural repurchase of grain products. Values for the remaining years are determined by means of physical-volume index II (row H of this table).

ⁿ Barsov (1968), p. 78.

ᵒ Determined as the product of the constant-ruble value series II (row J) and the weighted, all-trade price index for industrial goods purchases given in Barsov (1969), p. 123.

ᵖ That is, the difference between the "gain" from inflation on marketed output of agriculture (row F minus row D) and the "loss" from inflation on agricultural acquisitions of industrial products (row L minus row J), which, rearranged, is (row F minus row L) minus (row D minus row J), or (row P minus row N).

TABLE 2. Nonrural[a] Accumulation and the Trade Balance of Agriculture in 1913 World Market Prices (in millions of rubles)

	1928	1929	1930	1931	1932
A. Nonrural accumulation[b]	2,744.4	4,676.5	6,337.6	7,954.0	8,016.1
B. Increment in accumulation		1,932.1	1,661.1	1,616.4	62.1
C. Trade balance[c] of agriculture	1,849.3	1,940.6	2,256.9	2,451.5	1,608.9
D. Increment in trade balance		91.3	325.3	185.6	−842.6
E. Trade balance as percentage of accumulation	64.3	41.5	35.7	30.9	20.4
F. Row D as percentage of row B		4.7	19.6	11.5	

[a] Excludes rural nonagricultural sector.
[b] Includes accumulation and productive consumption of the nonrural nonproductive subsector.
[c] Material export surplus.
Source: Barsov (1968), pp. 78–80.

net recipient of material products, and probably substantially so, throughout the First Five-Year Plan.

Inclusion of the net flow of services cannot but reinforce the point, for agriculture had little in the way of services to offer nonagriculture, while it certainly benefited from educational, medical, and other governmental services as well as from service industries proper, such as passenger transportation and communications (Barsov 1969, pp. 137–38). Consideration of the two missing flows, then, indicates strongly that the agricultural sector proper was a net recipient of real resources during 1928–32.

The net resource contribution of a sector may be conceived in two conceptually distinct but measurably equivalent ways.[6] It may be conceived as the net flow of goods and services in constant, base-period prices (e.g., table 1, row N), or it may be conceived as the net flow of funds through price, transfer, and financial channels, because a sector that receives a net real product and service contribution from the rest of the economy must simultaneously finance the real inflow. A sector may acquire the funds with which to finance a net inflow of real resources from the rest of the economy in any one, or some combination, of three ways. It may obtain funds through financial channels by borrowing or by drawing down its own financial assets. It may be a net recipient of transfer payments—that is, unrequited payments, such as remittances by urban workers to relatives in the agricultural sector. Finally, an advantageous change in the terms of trade may serve to finance the increased net inflow of real goods and services. Consideration of these three channels offers an independent measure of the net contribution of Soviet agriculture during the First Five-Year Plan.

Thus, it is possible to test Barsov's conclusion by considering whether or not it is consistent with what is known, or can be deduced, about pecuniary flows through price, transfer, and financial channels. The positive gain from a differential rise in prices favoring agriculture over the nonrural sector (table 1, row Q) is, of course, completely consistent. In fact, it is more than sufficient to have financed the import surplus for the three-year period 1929–31, even granting a substantial margin for a possible adverse change in the terms of trade with the rural nonagricultural sector (about which we have no evidence one way or the other). Indeed, during this three-year period, there is every reason to suppose that the algebraic sum of the two remaining entries—that is, net transfer receipts and net funds raised through financial channels—was negative, representing a net outflow of funds from agriculture. For 1932 the financial gain from higher prices on the goods agriculture sold was not adequate to finance the recorded growth in the physical quantities of the goods it acquired from the nonrural sector, and it follows as an accounting truism that it had to finance its purchases by obtaining funds through financial or transfer channels. These findings are consistent with what is known, or can be inferred, about transfer and financial flows during the period in question.

The most difficult item to pin down is the sign of net transfer receipts of the agricultural sector. There are four main flows to consider. First, personal and enterprise tax and other "voluntary" payments (including profit withdrawals from state agricultural enterprises and agencies) increased slightly more than fourfold between 1928 and 1932 (Barsov 1969, p. 125. Tax and voluntary payments increased from 984.8 million rubles in 1928 to 4,595.7 million in 1932). This outflow was offset to some unknown, but probably slight, extent by state direct transfer payments to individuals and in somewhat greater degree by personal remittances from relatives residing in urban areas. The provision of free state services (e.g., educational or medical) must be treated as an imputed transfer receipt by agriculture and affords another offset to tax and other voluntary payments. Finally, and most important, the state's investment in the state-farm system and in the establishment of the Machine Tractor Station (MTS) system, to service the expanding collective-farm sector, was financed almost exclusively by means of grants from the state, which may very well have been large enough to give agriculture a net inflow of funds in respect to these various forms of unrequited transfer payments, particularly in the later years of the period.[7]

Even if net transfers were negative during the three-year period 1929–31, it seems unlikely that this was large enough to offset the gain agriculture received from the favorable price trends described above. The implication is that the agricultural sector was able to advance funds to the nonrural sector through financial channels, an implication that is consistent with the many reports of official concern about the accumulation of cash balances by the agricultural population during 1929–31.[8] Similarly, official reports on the successful diminution of cash hoards in the countryside in 1932 imply that the population was drawing down its financial assets to finance the excess of its current-ruble outlays over current receipts in transactions with the nonrural sector (Barsov 1969, p. 115).

We may conclude with some confidence, therefore, that the agricultural sector was a net recipient of real resources during the First Five-Year Plan and that mass collectivization did not serve to facilitate the "extraction" of real resources from the agricultural sector taken as a whole. This conclusion rests, of course, upon acceptance of 1928 price weights. It should be noted in this connection that 1928 was the last year of the New Economic Policy, which permitted open markets for agricultural products. Since a continuation of the NEP represented one possible alternative to mass collectivization, there is good reason to consider 1928 prices as meaningful in the context of the argument.[9]

3

In the concluding chapter of the book, Barsov criticizes sharply the standard Western interpretation of the role of agriculture during Soviet rapid industrialization, and he is particularly unhappy about the concepts of "primitive socialist accumulation" and of "agrarian colonialism" that underlie some of these treatments. As a strictly empirical proposition, *given 1928 price weights and a type-of-product definition of the agricultural sector,* Barsov is correct in rejecting the standard interpretation as inconsistent with the facts. However, it does not follow that the agricultural population was not exploited, and Barsov confuses the issue by presenting his argument exclusively in terms of hypothetical labor-content price weights. Nonetheless, it is clear that we must revise our conception of the role of agriculture during the First Five-Year Plan as a consequence of Barsov's empirical research. Moreover, it is possible to use Barsov's disaggregated data series to ascertain why and how Soviet agriculture, taken as a whole, came to be a net recipient of real resources during this period.[10] Consideration of these factors also serves to provide a picture of the relations between the various subsectors of Soviet agriculture in these years, and particularly those between the state, private peasant, and socialized subsectors.

The net flow of resources to the agricultural sector may be analyzed from several different perspectives, and each helps to illuminate a different aspect of the relations between the various sectors and subsectors of the economy. First, a comparison of rows D and I in table 3 shows that the terms of trade turned in favor of agricultural products taken together. However, within the agricultural sector the terms of trade did turn against kolkhozes with respect to planned (obligatory) procurements (compare rows A and I), but the rise in prices on the open collective-farm market more than compensated for it.[11] What this means is that, thanks to inflation on the open market, the peasants were able to shift a part of the burden thrown on them by the state to the nonrural population. It is unfortunate that the available data do not permit us to ascertain more precisely the relations between the state and the rural and nonrural populations.

Second, the private subsector of agriculture recorded a very substantial real volume import surplus with the nonrural sector (table 4, row F), which reflected mainly spending on industrial consumer goods financed by income earned from sales on the collective-farm market. Moreover, the state succeeded in controlling trade in manufactured goods in the rural area to a much greater extent than it did in the cities, where private trade continued to flourish (Barsov 1969, pp. 27–29). Consequently, what manufactured goods were available in the countryside—and the volume did of course decline sharply—were sold at lower prices than would otherwise have been the case. Thus, the private household sector may be viewed as principally responsible for the size of the net import surplus of agriculture in the years covered by table 4 (row F), even though the constant-ruble value of both sales and purchases declined. In this sense, the import surplus of agriculture may be attributed to the incompleteness of collectivization, which permitted the peasantry to continue private production and the marketing of products on the open market to the urban population.

Third, there was a substantial increase in the flow of industrial products to the agricultural sector, particularly to sovkhozes and the MTS system (table 3, row L). These products were also made available at favorable prices (row H), which contributed measurably to the favorable change in the terms of trade for the agricultural sector taken as a whole. As may be seen in table 4 (rows B and D), both the sovkhozes and the MTS recorded large physical-volume import

TABLE 3. Price and Quantity Indices for Agricultural Trade, 1928–32 (1928 = 100)

	1928	1929	1930	1931	1932
Agricultural commodities					
A. Planned procurement price index[a]	100.0	110.6	115.7	118.7	109.3
B. Decentralized procurement price index	100.0	—	—	—	354.3
C. Private trade (uncontrolled) price index	100.0	233.2	525.3	814.6	3005.7
D. All-trade (weighted) agricultural price index	100.0	117.2	180.0	198.8	313.5
E. All-trade physical-volume index	100.0	109.5	127.9	131.6	101.9
Industrial (nonrural) commodities					
F. State and cooperative rural retail price index	100.0	98.6	107.4	130.1	284.5
G. Private trade price index (1927/28 = 100)	100.0	139.3	218.2	392.8	845.7
H. Wholesale price index on "means of production"[b]	100.0	100.0	100.0	100.0	100.0
I. SII-trade (weighted) industrial price index	100.0	100.5	109.5	171.2	240.8
J. Physical-volume index state and retail trade	100.0	131.9	142.3	118.3	108.2
K. Physical-volume index private trade	100.0	65.6	89.5	73.7	26.8
L. Physical-volume index wholesale producer goods	100.0	120.5	154.2	240.8	239.2
M. Physical-volume index all trade	100.0	122.2	134.7	130.4	120.7

[a] All price indices use as a comparison base all-trade (weighted) prices in 1928 (or 1927/28) for agricultural (or industrial) trade.
[b] Direct state supply of equipment and materials at wholesale prices to sovkhozes, the MTS, and, for state-financed purchases only, to kolkhozes.
Sources: Barsov (1969): Rows A through D, p. 108; rows E and I, p. 123; rows F through H, pp. 112–15; rows J through M, table 11, pp. 118–19.

TABLE 4. Material Trade Balance by Agricultural Subsector, 1930–32 (in millions of rubles, 1928 prices)

	1930	1931	1932
A. Export surplus: kolkhozes only	+631	+1,500	+ 876
B. Export surplus: MTS	− 75	− 580	− 762
C. Export surplus: kolkhoz sector (A + B)	+556	+ 920	+ 114
D. Export surplus: sovkhozes only	−472	−1,018	− 934
E. Export surplus: socialized sector (C + D)	− 84	− 98	− 820
F. Export surplus: private sector	−825	− 659	− 653
G. Export surplus: nonstate sector (A + F)	−194	+ 841	+ 223
H. Export surplus: state sector (B + D)	−547	−1,598	−1,696
I. Export surplus: all agriculture (E + F) or (G + H)	−741	− 757	−1,473

Note: Figures shown with pluses represent a net flow from agriculture to the nonrural sector. Those with minuses indicate a net flow from the nonrural sector to agriculture. Source: Barsov (1969), table 13, pp. 142–43, converted to 1928 price weights, and table 1, rows D and J, above.

surpluses with the nonrural sector, and the combined effect was to swamp the real volume export surplus of kolkhozes (rows A, C, and E). Put differently, the "squeeze" applied to kolkhozes was offset by the net flow of real resources into the MTS and sovkhozes. Thus, the state was successful in diverting resources within the agricultural sector to capital formation in the state subsectors.

Finally, the state was undoubtedly successful in procuring products from kolkhozes "on the cheap" (see table 3, row A, and table 4, rows A and C), and the export surplus of kolkhozes (only) more than compensated for the import surplus of the private sector in two of the three years for which data are available (row G). From this perspective, the import surplus of agriculture may be attributed to state investment in the state subsectors of agriculture. However, the state's investment in sovkhozes and the MTS system failed to offset peasant destruction of the agricultural capital stock, and tractive power per unit of land area declined sharply during the First Five-Year Plan (Barsov 1969, p. 85, n.53). Moreover, although grain procurements increased remarkably between 1928 and 1931, from 157.4 million centners to 237.3 million (Barsov 1969, p. 103), state procurements of many other products declined sharply, most notably animal husbandry products and certain industrial crops (e.g., sunflower seed, hemp seed and fiber, flax seed) (Barsov 1969, table 10, p. 113). The increase in grain procurements reflected this adverse change in the composition of agricultural output and marketings, not the success of state procurement policy. It has been shown, in fact, that the entire increase in state grain procurements is more than explained by the decrease in fodder requirements cause by the wholesale destruction of livestock herds by the peasantry in hostile response to the collectivization drive.[12] The aggregate volume of agricultural procurements increased much less significantly and less permanently than for grain alone, and this temporary increase was, as has been seen, accompanied by a more than compensating increase in the supply of industrial products to the agricultural sector.

Ultimately, therefore, although the state did succeed in raising real resources from the peasantry and via the peasantry for investment purposes, the destruction occasioned by resistance to collectivization obliged it to turn around and use those resources for replacement investment in agriculture. This inflow, together with the net inflow to the private sector that was financed by the favorable change in the terms of trade with the nonrural population, caused the agricultural sector taken as a whole to become a net recipient of resources during the First Five-Year Plan.

The widely held conception of Soviet agriculture as a net contributor to rapid industrialization was very largely a result of the paucity of data for the sector as a whole and for the individual subsectors. As I have argued elsewhere,[13] a number of the interpretations put forward were also flawed by faulty theoretical modeling, particularly with respect to the concept of an economic surplus. In addition, observing both the unmistakable hardships collectivization imposed upon the Soviet peasantry and the undoubted success of the industrialization drive, investigators were led to assume that the two phenomena were causally related, for where else could the resources devoted to industrialization have come from? That many Soviet leaders and planners expressed an intent to "milk" the agricultural sector in support of rapid industrialization made this assumption all the more plausible.[14]

4

Whatever its merits may have been on other grounds, mass collectivization of Soviet agriculture must be reckoned as an unmitigated economic policy disaster. As with any kind of economic disaster, such as a tornado, there was no way in which the economy as a whole, and thus the state, stood to benefit, although certain fortunately placed individuals may have done so at the expense of others. Agricultural output increased only marginally over the entire period of the 1930s,[15] while labor productivity, yields, and rural and urban consumption per capita declined.[16] Despite considerable state investment in state farms and the MTS, tractive power available to agriculture declined precipitously between 1928 and 1933, thanks to the slaughter of livestock by the peasants.[17] The Soviet official history of World War II explicitly singles out Stalin's agricultural policies for criticism, for agriculture was one of the least-developed sectors of the economy and thus a major handicap at the outbreak of war.[18] The long-term consequences of collectivization (and of World War II) have also proved exceptionally difficult and costly to reverse, and success is not yet within reach despite two decades of economic, administrative, and social reforms in the countryside.[19]

The evidence suggests that the oppressive state agricultural procurement system, rather than serving to extract a net contribution from agriculture as a whole, should be credited with preventing the collectivization disaster from disrupting the industrialization drive. The squeeze on the kolkhozes, and on the peasantry generally, served to offset, at least partially, the adverse effects of the collectivization drive. The level of agricultural procurements was maintained in the face of extreme hardship in the countryside—hardship attributable partly to peasant resistance to collectivization and partly to administrative ignorance and confusion about how to reorganize agricultural production (Barsov 1969, pp. 193–94). That the terms of trade changed in favor of agriculture does not in the least mean that the peasantry became better off in consequence. On the contrary, what it means is that the peasantry was able to shift a portion of the real cost of collectivization and industrialization to the urban population, mainly through the uncontrolled collective-farm market. Whether or not this was sufficient to equalize the burden between the two sectors remains at issue. Barsov's own computations on this heading will not persuade anyone who is not prepared to adopt his particular operational definition of the labor theory of value.

Despite this shortcoming, Barsov has made a very important empirical contribution to our understanding of the process and consequences of mass collectivization. It is clear that, as an economic measure at least, mass collectivization was counterproductive even in the short run.[20] Since there has never been any disagreement among Western scholars with respect to its adverse long-run consequences, mass collectivization is thereby deprived of any economic rationale whatever. This suggests that a continuation of the New Economic Policy of the 1920s would have permitted at least as rapid a rate of industrialization with less cost to the urban as well as to the rural population of the Soviet Union.

NOTES

1. This statement of the "standard" hypothesis is somewhat oversimplified. There are in fact several versions, which differ from one another mainly because of differences in the way in which the "agricultural sector" has been defined. Alec Nove, for example, considers primarily the relation between the peasantry and the state in *An Economic History of the U.S.S.R.* (London, 1969), pp. 148–86. Alexander Erlich adopts essentially the same approach in *The Soviet Indstrialization Debate, 1924–1928* (Cambridge, Mass., 1960), pp. 119–21. However, the main concern of most economists has been the relation between the agricultural sector taken as a whole and the nonagricultural sector, and this is the form in which the hypothesis has passed into the general literature on economic growth. See, for example, Paul Baran, *The Political Economy of Growth* (New York, 1962), pp. 266–71; William H. Nicholls, "The Place of Agriculture in Economic Development," in Carl K. Eicher and Lawrence W. Witt (eds.), *Agriculture in Economic Development* (New York, 1964), pp. 22–24; Bruce F. Johnston and John W. Mellor, "The Role of Agriculture in Economic Development," *American Economic Review* 51, no. 4 (September 1961):579; Charles K. Wilber, "The Role of Agriculture in Soviet Economic Development," *Land Economics* 45, no. 1 (February 1969):87–96. For a Soviet view, see *Politicheskaia ekonomiia: Kommunisticheskii sposob proizvodstva* (Moscow, 1963), p. 286. For an excellent statement and analysis of the standard hypotheses, see Robert W. Campbell, *The Soviet-Type Economies Performance and Evolution* (3d ed., Boston, 1974), pp. 62–76, which appeared after this manuscript had been drafted.

2. Jerzy F. Karcz, "From Stalin to Brezhnev: Soviet Agricultural Policy in Historical Perspective," in James R. Millar (ed.), *The Soviet Rural Community* (Urbana, Ill., 1971), esp. pp. 37–60; Z. M. Fallenbuchl, "Collectivization and Economic Development," *Canadian Journal of Economics and Political Science* 33, no. 1 (February 1967):1–15; James R. Millar, "Soviet Rapid Development and the Agricultural Surplus Hypothesis," *Soviet Studies* 22, no. 1 (July 1970):77–93; James R. Millar and Corinne A. Guntzel, "The Economics and Politics of Mass Collectivization Reconsidered: A Review Article," *Explorations in Economic History* 8, no. 1 (Fall 1970):103–16.

3. A. A. Barsov, *Balans stoimostnykh obmenov mezhdu gorodom i derevnei* (Moscow, 1969), and "Sel'skoe khoziaistvo i istochniki sotsialisticheskogo nakopleniia v gody pervoi piatiletki (1928-1933)," *Istoriia SSSR*, no. 3 (1968):64–82 (hereafter Barsov 1969 and Barsov 1968 respectively). Barsov has evidently exploited fully the statistical data available in published sources pertaining to the period, and the bibliography that may be compiled from his footnote citations is essentially definitive. However, and more important, Barsov extensively uses new data series not previously available in published form, derived from the Tsentral'nyi gosudarstvennyi arkhiv narodnogo khoziaistva SSSR (esp. fonds 1562, 4372, and 7733), which was founded in 1961. For a brief description of this new archive,

see Patricia K. Grimsted, *Archives and Manuscript Repositories in the USSR: Moscow and Leningrad* (Princeton, N.J., 1972), pp. 133–34.

4. There are two related but separable issues involved in the standard hopothesis on the contribution of Soviet agriculture. One pertains to the actual net flow of real resources between agriculture and nonagriculture (however defined) and is pertinent to the questions addressed by the typical two-sector growth model. The other has to do with the welfare implications of the net flow—for example, for the agricultural population. Subject to the qualifications set forth below in the text and notes, the first issue lends itself to straightforward empirical measurement. The second, however, involves a choice of value standard and must therefore be answered using data (such as hypothetical price weights) not contained in the actual historical record. Since Barsov's choice of value standard is not likely to gain acceptance among Western students of the period, his principal contribution consists in the collection and reconstruction of the actual data series and therefore is pertinent to the first issue. Thus this review is focused on the question of the measurement of the net resource contribution of agriculture, as opposed to the issue of peasant welfare.

5. This is sometimes referred to as the index number problem, or, more technically, the formula error. The comparison of any two years, for example, involves two sets of quantities and two sets of prices. The quantity change may be measured using as weights prices in either the base or the given year. Ordinarily, the two alternative formulas will not yield answers that agree precisely, and the difference can be quite substantial. However, since the two formulas stand on an equal footing, there is no basis for choosing between them. Obviously, some other set of price weights, drawn from a third time or place, will be likely to yield a third answer.

6. For a detailed explanation, see Millar, "Soviet Rapid Development," esp. pp. 87–92.

7. Ia. I. Golev, *Sel'skokhoziaistvennyi kredit v SSSR* (Moscow, 1958), pp. 19–21; V. P. D'iachenko et al., *50 let sovetskikh finansov* (Moscow, 1967), pp. 49–50; Barsov (1969), p. 82.

8. A. N. Malafeev, *Istoriia tsenoobrazovaniia v SSSR (1917–1963 gg.* (Moscow, 1964), pp. 131–32, 172–73; M. Atlas *Razvitie gosudarstvennogo banka SSSR* (Moscow, 1958), pp. 129–30; Barsov (1969), pp. 115–24.

9. It would be extremely useful to be able to calculate the trade surplus of agriculture using price weights drawn, say, from 1932, because the size of the discrepancy between it and the 1928 price-weight index could serve as a measure of realiability. Unfortunately, Barsov does not provide price data for the years following 1928. It is doubtful, however, that the discrepancy would be larger than exists between the 1913 and the 1928 price-weighted indices.

10. As was indicated above, different sectoring criteria and different price weights may be expected to yield different concepts and measures of the "contribution" of agriculture. It is possible, therefore, that what I have called the standard interpretation of the role of agriculture may be valid for some subset of sectoring criteria and price weights. However, in my

opinion the sectors designated by Barsov are appropriate to an attempt to measure the contribution of the agricultural sector to economic development, conceived within the framework of a two-sector growth model. In addition, 1928 price weights are all that are available from the actual historical period.

11. Much depends, of course, on the reliability of the wholesale price index for "means of production," which indicates constant prices on equipment and materials directly supplied by the state to sovkhozes, the MTS, and for state-financed purchases only to kolkhozes (see table 3, note b). One of the (anonymous) referees of this essay called attention to the relatively high prices of tractors in 1928. He also suggested that this index may have been applied (inappropriately) to construction costs and other elements where price controls would have been much less effective than for equipment and materials. The latter criticism, if correct, implies that the favorable change in the terms of trade for agriculture may be overstated, and possibly substantially so. There does not appear to be any way to resolve this question directly. However, as I pointed out in the text above, the available data on transfers, financial flows, and the change in the terms of trade are consistent with a net import surplus for the agricultural sector. Moreover, the generally high quality of Barsov's works provides another reason for placing confidence in the sign of the change in the terms of trade, if not the precise magnitude of the change.

12. Karcz, "From Stalin to Brezhnev," p. 42.

13. Millar, "Soviet Rapid Development," pp. 78–82.

14. See, for example, Alexander Erlich, "Stalin's Views on Economic Development," in Ernest Simmons (ed.), *Continuity and Change in Russian and Soviet Thought* (Cambridge, Mass., 1955).

15. Gross agricultural output exceeded the precollectivization 1928 level only in 1937 and 1940, according to Soviet official figures; see, for example, *Narodnoe khoziaistvo SSSR v 1958 godu* (Moscow, 1959), p. 350. Western estimates have presented an even bleaker picture; see Arcadius Kahan, "Soviet Statistics of Agricultural Output," in Roy D. Laird (ed.), *Soviet Agricultural and Peasant Affairs* (Lawrence, Kans., 1963), pp. 134–60.

16. Barsov (1969), pp. 84, 87, 90; Iu. V. Arutiunian, "Osobennosti i znachenie novogo etapa razvitiia sel'skogo khoziaistva SSSR," in *Istoriia sovetskogo krest'ianstva i kolkhoznogo stroitel'stva v SSSR* (Moscow, 1963), p. 409. According to Arutiunian, average annual agricultural output per capita changed as follows (1926–29 = 100): 90.3 in 1913; 100.0 in 1926–29; 86.8 in 1930–32; 90.0 in 1938–40; and 94.0 in 1950–53.

17. Iu. A. Moshkov, "Zernovaia problema v gody kollektivizatsii sel'skogo khoziaistva," in *Istoriia sovetskogo krest'ianstva i kolkhoznogo stroitel'stva v SSSR*, p. 272; Barsov (1969), p. 85, n.53.

18. *Istoriia Velikoi Otechestvennoi voiny Sovetskogo Soiuza, 1941–1945*, vol. 6, p. 43.

19. It has frequently been argued that mass collectivization did at least serve to ensure an adequate flow of labor out of the countryside to fill the growing number of industrial occupations. It would be inappropriate to

include the net flow of labor between agriculture and the nonrural sector as they are defined by Barsov, for it would involve double counting where sectors are identified by type-of-product criteria. It would, of course, be suitable where geographical criteria are used. However, as an economic rationale for collectivization, the mobilization-of-labor argument is without force. In the first place, there is no evidence to suggest that the supply of labor was deficient prior to the initiation of collectivization. In the second place, it is clear that collectivization encouraged an excessive off-farm flow of labor and population, and its continuation at the present time remains one of the most intractable obstacles to the modernization of Soviet agriculture today. On this subject, see Norton T. Dodge, "Recruitment and the Quality of the Soviet Agricultural Labor Force," in Millar, *Soviet Rural Community,* pp. 180–213.

20. It must be remembered, of course, that we remain essentially in the dark with respect to the balance of trade during the Second Five-Year Plan, and, according to Barsov, who has seen the archival material available for that period, we are likely to remain ignorant. Very little information apparently exists, and what is to hand is evidently insufficient to permit the reconstruction of the necessary price and physical-volume time series (Barsov 1969, pp. 186–90). Consequently, the force of this conclusion obtains (with the reservations noted above) primarily for the period 1928–32. However, Barsov's findings do appear to be consistent with Bergson's findings for the 1937 data, which suggest that agriculture contributed considerably less to Soviet capital formation than had previously been supposed. See Abram Bergson, *The Real National Income of Soviet Russia since 1928* (Cambridge, Mass., 1961), p. 257. On this same point, see also Karcz, "From Stalin to Brezhnev," pp. 48–51.

5

Was Stalin Really Necessary?
A Debate on Collectivization

Introductory Remarks

JERRY F. HOUGH

In all scholarship fields there are certain questions or subjects which for a time become the focus of intense interest and study by a disproportionate number of the best minds in the field. In Soviet studies of the last decade, the question, that more than any other, has caught the attention of a generation of scholars and provided the basis for exciting reanalysis and debate has been the nature of the 1920s and the First Five-Year Plan—that is, the origins of the Stalin system and the validity of the basic assumptions of the total-itarian model which embodied our understanding of those origins.

There have been a number of major (and, of course, contro-versial) attacks upon our fundamental assumptions about the Soviet system. It has been argued that Lenin came to accept NEP as the long-term road to communism rather than temporary retreat; that Bukharin's program rather than Stalin's represented the logical cul-mination of Leninism; that "the revolution from above" of 1928–29 actually had many societal sources; that there was little need for massive renewal of capital stock in the First Five-Year Plan period and that relatively little occurred; that women were perhaps the major "source of accumulation" during the early industrialization drive; that Lysenko's enshrinement as genetics czar had little relationship to Marxist ideology other than an ex post facto one. All of these propositions have been forcefully advanced—and challenged—by leading scholars of the last decade.[1]

Of all the events of the 1920s and early 1930s, however, none has received more serious reconsideration than the collectivization decision of 1928–29. At the center of attention has been not only

From *Problems of Communism* 25 (July-August 1976):49–66, with Alec Nove. Reprinted by permission, with minor editorial changes.

the process by which the decision was taken but, more important, the relationship of the decision to the industrialization drive and "the Soviet model of economic development." One of the leading figures in that reconsideration is James R. Millar of the Department of Economics at the University of Illinois (Urbana), and he has been asked to begin this discussion with a summary of the revisionist position as he sees it.[2] The other participant in the debate is one of the most distinguished economists in the history of Soviet studies, Alec Nove of the University of Glasgow. The actual title of the debate is taken from the title of a famous article which he wrote in 1962.[3]

What's Wrong with the "Standard Story"

JAMES R. MILLAR

There are several possibilities as to what the somewhat elliptical title "Was Stalin Really Necessary?" actually means. One is: Was Stalin somehow inevitable? Historians of the Soviet period have almost all tended toward some degree of determinism in answering this question and have suggested that to some extent Stalin represented the culmination of forces set in motion at a much earlier date—say, at the turn of the century. But I am not going to charge Alec Nove with asserting some kind of historical inevitability. I take the title to mean: Was collectivization really necessary? Was it necessary in order to achieve the ends—that is, to achieve the rapid rate of industrialization—that the Soviets, in fact, achieved? As we proceed, I want to change the question from Was it necessary? to Was it optimal, given the development objectives of the Soviet leadership?

In dealing with this question, I could follow one of two strategies. I could attack on a very narrow corridor in hopes of overpowering my adversary with detailed statistics and highly abstruse formulations, or, on the contrary, I could attack broadly—launch a broadside against the standard interpretation for which the answer to the question Was Stalin really necessary? is the culmination. I have elected the latter course—to take a running shot at the overall interpretation of what I am calling the "standard story" of the role of agriculture in industrialization in the Soviet Union. We shall begin at the beginning and we shall conclude at the end of the First Five-Year Plan. Along the way, I hope to attack a number of elements of what I consider to be the standard interpretation.

The most convenient recent summary of the standard story can be found in the new textbook by Paul R. Gregory and Robert C.

Stuart, *Soviet Economic Structure and Performance,* which is based
on the work of most of the economic historians who studied the
Soviet Union in the 1950s and early 1960s.[4] In abbreviated form,
the story goes something like this: Once the Bolsheviks had gained
control, once the civil war had come to a close and it became obvious
that it would be impossible to establish an economy on the principles
underlying war communism, the New Economic Policy (NEP) was
introduced. Yevgeniy Preobrazhensky, among others, began to attempt to reconcile himself to the institutions of the New Economic
Policy.[5] He noted that the policy established a mixed economy, and
he argued that the socialist sector would obviously have to grow more
rapidly than the private sector during NEP if the socialist revolution
was to have a favorable outcome.

According to the standard story, however, Preobrazhensky said
much more than this. He is said to have claimed the need for very
rapid industrialization and to have developed the concept of "primitive socialist accumulation," which is translated in the standard story
to mean "exploiting the peasants in support of industrialization."
The story goes on to say that Nikolai Bukharin—perhaps the other
major theorist of the period[6]—retorted with the argument that if the
terms of trade were turned against the peasantry, or if the peasants
were taxed heavily in any other way, the peasants would simply
withdraw from the market, as they already allegedly had done during
the "scissors crisis" of 1922–24.[7]

Thus, the historical issue is presented as a dilemma. For the
purposes of military defense against a possible renewed intervention
by the West and for the purposes of establishing socialism in the
Soviet Union, it was necessary for the economy to industrialize and
modernize rapidly. The means proposed to do it—that is, taxing in
one form or another the 80 to 85 percent of the population who
were peasants—was said to be not feasible, for the peasantry would
withdraw from the market, and, doing so, would sabotage the possibility of rapid industrialization.

The standard story then turns from the dilemma of NEP to
the grain crisis of 1927–28. Marketings of grain were off sharply at
this time, and "emergency measures" were taken in 1928 to confiscate
hoards of grain from the peasantry. These emergency measures were
ultimately followed by collectivization. According to the argument,
the First Five-Year Plan, which had been approved in 1927, did call
for a high rate of industrialization, and, just as had been foreseen,
the peasants began—whether for political or economic reasons—to
sabotage the hopes of industrialization in Soviet Russia.

Stalin then is said to have thought of something Preobrazhensky had not—coercion. He thought of forcing the peasants into the collective farm and thereby depriving them of discretion over the level of sowings and over the share of marketings. The state was therefore able to ensure rapid industrialization at the expense of the peasantry. The story asserts that collectivization *did work* in this sense, that it did permit the extraction or the mobilization of a surplus from the peasantry (grain marketings rose sharply during the First Five-Year Plan), and that this squeeze on the peasantry was a significant factor among the sources of rapid industrialization. Preobrazhensky was right, it is said, in terms of where the resources had to come from, but he didn't think of collectivization. Stalin was right *and necessary* because he saw that the extraction of the surplus required coercion, since peasants would not surrender the resources voluntarily, and because he was willing to supply the coercion.

That, briefly, is the standard story, and in many ways it is a neat one—easy to teach and easy to remember. Here was Preobrazhensky who had the principles clear as to what was necessary. There was Bukharin who pointed out the fatal flaw in the argument. While in Preobrazhensky's presumed view, this left a hopeless situation. Stalin arrived to reresolve Preobrazhensky's dilemma. Collectivization was a necessary step if the Soviet Union was to achieve the rate of industrialization that it did in the 1930s. If the *only* way to achieve that rate of industrialization was through collectivization—if it was the single means available—the word "necessary" would acquire the same value, or meaning, as the word "optimal." From this it would follow that Stalin himself was also necessary—at least *given* the end. Necessary, but, of course, not necessarily desirable.

This is the standard story. What is wrong with it? The answer is—amost everything. Almost every single proposition, every fundament of the story, is either misleading, false, or wrong-headed.

The first problem with the standard story is that Alexander Erlich's famous article on Preobrazhensky contains more of Erlich (and of John Maynard Keynes) than it does of Preobrazhensky.[8] Erlich read a great deal more intelligence, consistency, and meaningfulness—particularly contemporary economic meaningfulness—into Preobrazhensky's writings than was ever there, and particularly more than was ever there during the time of the industrialization debate itself, for Preobrazhensky continued to refine his arguments long after the original debate was over.

Preobrazhensky spoke of primitive socialist accumulation, and many mistakenly think that this concept is merely analogous to Marx's primitive capitalist accumulation. (The people who say this have not understood what Marx meant by primitive capitalist accumulation.) What Preobrazhensky called for in his discussion of primitive socialist accumulation was simply the New Economic Policy. He says so very clearly in several footnotes in the text of *Novaya ekonomika* (The new economics). His proposal was little more than that the terms of trade be turned against the peasantry as a way of financing industrialization.

The reason for Preobrazhensky's proposal was very simple. Given the size of the private sector and the size of the public sector, socialism could succeed in Russia only if the public sector were to grow more rapidly than the private. Otherwise, the country would lapse back into a private economy. He argued for a more rapid public growth, and this required intercepting surplus value created in the private sector and transferring it into the public sector. Preobrazhensky also called for "self-exploitation" by the workers in the public sector. In his view, therefore, rapid growth required not just exploitation of the peasants—the proletariat would also have to make sacrifices to finance industrialization. Preobrazhensky made a very important point that people in public finance will recognize: given the fact that the premodern direct taxes associated with the czarist regime had been abandoned, the most efficient form of taxation was almost certainly some kind of indirect taxation, whether imposed through an indirect sales tax or by turning the terms of trade against the peasantry. On this point Preobrazhensky was right in terms of modern fiscal theory, but he was more correct generally than most people have realized, as we shall see.

In this debate, Bukharin argued that the peasants would withdraw from the market in the face of such taxation. There is no evidence at all for his assertion. On the other hand, numerous studies of Russian peasant behavior in the nineteenth century and early twentieth century by Russian scholars (one notable example is A. V. Chayanov[9]) suggest that the peasantry would *not* react in this way. In fairly undeveloped countries, peasants do respond to changes in relative prices rather quickly (usually given a year's lag, of course). Consequently, if the terms of trade turn against a *particular* product, the peasants will quit producing and/or marketing it and transfer their efforts to other products. This is true and well established. But what happens when the terms of trade *turn as a whole against the peasantry?* They maintain or even increase their production and their marketings (or leave the farm for nonrural employment, but only where it is available). When, for example, the peasant family suffers an adverse change in its economic situation through the addition of an extra unproductive mouth to feed (whether a baby or an invalid doesn't matter), the response is for the working members of the family to work harder.[10] This effort of the family to maintain its standard of living in the face of a general adverse economic change takes place not only when there is the birth of a child but also when there is a new tax, an across-the-board change in the terms of trade, and so forth. This is true not only of the Russian peasantry but of every agricultural population for which any investigation has been made. For example, it was true of farmers in the United States during the 1930s. What's more, it was true of the Soviet peasants during the 1922–23 "scissors crisis," for, contrary to a widespread misconception in the profession today, they did not withdraw from the market then.[11]

One of the factors that made many people feel the peasants would withdraw from the market was a fallacious notion of peasant self-sufficiency. The problem is partly that, as W. W. Rostow once entitled an article, "Marx was a city boy."[12] So were the Bolsheviks, and so have been most Soviet and Western students of the period. They have not understood that there is no such thing as a self-sufficient peasant household, and there wasn't in Russia in the 1920s. Many have a notion that agriculture receives nothing from industry but a few luxuries like a pair of trousers or sugar. But the peasants also need kerosene, matches, soap, salt, condiments, steel for plows, milling services, and a number of other goods and services that a peasant community cannot produce, or at least can in no way produce efficiently.

Indeed, the peasants often weren't even self-sufficient in agricultural products. We have a false picture of a peasant farmer who produced a full range of agricultural goods and marketed a little bit on the side, but that's not the way it was. In the 1920s as well as in the late nineteenth century, certain peasants produced grain or industrial crops like cotton or flax for the market, and these peasants had to purchase other farm products from other peasants. There were others—in fact, most peasants—who produced the animal husbandry products, fruit, and vegetables for local or urban markets. The production functions and interdependencies of even the poorest peasants in the country were, therefore, very complicated.

If we turn to the grain crisis of 1928, then the standard story clearly is right in suggesting that this event persuaded many Bolsheviks that the end of the NEP had come—that the New Economic Policy had either served its usefulness or that the peasants had decided to sabotage Bolshevik plans. The Bolsheviks were city boys. They didn't understand the peasants, they didn't like the peasants, and there were an awful lot of peasants. Thus, the Bolsheviks were quite prepared to accept an alarming and sinister explanation for the falloff in grain marketings.

However, if the standard story suggests that Draconian measures were necessary to solve the 1928 grain crisis, then it is wrong. As the late Jerzy Karcz has argued—although this is somewhat more controversial—the grain crisis really was a consequence of unfavorable price policy with respect to grain products. The somewhat neglected Soviet economist of the 1920s, Yuriy Larin, pointed out that the peasants considered their animals (as well as their alcohol) their banks, and when grain prices were low, they put grain in these "banks."[13] In fact, an unfavorable price relationship had developed between grain and livestock prices during the 1920s, and simultaneously there had occurred a gradual falloff in the marketings of grain during the period. An adjustment of prices within the agricultural sector might well have solved the grain marketing problems rather easily, but the Bolshevik leadership certainly did not understand this.

The final aspect of the standard story—and the crucial one from the point of view of the argument about the necessity of Stalin— is the belief that Preobrazhensky was at least right in suggesting that industrialization would occur at the expense of the peasantry. It is argued that since grain marketings *did* increase and the country *did* industrialize rapidly, industrialization must have been carried out at the expense of the peasants—that is, with resources extracted from them.

Yet, as a Soviet economic historian named Barsov has recently shown, Soviet agriculture did not contribute in any significant measure to industrialization during the First Five-Year Plan. Although Barsov's is a very serious and careful analysis, his conclusions may be questioned in the West because of his (Marxist) methodology.[14] However, as I have shown elsewhere,[15] when his data are reworked according to Western conventions and measured in 1928 prices, the contribution of Soviet agriculture—strictly defined as a Western, non-Marxist economist would define it[16]—*actually turns out to have been negative.* The case seems to be even stronger than Barsov realized. Agriculture was a net recipient of real resources in the First Five-Year Plan from 1928 through 1932. Far from there being a net flow of resources out of agriculture into the industrial sector, there was a reverse flow—and a reverse flow of some consequence when measured in 1928 prices. What is most surprising of all is that the terms of trade did not turn against agriculture during the First Five-Year Plan. *Prices changed—and significantly so—in favor of the agricultural sector.*

How did this favorable change in the terms of trade occur in the face of the terrible suffering? Why weren't the peasants better off? The favorable change in the terms of trade for the peasantry does not mean that the peasants were better off. It simply means that they were able to pass a portion of the burden placed upon them by collectivization, and by the procurement system erected upon it, onto the urban sector.[17]

What really happened? How did this flow of resources into agriculture take place, and how did people overlook it? In the first place, both the Bolsheviks and Western scholars have focused far too exclusively upon a single crop—grain. This crop may have been the most important from the standpoint of the Bolsheviks, but from the standpoint of the peasantry that wasn't the case. Before collectivization most peasants did not market grain at any time. When they marketed, they marketed animal husbandry products or other products raised on the plot. Grain was a major item marketed by some farms, but it was not the item marketed by the majority of peasant farms.

The focus on grain was one of the factors that led people to think that collectivization was successful, at least initially. While grain marketing did rise substantially, Jerzy Karcz has shown that if one takes livestock losses caused by peasant defiance of collectivization and multiplies that figure by official Soviet feeding norms of the period, one arrives at a surplus of grain for marketing purposes that is greater than the actual increase in grain marketings. That is, the animals that were slaughtered did not eat grain, and this left more grain available for marketing.[18] Of course, it also left less in the way of animal husbandry products to market, so the value of total marketings fell.

In the second place, Stalin's compromise with the peasantry, which left the private plot and the collective-farm market in existence, allowed the peasants to charge very, very high prices to the urban area for the products from their own private plots. If one thinks of exploitation in terms of the total Soviet population—urban and rural—the collective-farm market served as a valve tending to equalize the burden on the two sectors. Peasants on their own private account—their own private purchases and their own private sales—produced a net inflow of material resources during the First Five-Year Plan.

In the third place, people neglected the fact that the state was obliged to invest heavily in the Machine Tractor Stations and in the state farms in order to compensate for the loss of draft power caused by the slaughter of livestock. The state was obliged not only to produce more tractors than it had intended (and to finance their purchase and delivery to agriculture) but also to import more tractors than had been originally planned.

Thus, resources came into agriculture in the form of capital investment in the Machine Tractor Stations and the state farms, plus an increased and continuing charge for intermediate inputs such as fuel, lubrication, machine maintenance, and so forth. Material resources also flowed into agriculture in the form of peasant purchases of real products. There was only one subsector of agriculture from which there was a net outflow—the collective farm taken by itself, independent of the Machine Tractor Stations and the peasant private plots. But this outflow was not sufficient to counterbalance the reverse flows. The fact that analysts have focused on the collective-farm sector alone is one of the reasons for the misunderstanding of this period.

In short, rather than Stalin's collectivization program being necessary to finance industrialization, rapid industrial development actually took place during the First Five-Year Plan without any net accumulation from agriculture—in fact, with a net overflow of resources *to* agriculture. While it might seem striking that the successful Soviet industrialization drive was accompanied by a turning of the terms of trade in favor of agriculture, the same pattern is found in the industrialization of Western countries prior to the 1930s. Throughout the nineteenth century and the early part of the twentieth century, productivity changes everywhere (included in the United States) were occurring predominantly in the industrial sector, not the agricultural. The only way the agricultural sector could survive was for the terms of trade to change gradually in its favor, so that it could share the productivity gains made in the industrial sector. It is only with the development of mechanization, pesticides, herbicides, and hybrids that the possibility of an agriculture-first policy has arisen, and this means only *since* the 1930s.[19]

What there is evidence for in the late 1920s in Soviet agricultural policy is complete incompetence. There is no evidence whatsoever to indicate that the peasants would have withdrawn from the market even had the terms of trade been turned against them, and there is no evidence that the terms of trade even *had* to be turned against them. Collectivization was not necessary for the industrialization drive, and it was not optimal either. It was instead a disaster just like a hurricane or any other natural disaster. Economically, no one gained from collectivization, including those promoting rapid industrial development.

The "Logic" and Cost of Collectivization

ALEC NOVE

Was Stalin really necessary? and Was collectivization really necessary? are not quite the same question, although I agree they are related. I accept straightaway that there were alternatives to the policy being followed and that in certain respects collectivization was just the disaster that my colleague says it was. But it was very difficult for the Bolsheviks to accept any alternative. There are circumstances in which people who have a particular set of beliefs do not regard a particular practical alternative as a practical alternative. If there is a genuine alternative for me to eat either a cheese sandwich or a ham sandwich, this is not an alternative for a rabbi.

In a review of my book, Alexander Gerschenkron strongly objected to the use of the term "necessity,"[20] and perhaps it can be misleading. Certainly, as my article made clear, it has nothing to do with "desirability" as I use it and nothing to do with inevitability. For Poland to survive as an independent state in the eighteenth century, it was necessary to make major political changes. They were not made, and Poland did not survive as an independent state at that time. Moreover, there are in the world a number of different "necessities"—or, in Russian *zakonomernosti,* a nice word for which there is no easy English translation. There are trends and there are tendencies, which have an inner logic and which work themselves through. But, of course, they can be contradicted by other trends and tendencies, and at various crossing points in the processes of history it is by no means obvious what the outcome will be. Yet one still can identify a series of regularities, a series of tendencies, which I think makes the word "necessity" meaningful.

Whatever word is used, the essence of the argument about Stalinism in general rests on the totalitarian logic of the seizure of power by a small socialist minority in an overwhelmingly peasant country. There is the logic of the one-party state. There is the logic of trying to change society from above, which *is* part of the seizure of power by the Bolsheviks in the name of building socialism in a peasant country. There is the logic of the tough, organized bureaucracy which the party *had* to become in order to carry out these changes. There is also involved here the Russian autocratic tradition—a tradition of which Stalin was acutely aware. (He thought that there was a necesssity for a substitute czar and naturally preferred, for good personal reasons, that the mantle be his rather than anybody else's.) All of this was exacerbated by the sense of isolation, the sense of danger, and the consequent need for speed as perceived by Stalin and his cohorts. This is not an excuse, of course, for the *wild* excesses that, in fact, occurred during the First Five-Year Plan in a race that was run much too fast. Still, the felt need for speed really was genuine.

So far as agriculture is concerned, and I happily concentrate on that aspect of the question, we must begin with the fact that peasant attitudes really went back to medieval times. It is interesting to note that the peasant program which the Bolsheviks found it politically convenient to adopt at the time of the revolution included a ban on the purchase and sale of land, a ban on employment of labor, and a gearing of the size of the family holding to the number of people available for work and the number of mouths to feed. This program reflected the pre-Stolypin reform attitudes which still were dominant in the minds of the peasants,[21] but such attitudes also represented a problem for the Bolsheviks as they contemplated rapid change in the face of what appeared to them to be an obsolete peasant agriculture.

I recall a conversation with a former official who said, "You know, at the time when we were imposing on the peasants a policy which we knew they didn't like, some of us who knew our history remembered the potato riots under Catherine." Catherine II had ordered the Russian peasants to grow potatoes, which was, of course, the right thing to do. Peasants, being a lot of conservative dunderheads, refused, whereupon Catherine ordered that any peasants not growing potatoes be whipped. After a while, the peasants, having been whipped, planted potatoes and within a number of years were happily eating them. If the Bolsheviks were convinced that the peasants still were outmoded in their thinking and didn't know what was good for them, then it surely must have seemed as proper for the Bolsheviks as for the czars to make the peasants do something for their own good.

We must also recognize that the effect of the revolution on agriculture was profoundly reactionary. The commercial estates were largely wrecked and redivided, and many, though not all, of the peasant holdings that were consolidated as a result of the Stolypin reforms were also divided. Back it all went into the three-field medieval system—strips, periodic redistributions in some cases, etc., etc. This was an antique system of agriculture, and everybody, including Chayanov, agreed that it was even inconsistent with efficient small holdings, let alone large-scale production.[22] The Bolsheviks may have overestimated the technical advantages of large-scale agriculture, as Marxists have tended to do in the past, but the extent to which they were wrong was perhaps disguised from them by the fact that the existing arrangements in agriculture were very, very obsolete.

The statement that agriculture was not self-sufficient in the 1920s, if taken literally, is, of course, perfectly true. If, however, the statement seems to imply that there was not a reversion to greater self-sufficiency as a result of the revolution, then obviously the statement is wrong. Jerzy Karcz, Robert Davies, I myself, and others have joined in discussions about the measure of marketings, but in the end I am convinced by the following simple argument. In 1913—admittedly a very good year—the total of all out-of-the-village marketings was something like 21 million tons. Stalin claimed that by 1928–29 they had fallen to 12 million. The difference of 9 million tons equals the level of exports in 1913, and exports in 1926–27 were negligible.[23] Since the size of towns was approximately the same in 1913 and 1926, it seems to me that what, in fact, happened is that the peasants and their animals—and I acknowledge that the focus is on grain alone here—were eating what was once exported. It seems to me that the peasants regarded themselves, quite properly, as beneficiaries of their own acquisition of land and as a result ate better than before the revolution. They *were* eating a potential exportable surplus. There is no doubt whatever that if the economic conditions of a family decline, if an extra mouth exists to feed, people will make an effort to feed it, but there should not be a confusion between production response and selling on the market. What the Bolsheviks were concerned about was marketings. While peasants are not completely self-sufficient, they can at the margin make the decision to shift more toward consumption rather than take produce to the market. Industrial workers are in a different position. If you are working more and producing more ball bearings, you can't eat them. You *can* eat more cabbage and meat.

One can view primitive socialist accumulation—however defined—as a means of mobilizing agricultural exports to pay for the imports of capital goods from the West. That is just one way of looking at the first stages of industrialization from the vantage point of the Soviet leadership—and not an entirely unrealistic way of looking at it. Now, James Millar very properly says that there were alternative means of getting more marketings, and I'm sure there were. The problem is—what would the consequences of the alternatives be? It seems that both Bukharin and Preobrazhensky did run into a dilemma, for Preobrazhensky said more than that there was a need to turn the terms of trade against the peasant. He also said that there is a terrible danger from kulaks. And what on earth is a kulak? A kulak is a prosperous peasant. So long as you have this attitude (which Bukharin at first didn't have, but which even he later came to share, or said that he did), you must base yourself and the health of agriculture on the middle peasant. What is a middle peasant? A moderately unsuccessful one.

So long as all the Bolsheviks, including Bukharin (at least after 1925), agreed that the emergence of a powerful, commercially minded peasantry was a deadly danger to them, they had closed off one potentially viable alternative. This is my point about rabbis and ham sandwiches. If this alternative—which did exist and which may have been a much healthier one even for accumulation (I'll grant that)— was foreclosed, the Bolsheviks were in a fix. I'll also grant at once (and this is in my book) that their fix was rendered considerably worse by the price policy they adopted in agriculture. The grain crisis of the winter of 1927–28 was due much more to price relationships, which were very unfavorable to grain, than to any other single cause in the short run. That I completely accept. But in the longer run, the general level of productivity of agriculture was limited by the settlement of the revolution. The belief that the successful peasant was a kulak and an enemy prevented what would otherwise have been the natural development of a prosperous, commercially minded peasant agriculture.

The Bolshevik's range of choice was also limited by their attitude toward the market. The whole price policy of the second half of NEP was inconsistent with the maintenance of any sort of market equilibrium, and a number of persons at the time made this point. However, most of the Bolsheviks (though not Bukharin, I think) followed Preobrazhensky in regarding the market as the enemy. They saw no reason to make the adjustments required in order to maintain equilibrium. They would say: "The markets, the traders, the uncontrolled part of the economy are something we have tolerated since 1921 through dire necessity, but really we ought to fight all this." Preobrazhensky only accepted NEP because there was no alternative. As Bukharin pointed out, he saw a *conflict* between socialist planning and what he called "the law of value" (i.e., the market).[24] This kind of approach awoke responsive chords among the Bolsheviks because they were who they were. This is also part of the pattern we are discussing.

Finally, it should be recognized that, while the solution adopted was partly due to Stalin's personal predilections for violence and to the spirit of enthusiasm of the First Five-Year Plan, the Bolsheviks were the first ever to try such a policy, and they had few guidelines. Western economics at the time was interested in equilibrium and in the explanation for trade cycles. The word "growth" was never mentioned, and discussion of appropriate investment strategies for development was unheard of. Development economics was born in the West after World War II. I don't want to excuse the absurdities of some of Stalin's policies, because a number of people warned him that they were absurd and were rewarded with prison. But at the very least, we have to admit that had he, in fact, studied Western economists of the time, he would have learned very little that was of the slightest relevance to the problems the Bolsheviks were facing.

Now, what about the role of agriculture as a source of accumulation? This is a difficult question because we have here a distinction between intention and outcome, and we also have the problem of measurement in the wake of a disaster. It is not a source of disagreement that there was a disaster. Indeed, even Stalin would probably agree about that. It was, of course, not intended that one-half of the horses and most of the livestock in the USSR should be slaughtered in three years. It was an appalling situation.

So far as intentions are concerned, it is clear that Stalin and his cohorts were discussing ways and means of mobilizing material and financial resources largely, although not exclusively, from agriculture. The term "pumping over" (*perekachka*) was widely used in the discussions. When Stalin began his policy of industrializing rapidly in tandem with "soaking" the peasants, Bukharin called it "military-feudal exploitation of the peasantry" (this is the language he used in 1928).[25] In the outcome, Stalin et al. may have been wrong, but that they *thought* they were soaking and exploiting the peasantry was certainly the case, even though the text of the Frist Five-Year Plan (an absurd document in this respect) indicated that not only accumulation but also consumption would go up at a fast rate.

So far as outcome is concerned, I think we agree that the agricultural disaster resulting from the slaughter of farm animals and the precipitous decline in farm output completely transformed the situation. It is perfectly true, therefore, that (1) the total amount the Bolsheviks could get out of agriculture was notably less than they expected, and (2) the amount that they had to put in (primarily as the result of the slaughter) was greater than they expected. All this is completely true.

However, I have looked at Barsov and puzzled over the implications of his argument that the burden of industrialization was carried on the shoulders of the working class. I put this argument to one of the Russian émigrés, and he said, "Oh, my God. *Who starved during this period?*"

What then, is wrong with the argument that is put forward?

First, it all ends in 1932, because Barsov ends his article with 1932. If one carried the analysis on through 1935, one would find a reduction in the investment in agriculture in the years following 1932. Moreover, the free market prices were extremely high in 1932–33 (25–30–35 times higher than the official prices for foodstuffs), which certainly benefited those peasants who were able to get to the nearest town and sell their cabbage or some flour. By 1935 these prices were very sharply reduced, and I strongly suspect that if we had the average prices of these years, they would be much lower than in 1932. Thus, it may very well be that emergency inputs to maintain agricultural production in the wake of the draft-animal disaster were followed by a much more effective mobilization of agricultural products in subsequent years.

Indeed, I think that if the relevant figures were available, they would show that the maximum degree of exploitation of the peasantry—in the sense of pumping resources out of agriculture while providing the minimum returns for people and the minimum of technical inputs—took place from 1948 to 1953. In the late Stalin period the government was still paying for compulsory procurements the same prices or almost the same prices as in 1928, and delivery quotas were higher. The undersupply of inputs to the peasants at the time was appalling.

Second, I am much bothered by the argument with respect to the prices of 1928 and the alleged improvement in the terms of trade thereafter. Part of the problem is a suspicion that such improvement is notably weighted by the relatively low prices of industrial inputs into agricultural *production* (e.g., items such as tractors), and that it does not necessarily reflect the kind of prices peasants had to pay for consumer goods. If one looks at Malafeyev's book,[26] for instance, one finds that prices were rising toward the end of the First Five-Year Plan, and always more rapidly for rural areas than for urban areas.

An even greater problem is the fact that this was a time of grave shortage. Precisely by the end of 1932, and even worse in 1933, a number of things could not be bought at any price. For a peasant, trousers were by no means unfavorably priced in relation to the price he was able to get for the cabbage he sold in town, but, most unfortunately, there were no trousers to be had. The price system in 1932–33 was unbelievably complicated, with some goods rationed, others distributed through closed shops which were accessible only to those with special cards, and so on. Under those conditions, what on earth did prices mean? I know there is also evidence about the volume of movements of goods, but I am worried about these prices

TABLE 1. Food Consumption, 1928–32 (kilograms per capita)

	Bread and Grains	Potatoes	Meat
Urban			
1928	174.4	87.6	51.7
1932	211.3	110.0	16.9
Rural			
1928	250.4	141.1	24.8
1932	214.6	125.0	11.2

Source: Yu. A. Moshkov, Zernovaya problema v gody sploshnoy kollektivizatsii sel'skogo khozyaystva SSSR—1929–1933 gg. (The grain problem in the years of all-round collectivization of USSR agriculture—1929–1933) (Moscow: Izdatel'stvo Moskovskogo Universiteta, 1966), p. 136.

which have to be used as weights. The analysis just doesn't seem to square with the realities of the time.

It does seem to me that figures on food consumption graphically illustrate who actually bore the brunt of the worsening situation. From table 1, one can see that by 1932 there was a very sharp decline in the quality of food consumption in the towns, with the population filling their bellies with more bread and potatoes and eating less of the better food (specifically meat). On the other hand, the rural population ate less of *everything* by 1932, and this was before the famine of 1933. These figures suggest that the burden was not borne primarily by the urban population (although unmistakably a decline in the income of the urban population contributed substantially to the high level of investment in agriculture).

Finally, one should not forget the export of labor from the villages. This was both planned and unplanned, and it was massive. Life in the villages was so miserable, and people were so frightened of being labeled kulaks and arrested, that perhaps up to ten million of them fled to the construction sites and factories that were being built. I don't quite know how to measure it, but it was an important contribution of agriculture to industrialization. The peasants' arrival helped to depress the per capita consumption figures (and the labor productivity) in the cities, thereby creating the impression that the original urban inhabitants suffered more than they did.

In conclusion, let me repeat once more my belief that the actual collectivization program carried out by Stalin, which was a most dreadful thing, was not inexorably predetermined and that it was not morally justified by the outcome of the industrialization drive of the 1930s. One can say that the events which occurred have a pretty powerful explanation, given the nature of the Bolsheviks, the extent to which other alternatives seemed closed to them, and the extent to which they were ideologically predisposed in certain directions. The survival of the regime, given the Bolsheviks' aims and their rapid industrialization program, required a harsh, autocratic type of regime. Yet, as Roy Medvedev has contended in his book,[27] if there is an inherent logic in a cult of personality, much depends on the nature of the personality. When Stalin was in a position to make arbitrary and personal decisions, he went in for wild excesses, both in economic policy and, of course, in terror. Not for a moment, and certainly not in my article, did I suggest that this was in any sense necessary. This was Stalin showing the face of an oriental despot and behaving in a manner which only became possible after he had succeeded in getting into power, having shown a more moderate and human face while doing so.

Rejoinders

JAMES MILLAR

It seems to me that the disagreements between Professor Nove and me are of two different types. In the first place, our images of the Russian countryside in the 1920s are somewhat different. I don't agree, for instance, that Chayanov's studies demonstrate the antique nature of Russian agriculture. On the contrary, the implication of Chayanov's argument is that peasant agriculture could have survived the Soviet regime, as it had the czarist, had it not been for the Bolsheviks' misperceptions of the peasantry.

I also do not agree that the decline in marketings can be attributed simply to increased peasant consumption. The great famine of 1921–22 caused a very sharp reduction in animal stocks, and these had to be rebuilt in 1923–24, naturally at some cost in grain. Moreover, the international grain market was a disaster during the 1920s, particularly during the early part of the 1920s. The international price of grain had fallen precipitously, and the Soviet regime had not established an institution to organize the export of grains in these conditions. (The regime did put together an organization to export flax, and this did help to create the necessary demand to maintain the production and sowings of flax.) It does seem absolutely clear to me that the peasants were not self-sufficient and that a turning of the general terms of trade against them would have increased marketings, not just production.

I might add that I also do not believe that the labor which

moved out of agriculture in the First Five-Year Plan should be considered a contribution to industrialization. There is no evidence of a shortage of labor in Soviet Russia of the 1920s and the 1930s, nor any evidence of a need to take extraordinary measures to mobilize labor from the countryside. The experience of most developing countries both before and since the Soviet industrialization drive has been an excessive off-farm flow of population, and this without collectivization or anything like it. The unskilled, uneducated Soviet peasants who poured into the cities at that time were in many ways more of a nuisance than a help.

But much more important than any disagreements between us on interpretation of detailed questions is, I think, a fundamental methodological difference in our approaches. Professor Nove is concerned with explaining how things happened, and he is trying to say that, given the Bolsheviks, given the circumstances they faced, given their understanding of the agricultural situation, given the backwardness of Soviet agriculture, given the world situation—given all these factors, how could anything else have been decided?

It seems to me, therefore, that Professor Nove comes perilously close to a determinist position at times, but I am not concerned with arguing this point. I am trying not only to explain what happened but to evaluate it as a means-end relation. Professor Nove uses "necessity" in two senses: first, as a "tendency that has an inner logic"; second, as something that is needed. It was this latter meaning of "necessity" that he had in mind when he cited the example, "For Poland to survive as an independent state in the eighteenth century, it was necessary to make major political changes." And it is this latter meaning of "necessity" that primarily interests me. I don't care whether or not Bukharin or Preobrazhensky or Stalin or anyone else considered the various alternatives, for that is irrelevant in *evaluating* the appropriateness (optimality) of collectivization as a means to achieve the goal of rapid industrialization. My interest is in assessing whether collectivization or some similar coercive "squeezing" of the peasantry was needed for the Soviet rapid industrialization program to succeed.

The essence of my argument is that collectivization could not have been necessary for rapid industrialization for the simple reason that it did not, in fact, contribute net resources to the industrial sector. An analysis in terms of "surplus" is very confusing to anyone raised in neoclassical economic analysis, for what we are talking about is a *net* surplus, a *net* of the movement of goods flowing out of and into agriculture. We are putting prices on these counterflows and measuring the *net* difference. The approach is akin to measuring an export or an import surplus in a country's foreign trade and treating agriculture and nonagriculture as though they were different countries. In my opinion, Professor Nove is right about the contribution of capital stocks (in contrast to consumer goods) to the improvement in the terms of trade, but since the argument concerns agriculture versus nonagriculture, the fact that many of the resources flowing into agriculture were directed toward maintaining production simply buttresses my case.

Our knowledge about the net flow between agriculture and the nonagricultural sector after 1932 is, unfortunately, rather meager. Not only does Barsov's main study stop in that year, but on the basis of an examination of the archives, he says we never will have a definitive understanding of the question because some of the necessary data were not collected.[28] In any case, the "standard story" has always focused on the First Five-Year Plan, not the Second, and it is already a significant revision of the standard theory to say that the contribution of agriculture was postponed until after 1932. I personally am doubtful that the situation changed much after 1932. So far as the postwar period is concerned, I thought that no one argued that collectivization was beneficial to the industrialization drive over a fifteen- to twenty-year span. Collectivization was supposed to have solved an immediate procurement problem, but at a long-term cost to the economy as a whole. As recent developments in the Soviet Union have shown, so many raw materials for industrial production come out of agriculture that there is no way to discriminate sharply against the agricultural sector without in the end discriminating against overall growth.

In my opinion, we don't really know about the relative suffering produced by collectivization. That is, we don't know how the burden was shared between the agricultural and nonagricultural populations. We just know that both suffered losses in real wages and probably losses in real income. The measure in Nove's table 1 is not definitive, but I don't disagree with it. It is not relevant to the issue between us.[29] In any case I certainly never said or meant to imply that the burden was placed primarily on the working class. It fell on both classes. *The crucial point is that so much of this suffering was completely unnecessary and contributed in no way to industrialization.*

In conclusion, let me emphasize one point very strongly. One of the reasons that I have been attacking the standard story is that the question at hand is not merely of historical interest. The standard story has worked its way into the accepted Western developmental literature as "the Soviet model for economic development." This model (one famous version is the Ranis and Fei model[30]) describes an experience of industrialization in which very rapid growth is achieved, with the agricultural sector playing a real and substantial role as a source of investment resources. But if this model does not describe the actual Soviet experience—and it doesn't—we are left with the question: How *did* the Soviet Union achieve rapid industrial development? Once we get rid of some simple notion that the Soviets extracted resources out of a particular sector, we may be able to start thinking about this question seriously and come to some accurate understanding of what the Soviet model for economic development really was.

ALEX NOVE

It is, I think, wrong to say that I am arguing for a determinist position so far as the initiation of collectivization is concerned. I have contended that there were powerful objective reasons for a despot to be in a position to act and that there were powerful ideological reasons for him to be suspicious of any agricultural policy that created a strong and independent peasantry. But almost by definition, a despot has a range of choices. Of course, Stalin had around him a group of people—a stratum of semieducated, tough commissars whom he represented and whose interests on the whole they thought he was defending until he killed half of them—but some of the choices were his own.

I have also emphasized that some aspects of the collectivization program were counterproductive in the literal sense. There is nothing to be gained from taking grain away from starving peasants and then exporting it in order to buy machinery which was then wrecked by former peasants who hadn't been taught how to use it. This kind of thing is completely counterproductive, and obviously it occurred.

I recall listening to a woman who was defending a Ph.D. thesis at Moscow University. In the course of discussion, she said: "I would regard the Soviet agricultural model not as a model for socialism in agriculture but at best as a tragic necessity. We must hope that no other socialist country would be compelled to follow that road." She said it to an audience of 100, none of whom rose to object. "At best," therefore, "a necessary tragedy"—and the word "necessary" in this connection can very well be argued about, for in the end Stalin's course proved so counterproductive with respect both to the agricultural sector and to the aims of the First Five-Year Plan. I agree entirely that there could well have been an unexplored range of possibilities, for example, in the form of increased taxation. It is one of the astonishing features of the 1920s that the taxation on the peasants was always rather low, until it became penal as part of the policy of destroying individual peasant farming.

Yet, it does seem to me that the collectivization decision should be treated with some historical perspective. The policy of rapid tempos—of breaking out of what the pro-Stalin Bolsheviks believed to be the vicious circles that were holding them back—is quite understandable. It is quite logical that they should have tried. Moreover, if one adopts a particular strategy for good or for ill, then along with that strategy inevitably go a number of disadvantages which can be seen as costs of the chosen strategy. Look at the Western war economy and all its bureaucratic deformations. If one assumes that a strategy is rational—which it may not be—the errors and waste with which it is associated also in a paradoxical way have a rationality of their own. In a "great leap forward" strategy, at least some—though not all—of the waste and deformations, including excesses on the part of overenthusiastic comrades, must be expected.

So far as the burden of the industrialization drive is concerned, I agree, of course, that it was not limited to the peasants. (After all, the high free market prices were paid not by the state but by the urban citizens.) Nevertheless, I continue to worry about any calculation based on 1928 prices. In any other circumstance, the consequences of collectivization would naturally have included much higher prices of agricultural products simply by reason of the extreme shortages. The use of highly artificial prices both for outputs and inputs can produce very misleading results.

The best indicator, I think, is the relative welfare, the relative income, of different strata of the population. One must study the relativities and dynamics of peasant and urban incomes during and after collectivization. At the time of Stalin's death, the difference in income between the urban worker and any kolkhoz peasant not within very easy reach of the market was very strongly in favor of the urban worker, whatever way one weighs the evidence.

If one looks at the post-Stalin statistics, one sees a trend in the direction of evening out this difference to a very considerable extent. Today, the difference is much smaller and more the kind one would expect in a society at the Soviet Union's level of development. A fiscal reflection of this change is the gigantic budgetary subsidy that is given to maintain the difference between the quite high purchase prices for meat at the farms and the lower retail prices for meat in the shops. Instead of a high turnover tax revenue originating through the resale of agricultural products obtained at low prices, this particular item of revenue probably is insignificant today.

It is only with such an evening-out of the income difference that one can say the original Soviet method of socialist construction — if that is the name to give it — was finally, by stages, abandoned. Industrialization involving the pressing down of peasant standards — or in a sense, the exploitation of agriculture — cannot be said to have ended until sometime in the late 1960s.

A Moderator's Afterthoughts

JERRY F. HOUGH

Few debates have, I think, been so successful as this one in clarifying issues and advancing our understanding. The debate makes clear that several quite separate issues have been intertwined in our arguments about the collectivization phenomenon. The first question is the historical one: Why did it occur? Clearly this is a question that interests Professor Nove very much and Professor Millar very little. On this question, Professor Nove's real protagonists would seem to be those scholars, such as Moshe Lewin and Stephen Cohen, who see Bukharin's program in the late 1920s as the true Leninist one and who see NEP as a viable (maybe even natural) long-term Bolshevik alternative. While Professor Nove obviously believes that Bukharin's program was economically viable (and even desirable), he seems to be saying that that program was not politically viable and that any Bolshevik would have been pushed toward something like collectivization at the end of the 1920s.

The second question is: Who suffered most as a consequence of collectivization? To me, the most important contribution of the debate was to clarify that this question can be quite distinct from the question: Which sector contributed most to industrialization? A regime may willingly or unwillingly invest so much in agricultural mechanization that little "net surplus" is received from the agricultural sector, but, of course, peasants can't eat tractors. Undoubtedly, the question of relative suffering is partly a metaphysical one (What did groups receive in comparison with what was proper or "natural" for them to receive?), and undoubtedly any accurate analysis of it would have to be quite subtle and differentiated. Many peasant youths surely rejoiced at the newly created opportunity to move to city jobs, and those peasants near the cities suffered less than more remote peasants. Cotton farmers fared better than those in the non-black-earth region. Similarly, those workers who became Stakhanovites or who simply took advantage of new programs to raise their skills or even to receive higher education are in a much different category from those who remained unskilled. The gross distinction that may make the most sense is one based on age (the young being seen as beneficiaries in overall terms, the middle-aged and the old as the greatest losers), but in general terms Professor Nove must be right in emphasizing that conditions were not good in the villages. Whatever the relative costs borne by the urban and rural family in statistical terms, the urban family, unlike the peasant, often had an unemployed wife who could go to work in an effort to maintain family standards of living.

The third question—or set of questions—involves the concerns that interest Professor Millar most: Did the suffering of the peasants and workers at least "buy" a rapid rate of industrial growth for the Soviet Union? Was collectivization or something like it necessary for such growth, at least given the regime's reluctance to seek large-scale foreign investment? If it turns out that, whatever the intentions of the leadership, agriculture did not provide much (if anything) in the way of a net surplus to the industrial sector, what was going on that explains the very high rates of industrial growth? What was the "real" Soviet model of economic development in the sense of the way in which resources were actually mobilized for the industrialization drive? Professor Millar is surely right in holding that this is a question which deserves a most serious reexamination on the basis of new data. It is a question of vital interest not only to historians of the Soviet period but also to theorists of economic development in general—and to those charged with promoting such development in the Third World.

NOTES

In recent years a number of analysts have sought to gain a better understanding of the present Soviet political system by reexamining some of the traditional interpretations of the formative years of the USSR. This debate on Soviet collectivization between the noted economists James R. Millar and Alec Nove grew out of this effort. Originally an oral exchange of views, the debate took place on November 10, 1975, at Duke University, Durham, North Carolina. It was jointly sponsored by the Department of Political Science and the Committee for Russian and East European Studies, with a special helping hand from Professor Vladimir Treml of the Department of Economics. The moderator was Jerry F. Hough of the Department of Political Science, who transcribed and edited this record of the debate and added some afterthoughts of his own.

1. The propositions are advanced, respectively, in Moshe Lewin, *Lenin's Last Struggle* (New York: Pantheon Books, 1968); Stephen F. Cohen, *Bukharin and the Bolshevik Revolution* (New York: A. A. Knopf, 1973); Sheila Fitzpatrick (ed.), *The Cultural Revolution in Russia, 1928-1931* (Bloom-

ington: Indiana University Press, 1978); David Granick *Soviet Metal-Fabrication and Economic Development* (Madison: University of Wisconsin Press, 1967); Gail Warshofsky Lapidus, *Women in Soviet Society* (Berkeley: University of California Press, 1978); David Jaravsky, *The Lysenko Affair* (Cambridge, Mass.: Harvard University Press, 1970).

2. The other two major proponents of a revisionist position in this area are Moshe Lewin and (especially) the late Jerzy F. Karcz. See Lewin, *Russian Peasants and Soviet Power* (London: George Allen and Unwin, Ltd., 1968); Karcz, "Thoughts on the Grain Problem," *Soviet Studies* 18, no. 4 (April 1967):399–435; Karcz, "Back on the Grain Front," ibid. 21, no. 2 (October 1970):262–94; Karcz, "From Stalin to Brezhnev: Soviet Agricultural Policy in Historial Perspective," in James R. Millar (ed.), *The Soviet Rural Community* (Urbana: University of Illinois Press, 1971), pp. 36–70; Millar, "Soviet Rapid Development and the Agricultural Surplus Hypothesis," *Soviet Studies* 22, no. 1 (July 1970):77–93; Millar, "Mass Collectivization and the Contribution of Soviet Agriculture to the First Five-Year Plan," *Slavic Review* 33, no. 4 (December 1974):750–66.

3. *Encounter* (April 1962):86–92. The article was republished in Alec Nove's collection *Economic Rationality and Soviet Politics, or Was Stalin Really Necessary?* (New York: Praeger, 1964).

4. Paul R. Gregory and Robert C. Stuart, *Soviet Economic Structure and Performance* (New York: Harper & Row, 1974), esp. chaps. 2, 3, 4, and 12.

5. Yevgeniy Preobrazhenskiy, *The New Economics,* trans. Brian Pearce (Oxford: Clarendon Press, 1965).

6. See the very full discussion in Stephen F. Cohen, *Bukharin and the Bolshevik Revolution: A Political Biography, 1883-1938* (New York: Vintage Books, 1975), esp. chaps 5 and 6.

7. The "scissors crisis" was considered a crisis by the Bolsheviks because they expected that the sharp adverse change in the terms of trade that occurred in 1922–23 for agriculture would cause the peasants to cease bringing their products to market, thereby creating great hardships for the urban population. It was apparently Leon Trotsky who first described the situation as the "scissors crisis." The phrase was based on the fact that two indexes which were being used to measure the "adverse" change in the purchasing power of agricultural income, when portrayed on a graph, crossed each other and thus resembled an open pair of scissors.

The most recent examination of the original data, of the price indexes, and of the various interpretations put forward by Soviet economists at the time of the crisis shows that the peasants did not in fact withdraw from the market and that there was little reason to suppose that they would have done so subsequently. This study also argues that the data and indexes used in the famous scissors diagram are quite unreliable for measuring changes in the purchasing power of agricultural incomes. See Corinne Ann Guntzel, "Soviet Agricultural Pricing Policy and the Scissors Crisis of 1922-23" (Ph.D. diss., University of Illinois, 1972).

8. Alexander Erlich, "Preobrazenski and the Economics of Soviet In-

dustrialization," *Quarterly Journal of Economics,* no. 1 (February 1950): 57–88.

9. A. V. Chayanov, *The Theory of Peasant Economy,* ed. Daniel Thorner, Basile Kerblay, and R. E. F. Smith (Homewood, Ill: Richard D. Irwin, 1966).

10. This is also true with respect to labor. In the urban sector of the Soviet Union during the 1930s the real wage fell. What was the response of the urban family? More members of the family entered the work force, and those who already had jobs worked longer hours in an attempt to maintain per capita family consumption.

11. See Guntzel "Soviet Agricultural Pricing Policy," esp. chap. 3. For an example of an unsupported assertion to the contrary, see William L. Blackwell, *The Industrialization of Russia* (New York: Thomas Y. Crowell Co., 1970), pp. 84–85.

12. W. W. Rostow, "Marx Was a City Boy, or Why Communism May Fail," *Harper's Magazine,* February 1955, pp. 25–30.

13. Yuriy Larin, *Sovetskaya derevnya* (The Soviet countryside) (Moscow: Izdatel'stvo Ekonomicheskaya Zhizn', 1925), p. 217.

14. A. A. Barsov, *Balans stoimostnykh obmenov mezhdu gorodom i derevney* (The balance of value exchanges between the city and the countryside) (Moscow: Nauka, 1969); see also "Agriculture and the Sources of Socialist Accumulation in the Years of the First Five-Year Plan (1928–1933)," *Istoriya SSSR,* no. 3 (1968):64–82. For a sympathetic Western confirmation of Barsov's findings, see Michael Ellman, "Did the Agricultural Surplus Provide the Resources for the Increase in Investment during the First Five-Year Plan?" *Economic Journal* 85 (December 1975):844–64.

15. Millar, "Mass Collectivization."

16. In such a definition a type-of-product distinction is made—that is, the agricultural sector is defined to include enterprises or portions of enterprises producing agricultural products only, and rural enterprises producing nonagricultural prodcuts are treated properly as part of the industrial sector. This is in opposition to a simple geographical distinction between urban and rural areas.

17. The terms of trade changed gradually but significantly in favor of American agriculture, for example, during nineteenth- and early twentieth-century U.S. development. This does not mean that American farmers were made better off than American industrial workers as a result. It merely means that the greater productivity gains of the industrial sector were shared in this way with the agricultural sector, where productivity increases were smaller. The real income of farmers remained below that of workers throughout the period. The "favorable" change in the terms of trade for American agriculture merely helped to keep the gap between the two from widening. See Ralph A. Loomis and Glen T. Barton, "Productivity of Agriculture, United States, 1870–1958," *Technical Bulletin* (U.S. Department of Agriculture), no. 1238 (April 1961), esp. table 7 and pp. 28–38.

18. Karcz, "From Stalin to Brezhnev," pp. 42–46.

19. Loomis and Barton, "Productivity of Agriculture," esp. pp. 9–11, and 28–29.

20. Review of Nove (see n. 3) in *Economic History Review,* no. 3 (April 1965):606–9; reprinted in Alexander Gerschenkron, *Continuity in History and Other Essays* (Cambridge, Mass.: Harvard University Press, 1968), pp. 485–89.

21. The reform introduced by P. A. Stolypin in 1906–11 was intended to break up traditional peasant communal-land tenure and gradually replace it by private ownership of land.

22. See n.9.

23. The marketing figures are discussed in the two Karcz *Soviet Studies* articles cited in n.2 and in R. W. Davies, "A Note on Grain Statistics," *Soviet Studies* 22, no. 1 (January 1970):314–29.

24. See the discussion in Alev Nove, "Some Observations on Bukharin and His Ideas," in S. Abramsky and Beryl J. Williams (eds.), *Essays in Honour of E. H. Carr* (London: Macmillan Press Ltd., 1974), pp. 183–203.

25. Quoted in V. M. Molotov, "On Two Fronts," *Bolshevik* (January 21, 1930):14. See Cohen, *Bukharin and the Bolshevik Revolution,* pp. 306–7.

26. A. Malafayev, *Istoriya tsenoobrazovaniya v SSSR* (History of price formation in the USSR) (Moscow: Mysl', 1964), p. 148.

27. Roy A. Medvedev, *Let History Judge: The Origins and Consequences of Stalinism,* ed. David Joravsky and Georges Haupt (New York: Knopf, 1972).

28. Barsov, *Balans,* pp. 186–90. However, see "The NEP: The Leveling of Economic Relations between the City and the Countryside," in M. P. Kim (ed.), *Novaya ekonomicheskaya politika* (New economic policy) (Moscow: 1974), where he attempts some analysis of the Second Five-Year Plan period.

29. See n.17. The lower real income of American agricultural workers during the nineteenth century does not imply that industrial growth occurred at the expense of the agricultural sector. The truth is quite the opposite.

30. Gustave Ranis and John C. H. Fei, "A Theory of Economic Development," *American Economic Review* 51, no. 4 (September 1961).

6

Post-Stalin Agriculture: Performance and Prospects

The Soviet village is indeed the weakest point of the Soviet system, its Achilles' heel. It will have a great part in the ultimate destruction of Soviet power.

—Naum Jasny

Agriculture is often described as the Achilles' heel of the Soviet economy. But while this is true, it is less often remembered that Achilles could after all walk upon his heel.

—Peter Wiles

These statements by Jasny and Wiles illustrate a salient continuity of the post-Stalin period.[1] The Soviet rural village remains the "weakest point" of the Soviet economy. But Soviet society continues to walk upon its Achilles' heel. In fact, Soviet agriculture has made greater progress since 1953 than anyone anticipated, and the "Malthusian wolf" is farther than ever from the door. In the twenty-five years since Stalin's death, agricultural output has increased at a very respectable annual average of at least 3.5 percent,[2] while population growth has averaged only about 1.4 percent per annum.[3] Compared to the many countries that have had difficulty maintaining a significant growth rate of food products per capita, the USSR is clearly exceptional. Growth and the diversification of Soviet agricultural output since Stalin's death has made possible a significant enrichment of the average Russian's diet. Food consumption per capita, for example, has increased (in constant rubles) 100 percent since 1951, and this reflects eating better quality products more than it does merely eating more.[4] The magnitude of the change since Stalin is measured by the fact that per capita production of agri-

From *The Soviet Union since Stalin,* ed. Stephen F. Cohen, Alexander Rabinowitch, and Robert Sharlet (Bloomington: Indiana University Press, 1980), pp. 135–54. Originally titled "Post-Stalin Agriculture and Its Future." Reprinted by permission, with minor editorial changes.

cultural products in 1953 had just regained the prewar 1940 level, which was itself only at approximately the 1928 level. And the 1928 level of per capita consumption had probably been less than that of 1913.

The ambitiousness and high priority of the goal of enriching Soviet diets, rather than policy failure, are responsible for having converted the Soviet Union from a modest net exporter into a regular and significant net importer of agricultural products during the last decade. These large imports of grain, however, reflect only one dimension of the Soviet agricultural problem today—the liability of Soviet field crops, and especially grains, to sharp year-to-year fluctuations. Variability of this sort is not new, of course. What *is* new is the decision to import grains to compensate for harvest shortfalls. It was Nikita Khrushchev who reversed long-standing Soviet policy and ordered imports on a significant scale to offset the otherwise adverse impact that the poor 1963 grain harvest would have had on Soviet livestock herds, which, in turn, would have undermined planned increases in per capita production of animal husbandry products. Although Khrushchev soon fell from power, the precedent has remained. In 1975 the Soviet Union experienced a shortfall of eighty million metric tons of grain—equal to approximately 40 percent of the total and bountiful harvest of 1973, or 80 percent of the best Western estimates of the 1972 year-end grain stock inventory.[5] Imports to compensate for this disaster cost an enormous amount of foreign exchange that in earlier years would have been reserved to import Western technology, and they completely unsettled international grain markets.

The changes that have taken place in Soviet agriculture since Stalin, then, have been of fundamental significance to the Soviet consumer, and they have raised agriculture from the bottom to very nearly the top of the nondefense priority list. In this essay we shall examine Soviet agriculture in both historical and world perspectives. The concluding sections attempt to assess the nature of the problems Soviet agriculture faces and the prospects for their satisfactory resolution.

Disappearances and Reappearances: The Historical Record

The contemporary model of Soviet socialist agriculture shares historical features with previous models, but it is very different today from the Stalinist model of the early 1950s. The similarities over time are not so much the result of continuously acting forces as they are of recurring reactions, or historically ingrained responses, to particular types of problems. The concept of "continuity and change" is inadequate for describing the development of contemporary Soviet agricultural institutions, since even the changes that have taken place in recent years provide a certain continuity with the past. Particular solutions tend to reappear over time. Thus, much that once "disappeared" has in fact "reappeared" in contemporary Soviet agriculture.

A recent official history of Soviet agriculture provides a completely new periodization, one that obscures the fundamental contours of the Soviet experience. According to this work, Soviet agricultural history is divided into four periods.[6] The first runs from the revolution of 1917 through 1925, and it therefore mixes war communism with the radically different period of the New Economic Policy (NEP). The second period stretches from 1925 to 1941, which buries 1928, a critical turning point on the road to rapid industrialization; forced, mass collectivization; and the purges. The only virtue of 1925 as a dividing point is that statistics on agricultural output for the 1930s look better with 1925, rather than 1928, as a base year. The only traditional break that these articles provide is 1941, the outset of World War II, but this period is extended beyond Stalin's death to 1964, the year Khrushchev was removed from power. Stalin and the hero of de-Stalinization are obliged to share the same historical period! The final period is Brezhnev's, and the years 1965 through 1976 are represented by myriads of statistics revealing rapid growth rates of both inputs and outputs. Throughout this revision of Soviet agricultural history neither Stalin nor Khrushchev is mentioned by name, and yet each left a clear and easily read mark on the institutional structure of contemporary Soviet agriculture.

The only other figure of comparable significance was, of course, Lenin, who was obliged to use his enormous personal authority to the limit to introduce the NEP early in the 1920s. Money, markets, and normal trade relations had disappeared in the revolution and civil war, and the NEP restored these institutions to the dismay of many Bolsheviks. The NEP also allowed the peasant family farm to flourish, with all that implied in the way of complex production functions, "self-exploitation" of family labor, and smallness of scale in production units.

The NEP was a period of growing pecuniary relations among members of the rural popoulation and urban, industrial, and governmental transactors. By all objective measures NEP agriculture was a success. Prewar output levels were restored relatively quickly, the composition of agricultural output improved markedly, and the peasant producers showed themselves to be highly sensitive to market forces.

Mass collectivization at the close of the 1920s not only put an end to private middle-man activities, it also depecuniarized the rural sector by converting almost all economic transactions into in-kind payments to Machine Tractor Stations (MTS), to members for work performed, and as obligatory deliveries to the state. Collective-farm agriculture was imposed upon the rural population, and administrative measures replaced the market as the primary means for allocation of resources. Peasant resistance to collectivization led ultimately to a compromise that allowed peasant families, on condition of working a minimum number of days on the collective farm, access to tiny plots of land upon which they were allowed to continue private activity—mainly horticulture and animal husbandry. Thus, with mass collectivization there reappeared the "hungry plot" of post-Emancipation Russia, a plot too small to live on but large enough to provide an effective incentive to get the lord's land worked. Collective-farm agriculture was imposed on the apparent assumption that it would facilitate the extraction of an agricultural surplus to finance rapid industrialization. Nothing of the sort took place.[7] Agricultural output fell in absolute value, the composition of agricultural output deteriorated, and many in the countryside and elsewhere starved.

World War II interrupted recovery from the mistakes and excesses of mass collectivization, and postwar recovery favored the industrial-urban sector once more. By the time Stalin died in 1953, the rural sector was relatively (and perhaps even absolutely) more backward than it had been in 1928. This was the apogee of the Soviet unbalanced growth path, and since 1953 repeated attempts have been made to restore balance.

The first attempts by Stalin's heirs to address the agricultural problems he left to them did not involve significant institutional change. On the contrary, Nikita Khrushchev started out merely tinkering with the system Stalin had created in the 1930s. Agricultural procurement prices were increased and taxes reduced. Farmer earnings increased noticeably as a result, but the fundamental system of collective-farm, team cultivation with residual determination of farmer earnings, along with the MTS system, the four-track agricultural procurement system, and the coexistence of a tiny private agricultural system remained the salient organizational features. What *was* new was a promise by the state to adhere to "socialist legality" in its dealings with farms and farmers, a decision to create material incentives for workers, and a realization of the centrality of agriculture for improvement in the standard of living of urban households.

Farm output did increase appreciably between 1953 and 1957, but the increase was attributable in large part to the concurrent and almost incredible expanded cultivation of marginal lands in the remoter regions of the USSR. The Virgin Lands campaign brought into cultivation an area equal to the total cultivated area of Canada. This innovation was structural in only one respect. These lands were opened mainly by the creation of state farms, and the role of the state farm has grown continuously thereafter. Subsequently, the growth of the state farm sector has been a result of the conversion of weak collective farms into state farms. State farms cultivate a larger share of total arable land than collective farms today, and this trend continues.[8] State farms are organized on the model of state industrial enterprises, of course, so that this innovation was both important and costly to the state budget.

The development of the Virgin Lands was in large part a stopgap measure designed to increase total agricultural output rapidly in the expectation that the regularization of the Stalinist model of collective agriculture would soon produce results. The attempt to make Stalin's model of socialist agriculture work failed to meet expectations, however, and it was overturned in 1958. Like Lenin and Stalin before him, Khrushchev broke with previous agricultural policy and introduced radical changes in the institutional structure of agricultural production.

In 1958 the MTS system was abolished, and the old four-channel agricultural procurement system was also abandoned. Both changes substituted pecuniary for in-kind transactions. Since 1958 all taxes on agriculture have been paid in money, and farms have been obliged to purchase capital equipment and farm inputs from state agencies. Brezhnev and Kosygin continued the process of pecuniarization and intensification of Soviet agriculture, but with even greater emphasis upon research and development, mechanization, and the use of mineral fertilizers and pesticides. Financial discrimination against the collective farm has also been abandoned and farmer earnings have been increased and stabilized by a minimum guaranteed annual wage and access to the state pension system. The difference between Khrushchev's policies toward agriculture and those of his successors has been mainly a matter of acceleration and greater consistency. Nowhere is this more evident than in the priority that has been accorded to livestock production under Brezhnev and the consequent very large imports of grain and fodder from the West to support it. Per capita meat consumption has become the primary symbol of agricultural success in the USSR.[9]

A new model for agricultural production has been building therefore since 1958 under Khrushchev and Brezhnev. It has two prominent aspects: intensification of production and pecuniarization of transactions within the agricultural sector, and between it and the other sectors. The farm, whether collective or state, remains very large (although the operational unit is much smaller and has remained about the same throughout the period), which is a legacy both of the Stalinist model and of even more ancient Bolshevik mythology about increasing returns to scale in agricultural production. But the economic context in which Soviet farms operate today is essentially a socialist market environment, a reappearance, in effect of a prominent feature of the NEP. Dealings with farm workers, with state procurement agencies, with state industrial enterprises on both input and output sides, are all carried out in pecuniary, quasi-market terms. These changes are particularly important as an index of the change in policymakers' attitudes toward agriculture specifically and toward economic problems generally.

It is a shock to return, for example, to Stalin's last official pronouncements on Soviet agriculture. Consider his response to the recommendation of two prominent Soviet agricultural economists to sell the MTS system to the collective farms:

> The outcome would be, first, that the collective farms would become the owners of the basic instruments of production; that is, their status would be an exceptional one. . . . [Would not one] say that such a status could only dig a deeper gulf between collective-farm property and public property, and would not bring us any nearer to communism . . . ?

> The outcome would be, secondly, an extension of the sphere of operation of commodity circulation. . . . What do Comrades Saina and Venzher think—is the extension of the sphere of commodity circulation calculated to promote our advance towards communism?[10]

Twenty-five years later this traditional Bolshevik (and Marxist) animus toward commodity production and exchange has almost completely disappeared. Although still not as prominent as during the NEP, markets, prices, and other pecuniary institutions are playing more significant roles than at any time since. Moreover, trained economists have access to statistical data unavailable prior to 1957,[11] and a reformation has taken place in the interpretation of Marx. Economists, sociologists, and others have had much greater freedom than ever before to find their own citations in the writings of Marx, Engels, and Lenin to support their analyses and reform proposals. As a result, much less nonsense is written these days about agriculture than was the case only a decade or so ago.

Viewed in historical perspective, then, recent developments in Soviet agriculture are clearly favorable to rationalization. A more pragmatic and less ideologically rigid approach has gradually gained ground. Current institutional arrangements are far more conducive to growth and efficiency than at any time since collectivization. Finally, beginning in 1958, the sector has experienced the longest period of organizational stability and continuous growth in the history of the Soviet regime.

Soviet Agriculture in World Perspective

The performance of Soviet agriculture is ordinarily evaluated in the light of American agriculture. In the first place, this is because analysts are frequently concerned with Soviet strategic capabilities and because such comparisons are thought to reveal something about the superiority of the American economic system. In the second place, although the Soviet Union has inferior natural conditions for agriculture, there remain numerous physical similarities in the practice and potential of agriculture in the United States and in the USSR. Both countries occupy large land masses and contain relatively small populations. Thus, the kind of intensive farming that characterizes most of Asia is not relevant to an assessment of Soviet agriculture. The sort of medium intensity of cultivation that is typical of the United States is suitable for the USSR, too. Moreover, both countries have large economies, measured in terms of total GNP, and both also rely upon international trade for only a small proportion of their needs. Even so, an unqualified direct comparison of Soviet and American agricultural performance can be quite misleading with respect to the gravity of Soviet problems. To correct this bias, it is useful to compare the USSR with the typical developing country.

With few exceptions, the situation confronting the developing nations of the world is very different from that confronting Soviet leaders.[12] Although the Soviet Union shares with many developing countries the fact that it has been converted from a regular exporter of grains to the industrial countries into a net importer, this does not mean in the Soviet case a diminution in capacity to feed the population. It reflects instead an enrichment of the diet at a rate greater than can be sustained by domestic production year in, year out, and this itself is a characteristic result of the practice of over-commitment planning in the Soviet economy as a whole. It also reflects a new priority of the household sector of the economy.

Unlike the Soviet Union, the typical developing country is small in size and tends not only to be overpopulated but to be experiencing very rapid population growth as well. The rate of growth of population in the Soviet Union is not much greater than in the United States. Given that the demand for food products ordinarily grows less rapidly than personal income (i.e., that the income elasticity of demand for agricultural products is less than unity) and that this disparity tends to enlarge with economic development, the problem of satisfying the Soviet population's demand for food products is essentially a matter of time and cost and is not problematic in itself.

Unlike most developing countries, the Soviet Union is not a newly independent colonial country and is not characterized by existing or potentially serious political unrest, problems which tend to inhibit rational agricultural policy-making in many underdeveloped countries. Moreover, less than 40 percent of the Soviet population is rural today, and, despite disadvantages, the rural sector is literate and has access to health care unparalleled in the typical developing country. The Soviet Union is no longer primarily an agrarian economy, and the high level of development of the industrial sector and the relatively high degree of education of the rural population are mutually supportive prerequisites for modernization of agricultural production.

Soviet agriculture is, then, in a reasonably favorable position when viewed in the context of the developing economies of the world, and indeed it does not compare unfavorably with many developed economies in many respects. Certainly the agricultural problems and prospects of the island economies of Japan and England are hardly comparable. What the Soviet Union shares with many developed economies is the fact that agricultural production is relatively high-cost and highly subsidized. In fact, a global view reveals a handful of low-cost agricultural producers, notably the United States, Canada, Australia, and Argentina, whose governments are obliged in most years to deal with agricultural surpluses because the high-cost producer countries are sheltering and subsidizing their farmers.[13] The subsidy of the Soviet case is very large, but it stems more from strategic and ideological preferences for autarky than from the political influence of farmers.

A Comparison of Agricultural Performance in the United States and the USSR

Soviet agriculture has two very clear disadvantages that need to be dealt with at the outset. The U.S. economy is more highly industrialized than is the Soviet economy. Partly for this reason and partly for reasons of a different ordering of priorities, modernization of agriculture began significantly earlier in the United States. Climatic and other natural conditions in the Soviet Union are much less favorable to agriculture than is the case for the United States, which has a longer growing season, more uniform and reliable rainfall, smaller year-to-year variations in mean temperatures, and other conditions. The north-south temperature gradient is steeper in the United States as well, which permits some year-round growing zones. Nowhere in the vast stretches of the USSR are there to be found agricultural regions as richly favored as those of Iowa or Illinois.

Although these climatic differentials between Soviet and North American agriculture explain a portion of the differential performance of agriculture in each, they ought not be exaggerated. D. Gale Johnson, an authority of long standing, has argued persuasively that he does not "believe that soil and climatic conditions have been a major factor in restraining output growth. Nor do climatic conditions that prevail in the Soviet Union require the large year-to-year variability in total farm output that actually exists.[14]

Long-term comparison, from 1951 to 1975, indicates that growth in total agricultural output in the Soviet Union has outpaced that of the United States. The average annual rate of growth of total agricultural output was 3.5 percent, or a bit better, for the USSR and only 1.6 percent for the United States for these years.[15] As population growth rates have been very similar, the gap in per capita production of agricultural products has clearly been narrowing. The very magnitudes of output changes are quite impressive for the Soviet Union. For example, grain output averaged 88.5 million metric tons annually during 1951–55. By 1971–75 it had climbed to 181.5 million tons (or nearly 190.1 if the very poor 1975 harvest is excluded). The average for the first three years of the Tenth Five-Year Plan, 1976–78, has been almost 210 million tons. Similarly, total meat production more than doubled between the early 1950s and the current period, and equivalent increases were obtained for many other desirable food products such as milk, eggs, and vegetables.[16]

When one recalls that per capita production of agricultural products in 1953 was no greater than it had been in 1928, the increase over the past twenty-five years speaks for itself, but closer examination

TABLE 1. Output, Inputs, and Total Productivity in U.S. and Soviet Agriculture, 1951–75[a]

	Average annual rate of growth (percentage)			
	1951–60	1961–70	1971–75	1951–75
United States				
Output	2.1	1.1	1.8	1.6
Inputs	0.2	−0.1	0.2	0.1
Total productivity	1.9	1.2	1.7	1.5
USSR				
Output (three-year moving average)	4.9	3.0	0.9	3.4
Inputs	2.7	2.0	2.0	2.3
Total productivity	2.2	1.0	−1.1	1.0

[a] The base year for the calculations shown is the year before the stated initial year of period.
Source: Douglas B. Diamond, "Comparative Output and Productivity of U.S. and Soviet Agriculture" (ms., Conference on Soviet Agriculture, Kennan Institute for Advanced Russian Studies, Washington, D.C., November 6, 1976), fig. 5A.

points up several serious problems. First, the average annual rate of growth of agricultural output appears to be slowing down, falling from 4.9 percent per annum in the 1950s, to 3.0 percent in the 1960s, to an average of just short of 1.0 percent during the first half of the 1970s.[17] Although the very poor crop year of 1975 influences this low rate substantially, the trend is not encouraging, and it is highly unlikely that the rapid rates of growth that were obtained in the immediate post-Stalin years can be reestablished.

Moreover, if we apportion the increases in agricultural output since the early 1950s between increases in the physical quantities of the conventional inputs (land, labor, and capital) and the increase in the jointly measured productivity of these inputs, it may be seen that most of the growth is attributable to the growth of inputs rather than to growth in total productivity (see table 1). By contrast, total factor productivity has apparently increased at a somewhat more rapid rate in the United States. Although these measurements present difficulties and are not entirely reliable, it would appear that the already very large productivity gap that existed at the close of the Stalin period has not been narrowed. The increases that have been obtained in Soviet agricultural output have been purchased mainly by means of increasing the quantity of resources used in production.

In addition to the land resources added by the Virgin Lands campaign, very large investments have been made in Soviet agriculture. Since the late 1960s the share of gross fixed capital formation allocated to agriculture has been in the neighborhood of 25 percent. If investment in all branches of the economy that are supportive of agriculture, such as agricultural machinery manufacture and fertilizer production, is included, the share of investment in 1976 exceeded 34 percent of gross investment in the entire economy.[18] Soviet economists have been distressed to discover that the productivity of capital has been declining precipitously over the years, and the marginal product of capital is low enough now to raise questions about the usefulness of continued heavy investment.[19] As a consequence, the enormous investment of recent years has not led to a significant release of labor from agricultural employments, and the Soviet economy remains highly labor intensive despite growing capital intensity.

It is possible to obtain a rough comparison of the manpower requirements of agricultural production in the Soviet Union and the United States. In the United States, 4.6 percent of the total labor force was employed *directly* in agricultural employments in 1975. The figure for the Soviet Union (including those engaged on the private plots) was 25.4 percent.[20] The absolute figures for 1972 were 29.0 million worker years in the Soviet Union and 3.8 million in the United States. Of course, American farmers utilize more farm inputs that have been purchased from other sectors and a larger and more sophisticated distributional network for their output. When all labor inputs are counted, including those incorporated in the inputs farms purchase and those involved in processing, transporting, and marketing food and fiber products, the total labor input in Soviet agriculture was 43.9 million worker years in 1972, as against 12.1 million worker years in the United States that year.[21]

Comparison of Soviet and American agriculture, then, reveals what appears to be an inordinate absorption of current resources of labor, land, and capital in Soviet agriculture to produce a still inadequate and thus very costly output. The comparison raises two questions. First, why has the enormous economic effort of the last twenty-five years yielded so modest and variable a return? Second, what is the current Soviet leadership doing about the productivity gap, and how successful are their efforts likely to be?

Problems, Policy, and Prospects of Post-Stalin Agriculture

A survey of informed Western opinion reveals a striking consensus regarding the causes of inefficiency and low-productivity in Soviet agriculture today, although each expert ordinarily emphasizes different specific problems. The long list of specific problems may be grouped under four broad headings: (1) undercapitalization; (2) adverse composition of the agricultural labor force; (3) irrational price and wage formation practices; and (4) "systemic constraints," by which I mean certain irrational administrative practices and preferences that have acquired an aura of sanctity by reason of either ideology or simple bureaucratic inertia.

Soviet agriculture is undercapitalized in a relative sense only—relative to the United States[22] and relative to the output targets that have been set for the sector. If one takes into account the need for investment in rural infrastructure, that is, in rural road networks, retail outlets, and so forth, then it is obvious that Soviet agriculture trails far behind levels in the United States. Moreover, the limits set by climatic constraints will require relatively heavy investment in mechanization to speed planting and harvesting, in research and development of hybrids, and in new techniques of cultivation, areas much neglected during Stalin's years. Soviet soils are relatively poor also, and their quality has deteriorated through a general absence of proper soil and grassland management. Continued rapid expansion of livestock herds will require sustained heavy investment in facilities, transport, research, and veterinary medicine. Thus, continued heavy investment in Soviet agriculture is necessary, but it will not be easy to find the funds.[23] Even more troublesome, Soviet agriculture is already quite capital intensive by Western standards. A Western analyst recently described it as "two to three times as capital intensive as countries on a similar level of per capital income but subject to the discipline of market prices."[24] Both the average and the marginal products of capital are low and declining by all reports. For example, the energy capacity of Soviet agriculture doubled and productive capital per worker increased two-and-one-half times between 1965 and 1975, but gross production increased only by a third over the same decade.[25] Additional capital investment can only be justified, therefore, by substantial increases in yields, productivity, and efficiency.

This brings us to the second problem area—the agricultural labor force. Increased mechanization, the use of complex chemical compounds such as pesticides and fertilizers, cultivation of new hybrids, development of adequate soil maintenance programs, and upgrading farm management all require a highly educated and well-motivated labor force. Unfortunately, the age, sex, and educational composition of the agricultural labor force is highly disadvantageous.[26] The rural population has a higher proportion of nonworking-age population (young and old taken together) than the urban, which reflects the departure of able-bodied youth to urban-industrial pur-

suits. The agricultural population is 65 percent female as well, and
the able-bodied woman of child-bearing age is less likely than her
male counterpart to devote full time to work on the collective. Women
are also less likely to seek to acquire high-level skills, mainly because
the burdens of child-rearing, housekeeping, and private plot husbandry occupy much of their time. There is a bitter irony too about
the provision of educational facilities for rural youth. Education is
the primary lever for upward mobility in the Soviet Union generally,
and this applies with even greater force in rural areas. Education
opens opportunities for nonrural employments and thus tends to
promote the exodus of the more talented and ambitious young people—even where the education provided is specific to agricultural
job descriptions.

What makes the problem of the agricultural labor force so
intractable is the relative backwardness of the rural sector. Though
the degree of backwardness has lessened markedly since 1953, it still
extends to all aspects of Soviet rural life, from the most private to
the most public. Relative backwardness is characteristic of developing
economies, but the Soviet experience is extreme. Recent sociological
surveys in the countryside reveal not only that the young want to
leave for industrial occupations but that their parents want them to
do so as well.[27] Unlike American farm families, who groom one or
more of their children to take over the private family farm, the Soviet
rural family has only a small personal stake in farming and little
motivation other than family cohesiveness to encourage bright, ca-
pable young people to stay in farming. As an old woman kolkhoznik
put it in one of the Savchenko's stories: "Everybody is attracted to
the cities. . . . Only old people and women are left. . . . and after we
die nobody will be left."[28]

The total rural population, however, remains large, and despite
the decline that can be expected, there is no reason for despair if
rural employments and rural life can be made attractive enough to
slow the decline to a reasonable rate. It would certainly make no
sense to attempt to arrest it altogether. Much has been done to
improve the quality of rural life, but much more remains to be done.

Although the current institutional structure of Soviet agriculture
is much more favorable to efficient production than at any time since
the initiation of collectivization, procurement prices paid to Soviet
farms, prices charged in state retail outlets for agricultural products,
and urban-rural income differentials are still not economically rational—that is, they do not serve as correct indicators of true scarcities and thus do not call forth appropriate producer behavior. However, the very fact that all transactions in the agricultural sector have

been put in pecuniary terms makes this irrationality obvious not only to the Western observer but to any concerned Soviet policymaker as well. For example, Soviet agricultural products may be the most highly subsidized in the world.[29] Retail prices on many food products are too low relative to available supplies and therefore relative to nonagricultural goods as well. Wholesale prices (procurement and transfer prices) on a variety of agricultural products have no reasonable relationship either to each other or to retail prices, and so it goes.

Realigning state retail prices would be easier if the leadership had not promised repeatedly since 1954 to hold food prices constant. Thus, any adjustment in relative agricultural prices can take place only by lowering certain prices, and this would be possible only if reductions in the cost of producing these (relatively) overpriced goods could be expected.[30] Recent experience has shown that this is not a reasonable expectation—for prices of most agricultural inputs are in fact inflating. The situation is not promising.

However, the logic of relative prices is very forceful, especially now that the sector has been pecuniarized. Money represents power—purchasing power—in the Soviet Union, as it does elsewhere. And like it or not, managers of state and collective farms cannot but be tempted to bend in the direction prices point. In the absence of a major step backward to Stalinist measures—and this most unlikely—the pressure to rationalize agricultural prices is inexorable. Since unit costs of agricultural products are not likely to fall, retail food prices will eventually have to rise to permit a more rational structuring of the whole gamut of agricultural prices.

Rural-urban wage differentials present a somewhat different problem, however, and it falls into the fourth category of problems listed above. There is little question that the adverse wage differential has decreased during the last twenty-five years, but the change has hardly been radical. The wage on state farms has increased from less than 50 percent of the industrial wage to about 80 percent, and earnings on collective farms have increased from about 25 percent to 60 percent.[31] This kind of differential is typical of developed economies, but it is possible that in the Soviet case it ought to be reversed. Solution of the problem of creating an educated, well-motivated agricultural labor force in an economy in which private farming does not exist may require a differential that favors rural employments. But here we run into a "systemic constraint"—the fact that the Soviet Union is unabashedly a workers' state, and this has typically been interpreted to refer primarily to the industrial worker.

This essentially ideological distaste for a differential wage favoring agricultural employments is only one of a number of systemic constraints on progress in Soviet agriculture. A similar constraint, imposed for similar reasons, is the reluctance to permit the private sector of Soviet agriculture to operate at an optimal level. Soviet leadership has come to realize, mainly through Khrushchev's unhappy experience, that there is sufficient interdependence between public and private agriculture for discrimination against the private sector to rebound upon the public. The current leadership has been willing to tolerate the continued existence of private plot agriculture. Although many of the claims that have been made in the West about the greater productivity of private agriculture in the Soviet Union have been greatly exaggerated, it is nonetheless obvious that the current allocation of resources between the two sectors is not optimal. More important than enlargement of the area of individual private plots, which might be useful to some extent, would be the production and sale of small-scale implements, such as small motorized units, and of other agricultural supplies to improve the efficiency and output of private agriculture.

Most Western observers have been highly critical of the scale of Soviet agricultural enterprises, and the fact that so few private agricultural ventures in the capitalist West are of anything like the scale of the typical sovkhoz or kolkhoz is itself a sign that diminishing returns to scale set in early in agriculture. Bolshevik faith in the benefits of scale seem to be unshakable and impervious to experience either there or in the world at large. There is no reason, however, why the actual operating unit, the brigade, for example, could not be of optimal size, with farms remaining as large as they are today for other reasons. The problem is not really the large size of the typical farm but a failure to delegate sufficient responsibility and decision-making authority to units that are more nearly optimal in scale.

This brings us to three systemic traits that all observers of Soviet economic affairs are familiar with, traits that are not specific to agriculture at all and that are firmly rooted in Stalinist central planning. They are the tendencies to overcentralize decision making, to overcommit resources in the planning process, and to make decisions with a very low time horizon. Taken together, these three mutually reinforcing traits, which have thus far proven resistant to post-Stalin reform attempts, represent the most formidable obstacle to the evolution of efficient agricultural production. Excessive centralization is an even greater problem when it comes to planning and organizing agricultural production than it is for industry, because the variability of conditions of production (soils, climate, terrain, moisture, and so forth) is much greater in agriculture.

Overcommitment of resources is itself largely the outcome of the high degree of centralization of decision making and the mistrust of local adaptation of plans to local conditions. But it has become a sort of Soviet bureaucratic habit as well. The underlying notion seems to be that high targets serve as *means* as well as *ends*. The large grain imports of the 1970s, for example, have resulted from the fact that targets for the growth of livestock herds were set at unattainable levels, given any reasonable projection of sustainable rates of growth of the fodder base. What is unusual in this case is not that the targets were set so high but that these ultimately consumer-sector targets attained the degree of priority to permit the expenditure of large quantities of precious foreign exchange.

Finally, despite the five-year format of Soviet planning, managerial decision making at all levels ordinarily operates within a much shorter time horizon. The attempt to get results soon, if not immediately, contributes to a failure to optimize in the medium and longer run. It leads to allocation by priority and the consequent neglect of low priority areas. It also contributes to overcommitment planning, for it induces Soviet administrators to set targets that are not attainable on a sustained basis.

The Future of Soviet Agriculture

The problems cataloged above lead most Western students of Soviet agriculture to be pessimistic about the outlook for continued rapid growth of Soviet agricultural production. The agricultural labor force is certain to decline, the rate of capital formation in agriculture and agriculture-related industries cannot increase, and a decrease is more likely judging from the Tenth Five-Year Plan.[32] Expansion of the land area under cultivation is most unlikely, and current investment in reclamation and restoration of arable land and pasturage is unlikely to add as much to the total available as long-term neglect and heavy usage will require to be withdrawn from use.[33] Continued growth of agricultural output will necessarily depend, therefore, upon increases in total factor productivity, that is, increases in productivity of the conventional inputs taken together. Since total productivity has never increased in the past at the 3 to 3.5 percent rate required to match average annual growth of output during the last quarter century, it follows inescapably that the rate of growth in agricultural production over the next five to ten years will be lower. It also follows that Soviet agriculture will remain high-cost agriculture, for it is going to absorb large quantities of scarce resources, especially investment resources.

Meanwhile, the Soviet consumers' income continues to grow, and they have come to expect expanding supplies of high-quality farm products such as dairy products, fruits, vegetables, and beef. Failure of food output to grow commensurately with income and the still relatively high elasticities of demand for these high-quality products are going to be very disturbing to consumers and political leaders alike, and there is no feasible way to avoid some enlargement of the gap between the way Soviet consumers would like to divide their income among the various types of farm products and the actual composition of Soviet farm output. Raising prices to ration the scarcer products may indeed prove to be politically unwise as the current leadership seems to believe. Hence the dilemma for them. Thus, agriculture will remain for the foreseeable future *the* central domestic focus of political and economic attention. It seems safe in the light of these considerations to conclude that the USSR will continue to import from the West substantial quantities of grains, especially fodders (including soybeans), and perhaps of meat products as well.

In many ways and for many reasons the situation of Soviet agriculture is bleak. However, I am not myself prepared to paint the future of Soviet agriculture in too somber a color. Admitting to the problems outlined above, let me stress a few of the offsetting factors for post-Stalin agriculture. First, the current institutional structure of agricultural production is much more conducive to the development of efficiency than has been the case since the end of the 1920s. Second, Bolshevik ideology is an optimistic doctrine because it implies that solutions to all economic problems *do exist;* they need only be found. Third, Soviet leaders from Lenin forward have demonstrated an ability to get results if the goals have sufficiently high priority, and Soviet agriculture has, in my opinion, attained the requisite degree of priority. Finally, it is well to remember that, historically, most Western medium-term predictions of the growth of Soviet agriculture have been wrong, and almost always on the low side. Wishful thinking may be part of the explanation. But an inability to realize just how high a price Soviet leaders have been willing to pay (and impose) to achieve their goals has also been a factor. This might be labeled a "systemic advantage" of the Soviet-type economy.

Long-term comparison of output growth in the United States and the Soviet Union, say from 1913 to the present, which is long enough to wash out a large portion of the effects of short-term variation in growth in each system, reveals a small but significant differential advantage for the Soviet Union.[34] Thus, although a continuation of the rate of growth of agricultural production over the next five to ten years at the 3.5 to 4 percent rate of the last twenty-five years would be unrealistic, a rate of growth in the neighborhood of 2 to 2.5 percent is not impossible or unreasonable, and unexpectedly good weather could lead to an even more favorable outcome. Thus far, the Tenth Five-Year Plan is off to a good start, thanks to several good crop years. Finally, in a world in which aggregate demand for food products is expected to grow rapidly, more rapidly, some claim, than can be supplied,[35] it is encouraging to know that the Soviet Union is potentially self-sufficient and is investing heavily in the food sector. It just might prove to be a good investment.

NOTES

1. This essay is based upon a number of recent studies of Soviet agriculture. Most important are three papers presented at a conference on the future of Soviet agriculture that was held at the Kennan Institute for Advanced Russian Studies on November 16, 1976. These included my own paper, "Models of Soviet Socialist Agriculture"; D. Gale Johnson, "The 10th Five-Year Plan: Agriculture and Prospects for Soviet-American Trade"; and Douglas B. Diamond, "Comparative Output and Productivity of U.S. and Soviet Agriculture." Other significant recent studies of Soviet agriculture include the following: D. Gale Johnson, "Theory and Practice of Soviet Collective Agriculture" (University of Chicago, Office of Agricultural Economic Research, no. 75:28, December 1975); Jerzy F. Karcz, "Khrushchev's Impact on Soviet Agriculture," *Agricultural History* 40, no. 1 (January 1966); Alec Nove, "Soviet Agriculture under Brezhnev," *Slavic Review* 29, no. 3 (September 1970); W. Klatt, "Reflections on the 1975 Soviet Harvest," *Soviet Studies* 28, no. 4 (October 1976); Keith Bush, "Soviet Agriculture: Ten Years under New Management" (Radio Liberty, Munich, May 23, 1975); David W. Carey, "Soviet Agriculture: Recent Performance and Future Plans," and David M. Schoonover, "Soviet Agricultural Trade and the Feed-Livestock Economy," both in Joint Economic Committee, Congress of the United States, *Soviet Economy in a New Perspective* (Washington, D.C.: U.S. Government Printing Office, 1976). See also an earlier article of mine: "The Prospects for Soviet Agriculture," *Problems of Communism* 26 (May-June 1977):1–16, upon which I have drawn liberally for this essay. The epigraphs are from: Naum Jasny, "Kolkhozy: The Achilles' Heel of the Soviet Regime," *Soviet Studies* 3, no. 2 (October 1951):150–63; Peter Wiles, "The Soviet Economy Outpaces the West," *Foreign Affairs* 31, no. 4 (July 1953):566–80.

2. Diamond, "Comparative Output and Productivity of U.S. and Soviet Agriculture," fig. 5A.

3. Murray Feshbach and Stephen Rapawy, "Soviet Population and Manpower Trends and Policies," in *Soviet Economy in a New Perspective,* p. 115, table 1.

4. Gertrude E. Schroeder and Barbara S. Severin, "Soviet Consumption and Income Policies in Perspective," in *Soviet Economy in a New Perspective*, p. 623, table 2.

5. TsSU, *Narodnoe khoziaistvo SSSR v 1974 g.* (Moscow, 1975), p. 354; and Central Intelligence Agency, *Research Aid: The Soviet Grain Balance, 1960–73* (September 1975).

6. *Ekonomika sel'skogo khoziaistva* (1977): B. Maniakin and G. Makhov, "Pobeda Oktiabria i vosstanovlenie sel'skogo khoziaistva (1917–1925 gg.)," no. 8; "Pobeda sotsialisticheskogo sposoba proizvodstva (Tsifry i fakty)," no. 9; "Sel'skoe khoziaistvo v Velikuiu voinu i v poslevoennyi period (1941–1964 gg.)," no. 10; and "V usloviiakh razvitogo sotsializma (1965–76 gg.)," no. 11.

7. This point remains somewhat controversial. See, for example, James Millar and Alec Nove, "Was Stalin Really Necessary? A Debate on Collectivization," *Problems of Communism* 25 (July-August 1976): 49–66; and Millar, "Mass Collectivization and the Contribution of Soviet Agriculture to the First Five-Year Plan," *Slavic Review* 33, no. 4 (December 1974):750–66.

8. In 1976 there were 27,300 collective farms working an average of 3,600 hectares of sown area, as opposed to 19,600 state farms working an average of 5,900 hectares per farm. TsSU, *Naradnoe khoziaistvo SSSR za 60 let* (Moscow, 1977).

9. The importance of meat production as a symbol of success was first developed, I believe, by Arcadius Kahan.

10. J. Stalin, *Economic Problems of Socialism in the USSR* (Moscow, 1952), pp. 100–101.

11. Official compilations of statistical data were not published after 1938. An official statistical handbook did not reappear until 1957, the first of the *Narodnoe khoziaistvo* series that continues today.

12. Sterling Wortman, "Food and Agriculture," and David Hopper, "The Development of Agriculture in Developing Countries," both in *Scientific American* 235, no. 3 (September 1976). See also, Theodore W. Schultz, *Transforming Traditional Agriculture* (New Haven: Yale University Press, 1964).

13. D. Gale Johnson, *World Agriculture in Disarray* (London: Fontana/Collins, in association with the Trade Policy Research Centre, 1973).

14. Johnson, "The 10th Five-Year Plan: Agriculture and Prospects for Soviet-American Trade," p. 2.

15. Diamond, "Comparative Output and Productivity of U.S. and Soviet Agriculture," fig. 5A

16. *Pravda*, January 23, 1977, p. 2; *Ekonomicheskaia gazetta* 6 (1976):3–6; USDA, *Agricultural Statistics of Eastern Europe and the Soviet Union, 1950–70* (Washington, D.C., 1973); USDA, *USSR Agricultural Situation: Review of 1977 and Outlook for 1978* (Washington, D.C., 1978); speech by Premier A. Kosygin, November 4, 1978, AP Wireservice.

17. Diamond, "Comparative Output and Productivity of U.S. and Soviet Agriculture," fig. 5A.

18. Carey, "Soviet Agriculture: Recent Performance and Future Plans," pp. 586–87.

19. A. Pronin and M. Terent'ev, "Povyshat' effektivnost' ispol'zovaniia proizvodstvennykh fondov," *Ekonomika sel'skogo khoziaistva* no. 12 (1973):7–15; Folke Dovring, "Capital Intensity in Soviet Agriculture" (ms., Fifth International Conference on Soviet and East European Agricultural and Peasant Affairs, October 5–7, 1978, University of Kansas, Lawrence).

20. Diamond, "Comparative Output and Productivity of U.S. and Soviet Agriculture," fig. 8A.

21. For the complete analysis, see Millar, "The Prospects for Soviet Agriculture," table 3, p. 9.

22. Fixed capital (excluding land) per worker is actually higher in agriculture than in industry in the United States, which is not the case for the Soviet Union. For a discussion, see A. M. Emel'ianov, "Problemy tempov rosta i povysheniia effektivnosti sel'skokhoziaistvennogo proizvodstva," *Izvestiia akademii nauk SSSR: seriia ekonomicheskaia* no. 6 (1970):20–33.

23. The share of total net fixed investment that agriculture has absorbed (directly) has increased from 19.6 percent in 1961–65 to the 26.9 percent that is called for in the (current) Tenth Five-Year Plan. The latter is only marginally above the rate that was achieved on average annually during the Ninth Five-Year Plan, and there would appear to be no way to increase the share further. Most of the potentially arable land in the Soviet Union is already under cultivation, and current plans for reclamation and restoration will not be sufficient to do much more than offset the withdrawal of exhausted marginal lands. Carey, "Soviet Agriculture: Recent Performance and Future Plans," p. 590; Hopper, "The Development of Agriculture in Developing Countries," esp. p. 199.

24. Dovring, "Capital Intensity in Soviet Agriculture," p. 19.

25. Cited in ibid., p. 2.

26. For an excellent general discussion, see Norton T. Dodge, "Recruitment and the Quality of the Soviet Agricultural Labor Force," in James R. Millar (ed.) *The Soviet Rural Community: A Symposium* (Urbana: University of Illinois Press, 1971). More recently, see Central Intelligence Agency, *Research Aid, USSR: Some Implications of Demographic Trends for Economic Policies* (January 1977); and Stephen Rapawy, "Estimates and Projections of the Labor Force and Civilian Employment in the USSR: 1950 to 1990" (U.S. Department of Commerce, Bureau of Economic Analysis, 1976), pp. 19–20, 61–63.

27. See, for example, V. N. Kolbanovskii (ed.), *Kollektiv kolkhoznikov, sotsial'nopsikhologicheskoe issledovanie* (Moscow, 1970), esp. chaps. 6 and 7.

28. V. Savchenko, "Pis'mo," *Novyi mir* no. 4 (1966):118, as cited by Dodge, "Recruitment and the Quality of the Soviet Agricultural Labor Force."

29. The subsidy has been running at about 85–90 percent of the level of explicit Soviet defense expenditures and represents approximately 28

percent of national income originating in agriculture. Constance B. Krueger, "A Note on the Size of Subsidies on Soviet Government Purchases of Agricultural Producers," *ACES Bulletin* 16–17, no. 2 (Fall 1974).

30. This was Soviet experience historically with respect to the production of a wide variety of nonagricultural products of mass consumption, and this expectation has informed Soviet price policy for a very long time. For the best general discussion and history, see A. N. Malafeev, *Istoriia tsenoobrazovanniia v SSSR, 1917–1963* (Moscow, 1964). See also the various price indices presented in the standard Soviet statistical handbooks.

31. Based on Norton T. Dodge, "The Soviet Agricultural Labor Force, Recent Trends" (ms., Fifth International Conference on Soviet and East European Agricultural and Peasant Affairs, October 5–7, 1978, University of Kansas, Lawrence), table 2, p. 14.

32. See Carey, "Soviet Agriculture: Performance and Future Plans," esp. p. 590.

33. Klatt, "Reflections on the 1975 Soviet Harvest," pp. 489–91.

34. Soviet growth was measured over the period at an average annual rate of 3.4 percent, against 3.0 percent for the United States. This is a very conservative measure of the difference, because the impact of war and depression on the two systems were not really offsetting in all likelihood as the analysis implies. Herbert Block, "Soviet Economic Power Growth-Achievements under Handicaps," in *Soviet Economy in a New Perspective,* esp. p. 268.

35. See, for example, Food and Agricultural Organizations of the United Nations, *The State of Food and Agriculture 1974* (Rome, 1975).

PART 2

Financing the Soviet
Economic Experiment

7

History and Analysis of Soviet Domestic Bond Policy

On January 21, 1918, the new Bolshevik regime repudiated the internal as well as the external debt of the czarist and provisional governments that had preceded it. That the Soviet government subsequently made extensive use of domestic bond financing is not widely known, and its policy in this field has received little attention in the Western literature.[1] The purpose of this essay is to provide an analytical history of Soviet domestic bond policy.

Until the early 1960s the Soviet state budget (*Gosbyudzhet SSSR*), which is a consolidated budget for all governmental units, ordinarily recorded an annual deficit.[2] In the early years of Bolshevik rule deficits were apparently financed by direct currency issue. Domestic state bonds were first issued in 1922, at the close of the civil war, as part of a program designed to restore monetary stability. By the mid-1920s state domestic bond sales had become the principal mode of financing budget deficits, and this continued to be the case, with only temporary exceptions (notably during the war years of 1941–42[3]), up to and including 1957.

The share of gross proceeds from bond sales in total budgetary sources provides a rough measure of the relative significance of domestic bond financing.[4] Gross bond proceeds rose from an average of 6.8 percent of budget sources during the late 1920s to a peak of 13 percent in 1931, at the height of the industrialization drive. The share declined to between 5 percent and 6 percent for the remainder of the 1930s, but it again reached 13 percent in 1943, the most difficult war year. Between 1946 and 1956 the share varied between 6 percent and 9 percent. However, with the termination of the mass subscription bond series in 1957, the share fell to less than 1 percent in 1963. Since 1963, proceeds from bond sales to the public have

From *Soviet Studies* 27, no. 4 (October 1975):598–614. Reprinted by permission, with minor editorial changes.

been treated as a source of funds to the state bank (*Gosbank*) rather than to the state budget.[5]

The Soviet state budget relied heavily upon domestic bond financing during rapid development, war, and postwar reconstruction, and apparently it did so for reasons common to developing and wartime economies. Changes in the Soviet expenditure-revenue gap and tax structure over the course of development and war do not differ materially from the budget patterns of nonsocialist countries under similar circumstances.[6] However, there are a number of unusual and, indeed, unique features of Soviet domestic bond policy; and examination of these also helps to explain the virtual abandonment of domestic bond instruments in the late 1950s.

The first section below briefly describes the evolution of Soviet domestic bond policy. The principal characteristics of the mass subscription bond, which generated the bulk of bond proceeds from 1929 onward, are described and analyzed in the second section. The third section seeks to identify and evaluate the main determinants of Soviet domestic bond policy.

History

The main features of Soviet domestic bond issues are summarized in table 1.[7] There are a number of trends that stand out in sharp relief. As might be expected, issue amount (col. 5) and term to maturity (col. 21)[8] increase over time. The growing and eventually dominant role of the mass subscription bond, which was sold on a ten-month installment plan and usually by payroll deduction, is also obvious. More surprising, however, are the accompanying downward trend in coupon and premium rates offered to the public (cols. 18, 19, and 20) and the frequent resort to conversions and other adjustments in face value, maturities, and rates of return of outstanding issues (cols. 22 and 23.) Of interest also is the fact that the Soviet state budget came increasingly, and eventually exclusively, to rely upon lottery devices to determine the returns, if any, to bondholders (col. 20).

The evolution of Soviet domestic bond policy may be divided into a number of more or less distinct periods. The first, 1922 to 1927 or 1929, was one of experimentation and of relatively high-cost, short-term borrowing through open-market channels. The variety of different issues during this period was a consequence, according to one Soviet source, of the inexperience of policymakers in financial affairs.[9] The earliest bond issues were in-kind or gold-backed, which is explained by the fact that they were marketed during a period of severe monetary instability. No such guarantees were ever again offered once stabilization had been assured. Early issues were also sold on the market at discount, but this practice was also soon abandoned.

The state budget experimented during the 1920s with bonds earmarked for sale to particular classes of Soviet society. Because of its relative size and remoteness, both geographically and politically, the peasantry was the main object of this technique (col. 9), but special issues were also directed to workers and the Nepmen.[10] Class earmarking was abandoned after 1927, apparently because it was not successful. A large portion of the issues that were earmarked for sale to the peasantry, for example, were in fact purchased by the urban population.[11]

Another type of bond was issued in the 1920s by the state budget that was earmarked for sale to productive enterprises (col. 6). This reflected the difficulty encountered in attempting to market bonds to the population at large, for it was apparently easier to sell bonds to enterprises.[12] But it also represented an early attempt to control and/or reduce enterprise liquidity selectively. With the development of the control functions of the state bank with respect to enterprise receipts, outlays, and deposits, and the success of the mass subscription bond, bond sales to enterprises were terminated after 1929.[13]

The use of a lottery device of some sort to enhance the attractiveness of Soviet domestic bonds was common from the earliest issues (col. 20), and it is a technique that has been widely utilized elsewhere. State lottery and premium bonds were very popular in Britain, for example, prior to 1823, when the practice was prohibited by act of Parliament.[14] In Britain a lottery device was ordinarily utilized merely to distribute premiums over and above a coupon rate, and several Soviet issues of the 1920s operated similarly. However, the last such combination was offered in 1929. Thereafter, bonds were either lottery or coupon bonds.

The first mass subscription bond, with provisions for payroll deduction and installment purchase, was issued in February 1927. It was a relatively small issue, but its success apparently surprised and greatly impressed officials of the state budget. Another, and larger, issue appeared in August of the same year, inaugurating a new period in the history of Soviet domestic bonds. The August issue was accompanied by a major propaganda campaign on the theme of rapid industrialization. Committees were organized in each factory, institution, and organization to encourage subscription.[15] The organization of subscription committees was not unlike that of certain

TABLE 1. Soviet State Budget Domestic Bond Issues

Column groups: columns 4–5 = Face value; columns 6–12 = To whom; columns 13–18 = Special features; columns 19–21 = Terms; columns 22–23 = Changes in terms.

1 Date	2 Description[a]	3 Series	4 Amount (million poods)[b]	5 Amount (million rubles)[c]	6 Enterprises	7 Savings banks	8 Nepmen	9 Peasants	10 Workers	11 Cooperatives and kolkhozes	12 General population	13 In-kind–backed	14 Gold-backed	15 Use to pay in-kind tax	16 Pledge as collateral[d]	17 Subscription payroll deduction	18 Sold at market discount	19 Coupon rate (%)	20 Lottery premium rate (%)	21 Term (max.)[e] of loan	22 Adjustment[f]	23 Year
May 1922			10.0								X	Rye	X	X			95/100	6	X	0.8		
Oct. 1922			100.0	10.0	X						X	Rye, Sugar		X			95/100		X	10.0		
Mar. 1923			1.0																	0.11		
Nov. 1923				10.0	X								X				85/100	5	8	6.0		
Feb. 1924				5.0			X	X					X					6	X	2.9		
Mar. 1924				10.0					X				X					5	X	5.0		
Apr. 1924				1.0	X		X										82/100			1.0		
Feb. 1925				30.0														10	X	4.6		
Oct. 1925				10.0				X						X				12		2.0		
June 1926				10.0	X						X							6	8	6.0		
Sept. 1926				3.0				X			X			X					X	5.0		
Feb. 1927				10.0												X			10	8.0		
Mar. 1927				2.5	X													12	7	3.0		
June 1927				20.0							X				X	X		6	8	10.0		
June 1927				20.0							X				X	X		6	6	10.0		
Aug. 1927				20.0							X							6	7	10.0		
Dec. 1927	I			15.0				X			X					X		6	X	3.0		
July 1928	I	{1, 2}		55.0							X							11	X	10.0		
Sept. 1928	I			30.0	X						X				X	X		6	8	10.0	Cv	1938
Oct. 1928				50.0							X								X	15.0	Cv	1936
Mar. 1929				5.0							X				X	X			X	10.0	Cv	1938
July 1929	I	{1, 2}		75.0							X							0.0		10.0	Cv	1936
Nov. 1929				12.5	X						X				X	X		6	12	5.0	Un	1930
Jan. 1930				5.0							X				X	X			X	10.0	Un	1930
July 1930	I+U	{1, 2}		170.0							X							10	X	10.0	Un	1930
Mar. 1931				370.0		X					X				Rs	X				10.0		
June 1931	I	{1, 2}		160.0							X				Rs	X		10	X	10.0	Cv	1936
Feb. 1932	I			10.0							X				Rs	X			X	10.0	Cv	1938
June 1932	I	{1, 2}		320.0							X				Rs	X		10	X	10.0	Cv	1936
May 1933	I	{1, 2}		300.0 / 350.0							X				Rs	X		10	X	10.0	Cv	1936

Date	Type	No.	Amount		Rs		Term		%	Type	Year
Mar. 1935			30.0	X							
May 1935	I	1	350.0	X	Rs	X	8	X	10,0	Cv	1938
		2		X	Rs	X		X	10,0	Cv	1936
July 1936	I+C	1	400.0	X	Rs	X	4	X	20,0	Cv	1948
		2		X	Rs	X		X			
July 1937	D	1	400.0	X		X	4	X	20,0	Cv	1948
Apr. 1938	C	2	240.0	X					20,0	Cv	1947
July 1938	I	1	500.0	X		X	4	3	20,0	Cv	1948
		2		X				X			
Aug. 1939	I	1	600.0	X		X	4	4	20,0	Cv	1948
		2		X		X		X			
July 1940	I	1	800.0	X		X	4	X	20,0	Cv	1948
		2		X		X		X			
June 1941	I	1	950.0	X		X	4	X	20,0	Cv	1948
		2		X		X		X			
Apr. 1942	W	1	1,000.0	X		X	2	4	20,0	Cv	1948
		2				X		4			
June 1943	W	1	1,200.0	X		X	2	4	20,0	Cv	1948
		2									
May 1944	W	1	2,500.0	X		X	2	4	20,0	Cv	1948
		2						4			
May 1945	W	1	2,500.0	X		X	2	4	20,0	Cv	1948
		2									
May 1946	R	1	2,000.0	X		X		4	20,0	Cv	1948
May 1947	R	2	2,000.0	X		X		4	20,0	Cv	1957
Dec. 1947	C		—					4			
Feb. 1948	C	1	2,980.0	X		X	2	3	20,0	Pp	1957
		2						2			
May 1948	R		2,000.0	X		X		4	20,0	Pp	1957
May 1949	R		2,000.0	X		X	4	4	20,0	Pp	1957
May 1950	R		3,000.0	X		X	4	4	20,0	Pp	1957
May 1951	4		3,000.0	X		X	4	4	20,0	Pp	1957
May 1952	4		1,500.0	X		X	4	4	20,0	Pp	1957
June 1953	4		1,600.0	X		X	3	3	20,0	Pp	1957
June 1954	4		3,200.0	X		X	4	2	20,0	Pp	1957
May 1955	4		3,200.0	X		X	5	2	20,0	Pp	1957
May 1956	5		1,200.0	X		X	5	2	5,0	Pp	1957
May 1957	5							3	20,0		
July 1966			—								

a I = industrialization; U = unification; C = conversion; D = defense; W = war; R = reconstruction; 4 = Fourth Five Year Plan; 5 = Fifth Five Year Plan.

b One pood equals 36 lbs., or 16.38 kg.

c 1960 rubles (i.e., the decimal place was moved one place to the left in 1960).

d Rs = restricted.

e See discussion of retirement schedules in the text; 2;9 = 2 yrs., 9 mos.

f Un = unified; Cv = converted; Pp = postponed.

g This and all subsequent subscription bond issues up to and including 1941 were described as "all-win" lotteries, for all bondholders stood to win something over the course of the loan.

Sources: V. P. D'yachenko et al. (eds.), Finansovo-kreditnyi slovar' (Moscow, 1961), pp. 297–305; L. B. Valler, "Razvitie gosudarstvennogo kredita v SSSR," in P. Ya. Dmitrichev (ed.), Gosudarstvennye zaimy v SSSR (Moscow, 1956), pp. 20–43; M. Yu. Nakhmanovich, "Gosudarstvennye zaimy SSSR i ikh rol' na razlichnykh etapakh razvitiya narodnogo khozyaistva. Gosudarstvennye zaimy i denezhno-veshchevye loterei v sovremennykh usloviyakh," in P. A. Chetverikov (ed.), Sberegatel'nye kassy SSSR za 50 let (Moscow, 1972), pp. 42–58.

community charity drives in the United States today, in which members of the committee make personal visits to potential donors. However, the Soviet authorities definitely followed "hard sell" methods which proved to be very effective in mobilizing informal and formal pressure upon potential purchasers. A measure of the success of the bond subscription committees may be seen in the fact that this and all subsequent mass subscription bond issues were oversubscribed, and frequently by a considerable margin.[16] In effect, the development of the subscription bond and the formation of bond promotional committees removed bond sales from the open market, thereby laying the groundwork for reducing expected rates of return below open-market levels.

Thus by the end of the 1920s the main outlines of Soviet domestic bond policy had been drawn and greatly simplified. From 1930 onward the mass subscription bond was the principal source of bond proceeds, and in that year the industrialization and peasant issues of 1927–28 were "unified." According to Soviet official sources this was not a conversion, properly speaking, for the differential rates of return on the bonds so unified were maintained by adjusting coupon rates on the substitute issue.[17] Although Soviet sources are silent on this matter, it does appear that maturities were uniformly extended by the unification.

Throughout the 1930s industrialization bond sale campaigns were conducted in the late spring or early summer of each year to promote mass subscription of ever-increasing issue amounts. The "industrialization" subscription bonds of the 1930s were offered in two distinct series, between which the potential purchaser could choose. One series promised a straight coupon rate. The other featured an unusual lottery bond in which all bondholders were assured of winning something (plus return of the face value of the bond) over the nominal term of the bond. These were called "all-win" bonds, and this feature, of course, constrained both the number and size of the large winnings.

All outstanding mass subscription bonds were converted in July 1936. All maturity dates were extended twenty years, coupon rates were reduced to 4 percent, and the expected rate of return on the all-win series was presumably also reduced.[18] The purpose of the conversion was to reduce current and future service charges. Steps had been taken in 1931 to reduce the "liquidity" of mass subscription bonds and thus to extend the effective term of these bonds. Bondholders were obliged by law to obtain special permission before being allowed to pledge their bonds as collateral for loans from the state savings bank system. However, in March 1937 these restrictions were removed.[19]

In addition to the annual mass subscription bond issue, during the 1930s the state budget continued periodically to issue a straight lottery bond that was sold on the open market and liquid in the sense that the holder could recover the face value of the instrument at any time from a state savings bank outlet. Hence, they were colloquially described as "market bonds." Issue amount were relatively small (see issues for March 1929, January 1930, and February 1932 in table 1), and they were intended for sale to the better-paid members of Soviet society. All outstanding issues were converted in 1938 into twenty-year "3% state lottery bonds."[20] The conversion was severely adverse.

In March 1931 a special ten-year, 10 percent coupon-rate bond was issued and earmarked for sale to the state savings bank. This instrument was designed to serve as the mechanism for transferring changes in the savings account liabilities to the state budget.[21] The earnings were utilized by the savings bank to finance its activities. It is not clear from available Soviet sources just what happened to this issue subsequently. Interest rates offered by the savings bank system on the various types of savings deposits held by the public were reduced in 1936, coincident with the conversion of outstanding mass subscription bonds. It seems likely, therefore, that additional issues (and/or conversions) took place after 1931, for bond transactions between the savings bank and the state budget continued until 1963, when the savings bank system became the direct responsibility of the state bank.

The last prewar industrialization bond issue was scheduled for June 1941, and it became, in effect, the first issue of the war period. Immediately upon the outbreak of war, pledging of subscription bonds was suspended indefinitely. The savings bank system was also instructed at this time to suspend repurchase of outstanding 3 percent state lottery bonds (of 1938). (The suspension was lifted for these "market bonds" in January 1946.) All exisiting savings account balances were frozen for the duration of the war as well.[22]

Several significant changes were introduced in the first "war bond" subscription campaign of April 1942. As had been the case in the 1930s, the issue was divided into two series. However, the coupon-rate series, reduced to 2 percent per annum, was offered exclusively to collective farms and (private) productive artels. The purpose of the special series, which was offered only with the four war bond issues (1942–45), was to restrict the liquidity and thus the discretionary purchasing power of these nonstate productive enterprises. In this sense, these special series were similar functionally to the issues earmarked for enterprises in the 1920s. The general population was offered only a lottery premium bond. According to a Soviet source, the population had demonstrated a preference in the prewar years for the lottery series, and it was therefore decided to abandon the coupon rate series.[23] The all-win principle was also replaced by a lottery system in which only a fixed portion of bondholders (probably 35 percent) stood to win anything over the nominal twenty-year course of the issue. This allowed increases in the size and number of large winnings. Finally, a straight retirement lottery was introduced, by means of which a certain fixed proportion of (nonwinning) outstanding bonds were to be retired each year, beginning with the sixth year of the issue.[24] The evidence suggests that these changes reduced the expected rate of return below that for the 1941 mass subscription bond, but the available data do not permit a more precise conclusion.

The first of five "reconstruction" mass subscription issues appeared in 1946, with terms identical to those for war bonds. At the close of hostilities the Soviet economy had still not regained the level of output and employment of 1940. Moreover, the population had greatly increased its holding of financial assets, particularly of hand-to-hand currency balances.[25] Concern about the probable impact of "pent-up" demand, coupled with plans for rapid reconstruction (and a poor harvest in 1946), led to a monetary reform at the end of 1947. The reform called for an exchange of hand-to-hand (paper) currency at the rate of one new ruble to ten outstanding. Savings deposits (which included the Soviet counterpart of the demand deposit) in excess of 3,000 rubles were reduced at a somewhat more favorable rate. (Money prices and wages remained unchanged.)

A conversion of outstanding state budget debt accompanied the monetary reform. The 1938 issue of 3 percent state lottery bonds (the "market" bond) was exchanged in December 1947, at an adverse rate of five rubles to one in face value, and the date of maturity was set forward twenty years. In February 1948 all outstanding mass subscription bonds, with the sole exception of the 1947 issue, were converted in face value at an adverse rate of three rubles to one. Lottery premium rates were reduced to 2 percent and maturities extended to twenty years. These conversions reduced government nonmonetary debt to approximately one-third the preconversion level, and debt service changes were reduced even more substantially for the immediately ensuing years.[26]

The adverse effect of the conversions of 1947 was offset to a considerable extent by a series of subsequent reductions in state retail prices. The retail price index for all commodities (1947 = 100) fell to 50 in 1952 and to 43 by April 1954. This represented a sharp change in price trends, for prices had risen at an average rate of 14 percent per annum between 1928 and 1947.[27] The trend reversal, of course, had a favorable effect upon expected rates of return on bond issues of the late 1940s and early 1950s. Issue sizes for mass subscription bonds were increased substantially for 1951 and 1952 with no reduction in the nominal rate of return (4 percent). The struggle for succession among Stalin's heirs may have been reflected in the sharp reduction in issue sizes for 1953 and 1954. However, the reduction doubtless also was a response to the rising cost of bond financing, and the lottery premium rate was indeed reduced from 4 percent to 3 percent. In 1955 and 1956 the state budget returned to the issue levels of the early 1950s, and the lottery premium was further reduced to 2 percent (with retail prices essentially constant). The reduction was accomplished by reducing the proportion of winning certificates to 25 percent, the elimination of the largest winnings category, and a change in retirement schedules.[28]

In April 1957 an official joint decree of the Communist party and the Council of Ministers announced the termination of mass subscription bonds after 1957. It was also announced that the state budget would henceforth cease to conduct premium lotteries for all outstanding mass subscription bonds. In effect, expected rates of return were taxed away. Moreover, annual retirement lotteries scheduled for the 25.8 billion rubles in outstanding mass subscription bonds were postponed for a twenty-year period.[29] This was, then, a final and drastic conversion of state debt and the third in little more than twenty years (1936, 1948, and 1957). The 3 percent state lottery bond (of 1947) was not affected by these rulings.

A final and relatively small (1.5 billion rubles) mass subscription bond issue was floated in May 1957. It promised a 2 percent lottery premium rate for a term of five years. This issue was designed to smooth the transition for the state budget, for its receipts had already been fixed by the 1957 plan. By implication, the decision to terminate mass subscription bond issues was taken quickly. It is interesting to note that organizers of the subscription campaign of 1957 were instructed that individual subscriptions were not to exceed two weeks' pay and that the bonds were not to be sold to those with incomes of less than 50 rubles per month.

According to the original decree, the retirement of pre-1957 subscription bonds was scheduled to begin in 1977 and to extend through to 1996. However, in May 1971 Brezhnev announced at the Twenty-fourth Party Congress a plan for "early" retirement of outstanding bonds. Retirement is now scheduled to begin in 1974 and to be completed in 1990. It calls for the retirement each year of 1.0 billion rubles in 1974–75, of 1.2 billion in 1976–80, of 1.5 billion in 1981–85, of 2.0 billion in 1986–89, and 2.3 billion in 1990.[30] Presumably, a lottery will be utilized to determine the order of retirements.

In November 1967 the last lottery was held to determine winners in the 3 percent state lottery bond issue of 1947. Meanwhile, a new 3 percent lottery bond had been issued in July 1966, which was sold "somewhat" above face value. However, holders of the 1947 bond (i.e., nonwinners) were permitted to exchange them without penalty (at face value) for the new issue, and 90 percent were reportedly so exchanged. On January 1, 1972, the total stock of 3 percent state lottery bonds (1966 issue) outstanding stood at 2.9 billion rubles.[31] Since these bonds may be freely bought or sold at any time at state savings bank outlets, it is clear that there are riskseekers among the Soviet population to whom the lottery principle is appealing. The expected rate of return on 3 percent lottery bonds is considerably less than the 3 percent per annum rate guaranteed on long-term savings accounts. (Savings account deposits totaled 53.2 billion rubles on January 1, 1972.[32])

Structure and Characteristics of Postwar Soviet Bond Issues[33]

The basic building block of all Soviet bond issues is the *razryad,* which may be best translated in this context as "subseries" or "order." For all postwar mass subscription issues, except the 1948 conversion issue, this basic unit was one million ten-ruble bond certificates, or ten million rubles face value. Thus, the 3.79 billion ruble issue subscribed in 1952 was composed of 379 orders (*razryady*). The 1948 conversion issue was composed of orders of 2.5 million twenty-ruble certificates (50 million rubles per *razryad*). The *razryad* is the basic unit for each issue because winnings and the order of retirement (i.e., the expected rate of return) are fixed in terms of it.

For all postwar mass subscription bonds, lotteries were held twice a year to determine winning certificates, and the number of winning certificates was fixed per *razryad* for each of the forty semiannual lotteries. Winning certificates were retired, and the stated value of winning included the face value of the bond. Thus, a certain preestablished fraction of each issue was retired each year in this way (see table 2). With the exception of the issues for 1955 to 1957, the size of total annual winnings and the number of certificates retired

TABLE 2. A Reconstruction of Winnings and Retirement Schedules, Soviet Domestic Bonds (1948–56) (millions of 1960 rubles)

Winnings & Retirement	%[a]	Total issue[b]	1948	1949	1950	1951	1952	1953	1954	1955	1956	1957	1958	1959	1960	1961	1962	1963	1964	1965	1966	1967	1968	1969	1970	1971	1972	1973	1974	1975	1976	1977	Total	% retired	Total to 1957
1947	4%		65	65	65	65	65	65	65	65	65	65	64	64	64	64	64	63	63	63	63	63	63									1,285			390
	Ret.		40	41	40	40	40	41	38	38	38	37	37	37	37	37	37	36	36	36	36	36	40									755	33	
1948	2%			41	40	40	41	41	41	41	38	41	37	37	37	37	37	36	36	36	36	36	27									810	20	257
	Ret.			41	41	41	41	41	41	41	41	41										67	1									560		
1948	2%			29	29	29	29	29	28	28	28	28	28	28	28	28	28	28	28	28	28	38	63									71		
1948	4%						4	4	4	4	4	4	4	4	4	3	3	3	3	3	2	74	36	67								1,290	33	356
1949	4%			66	66	66	66	66	65	65	65	63	63	63	64	63	64	63	63	63	63	74	38									760	33	333
	Ret.			40	40	40	40	40	40	39	39	39	37	37	37	37	37	37	36	38	74	46										1,365		
1950	4%				70	70	70	70	70	69	41	41	41	41	40	67	67	67	67	75	46	94										805	35	348
	Ret.				42	42	42	42	42	42	78	41	76	76	76	75	75	75	48	94	58											1,515		
1951	4%					50	50	50	50	50	50	49	49	49	49	48	48	48	95	58	101											965	35	377
1952	4%						78	99	99	98	96	96	96	96	96	95	60	60	103	101	64											1,920	35	345
1953	4%						63	63	99	99	63	62	62	62	104	60	104	103	66	64	36											1,215	35	112
1953	3%						107	107	107	107	107	107	68	68	104	68	66	66	36	36	28											2,075	35	93
1954	3%						69	69	69	69	36	36	36	36	36	36	36	28	28	28	40											1,335	35	86
1954	Ret.						28	28	28	31	40	40	40	40	40	40	40	40	31	31	31							40				720		
1955	2%										31	31	31	31	31	31	31	31	31	53	53	53				53	53	53	53	53		560		43
	Ret.											43	43	43	43	43	43	43	43	43	52	52				52	52	52	52	43		800	25	
1956	2%											43	43	43	43	43	43	43	43	43	43	43				43	43	43	43	43	52	620	25	
	Ret.																														43	1,060		
Subtotal			105	285	397	525	687	861	922	991	1,084	1,175	1,169	1,165	1,162	1,160	1,157	1,152	1,149	1,146	1,142	1,138	1,035	868	763	643	491	326	262	191	95				2,739
Retirement lottery																																			
1947		2,290						57	57	57	57	57	57	96	97	97	96	96	96	97	142	142	142	235	151	155	195	212	158	158	176			1,532	67	285
1948		2,800						56	56	56	56	56	56	146	61	61	146	146	146	146	235	235	235	36	195	195	195	158	158	176	364	364		2,241	80	224
1948		180								58	58	58	58	58	69	69	97	97	97	143	143	143	143	143	151	212	158	158	364	364	360			1,548	100	232
1948		2,300							58	61	61	69	61	69	87	102	121	121	153	151	151	151	155	195	158	158	176	364	360	360				1,631	67	183
1949		2,440								69	69	87	87	69	87	121	87	121	153	153	153	155	195	212	158	158	176	364	360					1,794	65	138
1950		2,760									95	95	95	95	87	95	153	167	167	212	212	212	176	176	364	360							2,262	65	87
1951		3,480										16	16	16	18	30	30	30	34	30	104	104	104	103	103	103							2,465	65	
1952		3,790											18	18	18	34	34	34	104	104	104	103	103	103									1,056	65	
1953		1,590												43	43	43	43	43	43	43	43	43	43										1,158	65	
1954		1,780																															2,598	75	
1955		3,470																														360	2,573	75	
1956		3,430																																	
Subtotal		30,310						57	191	232	301	388	483	538	685	769	864	930	1,002	1,186	1,251	1,346	1,448	1,351	1,112	1,103	1,208	1,270	1,058	900	724	360				
Grand total			105	285	397	525	687	918	1,093	1,223	1,385	1,563	1,652	1,703	1,847	1,929	2,024	2,082	2,151	2,332	2,393	2,484	2,483	2,219	1,875	1,746	1,699	1,596	1,320	1,091	819	360			1,149

Balance outstanding 1957 26,422[c]

[a] See text for an explanation of premium rates.

[b] Actual subscription total.

[c] The actual balance outstanding was 25,930 million rubles, which indicates that the reconstruction presented here is reasonably accurate. This figure comes from A. G. Zverev, *Gosudarstvennye zaimy i vklady v sberegatel'nye kassy* (Leningrad, 1957), p. 23.

Sources: L. B. Valler, "Razvitie gosudarstvennogo kredita v SSSR," M. A. Nadis and A. I. Yagodinsky, "Osnovnye usloviya i struktura gosudarstvennykh zaimov," and the addendum, all in P. Ya. Dmitrichev (ed.), *Gosudarstvennye zaimy v SSSR* (Moscow, 1956), pp. 20–43, 44–63, and 152–57 respectively.

in this way declined by a small amount in the eleventh and sixteenth year of the twenty-year nominal term. This was effected by reducing the number of twenty-ruble prizes (i.e., a ten-ruble return on a ten ruble bond).

Each postwar mass subscription bond issue also featured a second lottery to determine the order in which nonwinning certificates were to be retired during the nominal term of the issue. The retirement lottery was scheduled to be held once a year beginning in the sixth year from date of issue. The fraction of bonds retired per *razryad* by the retirement lottery increased in the twelfth and seventeenth years of the issue (table 2). Certificates not retired by either "winning" or "retirement" lotteries over the twenty-year course of the issue could be redeemed at face value from state savings bank outlets during the twenty-first year (only).

Although all postwar bond issues were for a nominal twenty-year term, the effective term was considerably less as a result of the two retirement mechanisms described above. It was Soviet practice to calculate the "average term" as the effective number of years that the funds made available by each issue remained at the disposal of the state budget. "Average term" was calculated in the following manner. The face value of bonds retired in each of the forty winning lotteries was multiplied by the number of years from the original date of issue that each lottery was held. Bonds retired in the straight retirement lotteries, which began in the sixth year of the loan, were treated in the same fashion. The sum of these two calculations was then divided by the face value of the total actual issue, yielding the average term in years. For example, the funds made available to the state budget by the 1952 mass subscription bond issue for a nominal twenty-year term were equivalent to a hypothetical loan for the same total ruble amount for a period of 12.6 years, absent interim retirements. Examination of the time shapes of bond retirement schedules for the postwar years (table 2) shows an extension in average terms brought about by bunching retirements via the retirement lottery in the later years.

The stated premium rate on all postwar (and presumably earlier straight lottery) bonds was determined on the basis of the average term computation. As mentioned earlier, the 4 percent lottery premium rate officially announced for the 1952 issue did not represent the expected rate of return. It is obtained instead by dividing the total winnings scheduled for the issue over its twenty-year nominal term by the average term, which yields the average annual payout. Dividing through by the actual issue ruble volume (times 100) yields the "average annual" interest cost to the state budget, or a little in excess of 4 percent for the 1952 issue. This number is obviously considerably in excess of the true expected rate of return on the 1952 issue. It is easy to see why earlier students of the Soviet economy overestimated expected rates of return on Soviet bond issues, for they were apparently unaware of the difference between nominal and average terms.[34]

Computation of the true expected rate of return to Soviet bond-holders, in conformity with Western practice, is, of course, rather complicated. This is a topic in itself,[35] so let me indicate here only the general outline of what is involved and of the outcome. First, only a certain fraction of bonds stood to be drawn in the winning lotteries over the nominal term of the loan (table 2). Purchasers, for example, of a ten-ruble 1952 certificate had a 0.35 chance of "winning" anything at all. There was a very small probability that they would win the largest prize available (2,500 rubles, less the 10-ruble nominal value of the certificate) in the first winning lottery, which was scheduled approximately six months following fulfillment of the subscription. In this instance, of course, the rate of return is astronomical. In fact, the rate of return obtained by *all winning bond-holders* over the twenty-year nominal term was relatively high, for the smallest winning was 10 rubles on the 10-ruble certificate in the fortieth lottery at the end of the twentieth year. However, there was, correspondingly, a 0.65 chance of recovering nothing more than the face value of the bond (barring conversion, postponements, etc.), and this might occur as late as twenty-one years from the date of purchase. Thus, the expected rate of return for any Soviet postwar mass subscription bond depends upon the opportunity rate of return that is selected to compute the negative rate of return on nonwinning bonds. Even if one uses as an opportunity rate of return the rate offered by the state bank system on long-term deposits (i.e., 3 percent for the latter part of this period), the expected rate of return that emerges is very low.

Downward adjustments in the reported premium rate on postwar mass subscription bonds (see table 1, col. 20) were effected by reducing the proportion of winning bonds per *razryad* and by eliminating large lottery prizes. Consequently, the decline in the stated premium rate reflects, but does not measure, a decrease in expected rate of return. Differential rates of inflation and the historical frequency of adverse bond conversions ought also to be taken into account in determining expected rates of return to bond purchasers. Only the first and the last mass subscription bond issues (February 1927 and May 1957, respectively) escaped conversion.

The only domestic bond in circulation in the Soviet Union

today is the twenty-year term, 3 percent lottery bond of 1966. All terms and conditions of its predecessor, the December 1947 conversion issue, were faithfully executed. The 1947 issue called for six "basic" winnings lotteries per year, with a top premium of 5,000 rubles on a 20-ruble certificate, and for an annual supplementary lottery with a top prize of 10,000 rubles. The 3 percent lottery bond could be purchased or sold at any time at state savings bank outlets, and all outstanding certificates participated in all "basic" annual lotteries. The annual supplementary lottery was restricted to bonds held at least nine months, as an incentive to long-term lending. Winning certificates were retired, so a certain fraction of the issue was retired each year. For the 1947 issue, 25 percent of all bonds sold were scheduled to be retired over the nominal twenty-year course of the issue. Nonwinning certificates could be redeemed at any time, but in no case later then January 1, 1970. The 3 percent premium return was calculated as described above for mass subscription issues. However, as the 3 percent state lottery bond had no provisions for a straight retirement lottery (i.e., in addition to the winning lotteries), the expected rate of return was considerably less than for mass subscription issues. The difference reflected, then an implicit liquidity premium.

A new 3 percent state lottery bond was offered for sale beginning in July 1966. It was similar to the 1947 issue in that it was also a nominal twenty-year bond and could be freely bought and sold at any time at state savings bank outlets. However, the 1966 issue is sold "somewhat" above face value and repurchased only at face value. Holders of outstanding (nonwinning) 1947 bonds were permitted to exchange them for the new issue at face value (between December 1, 1967 and June 1, 1968 only), and, reportedly, 90 percent of the 1.3 billion rubles' worth of bonds outstanding in November 1967 were so exchanged.[36]

The 1966 issue differed somewhat from the 1947 in certain other provisions. The supplementary lottery was abolished (and with it the largest prize of 10,000 rubles), and the number of "basic" lotteries was increased to eight per year. By rearranging the number of prizes, the fraction of certificates scheduled to win anything at all was increased from 25 percent to 30 percent. Ten- and twenty-ruble bonds are available, but winnings are calculated on twenty-ruble certificates (i.e., the ten-ruble certificate is half a bond).

The expected rate of return on 1966 3 percent state lottery bonds depends, of course, upon the opportunity return that is utilized to calculate the (negative) rate of return on nonwinning bonds. Presumably, the lowest savings bank rate (2 percent) (on what are essentially demand deposits) is appropriate in this instance since these are readily marketable bonds. Given this assumption, the expected rate of return on 3 percent state lottery bonds is less than 1 percent.[37]

An Analysis of Soviet Domestic Bond Policy

The development of the mass subscription bond at the end of the 1920s provided the state budget with what proved to be a very effective device for raising funds from the population during rapid industrialization, the war, and postwar reconstruction. During these years the sale of domestic bonds to the population ordinarily raised as much or more than was obtained by direct personal income taxes. The organization of bond subscription committees at the grass-roots level in all enterprises and institutions and the linking of bond promotion with major social and economic objectives effectively removed bond sales from the marketplace into an arena in which considerable "moral" pressure could be applied to potential subscribers. Moreover, installment purchase helped to minimize the immediate financial impact of bond subscription, and payroll deduction afforded an efficient means of enforcing timely payment.[38]

The extensive utilization of lottery devices may be explained as the outcome of several related factors. From the late 1920s onward the population offered the only source of private saving. Apart from the collective farms and certain (private) productive artels, productive enterprises were publicly owned, and other, nonfinancial devices had been developed to monitor and control enterprise cash balances and transfer enterprise retained earnings to the state budget. The principal target of domestic bond sales was, therefore, the population, for it alone owned discretionary cash balances. In nonsocialist countries, where the financial system is likely to be dominated instead by private financial and nonfinancial enterprises, extensive use of lottery bond instruments would be much less likely.

Both practical experience elsewhere and theory suggest that lottery devices may offer very successful means of tapping household savings.[39] Soviet experience is interesting in this respect, because the shift away from the "all-win" principle in the early 1940s was explained as reflecting the population's preference for taking larger gambles (i.e., a smaller chance of winning a larger prize). Lotteries, of course, provide entertainment as well as the chance to make a killing, and the large number of winning lotteries that were ordinarily held each year provided considerable action. During 1955, for example, some eighteen winning lotteries were held on subscription bonds and seven for 3 percent state lottery bonds. The sheer number of lotteries held in any given year may also have tended to exaggerate the likelihood of winning.

The history of Soviet domestic bond policy suggests an over-weaning official concern about service charges on outstanding debt. Steps were repeatedly taken to minimize and/or reduce these charges outright. The conversions of 1936, 1938, 1947, 1948, and 1957 were undertaken mainly for this reason, as was the systematic reduction in expected rates of return from 1929 onward. Extensive exploitation of lottery devices should be viewed in this light as well, for the determination of the expected rate of return on any given Soviet lottery bond is impossible in the absence of a complete decription of the time shapes of winnings and retirement.

The available data on bond receipts, debt service charges, and net funds raised by domestic bond financing, 1940–66, are presented in table 3. That mass subscription bond sales dominated state budget bond proceeds is obvious from an examination of rows D and E.

Debt service charges on mass subscription debt absorbed a little more than 40 percent of proceeds from new subscriptions in 1955 and 1956 (row K), and net proceeds from all bond sales had declined to between 4 percent and 5 percent of state budget receipts in these years (rows A and L). Debt service charges on mass subscriptions bonds issued prior to 1957 were scheduled to rise from 1.39 billion rubles in 1956 (row J) to a peak of approximately 2.5 billion in 1967–68 (see estimate in table 2). Had issues continued after 1957, at the 1956 level, service charges would have climbed to 2.5 billion rubles by 1962 instead.

The official reasons given for terminating mass subscription bond campaigns were (1) the growth of debt service changes and (2) the undesirability of increasing annual issue amounts beyond the 3.5 billion-ruble level of 1955 and 1956. "If the issue of bonds continues in larger volume than, for example, in 1956, this would be burden-some to the population. But if bonds are issued in smaller volume then it [bond proceeds] would almost entirely be absorbed by win-nings and retirement of outstanding issues"[40] This explanation as-sumes that the population regarded bond subscriptions in large part as simply a tax, which the very low rates of return on recent issues certainly justified. The first sentence implies official unwillingness to make new subscription bond issues more attractive by increasing the rate of return promised, and in any case, the increase required would certainly have been very substantial. The second sentence, if it means anything economic at all implies an official preference with respect to the redistributive consequences of financing forthcoming debt service charges by means of new issues. Faithful fulfillment of the

TABLE 3. Bond Proceeds and Service Charges, 1940–66 (in billions of 1960 rubles)

	1940	1941	1942	1943	1944	1945	1946	1947	1948	1949	1950	1951	1952	1953	1954	1955	1956	1957	1958	1959	1960	1961	1962	1963	1964	1965	1966
A. Gross proceeds state budget	18.00	17.70	16.50	20.40	26.90	30.20	32.50	38.60	41.10	43.70	42.30	47.00	49.80	54.00	55.90	56.40	58.60	62.70	67.20	74.00	77.10	78.10	84.30	89.50	94.40	102.30	106.30
B. Gross bond proceeds	1.15	1.15	1.53	2.55	3.26	2.90	2.47	2.57	2.39	2.76	3.10	3.68	4.26	3.04	2.65	3.68	4.43	3.53	1.06	1.49	0.91	0.80	1.17	1.31	0.11	0.18	0.22
C. B as % of A	6	6	9	13	12	10	8	7	6	6	7	8	9	6	5	7	8	6	2	2	1	1	1	1	—	—	—
D. Gross proceeds subscription bonds	0.90	0.83	1.22	1.79	2.63	2.31	2.06	1.90	n.a.	n.a.	2.64	3.26	3.60	1.73	1.62	3.02	3.28	1.85	0.32[a]	—	—	—	—	—	—	—	—
E. D as % of B	78	72	80	70	81	71	83	74	—	—	85	89	85	57	61	82	74	52	30	—	—	—	—	—	—	—	—
F. Proceeds 3% lottery bond	0.02	n.a.	n.a.	n.a.	n.a.	n.a.	0.04	0.02	0.04	0.06	0.06	0.06	0.06	0.09	0.11	0.12	0.14	0.07	0.08	0.16	0.06	0.04	0.06	0.07	0.11	0.18	0.22
G. Other bond proceeds[b] B−(D+F)	0.23	—	—	—	—	—	0.37	0.65	—	—	0.40	0.36	0.60	1.22	0.99	0.54	1.00	1.61	0.66	1.33	0.85	0.76	1.11	1.24	—[c]	—	—
H. Debt service charges (all)	0.28	0.34	n.a.	n.a.	n.a.	n.a.	n.a.	n.a.	n.a.	n.a.	0.51	0.68	0.90	1.17	n.a.	1.43	1.63	1.80	0.37	0.70	0.70	0.80	0.80	0.10	0.10	0.10	0.10
I. H as % of B	24	30	—	—	—	—	—	—	—	—	16	18	21	38	—	39	37	51	35	47	77	100	68	8	91	56	45
J. Debt service charges subscription bonds only	0.12	0.16	0.18	0.21	0.28	0.39	0.39	0.53	0.14	0.25	0.37	0.49	0.68	0.97	1.02	1.20	1.39	1.60	n.a.	n.a.	n.a.	n.a.	n.a.	—	—	—	—
K. J as % of D	13	19	15	12	11	17	19	28	—	—	14	15	19	56	64	40	42	87	n.a.	n.a.	n.a.	n.a.	n.a.	—	—	—	—
L. Net funds raised (all) (B−H)	0.87	0.81	—	—	—	—	—	—	—	—	2.59	3.00	3.36	1.87	—	2.25	2.80	1.73	0.69	0.79	0.21	0.0	0.37	1.21[d]	0.01	0.08	0.12
M. Net funds raised subscription bonds only (D−J)	0.78	0.67	1.04	1.58	2.35	1.92	1.67	1.37	—	—	2.27	2.77	2.92	0.76	0.60	1.82	1.89	0.25	—	—	—	—	—	—	—	—	—

[a] Terminated after 1957. The 1958 proceeds reflect the fulfillment of bond subscriptions contracted in 1957.

[b] Includes, principally, bond purchases by the state savings bank, the social insurance system, and for the war years, collective farms and nonstate productive artels. All proceeds from these sources were transferred from the state budget to the state bank after 1963.

[c] All bond transactions transferred to the state bank after 1963.

[d] The increase in this year reflects the fact that the 1957 subscription bond issue was retired in full by the end of 1962.

Sources: Row A: 1940–46, 1950: V. P. D'yachenko, "Sovetskaya sistema finansov i kredita v bor'be za sotsialisticheskoe pereustroistvo ekonomiki 1917–1957 gg. (ed.), Sovetskaya sotsialisticheskaya ekonomika 1917–1957 gg. (Moscow, 1957), pp. 581, 586; 1947–49, 1951–53: Franklin D. Holzman, Soviet Taxation (Cambridge, Mass., 1955), p. 222; 1955, 1960–65: Gosudarstvennyi byudzhet SSSR i byudzhety soyuznykh respublik (Moscow, 1966), p. 10; 1956–59: Gosudarstvennyi byudzhet SSSR i byudzhety soyuznykh respublik (Moscow, 1962), p. 7; 1966: Gosudarstvennyi byudzhet SSSR i byudzhety soyuznykh respublik (Moscow, 1972), p. 11.

Row B: 1940–46: D'yachenko, "Sovetskaya sistema finansov," pp. 581, 586; 1947–52: Holzman, Soviet Taxation, p. 222; 1953–54: Gosudarstvennye byudzhety soyuznykh respublik v pyatoi pyatiletke (Moscow, 1957), p. 5; 1955–60: Gosudarstvennyi byudzhet SSSR (1962), p. 9; 1961–65: Gosudarstvennyi byudzhet SSSR (1966), p. 11; 1966: Gosudarstvennyi byudzhet SSSR (1972), p. 12.

Row D: 1940–45: K. N. Plotnikov, Ocherki istorii byudzheta sovetskogo gosudarstva (Moscow, 1954), p. 316; 1946–47: A. Zverev, "Sovetskie finansy i stroitel'stvo sotsializma v SSSR," in Finansy SSSR za XXX let (Moscow, 1947), p. 76; 1950, 1955–58: Gosudarstvennyi byudzhet SSSR (1962), p. 9; 1951, 1954: Gosudarstvennye byudzhet (1957), p. 5; 1952: Narodnoe khozyaistvo SSSR v 1962 godu (Moscow, 1963), p. 635; 1953: Narodnoe khozyaistvo SSSR v 1958 godu (Moscow, 1959), p. 899.

Row F: 1940, 1950, 1955–60: Gosudarstvennyi byudzhet SSSR (1962), p. 9; 1946–54: A. G. Zverev, Gosudarstvennye zaimy i vklady v sberegatel'nye kassy (Leningrad, 1957), p. 36, and Plotnikov, Ocherki istorii byudzheta, p. 399, who gives the total for 1946–50; 1961–65: Gosudarstvennyi byudzhet SSSR (1966), p. 11; 1966: Gosudarstvennyi byudzhet SSSR (1972), p. 12.

Row H: 1940, 1950, 1953, 1955–56, 1958: Narodnoe khozyaistvo SSSR (1959), p. 900; 1941: R. W. Davies, The Development of the Soviet Budgetary System (Cambridge, 1958), p. 296; 1951: Plotnikov, Ocherki istorii byudzheta, p. 488; 1952, 1959, 1961–62: Narodnoe khozyaistvo SSSR (1963), p. 635; 1957: (Plan) A. G. Zverev, "Finansy SSSR za 40 let sovetskoi vlasti", in N. Laptev (ed.), Finansy i sotsialisticheskoe stroitel'stvo (Moscow, 1957), p. 77; 1960, 1965: Narodnoe khozyaistvo SSSR v 1969 godu (Moscow, 1970), p. 769; 1963–64: Narodnoe khozyaistvo SSSR v 1964 godu (Moscow, 1965), p. 770; 1966: Narodnoe khozyaistvo SSSR v 1968 godu (Moscow, 1969), p. 774.

Row J: 1940–53: Plotnikov, Ocherki istorii byudzheta, pp. 317, 488; 1946–56: Zverev, Gosudarstvennye zaimy i vklady; p. 25; 1957: (Plan) Zverev, "Finansy SSSR za 40 let," p. 77.

terms and conditions under which the outstanding debt had been floated would have entailed either a redistribution of income within the household sector in favor of exciting bondholders or a transfer of command over real resources from the state budget to existing bondholders. It would not have mattered in the first instance whether this was effected by additional bond sales or by some form of direct taxation and therefore, the official explanation either does not really address the question of why it was decided to abandon subscription bond sales, or it is simply irrational. It does suggest, however, official unwillingness to permit a redistribution of income in favor of existing bondholders at the expense of either current earned personal income or other budget outlays.

The decision to default on outstanding bonds cannot be interpreted as somehow "deflationary" in the long run,[41] unless the very improbable assumption is made that the state budget would otherwise have financed debt service and retirements by means of state bank overdrafts (i.e., by "printing" money). Historically, the state budget had had recourse to overdraft finance only in times of dire emergency since the early 1920s, as, for example, during the early years of World War II.[42]

The 1957 conversion was accompanied by the promise that mass subscription bonds would not be issued in the future. Consequently, the net effect was not disadvantageous to all bondholders. In exchange for forgoing the opportunity to participate in winning lotteries (i.e., the expectation of a possible positive return) and a twenty-year delay in redemption dates for bonds previously purchased, the population was promised relief from future bond subscriptions. The recommended subscription in 1956 was three to four weeks' pay, and installment payments during that year totaled 3.28 billion rubles (table 3, row D). The flow of debt service payments to the population on mass subscription bonds only was 1.39 billion rubles in 1956 and 1.60 billion in 1957 (row J). Thus, the complete abandonment of subscription bonds would have yielded a net gain of at least 1.7 billion rubles in *current* income to the population as a whole. The final 1957 issue reduced the actual gain to about 1.0 billion rubles in 1958.

Of course, only certain members of the population stood to "gain" in this way. The 1957 reform was particularly disadvantageous to the older members of the population who would have held a disproportionate share of outstanding bonds and had a much smaller chance of surviving the "freeze." Franklyn Holzman, in fact, interpreted the reform as an attempt by Khrushchev to gain the support of the young.[43] Perhaps this was in part the case, but the reform also effected a redistribution disadvantageous to high-income classes as well since bond sales had been based upon a progressive scale (i.e., the purchase of a fixed number of weeks' earnings). Thus, the 1957 reform produced an increase in disposable income, a reduction in the flow of unearned income relative to earned income, and an intergenerational and interincome class redistribution of income. Morris Bornstein may, therefore, have been correct in interpreting the reform as having "a favorable effect (from the viewpoint of the regime) on worker incentives."[44] It should be noted, though, that previous bond conversions would have had the same effect in some degree.

Holzman has put forward another reason to explain the abandonment of mass subscription bonds. Indeed, he predicted in 1955 an early termination of new issues on the basis of an estimate of the "tax burden" of these bonds.[45] This would seem to have been a case, unfortunately, of being right for the wrong reasons, for Holzman's prediction was founded on the mistaken assumption that state retail prices would continue to fall after 1954. For somewhat technical reasons, Holzman also underestimated the tax burden as at 1954.[46]

There can be little question that the tax burden of subscription bonds decreased between 1947 and 1954, as the state retail price level was reduced by more than one-half, but the downward trend ended in 1954. Also, the bond lottery premium was reduced from 4 percent to 3 percent in 1952 and again from 3 percent to 2 percent in 1955, and these reductions at least partially offset the favorable effect of earlier price declines upon expected rates of return. By 1957, the tax burden of mass subscription bonds had stabilized at a relatively high rate, even if the state savings bank rate is utilized rather than Holzman's hypothetical "market" rate. Thus, the tax burden argument cannot provide the impetus to the 1957 reform.

Instead, the decision to abolish bond subscriptions should be interpreted mainly as a decision to decrease taxes on the population, since the bond was in large part merely a tax. The decision to cease paying lottery premiums and to freeze outstanding bonds represented a decision to substitute a new tax to compensate partially for the loss of bond subscription revenue. But the net effect was to decrease taxes on the population, and this effect was augmented by a reduction in personal income tax rates in 1958.[47] To the extent that reduced taxation was reflected in a relative decline in state budget outlays, the net effect was to transfer purchasing power to the household sector and to do so in such a way that, in the long run, it benefited primarily the young and the lower-income classes.[48]

Ironically, to the extent that members of the population were

prepared to save some portion of the income released by the tax
burden of subscription bonds, the 1957 reform reflected a decision
by the state sector *to tax less and to borrow more,* by virtue of the
state's monopoly on all financial channels. In other words, the population was free to allocate some portion of the resulting current
(and future) increase in disposable income among the various financial channels available, and savings accounts had always offered a
higher rate of return, much greater liquidity, and, historically, a considerably smaller risk of confiscation. Increases in private savings
accounts today, of course, serve to finance (primarily) the state enterprise sector via Gosbank rather than the state budget.[49]

NOTES

1. Brief descriptions of domestic bond policy may be found in the
standard works on the Soviet state budget: Franklyn D. Holzman, *Soviet
Taxation* (Cambridge, Mass., 1955); R.W. Davies, *The Development of the
Soviet Budgetary System* (Cambridge, 1958). Passing reference to state
bonds may also be found in Alec Nove, *An Economic History of the U.S.S.R.*
(London, 1972); Maurice Dobb, *Soviet Economic Development since 1917*
(New York, 1966). See also Franklyn D. Holzman, "An Estimate of the
Tax Element in Soviet Bonds," *American Economic Review* 47 (June 1957):
390–96, which represents the only attempt that has been made to determine
the expected rate of return on Soviet domestic bonds. Unfortunately, these
sources are not only brief but inaccurate in certain respects.

2. Official Soviet sources report a budget surplus for all years since
1928–29, except for 1941, 1942, and 1943. However, these reports are based
upon the cash-flow budget, which includes the flow of funds through financial channels to the state budget. According to Western convention, the
Soviet state budget was rarely in surplus until very recent times (see Holzman, *Soviet Taxation,* pp. 228–30).

3. For a description of the alternatives utilized during the early war
years, see James R. Millar, "The Soviet War Budget" (ms.).

4. L. B. Valler, "Razvitie gosudarstvennogo kredita v SSSR," in P. Ya
Dmitrichev (ed.), *Gosudarstvennye zaimy v SSSR* (Moscow, 1956), p. 27;
Holzman, *Soviet Taxation,* p. 217 (table 47); table 3.

5. Yu. M. Belugin, "Razvitie sberegatel'nykh kass SSSR," in P. A. Chetverikov (ed.), *Sberegatel'nye kassy SSSR za 50 let* (Moscow, 1972), pp.
24–25.

6. For an analysis of nonsocialist budgets, see Harry H. Hinrichs, *A
General Theory of Tax Structure Change during Economic Development*
(Cambridge, Mass., 1966). For an examination of the Soviet case, see Donna
Bahry and James R. Millar, "Economic Development and the Changing
Tax Structure of the Soviet Budget" (ms.).

7. Table 1 omits certain domestic bond issues by agencies and organizations other than the state budget. Between 1923 and 1934 some nineteen

bond issues were floated by various commissariats, trusts, and societies, including one by the Moscow *ispolkom*. For a brief description of these issues, see V.P. D'yachenko et al. (eds.), *Finansovokreditnyi slovar'* (Moscow, 1961), tom I, pp. 304–5.

8. Almost all Soviet bonds provided for the retirement of a certain fraction of the outstanding issue in each year of the stated term. Terms to maturity given in table 1 are maximums and thus overstate effective terms, as is explained in the text below. The trend in maximum terms, in fact, understates somewhat that for effective terms.

9. Valler, "Razvitie gosudarstvennogo kredita v SSSR," p. 24.

10. This acronym refers to the middlemen who were permitted to operate during the period of the New Economic Policy of the 1920s.

11. Ibid.

12. Ibid.

13. Davies, *The Development of the Soviet Budgetary System*, pp. 227–28. For a thorough discussion of bank controls, see Christine Netishen Wollan, "The Financial Policy of the Soviet State Bank 1932–1970" (Ph.D. diss., University of Illinois at Urbana-Champaign, 1972), pp. 156–84.

14. For a brief description of lottery, or premium, bonds in the British Isles, see Harvey E. Fisk, *English Public Finance from the Revolution of 1688* (New York 1920), pp. 108–15. For more extended treatment, see C. L'Estrange Ewen, *Lotteries and Sweepstakes* (London, 1932).

15. A. A. Gerasimov, "Organizatsiya razmeshcheniya gosudarstvennykh zaimov," in Dmitrichev, *Gosudarstvennye zaimy v SSSR*, pp. 74–86.

16. Compare official issue amounts as given in D'yachenko et al., *Finansovokreditnyi slovar*, pp. 301–4, with actual subscription totals as given by Valler, "Razvitie gosudarstvennogo kredita v SSSR," pp. 27–43

17. D'yachenko et al., *Finansovokreditnyi slovar'*, M. Yu Nakhmanovich, "Gosudarstvennye zaimy SSSR i ikh rol' na razlichnykh etapakh razvitiya narodnogo khozyaistva. Gosudarstvennye zaimy i denezhno-veshchevye loterei v sovremennykh usloviyakh," in Chetverikov, *Sberegatel'nye kassy SSSR za 50 let*, p. 46.

18. Valler, "Razvitie gosudarstvennogo kredita v SSSR," pp. 30–31.

19. Ibid., p. 31; Nakhmanovich, "Gosudarstvennye zaimy SSSR i ikh rol' na razlichnykh etapakh razvitiya narodnogo khozyaistva," pp. 47–48.

20. Valler, "Razvitie gosudarstvennogo kredita v SSSR," pp. 30–31.

21. G. Eremeeva, *Razvitie sberegatel'nogo dela v SSSR* (Moscow, 1958), p. 63.

22. Valler, "Razvitie gosudarstvennogo kredita v SSSR," p. 35.

23. Ibid.

24. See table 2.

25. M. L. Tamarchenko, *Sovetski finansy v period Velikoi Otechestvennoi voiny* (Moscow, 1967), p. 40.

26. Valler, "Razvitie gosudarstvennogo kredita v SSSR," pp. 36–39.

27. A. N. Malafeev, *Istoriya tsenoobrazovaniya v SSSR, 1917–1963* (Moscow, 1964), p. 405.

28. See table 2.

29. A. G. Zverev, *Gosudarstvennye zaimy i vklady v sberegatel'nye kassy* (Leningrad, 1957), pp. 27–28. Note that all ruble figures given here and elsewhere are in "new" rubles (i.e., the decimal was moved one place to the left in 1960).

30. Nakhmanovich, "Gosudarstvennye zaimy SSSR i ikh rol' na razlichnykh etapakh razvitiya narodnogo khozyaistva," p. 52.

31. Ibid., pp. 52–54.

32. TsSU, *Narodnoe khozyaistvo SSSR, 1922–1972 gg.* (Moscow, 1973), p. 373.

33. The description that follows is based on table 2 and M. A. Nadis and A. I. Yagodinsky, "Osnovy usloviya i struktura gosudarstvennykh zaimov," and "Tirazhi vyigryshei i tirazhi pogasheniya po gosudarstvennym zaimam," in Dmitrichev, *Gosudarstvennye zaimy v SSSR*, pp. 44–63, 100–108.

34. See references given in n.1, esp. Holzman, "An Estimate of the Tax Element in Soviet Bonds," which presents the only previous attempt to calculate the expected rate of return on Soviet bonds.

35. The discussion that follows in the text is based upon an analysis of the 1952 and 1956 mass subscription bond issues and of the 1966 3 percent state lottery bond. A paper describing the results is available in draft form: James R. Millar and James A. Gentry, "Expected Rates of Return for Selected Post-War Soviet Domestic Bonds."

36. Nakhmanovich, "Gosudarstvennye zaimy SSSR i ikh rol' na razlichnykh etapakh razvitiya narodnogo khozyaistva," pp. 53–54.

37. This calculation ignores the fact that these bonds are sold at a slight premium.

38. According to Valler, "Razvitie gosudarstvennogo dela v SSSR," p. 40, n.1, the total funds actually raised by any given bond issue ordinarily fell somewhat short of the amount subscribed because of labor turnover.

39. See, for example, the works referred to in n.14, and Milton Friedman and L. J. Savage, "The Utility Analysis of Choices Involving Risk," *Journal of Political Economy* 61 (August 1948): 279–304.

40. Nakhmanovich, "Gosudarstvennye zaimy SSSR i ikh rol' na razlichnykh etapakh razvitiya narodnogo khozyaistva," p.51.

41. Franklyn D. Holzman, "The Soviet Bond Hoax," *Problems of Communism* 6, no. 5 (September-October 1957): 49.

42. For a discussion, see Millar, "The Soviet War Budget."

43. Holzman, "The Soviet Bond Hoax," p. 49.

44. Morris Bornstein, "An Estimate of the Tax Element in Soviet Bonds: Comment," *American Economic Review* 48, no. 4 (September 1958): 665.

45. Holzman, *Soviet Taxation*, pp. 207–9.

46. For a discussion, see Bornstein, "An Estimate of the Tax Element," pp. 662–64; Holzman, "Reply," *American Economic Review* 48, no. 4 (September 1958): 665–67.

47. *Pravda*, December 20, 1957, cited in Bornstein, "An Estimate of the Tax Element," p. 665.

48. The sharp decline in state budget defense outlays from 1956 to 1958

inclusive may be significant in this connection. Also, the index of state retail prices, which shows a small jump in 1958, reflecting the net effect of a sharp rise in prices of alcohol products and small declines in certain food items, notably meat, fish, and bread, seems to support the argument. See *Narodnoe khozyaistvo SSSR v 1958 godu,* pp. 900 and 770–71 respectively.

49. For a discussion see Christine N. Wollan, "A Sources and Uses of Funds Analysis of the Soviet State Bank," (ms., Central Slavic Conference, November 9, 1974, St. Louis, Missouri).

8

Financing the Soviet Effort in World War II

The Soviet economic effort in World War II has not received much study in the West, mainly because of the paucity of economic data. Texts on the economy of the USSR characteristically neglect the period altogether, with no more than a paragraph or two for the transition from the late 1930s to the early 1950s. Fortunately, it is now possible to begin serious analysis of the economics of the war effort. It is important to do so because the scope and magnitude of the war effort were clearly as great as the impact of rapid industrialization and mass collectivization. The purpose of this essay is to describe and analyze the way in which the cost of the war was financed, based on data which permit the reconstruction of the state budget for the war years.

The Soviet economic effort was unique in two respects. First, the magnitude of total war costs was undoubtedly greater than for any other participant in World War II, both absolutely and per capita. A Soviet economic historian has claimed that the war cost "two Five-Year Plans," excluding human costs.[1] This estimate may be a bit high as a measure of material costs, but not by so very much. Calculations by various methods yield estimates of the replacement cost of total material (nonhuman) war losses ranging from about three to a little more than seven years' earnings of the 1940 labor force.[2] Second, unlike any other major participant, a large share of total war costs was inflicted in the early years of the contest. Thus, a long, bitter war had to be fought with less than prewar economic capacity. Also, in contrast to the United States and Great Britain, for example, the outbreak of war could have no favorable effect on aggregate demand and employment, for the economy was already overextended as a result of rapid industrialization.

The contours of Soviet war finance were shaped mainly by the

From *Soviet Studies* 32, no. 1 (January 1980):106–23. Reprinted by permission, with minor editorial changes.

fluctuating tide of battle on the (German) Eastern front. Operation
Barbarossa was launched on June 22, 1941. In the first six months
of fighting German forces occupied territory which in the immediate
prewar wars had contained 40 percent of the Soviet population, 32
percent of the labor force of all state enterprises, and 33 percent of
the fixed capital assets of the state enterprise sector.[3] By December
2, when the "Last Heave" of the German army to take Moscow had
ground to a halt, Soviet economic capacity had been reduced by
almost one-third, and the precipitous fall in many vital economic
indices had yet to be arrested. Marshal Zhukov's successful, if hasty
and desperate, defense of Moscow dealt the German army its first
strategic defeat of the war in any theater,[4] and the respite it afforded
allowed the Soviet economic mechanism time to begin to rebound.
By the onset of the German summer offensive of 1942 the Soviet
economy was on its way to being fully converted to a war footing.
The output of essential war industries was already on the rise, and
plant and equipment evacuated to and beyond the Urals was beginning to come back into operation.[5] By this time the revamped Soviet
economy was much more efficiently geared for war than the German,
which was to begin total war mobilization in earnest only subsequently under Albert Speer.[6]

Most Soviet war historians divide the war period into two phases
at the middle of 1942. The principal economic indices, presented in
table 1, seem to support this practice, for the nadir in Soviet strategic
fortunes can be placed some time in late 1941 or early 1942. Note
the rapid rise in war production despite the drastic fall in national
income, gross industrial production, and average number of workers
and salaried officials in 1941–42. The cost of augmenting war production may be seen, in part, in the decline in capital investment
and retail turnover. It is also evident in the high proportion of gross
industrial production absorbed by war production during 1942–44.
The decline in national income and gross industrial production in
1945 reflected the early reconversion to peacetime production lines
and the decompression of controls over the labor force.

Financing the war effort has to do with the ways in which the
people (and organizations) may be induced to cooperate in making
the necessary resources available for the war effort. As long as the
central government has control of the banking and currency system,
the problem of financing a major war effort does not consist in finding
funds with which to pay for domestically produced war materials
and additional military personnel, but in avoiding or minimizing
untoward consequences of spending the huge sums modern warfare
requires and of the way in which the fiscal burden of the war is

TABLE 1. Principal Economic Indices, 1941–45 (1940 = 100)

	1941	1942	1943	1944	1945
National income	92	66	74	88	83
Gross industrial production	98	77	90	104	92
War production	140	186	224	251	173
Percentage of gross industrial production	n.a.	63.9	58.3	51.3	40.1
Gross agricultural output	62	38	37	54	60
Average annual number of workers and salaried officials	88	59	62	76	87
Capital investment (non-kolkhoz)	86	53	53	72	89
State and cooperative retail turnover (constant prices)	84	34	32	37	45

Source: Istoriya Velikoi Otechestvennoi voiny Sovetskogo Soyuza 1941–45 gg.. (Moscow, 1961), table 6, p. 45; and G. S. Kravchenko, Ekonomika SSSR v gody Velikoi Otechestvennoi voiny (Moscow, 1970), p. 351.

allocated among and influences the behavior of the various members and classes of society, present and future. The objective is to find an optimum combination of tax and financial instruments with respect to the expected incentive response of the public and of organizations.

Sources and Uses of State Budget Funds

The real cost of war must, of course, be paid currently. It is possible to trace the impact of war costs and of the structural changes in the Soviet war economy on the sources and uses of state budget funds for the war years. A statement of sources and uses of funds reveals where the money comes from to finance the various outlays of the state budget. All items are in money terms and reflect changes in prices as well as physical-volume outlays, for finance has to do with the raising and spending of funds.[7] This kind of statement is particularly revealing for the Soviet war effort because the state budget is so comprehensive in the USSR. It is a consolidated statement for all union, republic, and local governmental units, and it includes the main investment flows in the economy as well as military and non-defense categories of expenditure.

Nonfinancial Uses of Budget Funds

Nonfinancial state budget uses of funds may be classified into the four broad categories shown in table 2 (rows A, B, J, and P). Columns 10 to 14 provide percentage shares of these and various subcategories of sources and uses for selected years and for the war period, 1941–45.[8] Defense outlays (row A) rose from 33 percent of all budget nonfinancial uses of funds in 1940 to 59.7 percent in 1942, and averaged 51.4 percent for 1941–45. The shares of the other major outlay categories shrank correspondingly and, in the early years of the war, absolutely as well as relatively.

A comparison of the share of wartime defense outlays with 1940 defense outlays is somewhat misleading, for the share of defense outlays had already begun to rise sharply by 1940 in anticipation of war. In 1937, for example, defense outlays claimed only 17 percent of all budget nonfinancial uses of funds, while outlays on the national economy absorbed 40 percent (as opposed to 33.9 percent and 21.5 percent respectively for 1940 and 1941–45).[9] It should also be noted that the budget category "defense outlays" understates state budget expenditures for "war needs." Outlays connected with the conversion of plant, equipment, and manpower to war production are not included. Some considerable portion of government outlays to finance new investment and subsidies to state enterprises during the war, which are included here in row B, were also war-related. Moreover, neither research and development outlays nor the additional civilian administrative costs occasioned by the war are included in this line.

The second major outlay category, "outlays on the national economy," is composed of interest-free capital grants from the state budget to finance fixed capital investment and increases (or losses) in the working capital of state enterprises. The bulk of capital investment in the socialized sector of the Soviet economy had been financed in this way prior to the war (via *Stroibank*), and it therefore represented an adaptation to war conditions only by redirection of operations. The third category, "social-cultural outlays," needs no explanation, apart from noting that research and development expenditures and medical care and pensions for war wounded and dependents fall under this heading. "Administration," the fourth broad category, refers to the various political, economic, police, and other administrative personnel on the budget's payroll, notable chiefly because of the absolute as well as relative decline in this budget item.

The changes in budget outlay priorities revealed in table 2 reflect the change in the allocation of real national income occasioned by

TABLE 2. Soviet War Budget

(1)	(2) 1940	(3) 1941	(4) 1942	(5) 1943	(6) 1944	(7) 1945	(8) 1941–45	(9) 1946	(10) 1940	(11) 1942	(12) 1944	(13) 1941–45	(14) 1946
	(billions of 1960 rubles)								percent total — nonfinancial uses, row S				
Uses of funds, nonfinancial													
A. Defense outlays	5.7	8.3	10.8	12.5	13.8	12.8	58.2	7.4	33.3	59.7	52.8	51.4	23.1
B. Outlays on the national economy	5.8	5.2	3.2	3.3	5.4	7.4	24.4	10.6	33.9	17.7	20.6	21.5	33.0
C. All industry	2.9	3.0	1.8	1.8	3.1	4.4	14.0	7.0	17.0	9.9	11.8	12.4	21.8
D. Heavy and machine tool industry only	2.6	2.8	1.7	1.6	2.8	3.9	12.8	n.a.	15.2	9.4	10.7	11.3	n.a.
E. Agriculture (excludes procurement)	1.3	0.9	0.5	0.5	0.7	0.9	3.6	1.3	7.6	2.8	2.6	3.1	4.0
F. MTS only	0.8	0.6	0.3	0.3	0.4	0.5	2.1	n.a.	4.7	1.7	1.5	1.8	n.a.
G. Transport and communications	0.7	0.6	0.4	0.6	0.9	1.1	3.6	1.2	4.1	2.2	3.4	3.1	3.7
H. Housing and communal services	0.3	0.1	0.1	0.1	0.2	0.3	0.8	0.4	1.7	0.5	0.7	0.7	1.2
I. Trade and agricultural procurement	0.2	n.a.	n.a.	0.1	0.1	0.2	n.a.	0.3	1.1	n.a.	0.3	n.a.	0.9
J. Social-cultural outlays	4.1	3.1	3.0	3.8	5.1	6.3	21.3	8.0	24.0	16.6	19.5	18.8	24.9
K. Education and enlightenment	2.2	1.5	1.0	1.3	2.1	2.6	8.5	3.8	12.9	5.5	8.0	7.5	11.8
L. Health and physical culture	0.9	0.7	0.7	0.8	1.0	1.1	4.3	1.4	5.3	3.9	3.8	3.8	4.4
M. Grants to families	0.1	0.1	0.1	0.1	0.1	0.2	0.7	0.4	0.5	0.5	0.3	0.6	1.2
N. Social insurance	0.5	0.3	0.2	0.3	0.4	0.5	1.7	n.a.	2.9	1.1	1.5	1.5	n.a.
O. Social maintenance	0.4	0.6	1.1	1.3	1.7	2.0	6.6	2.1	2.3	6.1	6.5	5.8	6.5
P. Administration	0.7	0.5	0.4	0.5	0.7	0.9	3.1	1.2	4.1	2.2	2.6	2.7	3.7
Q. Total nonfinancial uses above	16.3	17.1	17.4	20.1	25.0	27.4	107.0	27.4	95.3	96.1	95.7	94.4	84.7
R. Other, unidentified uses of funds[a]	0.8	1.7	0.7	0.7	1.1	2.1	6.3	4.9	4.7	3.9	4.2	5.6	15.3
S. Total expenditures chargeable against ordinary receipts	17.1	18.8	18.1	20.8	26.1	29.5	113.3	32.1	100.0	100.0	100.0	100.0	100.0
T. Republic and local budget nonfinancial outlays	4.2	3.1	2.2	2.6	3.8	4.8	16.5	6.6	24.6	12.2	14.5	14.6	20.6

TABLE 2. (cont.)

(1)	(2) 1940	(3) 1941	(4) 1942	(5) 1943	(6) 1944	(7) 1945	(8) 1941–45	(9) 1946	(10) 1940	(11) 1942	(12) 1944	(13) 1941–45	(14) 1946
				(billions of 1960 rubles)					percent total—nonfinancial uses, row S				
Sources of funds													
U. Enterprise profit withdrawals	2.2	2.4	1.5	2.0	2.1	1.7	9.7	1.7	12.9	8.2	8.0	8.5	5.2
V. Turnover tax receipts	10.6	9.3	6.6	7.1	9.5	12.3	44.9	19.1	62.0	36.4	36.3	39.6	59.5
W. Total above (U + V)	12.8	11.7	8.1	9.1	11.6	14.0	54.6	20.8	74.9	44.6	44.3	48.1	64.7
X. Income tax from cooperatives, kolkhozes, etc.	0.3	0.3	0.2	0.3	0.3	0.3	1.7	0.3	1.7	1.1	1.1	1.5	0.9
Y. Income of the MTS	0.2	0.1	0.1	0.1	0.1	0.1	0.4	n.a.	1.1	0.5	0.3	0.3	n.a.
Z. Transfer of cash balances of socialized sector	—	2.0	—	—	—	—	2.0	—	—	—	—	1.7	—
AA. Direct taxes and fees from population	0.9	1.1	2.2	2.9	3.7	4.0	13.8	2.3	5.2	12.1	14.1	12.7	7.1
BB. Agricultural tax	0.2	0.2	0.1	0.4	0.5	0.6	1.8	n.a.	1.1	0.5	1.9	1.5	n.a.
CC. Income tax	0.4	0.5	0.3	0.6	0.9	1.1	3.4	n.a.	2.3	1.6	3.4	3.0	n.a.
DD. Housing and cultural tax	0.4	0.4	0.2	—	—	—	0.6	n.a.	2.3	1.1	—	0.5	n.a.
EE. Taxes on bachelors, one-person and childless families	—	0.0	0.1	0.1	0.2	0.3	0.8	n.a.	—	0.5	0.7	0.7	n.a.
FF. War tax	—	—	1.4	1.7	2.1	2.0	7.2	—	—	7.7	8.0	6.3	—
GG. War lottery receipts	—	0.1	0.2	0.3	0.5	—	1.2	—	—	1.1	1.9	1.0	—
HH. Money gifts to Red Army and Defense Funds	—	0.2	0.5	0.5	0.5	0.1	1.8	—	—	2.7	1.9	1.5	—
JJ. Total above (AA + GG + HH)	0.9	1.4	2.9	3.7	4.7	4.1	16.8	2.3	5.2	16.0	18.0	14.8	7.1
KK. Local taxes and collections	0.2	0.1	0.2	0.3	0.6	0.6	2.0	n.a.	1.1	1.1	2.2	1.7	n.a.
LL. Other republic and local nonfinancial income	0.4	0.5	0.3	0.4	0.5	0.6	2.3	n.a.	2.3	1.6	1.9	2.0	n.a.
MM. Social insurance contributions	0.9	0.7	0.6	0.7	0.9	1.0	3.9	1.2	5.2	3.3	3.4	3.4	3.7
NN. Total nonfinancial sources of funds above	15.7	16.8	12.4	14.6	18.7	20.7	83.7	24.6	91.8	68.5	71.6	73.8	76.6
OO. Other unidentified sources of funds[b]	1.2	-0.5	2.6	3.3	4.9	6.3	16.7	5.4	7.0	14.3	18.7	14.7	16.8
PP. Total nonfinancial sources of funds	16.9	16.3	15.0	17.9	23.6	27.0	100.4	30.0	98.8	82.8	90.4	88.6	93.4
QQ. Republic and local budgets	3.9	3.1	2.2	2.6	3.5	4.1	15.5	6.2	22.8	12.1	13.4	13.6	19.3

TABLE 2. (cont.)

(1)	(2) 1940	(3) 1941	(4) 1942	(5) 1943	(6) 1944	(7) 1945	(8) 1941–45	(9) 1946	(10) 1940	(11) 1942	(12) 1944	(13) 1941–45	(14) 1946
				(billions of 1960 rubles)					percent total—nonfinancial uses, row S				
RR. State budget deficit (or surplus), upper bound (Q − NN)	0.6	0.3	5.4	5.5	7.3	6.7	23.3	2.6	3.5	29.8	27.9	20.5	8.0
SS. State budget deficit (or surplus), lower bound (S − PP)	0.2	1.5	3.1	2.9	2.5	2.5	12.9	2.1	1.1	17.1	9.5	11.3	6.5
TT. Republic and local budgets (T − QQ)	0.3	0.0	0.0	0.0	0.3	0.5	1.0	1.2	1.7	0.0	1.1	0.8	3.7
Change in government debt													
UU. Net bond proceeds	0.9	0.8	1.4	2.3	3.0	2.5	10.0	2.1	5.2	7.7	11.5	8.8	6.5
VV. Net funds raised through Gosbank (designated cash deficit)	−0.6	2.1	2.0	0.9	−0.5	−0.3	4.2	−1.7	—	11.0	—	3.7	—
WW. Net funds raised through domestic financial channels (UU + VV)	0.3	2.9	3.4	3.2	2.5	2.2	14.2	0.4	2.9	18.8	9.6	12.5	1.2
XX. Discrepancy (SS − WW), use of funds not accounted for	−0.1	−1.4	−0.7	−0.3	0.0	0.3	−1.3	1.7					

[a] Residual: (S − Q)   [b] Residual: (PP − NN)

Source: Compiled from V. P. D'yachenko, "Sovetskaya sistema finansov i kredita v bor'be za sotsialisticheskoe pereustroistvo ekonomiki i postroenie kommunizma v SSSR," in L. M. Gatsovsky et al., *Sovetskaya sotsialisticheskaya ekonomika 1917–1957 gg.* (Moscow, 1957), pp. 581, 586; V. P. D'yachenko, "Finansy v sisteme voennoi ekonomiki," in I. A. Gladkov et. al, *Sovetskaya ekonomika v period Velikoi Otechestvennoi voiny 1941–45 gg.* (Moscow, 1970), pp. 419, 424; James R. Millar, "History and Analysis of Soviet Domestic Bond Policy," *Soviet Studies* 27, no. 4 (October 1975): table 3; K. N. Plotnikov, *Ocherki istorii byudzheta sovetskogo gosudarstva* (Moscow, 1954), pp. 324, 335, 340, 353, 418, 423, 425, 437; M. L. Tamarchenko, *Sovetskie finansy v period Velikoi Otechestvennoi voiny* (Moscow, 1967), pp. 30, 40, 46, 106. Note that row S is net of debt service charges (as estimated in Millar) and that rows PP and QQ are net of state bond proceeds (as given in Millar).

TABLE 3. National Income by Shares, 1940, 1942–45 (percentage of total in each year)

	1940	1942	1943	1944	1945
A. Capital investment	19	4	7	15	13
B. Consumption, including military personnel	74	67	60	61	69
C. War outlays, excluding consumption of military	7	29	33	24	18
D. Military consumption	4	11	11	11	n.a.
E. Total C + D	11	40	44	35	n.a.

Sources: M. L. Tamarchenko, *Sovetskie finansy v period Velikoi Otechestvennoi voiny* (Moscow, 1967), pp. 50–51; Ya E. Chadaev, *Ekonomika SSSR v period Velikoi Otechestvennoi voiny* (Moscow, 1965), p. 350; Kravchenko, *Ekonomika SSSR v gody Velikoi Otechestvennoi voiny,* pp. 228, 125.

the war effort. An official Soviet estimate of national income shares is reproduced in table 3. Capital formation fell from 19 percent in 1940 to a low of 4 percent in 1942. The prewar rate of capital formation was not regained at any time during the war. The share of consumption fell sharply also, but the decline was constrained by the large absolute decrease in real national income during the war (see table 1). Hence, war outlays, exclusive of military consumption, rose at the expense of investment and consumption, from 7 percent in 1940 to a high of 33 percent in 1943. If military consumption is included, the 1943 share reached 44 percent. Yet even this share understates the fraction of real national income that was absorbed by the war effort proper. The official history of the war states that "war needs" absorbed 55 percent of Soviet national income in 1942, as against 15 percent in 1940.[10] Presumably this figure includes not only the consumption of military personnel but also certain other items such as air defense of major cities, military construction, and perhaps wartime conversion of plant and equipment, as well as research and development outlays.

The figure for 1943 would have been correspondingly higher for the same reason. The war period witnessed an increased degree of concentration of budget outlays at the union level (table 2, row T). Republic and local government outlays fell from 24.6 percent of state budget nonfinancial outlays to 14.5 percent for the war period. It is of some interest, however, to note the fact that the degree of budget centralization so measured had been declining during the immediate prewar years (from a peak during the First Five-Year

Plan). The downward trend in the degree of centralization of budget outlays was resumed after the war and did not flatten out until the early 1960s.[11] Centralization during World War II represented, therefore, one of the mechanisms by which resources were made available for war needs, that is, by restricting local budgetary discretion.

Nonfinancial Sources of Funds

The impact of war also radically altered the relative shares of the main nonfinancial sources of budget funds (table 2). These sources include direct taxes and fees paid by the population, taxes on the income of cooperatives and kolkhozes, the "turnover tax," and enterprise profit withdrawals.[12]

In prewar years the turnover tax dominated total budget revenue. Price controls on rationed items and the decline in the production of consumer goods during the war caused turnover tax proceeds (row V) to decline in significance from 62 percent of total nonfinancial uses of funds (row S) to an average of 39.6 percent for 1941–45 (row V). Turnover tax receipts recovered substantially after 1944 with the opening of "commercial" stores and special restaurants (*glavosobtorga*), which were permitted to sell above-ration merchandise at or near market clearing prices.[13]

Before the war, enterprise profit withdrawals had been the second largest source of budget funds. These proceeds shrank from 12.9 percent of all nonfinancial uses of funds in 1940 to 8.5 percent during 1941–45, partly as a result of the loss of enterprises in occupied territory and the "down time" of evacuated plant and equipment, and partly as a result of temporary loss in plant efficiency due to war conversion, the shortage of skilled manpower, and inefficiency caused by prolonged working hours. This decline also reflected the successful attempt of the state to force down prices on war materials as overhead costs per unit declined and productivity increased.[14] The abolition of the "director's fund" (out of which enterprise managers had previously paid incentive premiums and financed minor capital improvements) for the duration of the war, served to compensate only marginally, by increasing the percentage-take of profit withdrawals.[15]

On July 3, 1941, both the agricultural and the personal income tax systems were revised and a war surtax added to each. The agricultural surtax was 100 percent across the board, with exemptions for rural families with members serving in the armed forces. The personal income tax surcharge was differentiated by social category, monthly wages, and the type of service the individual was rendering to the war effort. However, these changes proved inadequate. Insufficient additional revenue was generated, and these surcharges did not affect those not liable for either the agricultural or the income tax. Consequently, the surtax system was replaced by a special war tax on January 1, 1942, which was essentially a poll tax on all men and women over eighteen years of age (except servicemen and certain families on government relief), graduated according to income for urban workers and salaried officials and by geographical region for the agricultural population. Those eligible for military service, but not mobilized, were subject to a special surtax in addition. Few exemptions were permitted. The war tax was abolished on January 1, 1946. In November 1941 a special new tax had been introduced on bachelors and single-member and childless families. It raised a small amount of funds and, interestingly, was not abolished at the end of the war.[16]

As a result of these measures, direct taxes and taxes collected from the population (table 2, row AA) rose from 5.2 percent of all nonfinancial uses of funds in 1940 to a peak of 14.1 percent in 1944. In addition, during the war the population was encouraged to contribute money (and other valuables) to the Red Army and Defense Funds,[17] and four war lotteries were held to raise funds from the population (see rows GG and HH). If we include these two lines and social insurance contributions (row MM), then total direct taxes and transfers from the population rose from 10.4 percent of all nonfinancial uses of funds in 1940 to 21.4 percent in 1944 and averaged 18.2 percent during 1941–45 (row JJ plus row MM). Increased direct taxes, fees, and transfers from the population, then, helped to offset the diminution in profit withdrawals and turnover tax proceeds during the war years.

Direct tax receipts increased relative to indirect tax receipts during the critical early years of the war. Once the tide of battle had been turned, however, the prewar ratio was reestablished rather quickly. The direct/indirect ratio had been in decline from approximately the initiation of rapid industrialization. The war reversed the trend temporarily.[18] Similarly, the ratio of union budget to republic plus local budget sources of funds had been falling from the middle 1930s, and this trend was also temporarily reversed by World War II (row QQ).

Despite the curtailment of republic and local outlays, and the sharp rise in direct tax collections from the population and nonstate enterprises and organizations, the gap between nonfinancial uses and sources of funds increased in the war years. A somewhat unusual device was utilized at the outset of the war to minimize the reported deficit of the state budget. The deposit balance of all state enterprises, organizations, and institutions, totaling some two billion rubles, were frozen and transferred to the state budget.[19] This represented, of course, a net source of funds to the state budget, and one essentially unique to the Soviet-type economy, but its main significance was in promptly precluding the possibility of nonessential spending by these agencies.

Budget Funds Raised through Financial Channels

The Soviet state budget has access to a variety of domestic financial channels through which funds may be raised (or advanced and returned). The most important channels during World War II were the sale of various types of government bonds to the population and to nonstate organizations and enterprises and borrowing (via overdraft) through the banking system (Gosbank). Before and during the war, and until quite recently, the net increase (decrease) in privately held savings account balances was also transferred to the state budget by means of regular purchases (sales) of special government bonds by the savings bank system.

Two estimates of state budget deficits for the period 1940–46 are presented in table 2. Row RR may be viewed as the upper-limit estimate and row SS as the lower-limit estimate. It is impossible to determine precisely just what total of funds was raised through financial channels on a net basis because Soviet budgetary data are not presented fully in any official source. The upper-limit estimate is based on the difference between all itemized nonfinancial sources and uses of budget funds. The lower limit is based on reported total sources, less gross bond proceeds, and total uses chargeable against ordinary receipts, less debt service charges. Unfortunately, only data on subscription bond debt are available. The true deficit for any year, except 1941, lies between these two estimates.

There are, of course, several alternative ways in which a government deficit (or surplus) may be defined, and it is important to note that the official Soviet definition is based on a very narrow construction. A deficit (surplus) is declared only if total budget sources of funds, inclusive of gross bond proceeds, are less (more) than total uses of funds chargeable against ordinary revenue (inclusive of debt service charges). Thus a reported budget deficit means that the state budget is either drawing down its cash balance with Gosbank or "overdrawing" its Gosbank account, and conversely for a reported surplus. In other words, the Soviet definition is based on the cash-flow account. Consequently, a deficit was officially declared[20] only for 1941, 1942, and 1943 of the war years (see row VV). If, however, we measure the Soviet deficit as the difference between funds raised and funds advanced or returned through financial channels, then the state budget ran a substantial deficit in every war year, with a peak in excess of 17 percent of total nonfinancial outlays in 1942 and an average value in excess of 11.3 percent for 1941–45 taken together (rows RR and SS). As may be seen from row TT, the war deficit is attributable almost exclusively to the union budget.

The state budget was obliged, therefore, to rely much more heavily on financial channels during the war, especially during its early years, than had ordinarily been the case in the prewar period. Only 1931, one of the most difficult years of rapid development, is at all comparable in this respect.[21] Some portion of wartime deficits (row RR) may have been financed through international financial channels, specifically by drawing down foreign and gold currency balances and through direct borrowing. Lend Lease, for example, provided approximately five billion rubles.[22] Unfortunately, however, it is not possible to discover how, or indeed whether, these flows were recorded in the state budget.

Domestic financial channels afforded a substantial net source of funds during the war years. The available data (summarized in table 2, rows UU, VV, and WW) show that *at least* 18.8 percent of total uses chargeable against ordinary income (row S) in the peak year, 1942, was raised through financial channels. A minimum of 12.5 percent was obtained from domestic financial channels over the war years taken together.

The bulk of domestic funds was raised by means of bonds subscribed by the population. Four nominal twenty-year term war bond issues were subscribed for a total of 9 billion rubles,[23] and net subscription bond proceeds (including the last prewar issue of June 1941) totaled 7.56 billion rubles for 1941–45. As opposed to prewar debt issues to the public, only kolkhozes and cooperative organizations were offered interest-bearing debt. Private individuals, who subscribed the bulk of war bond issues, merely became eligible for possible cash lottery winnings over the nominal twenty-year term of the loan.[24]

The remainder of bond proceeds obtained during the war was derived from sales of 3 percent state lottery bonds ("market bonds") to the population and from bond purchases by the state savings bank and social insurance systems. Several special financial devices were utilized in this connection. First, existing private savings account balances were blocked for the duration of the war. Although this did prevent households from drawing out these balances, it also apparently discouraged voluntary new savings deposits, which increased

TABLE 4. Wartime Deficits as Percentage of Expenditures Chargeable to
Ordinary Revenue

Year ending March 31	Great Britain	Year ending June 30	USA	Year ending December 31	USSR Bounds Upper	Lower
1939/40	21	1940	41	1940	3.5	1.1
1940/41	62	1941	40	1941	1.5	7.9
1941/42	55	1942	60	1942	29.8	17.1
1942/43	49	1943	71	1943	26.4	13.9
1943/44	47	1944	52	1944	27.9	9.5
1944/45	45	1945	53	1945	22.7	8.4

Sources: Table 2 above; Statistical Abstract of the United States, 1946 (U.S. Government Printing Office, Washington, D.C., 1946), pp. 312–13; Great Britain, Central Statistical Office, Annual Abstract of Statistics, no. 84 (1935–1946) (London, 1948), pp. 213–15.

negligibly during the war despite the fact that new deposits were not subject to blocking and the institution of a special cash lottery for new depositors. Second, special savings accounts were established for all workers and salaried officials for the deposit of forgone vacation-period earnings. In effect, this was a form of deferred payment of a portion of wages and salaries, for vacations were suspended during the war. These special savings accounts, which accumulated in excess of one billion rubles by the end of 1945, were also blocked for the duration of hostilities.[25]

In addition to bond proceeds, the state budget raised substantial funds through the Gosbank. The state budget account at the outbreak of the war showed a balance of 0.8 billion rubles, which had accumulated by means of cash-flow surpluses of prewar budgets. This balance was run down in the early part of the war. The state budget was also obliged to borrow directly through the Gosbank a total of 5 billion rubles during the first three years of war (table 2, row VV). That is, the excess of budget uses chargeable to ordinary revenue over all other financial and nonfinancial sources of funds was simply paid out by the Gosbank on a budget overdraft. The process was reversed in 1944 and 1945 as the budget managed to run small cash-flow surpluses.

A rough-and-ready comparison of the role of deficit finance in the United States, Great Britain, and the Soviet Union is presented in table 4. Because differences in definitions and in fiscal year reporting cannot be completely ironed out, the comparison cannot be regarded as exact. It is clear, however, that the time patterns of budget deficits are similar for the three countries. Deficits are greatest in the early years of the war effort, and they diminish as the tax structure is geared to the war effort. This general pattern reflects Lord Robbins's dictum that "in war, time is more important than money—it is one priority which is virtually absolute."[26]

Even if we allow for a wide margin of error in the estimates of Soviet state budget wartime deficits, it is clear that the Soviet Union financed a greater portion of war outlays by means of direct and indirect taxation than did either Great Britain or the United States. Three factors may help to explain this outcome. First, a very deliberate and successful effort was made in the Soviet Union to hold down prices on armaments. In fact, in the later years of the war these prices were actually forced down as productivity increased. According to one Soviet source, some four to five billion rubles were "saved" in this way.[27] Second, the Soviet financial system was (and remains) undeveloped by Western standards, and Soviet peacetime practice both before and after the war suggests a very cautious and conservative approach to the use of financial instruments.[28] Moreover, the population represents the only source of private saving, and nonfinancial methods have ordinarily been used to transfer the net earnings of industrial and commercial enterprises to the state budget. Third, the governments of Britain and the United States were perhaps more cautious about increasing tax rates than the Soviet government. They were much more concerned, for instance, to maintain an effective system of pecuniary incentives during the war period, and they may have been concerned for more purely political reasons as well. As A. C. Pigou put it, "in a war on a great scale, it is generally agreed that a policy of finance through taxation alone, however excellent it might be in theory, is in practice out of the question, for the simple reason that the people would not stand it."[29]

An Overview of the Soviet War Budget

The main sources and uses of Soviet funds are charted in figure 1. The chart reveals that the steady, sharp rise in monetary defense outlays was financed largely by increases in direct taxes and collections from the population, and by extraordinary recourse to financial channels. As defense outlays tapered off after 1944, so did these two sources of funds. Of course, the increase in defense outlays was also financed in part by the decline in spending in nondefense categories. However, these latter items followed closely the movement of turnover tax receipts and profit withdrawals, traditionally the main sources of state budget proceeds. In effect, turnover tax and profit withdrawal receipts and nondefense outlays both followed the general course of

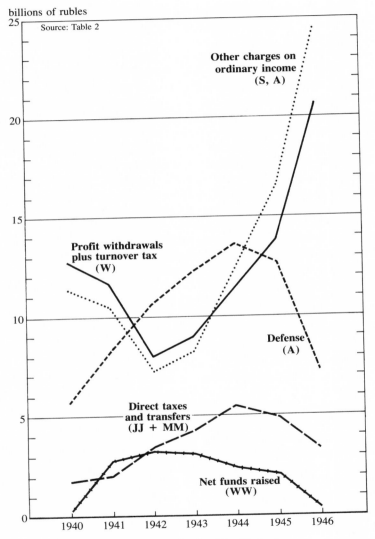

billions of rubles

Source: Table 2

Other charges on
ordinary income
(S, A)

Profit withdrawals
plus turnover tax
(W)

Defense
(A)

Direct taxes
and transfers
(JJ + MM)

Net funds raised
(WW)

1940 1941 1942 1943 1944 1945 1946

FIGURE 1. Soviet War Budget

total economic activity. The beginning of economic recovery in 1942 is clearly evident (see also table 1). The shift in priorities away from defense outlays at the end of 1944, as the tide of battle moved decisively in favor of the Soviet armies, is also evident. Note that this shift accelerated till the end of 1946.

Conclusion

The real cost of the war was borne, of course, by those who endured it and carried its scars afterward. Some twenty million lives, about 10 percent of the 1941 population, were lost.[30] An unknown number of Soviet citizens suffered from wounds, malnutrition, and war-related illnesses. The resources consumed by the war were obtained by means of a greater economic effort by the population and at the expense of investment, consumption, and nonmilitary government outlays (in that order). These sacrifices are all the more impressive given the tautness of the prewar economy and the enormous destruction and loss of capital stock that took place in the first six months of the war.

The reallocation of resources to the war effort was financed, in the strict sense of the word, primarily by new direct taxes and by borrowing. Observation of state budget practice before, during, and following the war reveals clearly official preferences with respect to choice among public finance instruments. Indirect taxation was clearly preferred to direct taxation, and financial instruments represented the least-preferred method of finance. Deficit financing was kept to a minimum during the war and was ended as soon as possible afterward.

The war, therefore, reversed three prewar trends. It increased the share of the central government (the union budget) in total governmental outlays; it increased the share of budget expenditures financed through financial channels; and it caused a sharp rise in the ratio of direct to indirect taxes as sources of budget funds. All three prewar trends were quickly reestablished shortly after the close of hostilities. In these respects, the popular description of the peacetime Soviet economy as a variant "war economy" is rather misleading. Both sources of funds and spending priorities were very different during World War II from those before or after it.

Raising real resources for and raising funds to finance the war effort are related mainly through systems of pecuniary incentives (e.g., the wage system, the price system, the accounting and budgetary systems) that operate within the economy. Although the Soviet economy had relied heavily on direct controls and directives from 1928

onward and did so even more heavily during the war,[31] it is clear
that a serious effort was made by planners to preserve pecuniary
institutions. The aim of financial policy was not to increase the rate
of saving of the population, for this was determined elsewhere. It
was instead to avoid a breakdown of incentives to work and to
contribute efficiently to the war effort. This meant providing an
equitable distribution of the goods available during the war and
creating the presumption that wartime forced saving would retain
purchasing power through and after the war.

That presumption was, of course, not borne out. Inflation did
take place during World War II in both product prices and money
wages. To the extent that official retail prices rose more rapidly than
money wages, and this was generally the case,[32] the result was to
increase turnover tax proceeds or to inflate profit withdrawals to the
state budget. As has been shown, these were not significant new
sources of funds to the budget. The impact of inflation was greatest
in the free markets, which included the collective farm market[33] and
various informal (legal as well as illegal) markets.[34] Inflation in these
markets redistributed the financial assets of the population from
buyers to sellers and thus predominantly from urban dwellers to rural
savers. The 1947 Monetary Reform, in effect, eliminated by confiscation a large part of the value of financial assets so acquired during
the war (and before).[35] The reform had disproportionately heavy
impact on hoards of cash compared with other assets and was justified
in part as a tax on war profiteers. Insofar as speculators and other
war profiteers would have been likely to avoid savings accounts and
war subscription bonds to evade detection, the incidence of the reform
would have been appropriate, but it also fell disproportionately on
the rural population, which was more likely to hold cash than the
urban. The systematic reduction in official state retail prices that
followed between 1948 and 1954[36] worked to the disadvantage of
the rural population also because it was not justified by a corresponding increase in the supplies of consumer goods. Thus, the urban
population benefited relatively because of the inefficient rural distribution system for these goods and because of their proximity to
queues. To some extent, therefore, the rural population was treated
as a whole as though it were composed of war profiteers.

Aggregate demand for consumer goods thus was redistributed
in the postwar years, in favor of the urban population, and demand
pent-up during the war was partly eliminated and partly redistributed
over time, via the gradual series of price reductions. These measures
no doubt had a weakening effect upon financial instruments generally
in the Soviet Union. And it is fair to say that Soviet financial policy

in the postwar years reveals a general neglect of financial instruments proper and an inclination to treat financial instruments as special taxing devices. As a result, the number and variety of financial instruments actually declined following postwar reconstruction.[37]

NOTES

1. M. L. Tamarchenko, *Sovetskie finansy v period Velikoi Otechestvennoi voiny* (Moscow, 1967), p.135.

2. See James R. Millar and Susan J. Linz, "The Cost of World War II to the Soviet People: A Research Note," *Journal of Economic History* 38, no. 4 (December 1978):959–62.

3. G. S. Kravchenko, *Ekonomika SSSR v gody Velikoi Otechestvennoi voiny* (Moscow, 1970), pp.123–25.

4. For descriptions of the military campaigns and the general history of the war, see Alan Clark, *Barbarossa: The Russian-German Conflict, 1941–45* (London, 1966); B. H. Liddell Hart, *A History of World War II* (New York, 1971); Albert Seaton, *The Russo-German War, 1941–45* (London, 1971). Alexander Werth's *Russia at War* (New York, 1965) is also useful.

5. The Soviet official history of the war puts the date of "full-conversion" as December 1942 (*Istoriya Velikoi Otechestvennoi voiny Sovetskogo Soyuza 1941–1945 gg.* [Moscow, 1961], table 6, p. 46). However, all major studies by Soviet scholars emphasize that the turning point for the war economy was in mid-1942. See, for example, N. Voznesensky, *Voennaya ekonomika SSSR v period Otechestvennoi voiny* (Moscow, 1947), p. 37, and Kravchenko, *Ekonomika SSSR*, pp. 349–50. Ya. E. Chadaev gives a description of the evacuation of the moveable equipment and furnishings of more than 1,500 industrial establishments and 10 million persons in advance of the German invasion in *Ekonomika SSSR v period Velikoi Otechestvennoi voiny (1941–1945 gg.)* (Moscow, 1965), p. 75

6. Alan S. Milward, *The German Economy at War* (London, 1965). See also Albert Speer, *Inside the Third Reich* (New York, 1971) and John K. Galbraith's review of this book, based upon his own immediate postwar interviews with Speer (as a member of the United States Strategic Bombing Survey), in *Economics, Peace and Laughter* (New York, 1971), pp. 220–30.

7. For a general discussion of the flow-of-funds approach, see John P. Powelson, *National Income and Flow-of-Funds Analysis* (New York, 1960) or Nathaniel Jackendoff, *Money, Flow of Funds, and Economic Policy* (New York, 1968).

8. The Soviet war effort proper ran from June 1941 until the middle of August 1945, or about two months more than four years. However, semiannual data are not available, and it is necessary to treat the entire five-year period as a unit.

9. V. P. D'yachenko, "Sovetskaya sistema finansov i kredita v bor'be za sotsialisticheskoe pereustroistvo ekonomiki i postroenie kommunizma

v SSSR," in L. M. Gatovsky et al., *Sovetskaya sotsialisticheskaya ekonomika 1917–1957 gg.* (Moscow, 1957), pp. 568, 574.

10. *Istoriya Velikoi Otechestvennoi voiny,* table 6, p. 46.

11. For an extended analysis, see Donna L. Bahry, "An Analysis of the Soviet Budgetary Process" (Ph.D. diss., University of Illinois at Urbana-Champaign, 1977).

12. The turnover tax was collected primarily on goods and services sold through state and cooperative retail outlets to the population. A small but indeterminate amount was raised during the war on wholesale turnover. According to Alec Nove, *An Economic History of the USSR* (London, 1972), p. 252, heavy industry purchases accounted for about 10 percent of turnover tax receipts in 1935, but wartime pricing policy would have tended to reduce this share because armaments were exempt. Enterprise profit withdrawals are a somewhat anomalous item, for it reflects the state's ownership of the means of production and thus its title to the profits state enterprises earn. It is convenient, however, to treat profit withdrawals as a kind of profit tax receipt of the government, rather than as a final distributive share of the state sector.

13. Tamarchenko, *Sovetskie finansy,* p. 40.

14. Ibid., p. 67; V. P. D'yachenko, "Finansy v sisteme voennoi ekonomiki," in I. A. Gladkov et al., *Sovetskaya ekonomika v period Velikoi Otechestvennoi voiny 1941–1945 gg.* (Moscow, 1970) pp. 419, 432–33.

15. D'yachenko, "Finansy v sisteme voennoi ekonomiki," p. 433.

16. Tamarchenko, *Sovetskie finansy,* pp. 71–75; D'yachenko, "Finansy v sisteme voennoi ekonomiki," pp. 438–41.

17. Households also contributed working days, government obligations, savings account balances, foreign currencies, precious metals and valuables to these Funds. Tamarchenko, *Sovetskie finansy,* p. 89.

18. James R. Millar and Donna Bahry, "Financing Development and Tax Structure Change in the USSR," *Canadian Slavonic Papers* 21, no. 2 (June 1979):165–74.

19. D'yachenko, "Finansy v sisteme voennoi ekonomiki," p. 419.

20. Tamarchenko, *Sovetskie finansy,* p. 30.

21. James R. Millar, "History and Analysis of Soviet Domestic Bond Policy," *Soviet Studies* 27, no. 4 (October 1975):598–99.

22. It is virtually impossible to put a ruble value on Lend Lease and other assistance from abroad, for the issue is complicated by the problem of selecting an appropriate exchange rate at the time and by the currency revaluation of 1960. Soviet sources claim that foreign assistance contributed approximately 4 percent of the value of domestic production during the war years. This estimate does not seem unreasonable. For discussions see Tamarchenko, *Sovetskie finansy,* p. 54, and Yu. G. Chernyavsky, *Voina i prodovol'stvie: snabzhenie gorodskogo naseleniya v Velikuyu Otechestvennuyu voinu 1941–1945 gg.* (Moscow, 1964), pp. 19–20.

23. D'yachenko, "Finansy v sisteme voenni ekonomiki," pp. 435–36; Tamarchenko, *Sovetskie finansy,* p. 82. The discrepancy between war bond subscriptions and the total funds raised by government bonds during the

war (Millar, "History and Analysis of Soviet Domestic Bond Policy," table 3) is explained by fulfillment of prewar bond pledges during the war period.

24. For a description, see Millar, "History and Analysis of Soviet Domestic Bond Policy," pp. 603–4.

25. D'yachenko, "Finansy v sisteme voenni ekonomiki," pp. 436–37.

26. Lionel Robbins, *The Economic Problem in Peace and War* (London, 1947), p. 35.

27. D'yachenko, "Finansy v sisteme voenni ekonomiki," pp. 419, 432–33.

28. For a discussion, see Millar, "History and Analysis of Soviet Domestic Bond Policy," pp. 606–14.

29. A. C. Pigou, *The Political Economy of War* (New York, 1941), p. 72.

30. About half were civilian detainees or military prisoners of war. Kravchenko, *Ekonomika SSSR*, p. 369.

31. As an example of the extent of direct controls in existence immediately prior to the war, voluntary departure from employment was abolished and the authority of the state to transfer workers among employments was established in two decrees of 1940. V. D. Kalinin, "Trud i kadry v promyshlennosti," in Gladkov et al., *Sovetskaya ekonomika*, p. 187.

32. See D'yachenko, "Finansy v sisteme voenni ekonomiki," p. 429, and Tamarchenko, *Sovetskie finansy,* pp. 53, 71. The only available direct Soviet estimate claims that real wages fell 60 percent during the war years. A. N. Malafeev, *Istoriya tsenoobrazovaniya v SSSR* (Moscow, 1964), p. 235.

33. Malafeev, *Istoriya tsenoobrazovaniya v SSSR,* pp. 230, 235.

34. D'yachenko, "Finansy v sisteme voenni ekonomiki," p. 430.

35. For a description of the reform, see "O provedenii denezhnoi reformy i otmene kartochek na prodovol'stvennye i promyshlennye tovary," in A. A. Poskonov (ed.), *Kreditnodenezhnaya sistema SSSR* (Moscow, 1967), p. 69.

36. *Narodnoe khozyaistvo SSSR v 1956 g.* (Moscow, 1957), p. 233.

37. Millar, "History and Analysis of Soviet Domestic Bond Policy."

9

Financial Innovation in Contemporary Soviet Agricultural Policy

At a very early stage of the Bolshevik experiment with economic planning it became obvious that the economy could not be made to function without the use of money and other financial instruments. In fact, a financial history of the Soviet economy would show a gradual but relentless expansion in the number and functions of financial instruments. This expansion has been gradual largely because Soviet economists, planners, and administrators had had both ideological (theoretical) and practical reservations about the appropriate uses as well as the potential abuses to which financial instruments can be put. The process has been relentless nonetheless, because for a number of essential economic functions the possible substitutes or alternatives to financial instruments are either impractical or nonexistent. Let me attempt to explain briefly the fundamental reasons for the ambivalence in Soviet financial policy. As ordinarily described, the essential functions of money in an economy are (1) as a unit of account, (2) as a medium of exchange, and (3) as a store of value. As a unit of account, money permits the aggregation and comparison of what would otherwise be incommensurable magnitudes, such as units of labor time, material inputs, final goods, and services. The need to keep track of enterprise receipts and disbursements was recognized quite early in Soviet history. The mandatory introduction of *khozraschet* (economic budgeting and accounting) for all state enterprises in 1921 ensured the accountability of enterprise managers for the uses to which enterprise funds are applied.[1]

Both the medium-of-exchange and the store-of-value functions, as opposed to the unit-of-account function, are quantitative functions

From *Slavic Review* 32, no. 1 (March 1973):91–114. Reprinted by permission, with minor editorial changes.

TABLE 1. Time Shapes of Expenditures, Receipts, and Wage Payments in Kolkhozes for 1965 (percentage of annual outlays or receipts)

Month (1)	Productive outlays		Money wage outlays		Money receipts	
	For the month (2)	Cumulative total (3)	For the month (4)	Cumulative total (5)	For the month (6)	Cumulative total (7)
January	2.6	2.6	9.4	9.4	1.0	1.0
February	4.0	6.6	10.5	19.9	1.5	2.5
March	4.9	11.5	6.3	26.2	2.8	5.3
April	5.6	17.1	7.7	33.9	3.2	8.5
May	7.1	24.2	5.1	39.0	3.6	12.1
June	9.0	33.2	7.6	46.6	4.7	16.8
July	10.2	43.4	11.0	57.6	7.1	23.9
August	11.8	55.2	9.3	66.9	9.4	33.3
September	13.1	68.3	9.1	76.0	12.7	46.0
October	14.8	83.1	7.9	83.9	16.9	62.9
November	15.9	99.0	8.6	92.5	18.6	81.5
December	1.0	100.0	7.5	100.0	18.5	100.0

Source: M. Z. Pizengol'ts, *Oborotnye sredstva kolkhozov* (Moscow, 1968), p. 155.

of money in the sense that each requires the existence of a stock of money (currency plus deposit accounts) that may be held by the various nonbank transactors for varying periods of time. The medium-of-exchange function is, in fact, really a short-term store-of-value function. In the short period (e.g., a month), transactors hold cash balances because the time shapes of their receipts and disbursements do not coincide. Monthly receipts may be bunched up and outlays spread rather evenly over the period, or vice versa (for example, see table 1). Transactor cash balances help, therefore, to cushion these time-shape discrepancies. In an economy in which specialization in production is highly developed, the alternative to the use of money as a medium of exchange—that is, barter exchange—is obviously infeasible. However, because money deposits represent potential command over resources, exercisable at the discretion of the holder, Soviet administrators have always viewed cash balances as necessary evils at best. Moreover, the discretion afforded the holder of a cash balance cannot be effectively controlled by controlling current sources of funds.

The longer-term store-of-value function of money results from the determination of some transactors to hold a portion of their wealth in cash, as opposed to interest-bearing or tangible assets. It is perhaps a less essential function than the medium-of-exchange function because of the multitude of substitutes available to transactors even in the Soviet economy. In any case, it is more relevant to households than to enterprises. But its discretionary aspect presents the same potential power to disrupt the planned allocation of resources.

Recognizing the necessity for the use of money, Soviet administrators have sought to minimize and control the discretion implied in a number of ways. First, till-cash is constrained to the bare minimum of hand-to-hand currency, if that. Second, as large a volume as possible of interenterprise transactions are conducted by offset settlement. Third, enterprises ordinarily hold their cash balances in special accounts earmarked for specific purposes, and interaccount transfer is not permitted. For example, the collective farm's cash balance on capital account may not be used to pay money wage obligations, even though it may for the period in question be an idle balance. Finally, the credit facilities of the Gosbank also serve to minimize the need for cash-balance accumulation.

Short- and long-term credit instruments represent an alternative to the advance accumulation of cash balances as a means of financing the difference between current-period outlays and receipts. Current outlays for productive needs and for capital investment may be financed by current borrowing. Expected future receipts may be used subsequently to retire these liabilities. Crediting facilities, therefore, reduce the need to accumulate cash balances in settlement and deposit accounts. Indeed, it would not be feasible to operate the Soviet enterprise sector without short-term credit instruments.

Even so, these other financial instruments have also always been regarded with considerable apprehension by Soviet policymakers. Access to credit, like title to cash balances, permits transactors to spend more, or less, than their current receipts during any given period, and it thus offers potential enterprise-level command over the allocation of resources. Short-term bank credit has always been available to state enterprises for seasonal and other purely short-term needs. However, until quite recently, Soviet policymakers have preferred to finance operating losses and additions to the enterprise capital stock, both fixed and working, by means of direct or indirect transfer payments from the state budget. Collective farms have represented the only significant exception to this policy for productive enterprises until recent times. Concern over the possible adverse effects of the availability of credit, whether in the form of a distortion of the planned allocation of final goods and services, inflationary pressures, or merely the unsanctioned use of funds, is revealed by the careful and very strict specifications required to obtain credit financing and by the extensive use of highly supervised line-of-credit financing methods. One other general aspect of Soviet financial policy deserves mention at this point. Since financial instruments are not ordinarily intended to have significant allocative effects, other than to support the planned allocation of resources, no attempt has been made to use the interest-rate charge as an allocative device. The main function of the interest charge has been to cover all or a portion of the cost to the lending institution arising from the particular transaction in question. This doubtless explains why long-term rates are invariably set below short-term rates. The interest charge has also been used as a kind of penalty device, for it is usually increased substantially for overdue notes.

In general, therefore, Soviet financial policy has always been conducted cautiously and conservatively in order to ensure that the potential discretion implied by the existence of financial instruments may not be used to undermine central control and the planned allocation of resources. Every attempt has been made to constrain the use of financial instruments to a supporting role in the planning process. This objective has not always been attained. What is more, as I shall argue below, the very conservatism of state financial policy has at times served to undermine other general policy objectives in the agricultural sector. The financial policy innovations to be discussed below represent, in substantial part, a response to this outcome. They are, however, also evidence of recognition of the need to expand the functions of financial instruments to meet the changing needs of the Soviet economy.

Financing in the Collective-Farm Sector

With the foregoing general observations in mind, let us turn first to a consideration of financial policy innovations in the collective-farm sector since 1953.

Financing Seasonal Needs. The time shapes of receipts and disbursements on current operating account for agricultural enterprises are highly seasonal. Table 1 illustrates this seasonality for collective farms during 1965. Receipts from sales and deliveries of field and animal husbandry products tend to be bunched in the second half of the year. Nonlabor productive expenditures also reach a crescendo in the latter part of the year, but they lead receipts throughout the year, as may be seen by comparing the cumulative monthly totals in columns 3 and 7. Wages and salary outlays are spread much more evenly over the year, and the cumulative total of these outlays leads that of receipts by an even more substantial margin.

The discrepancies in these time shapes must be financed somehow, and the different ways in which this can be done have significant implications for worker and managerial incentives and for central control over the uses of the funds so raised. Moreover, several important policy decisions of the 1950s and 1960s have had as an effect an enlargement of these time-shape discrepancies. From 1953 on koklhozes have been strongly urged to increase the share of money pay in total pay to kolkhozniki and to institute quarterly or monthly workday payments (for a good part of the year these are wage advances). The share of money pay in total pay to kolkhozniki rose from 25 percent to 92 percent between 1952 and 1967,[2] and most kolkhozes today do pay labor on a monthly basis. The abolition of the Machine Tractor Station (MTS) system in 1958, by transferring operating responsibility of farm equipment to the kolkhozes, greatly increased money operating outlays of the kolkhozes and shifted to the burden of financing the inherent lead in these expenses over receipts. Enlarged access to, as well as better terms for obtaining, short-term credit became necessary for the successful implementation of these two major reforms.

There are several ways in which the kolkhozes may finance seasonal needs for funds. One way, of course, is for the kolkhoz to accumulate past-period receipts in the form of operating and other special-purpose cash balances and to deplete these balances during the first half of the year. For example, in 1957 the total operating cash balance of all kolkhozes (on December 31) represented 14 percent of total money receipts for the year. An adverse consequence of the way in which the transfer of MTS equipment to kolkhozes was financed can be seen in the decline in this ratio to less than 6 percent in 1960. By 1966 the operating cash balance had recovered and represented 18 percent of total money receipts.[3]

The accumulation of cash balances has been particularly important for the payment of regular monthly or quarterly money labor advances, for until 1965 kolkhozes were not permitted to finance these payments with bank credit. The opening balance (January 1) of the special cash account for money labor payments has offered a significant potential source of funds for this purpose, representing somewhat better than 11 percent of the total annual money payments to kolkhozniki for 1958 and 1963 through 1967. This figure was considerably lower during 1959 through 1962, reflecting the adverse financial consequences of the MTS reform.[4] The importance of this account may also be seen in the fact that the upward trend in total money payments to kolkhozniki, which had been established at least as early as 1949, failed to continue in 1959–60.[5]

Kolkhozes may also finance a portion of seasonal needs by means of accrued obligations to members for labor payments. At one time this was an important and officially sanctioned source of funds to kolkhozes. Participating members of the kolkhoz were obliged to absorb a large share of seasonal time-shape discrepancies, for kolkhozniki were paid only as receipts became available. However, the increased priority of the agricultural sector and official concern about the adequacy of material incentives on kolkhozes in the post-Stalin period have produced heavy pressure on farm management to minimize use of this potential source of funds.

Trade credit afforded by supply organizations has provided a minor source of funds to cover seasonal needs, which reflects official disapproval of late payment for supplies. Much more important, since 1953, however, has been the provision of money advances by procurement agencies under contracts for the future delivery of farm products. Procurement agencies have financed these advances themselves largely by means of short-term bank credit. Thus, these agencies have served essentially as financial intermediaries for Gosbank, and the money advances they provide have been quite rightly viewed by Soviet financial specialists as "indirect bank credit." Kolkhozes have been eligible during the first half of each year for money advances up to a total of 30–40 percent of the value of contracted output, without regard to the financial condition of the farm and at no interest charge.[6]

Advances from procurement agencies increased both absolutely and relatively to direct bank credit on current account throughout the 1950s and the early 1960s and represented 83 percent of total direct and indirect credit extensions for productive needs in 1965.[7] The absence of strict, centralized bank control over these sources of kolkhoz funds ultimately proved unsatisfactory. Kolkhozes were eligible for advances without having to demonstrate legitimate need. Moreover, because many kolkhozes that produced a variety of outputs were eligible to receive advances from several different procurement agencies, effective centralized control was not possible. Due to concern over the possibilities for financial irresponsibility, and perhaps even impropriety, the system of procurement-agency advances began to be phased out in 1966. By 1967 advances had been reduced to 25 percent of total direct and indirect bank credit, and by 1969 direct bank credit had completely replaced indirect credit.[8]

Short-term direct bank credit has, therefore, only very recently become a principal outside source of funds to kolkhozes for financing seasonal needs. The fact that from 1956 through 1965 direct bank financing of seasonal farm expenditures declined considerably in relative significance reflected the continuation of very cautious bank policy and highly restrictive terms for kolkhoz short-term borrowing in the face of major reforms in the institutional structure of the kolkhoz which served to increase the farm's needs for seasonal financing.

Until 1959 the total volume of short-term credit legally extendable to kolkhozes by Gosbank was limited by the sum of the kolkhoz sector's current-account demand deposits.[9] That is, Gosbank was free to lend to kolkhozes only the current-account deposits of other kolkhozes. The reason for this restriction was, presumably, to ensure that short-term credit extensions to kolkhozes would not involve a net flow of funds from the rest of the economy. However, because the time shapes of receipts and disbursements are much the same for all farms, short-term credit was relatively scarce when most needed and relatively plentiful when least required by kolkhozes. As a result of this restriction the kolkhoz sector was frequently a net source of funds (on current account) to other sectors of the economy until 1959 (see table 5, row E). The restriction was abolished in 1959, presumably because of the (unanticipated) sharp decline in kolkhoz current-account cash balances that accompanied the MTS transaction of 1958.

Even so, short-term bank credit policy remained excessively restrictive. The abolition of the MTS system transferred to the kolkhoz a substantial category of seasonal expenditures (such as expenditures under the future year's crop) previously absorbed by the state budget, and dealings with the Repair Tractor Stations (RTS) were put on a cash basis. Meanwhile, administrative pressure on kolkhozes to pay regular monthly wages and to increase the share of money pay in total pay to farm members also greatly increased the need for seasonal credit facilities. Gosbank was, however, explicitly prohibited from advancing funds to kolkhozes for money wage settlements and advances. (Gosbank was also not permitted to finance obligatory payments to the government or the amortization fund transfer.) As a result, the system of agricultural procurement-agency advances became the principal source of outside seasonal financing.

Some easing of short-term direct bank credit conditions took place in 1961. The interest charge on short-term debt was reduced from 2 percent per annum to 1 percent (with a 3 percent penalty rate on arrears), and Gosbank was authorized to expand its coverage of seasonal needs where procurement-agency advances proved insufficient for farm needs.[10] The effect was, however, marginal. In December 1965 the entire system of short-term direct bank credit was overhauled. Gosbank was given primary responsibility for financing seasonal needs of kolkhozes, including money wage advances to kolkhozniki.[11] From 1966 on, procurement-agency advances declined precipitously in significance, accrued obligations of kolkhozes to their members for wages were reduced substantially, and the regular monthly payment of wage advances was, finally, assured.[12] Direct bank financing has also ensured much closer bank scrutiny of kolkhoz financial behavior.

Financing Working Capital. Let us turn now to a consideration of the financing of working capital accumulation in the kolkhoz sector. Investment in circulating capital represents a smaller share of total working capital for sovkhozes than it does for kolkhozes.[13] This difference reflects the "producer cooperative" status of the kolkhoz. The kolkhoz invests more heavily than the sovkhoz does in finished output, mainly because the kolkhoz has greater discretion over its disposition than the sovkhoz does. The kolkhoz must also maintain relatively large current-account cash balances to finance seasonal needs and for a variety of special purposes, the single most important of which is the special deposit for the payment of money wage advances.

The abolition of the MTS system in 1958 greatly increased the working capital requirements of kolkhozes. The total stock of working capital very nearly doubled between January 1, 1958, and January 1, 1959 (table 2, row A), and almost all of the increase was financed by the kolkhozes themselves—that is, without increased bank financing. Moreover, the share of working capital (January 1) financed by inside funds, or retained net income ("own" working capital, row C), as opposed to that received through financial channels, increased from 60 percent in 1958 to 81 percent in 1960 and remained almost as high through 1966. Thus the MTS reform placed a heavy burden on the collective, and short-term credit policy clearly failed to support the spirit of the reform, for many kolkhozes found themselves in extreme financial difficulties for this reason. Some Western commentators suggested at the time that one purpose of the MTS reform was to absorb the growing demand-deposit balances of kolkhozes, but this can clearly be seen now as a mistaken interpretation. The decline in current-account deposits was obviously contrary to the whole import of the post-Stalin price and incentive reforms in this sector.[14] It reflected, instead, the inability of kolkhozes, at least in

Table 2. Financing Working Capital: Kolkhozes (in millions of rubles)

	1958	1959	1960	1961	1962	1963	1964	1965	1966
A. Working capital assets (Jan.1)	5,001	9,524	9,269	9,008	9,597	10,895	11,234	12,674	14,887
Less debt outstanding:									
B. Equals: Own working capital (Jan.1)	2,981	7,064	7,495	7,259	7,558	8,468	8,711	9,704	11,381
C. Share of own working capital (in percentage) (B ÷ A) × 100	60	74	81	81	79	78	78	77	77
D. Line B as a percentage of gross money receipts	31	53	54	54	56	56	55	55	57

Source: Pizengol'ts, Oborotnye sredstva kolkhozov, p. 120.

Table 3. Structure of Outstanding Liabilities on Working Capital Account (in percentage)

	January 1			December 31	
	1960	1964	1966[a]	1965[a]	1968
A. Total value of working capital	100	100	100	100	100
B. Direct and indirect bank credit	7.1	8.2	3.8	5.8	8.4
C. Direct bank credit (Gosbank)	6.2	6.4	2.2	3.4	7.7
D. Procurement agency advances	0.9	1.8	1.6	2.4	0.7
E. Other obligations	22.5	19.6	15.3	18.8	12.1
F. Accrued wage obligations	15.1	16.5	13.2	16.6	9.7
G. Trade credit: other enterprises and organizations	7.4	3.1	2.1	2.2	2.4
H. Total liabilities on working capital account (B + E)	29.6	27.8	19.1	24.6	20.5

Sources: 1960, 1964, 1966: G. Belousenko, Oborotnye sredstva kolkhozov i kredit (Moscow, 1968), p. 53. 1965, 1968: K. S. Kartashova, Finansy, kredit i raschety v kolkhozakh (Moscow, 1970), p. 123.

[a] The percentage figures for January 1, 1966, and December 31, 1965, are misleadingly low, for they reflect the state's "forgiveness" of a substantial volume of short-term credit outstanding to "weak" kolkhozes in the latter part of 1965.

the initial years, to finance working capital at the necessary level. In this sense, it represented a failure of the state's financial policy.

An examination of table 3 reveals the small role that direct and indirect bank credit have played in financing working capital for collective farms. Conversion to the new policy of exclusive direct bank financing during 1966–68 did not materially increase the state's share. It has, however, affected the composition of liabilities to working capital account. Direct credit increased at the expense of indirect credit, and of the 7.7 percent figure for 1968, 3.2 percent represented long-term bank credit granted (mainly) to finance payment of guaranteed annual wages, as opposed to 0.6 percent in 1965.[15] This new credit avenue no doubt helps to explain (along with substantial agricultural procurement price increases) the favorable decrease in accrued wage obligations of kolkhozes to their members (see row F).

The kolkhoz has always been required to be much more self-sufficient with respect to working capital requirements than state enterprises, including sovkhozes. Whereas kolkhozes have had to finance approximately 80 percent of working-capital needs by means of inside funds, and bank credit (direct and indirect) has contributed only in the neighborhood of 6 percent, the comparable figures for all state enterprises and organizations have been approximately 38 percent and 45 percent during 1960–68. The share of inside financing of working-capital requirements for sovkhozes and other state agricultural enterprises has declined from about 59 percent in 1960 to 48 percent in 1968, and the share of state-bank direct credit increased correspondingly from 28 to 36 percent.[16] In addition, state enterprises have received direct budgetary grants to help finance annual increases in working-capital requirements. The increased role of bank credit in the financing of working-capital needs for state agricultural enterprises represents, in part, however, an attempt to phase out direct budget transfers in favor of short-term bank credit.[17] (This is true for other state enterprises as well.) We must conclude, therefore, that although recent reforms in short-term crediting policy have produced significant and desirable results, the kolkhoz sector remains seriously disadvantaged compared with state enterprises regarding access to short-term bank credit.

Financing on Capital Account. Let us turn now to a consideration of kolkhoz financing on capital account proper and the role of long-term bank credit. Over the years since Stalin's death, the object coverage (the types of expenditures for which credit is available, such as construction of farm buildings, equipment purchases) of long-term bank credit available to kolkhozes has been extended considerably and the terms and conditions gradually eased. With few exceptions long-term credit may be applied only to the financing of fixed-capital investment.[18] The first major reform in long-term loan policy came in 1955. The excessive red tape involved in loan approval and in the use of the line of credit so established was reduced somewhat. Access of "weak" kolkhozes to long-term borrowing was also enhanced to some degree. More important, state budget funding of Selkhozbank, which was at that time responsible for long-term loans to kolkhozes, was increased substantially. Finally, the interest charge was reduced from 3 percent per annum to 1.75 percent. (The penalty rate on arrears was also reduced to 3 percent, from 6 percent.) However, the maximum term on loans remained ten years.[19]

Before 1958, long-term borrowing by kolkhozes was primarily devoted to expenditures on improving farm livestock herds and facilities.[20] The abolition of the MTS system in that year made kolkhozes solely responsible for the acquisition of agricultural machinery and equipment as well, and coverage was accordingly enlarged. Expanded coverage and responsibility for kolkhoz investment projects put a strain on the facilities of Selkhozbank. The severely limited network of Selkhozbank outlets (448 as compared to 4,861 for Gosbank) and the duplication of work between Selkhozbank in the granting and administering of long-term credit and Gosbank in the granting and administering of short-term credit led to the abolition of Selkhozbank in 1959.[21] Gosbank assumed full responsibility from that time on for all bank financing available to kolkhozes.

Another major reform was introduced in 1961. The interest charge on long-term credit was reduced to 0.75 percent per annum (the penalty charge on arrears remained at 3 percent per annum), and, more important, the maximum term of payment was increased to fifteen years for certain long-lived objects. Terms and coverage were expanded again in 1964.[22]

Despite this series of reforms, long-term lending policy has remained highly conservative. Kolkhozes may not refund existing long-term debt (that is, take out a new loan to cover due debt), and prompt and full payment of the annual interest charge and due principal payment is required to retain eligibility for new loan extensions.[23] In substantial degree, therefore, access to long-term financing has depended on current-year performance of the farm, instead of on an evaluation of the expected remunerativeness of the proposed investment project. "Weak" kolkhozes are also, therefore, the least likely to obtain long-term financing. In recent years the irrationality of so strict a policy has apparently been recognized, and the kolkhoz may now (since 1965) petition a deferment of due payments without prejudice if it can be shown that the farm's financial difficulties are not a result of poor farm management.[24] There are, however, no data available that would permit an assessment of the liberality of Gosbank in granting such deferments.

That the excessively restrictive character of long-term bank credit policy has been, at least tacitly, recognized by Soviet authorities may be seen in the fact that, periodically, kolkhozes are "forgiven" all or a portion of the debt outstanding. In 1965, for instance, Gosbank was instructed to write off 1.450 billion rubles in outstanding long-term debt of the kolkhoz sector.[25] A debt "forgiven" in this way does not, of course, represent a net source of funds to the kolkhoz, for it must be applied simultaneously to the liquidation of existing debt. This will decrease principal and interest payments in subsequent periods, but the main advantage it has offered kolkhozes has been to reestablish their eligibility for new credit extensions. Kolkhozes were obviously very quick to exploit the possibility (see table 5, rows C and H, for the years following 1965), which strongly suggests that the extent of net borrowing by kolkhozes is constrained by state financial policy and not by the financial conservatism or satiety of kolkhozes.

The inadequacy of long-term bank credit in 1958 required, in fact, the creation of a special debt instrument to finance the acquisition by kolkhozes of the physical assets of the MTS system. Selkhozbank, which was at that time responsible for long-term lending to kolkhozes, was not adequately funded for the purpose. Moreover, since kolkhozes were obliged legally to accept and pay for the MTS assets allocated to them (at prices established by special raion commissions), the terms and conditions for regular long-term borrowing through Selkhozbank could not in any case have been observed, for a large number, possibly a majority, of the kolkhozes were not eligible for additional credit. Consequently, kolkhozes were permitted (with the permission of the respective *raiispolkomy*) to pay for MTS equipment in installments over a two- to three-year period (deferment up to a total of five years was also possible with the permission of the appropriate *oblispolkom*). No interest charge was required except for arrears, at 3 percent per annum.[26] These stiff terms imposed a severe financial burden on kolkhozes, and a number went under and had to be converted into sovkhozes. Those that survived did so by robbing Peter to pay Paul. Cash balances were depleted, including the special reserve fund for the payment of money advances to kolkhozniki, which set back sharply the program to increase the share of money pay in total pay and for the distribution of monthly money wage advances in subsequent years. New capital investment also had to

TABLE 4. Capital Account Sources and Uses of Funds, Kolkhoz Sector, 1953–66 (in current rubles, billions)

	1953	1954	1955	1956	1957	1958	1959	1960	1961	1962	1963	1964	1965	1966
Sources of Funds														
A. Indivisible fund transfer	0.867	1.121	1.322	1.673	1.682	3.042	3.334	3.196	3.203	3.430	3.390	3.600	3.920	4.450
B. Total transfers from current account	1.014	1.419	1.688	1.745	1.740	3.119	3.334	3.196	3.203	3.430	3.390	3.600	3.920	4.450
C. Direct money receipts on capital account	0.289	0.190	0.244	0.273	0.284	0.322	0.600	0.958	0.964	1.020	1.020	1.020	1.020	1.020
D. Total nonfinancial sources	1.303	1.609	1.932	2.018	2.024	3.441	3.934	4.154	4.167	4.450	4.410	4.620	4.940	5.470
E. Net funds obtained (+) or advanced or returned (−) through financial channels	0.014	0.127	0.149	0.221	0.282	1.476	0.259	−0.372	−0.108	0.130	0.190	0.747	−0.833	1.236
F. Total net sources	1.317	1.736	2.081	2.239	2.306	4.917	4.193	3.782	4.059	4.580	4.600	5.367	4.107	6.706
Uses of Funds														
G. Money capital expenditures, n.e.c.[a]	0.875	1.187	1.528	1.725	1.687	3.966	2.780	2.441	2.566	2.894	—	—	—	—
H. Money capital repair expenditures	0.165	0.185	0.216	0.247	0.262	0.381	0.683	0.703	0.657	0.630	—	—	—	—
I. Acquisition of working and productive cattle	0.209	0.254	0.201	0.335	0.437	0.503	0.662	1.025	0.994	1.127	4.540	5.370	5.900	—
J. Total money capital outlays	1.249	1.626	1.945	2.307	2.385	4.850	4.446	4.167	4.218	4.651	—	—	—	—
K. Discrepancy (F − J)	0.068	0.110	0.136	−0.068	−0.079	0.067	−0.253	−0.385	−0.159	−0.071	0.060	−0.003	−1.793[b]	—

[a] n.e.c.: not elsewhere classified. This item includes construction and the acquisition of equipment.
[b] Size of discrepancy is a result of the (unallocated) "forgiveness" of long-term debt.

be postponed in order for kolkhozes to pay for MTS assets, which, of course, represented no net increase in the capital stock available to them. In short, the way in which the MTS transaction was financed proved disastrous for the state's own policy goals in the kolkhoz sector.

The capital account sources and uses of funds for the kolkhoz sector for 1953–66 are displayed in table 4. A capital account sources and uses of funds statement tells one where the money came from to finance the capital outlays of the sector. The kolkhoz sector finances capital outlays partly by transfers of retained income from current account (row B), partly by direct receipts (row C) from sales of its existing capital stock (e.g., livestock herds), and frequently also by means of net borrowing (row E). Of course, if transfers and direct receipts (row D) exceed current capital outlays (row J), then the

---

Sources for Table 4:

Row A: 1953–58: S. Koriunov, *Nedelimye fondy i kapital'nye vlozheniia kolkhozov* (Moscow, 1960), pp. 15, 23; 1959–61: M. G. Vainer (ed.), *Effektivnost' kapital'nykh vlozhenii v sel'skoe khoziaistvo* (Moscow, 1963), p. 197; 1962–64: *Narodnoe khoziaistvo SSSR v 1962 godu* (Moscow, 1963), p. 330, *Nar. khoz., 1963* (Moscow, 1965), p. 341, and *Nar. khoz., 1964* (Moscow, 1965), p. 390, respectively; 1965–66: computed from gross income data in *Nar. khoz., 1965* (Moscow, 1966), p. 405, *Nar. khoz., 1967* (Moscow, 1968), p. 466, and percentage figures in Kartashova, *Finansy, kredit i raschety*, p. 36.

Row B: Includes row A plus, for 1953–55 only, retirement of long-term debt plus, for 1953–58 only, money payment for force-account construction. 1953: Ia. I. Golev, *Sel'skokhoziaistvennyi kredit v SSSR* (Moscow, 1958), pp. 35, 47; 1954–58: Koriunov, p. 23.

Row C: 1953, 1958: Koriunov, p. 15; 1954: partial data, Koriunov, p. 28; 1955–56: estimated from the annual average figure for 1955–57 given by R. V. Alekseeva and A. P. Voronin, *Nakoplenie i razvitie kolkhoznoi sobstvennosti* (Moscow, 1963), p. 19, the subtotal for 1956 (p. 69) and the known total for 1957; 1957–61: Vainer, p. 197, and Koriunov, p. 15; 1962: computed from S. I. Nedelin (ed.), *Organizatsiia finansov kolkhoza* (Moscow, 1964), pp. 46–47, and the 1962 indivisible fund transfer; 1963–66: same as 1962.

Row E: See table 5, row L.

Row G: 1953–55: Golev, p. 51; 1956: *Gosudarstvennyi bank SSSR k XXII s''ezdu KPSS* (Moscow, 1961), p. 61; 1957–58: Koriunov, p. 43; 1959: determined by subtracting known figures for 1956–58 and 1960 from the 1956–60 aggregate given in *Gosudarstvennyi bank SSSR*, p. 61; 1960–61: Alekseeva and Voronin, p. 105; 1962: Nedelin, p. 57.

Row H: 1953–55: Golev, p. 51; 1953, 1957–58: Koriunov, p. 43; 1956–60: Vainer, p. 47; 1960–61: Alekseeva and Voronin p. 105; 1962: Nedelin, p. 57.

Row I: 1953–55: Golev, p. 51; 1956, 1960: *Gosudarstvennyi bank SSSR*, p. 61; 1957–58: Koriunov, p. 43; 1959: 1956–60 aggregate in *Gosudarstvennyi bank SSSR*, p. 61, less 1956–58 and 1960; 1960–61: Alekseeva and Voronin, p. 105; 1962: Nedelin, p. 57.

Row J: 1959: computed from table 55, p. 200, in Alekseeva and Voronin; 1963–64: computed from index in I. Levchuk, *Dolgosrochnyi sel'skokhoziaistvennyi kredit* (Moscow, 1967), p. 104, and total for 1965 given by Kartashova, p. 82; 1965–66: Kartashova, p. 82.

sector must be advancing funds on a net basis to other sectors of the economy (see the negative entries in row E).

A comparison of row D with row J shows quite clearly that kolkhozes have been obliged to finance internally the greater part of money capital outlays throughout the period in question. Net funds obtained through financial channels (row E) were relatively substantial only in 1958 and 1966. The former reflects the assumption of deferred payments for the MTS transaction, and the 1966 figure is explained by the favorable impact of the 1.450 billion ruble debt write-off of 1965 on kolkhoz access to long-term loans. Of particular interest, the kolkhoz sector advanced funds on a net basis on capital account (that is, ordinary, or nonfinancial, sources of funds on capital account exceeded money capital outlays) in 1960, 1961, and 1965. The latter, of course, reflects the debt write-off, but 1960 and 1961 reflect the continuing burden of the MTS transaction and its inhibiting effect on money capital outlays, which declined in 1958–61 (inclusive). In most of the remaining years displayed, net funds obtained on capital account through financial channels represented less than 10 percent of money capital outlays. The fragmentary data available for 1966 and 1968 suggest, however, that the reforms of 1965 and 1966 may have liberalized long-term credit policy, but not as dramatically as might have been expected.[27]

Net Loanfund Financing: Kolkhoz Sector. The data presented in table 5 clearly indicate that loanfund financing has not played a significant role in financing either current or capital account outlays. In fact, loanfund financing appears to have played a rather equivocal role with respect to financing the major reforms that were introduced in the kolkhoz sector during the period of the ascendancy of Nikita Khrushchev. The somewhat fragmentary contemporary data available suggest that financial policy may have been better coordinated with the procurement price increases and the institutional reforms, such as the guaranteed annual wage reform, in subsequent years.[28]

The relative insignificance of net funds obtained through financial channels by kolkhozes (table 5, row M) may be seen in the fact that the item is negative for seven of the fourteen years covered (1953–66). Moreover, during this same period, total money receipts of collective farms rose from 4.96 to 23.1 billion rubles.[29] No comparable upward trend is evident in net money obtained on consolidated account[30] (row M). Between 1953 and 1966, kolkhozes advanced or returned funds through financial channels on current account (row E) in eleven of the fourteen years. This kind of behavior is explained partly by the increase in current-account cash balances and partly by very restrictive short-term credit policy. For the fourteen years covered in table 5, kolkhozes obtained funds through financial channels on capital account (row L) in all but three years: 1960, 1961, and 1965. These exceptional years were discussed in the preceding section. Behavior on consolidated account (row M) is, therefore, more erratic, depending as it does on the net effect of these two, usually contrary, patterns.

The result is that the sector has obtained net funds through financial channels in significant amounts only exceptionally and only as a result of specific high-level political decisions. In the absence of specific policy decisions, conservative financial policy has prevailed. It would also seem quite clear that this is the way Soviet authorities prefer it to be. Debt, like sin, is to be avoided at all cost. This may or may not have been a good rule for the upright Victorian family to follow, but it can hardly ever have made sense as a general rule of thumb for a productive enterprise. Conservative state financial policy has indeed severely restricted the liquidity of the kolkhozes, but it has also had the unintended effect of undermining the state's own attempts to increase capital investment and material incentives in the kolkhoz sector.

Innovation in Financial Policy toward the State Farm and Other Agricultural Organizations Sector

Innovation in state financial policy with respect to state farms (and other state agricultural organizations) has had an entirely different stimulus than that which has motivated reform in the kolkhoz sector. Expansion in the coverage and terms of financial instruments available to state farms has been provided mainly in order to reduce dependence on direct state budget transfers for the financing of operating cost deficits, increases in working capital requirements, and capital investment outlays. The stimulus has been, essentially, the financial implications of the central planning and management reforms announced by Premier Kosygin in September 1965, rather than the inadequacy of existing financial arrangements.

Unlike the kolkhoz, the sovkhoz has never been required to be self-sufficient—that is, to cover all expenses with sales receipts (*samookupaemost'*). As for other state enterprises, the base wage and salary bill has not depended on the economic performance of the farm. Sovkhozes have, therefore, been eligible for direct transfers of funds from the state budget to finance certain current operating

TABLE 5. Loanfund Financing: Kolkhoz Sector (in millions of new rubles)

	1953	1954	1955	1956	1957	1958	1959	1960	1961	1962	1963	1964	1965	1966
Current Account														
Loanfunds receivable (Dec. 31)														
A. Deposit balance	503.2	895.7	985.5	1,189.8	1,022.1	1,170.2	697.2	600.8	1,122.0	1,716.1	2,193.8	2,364.1	3,238.6	4,170.2
B. Increment loanfunds receivable	231.9	392.5	89.8	204.3	−167.7	218.8[a]	−586.6[a]	−96.4	521.2	594.1	477.7	170.3	874.5	931.6
Loanfunds payable (Dec. 31)														
C. Short-term debt	213.8	236.9	260.0	273.2	372.8	374.6	701.7	666.0	644.0	708.0	804.0	871.0	365.0	392.0
D. Increment loanfunds payable	39.8	23.1	23.1	13.2	99.4	1.8	327.1	−35.7	−22.0	64.0	96.0	67.0	−506.0	−27.0
E. Net funds obtained, current account (D − B)	−192.1	−369.4	−66.7	−191.1	267.1	−217.0	913.7	60.7	−543.0	−530.2	−381.7	−103.3	−1,380.5	−958.6
Capital Account														
Loanfunds receivable (Dec. 31)														
F. Deposit balance	530.0	614.0	698.1	776.8	625.6	465.7	324.9	279.3	474.0	689.6	893.8	835.7	943.8	1,053.6
G. Increment loanfunds receivable	121.0	84.0	84.0	78.8	−151.2	−159.9	−140.8	−45.9	195.0	215.6	204.2	−58.1	108.1	109.8
Loanfunds payable (Dec. 31)														
H. Long-term debt	1,133.1	1,343.7	1,576.2	1,876.1	2,007.1	2,173.0	2,355.9	2,378.3	2,645.6	3,101.6	3,605.9	4,404.4	3,890.1	5,255.3
I. Increment long-term debt	135.8	210.6	232.5	299.8	131.0	165.9	182.9	22.4	267.3	456.0	504.3	798.5	−514.3	1,365.1
J. Deferred liability, MTS purchase	—	—	—	—	0.0	1,150.0	1,085.0	645.0	465.0	355.0	245.0	135.0	20.0	0.0
K. Increment deferred liability	—	—	—	—	—	1,150.0	−65.0	−440.0	−180.0	−110.0	−110.0	−110.0	−110.1	−20.0

TABLE 5. (cont.)

	1953	1954	1955	1956	1957	1958	1959	1960	1961	1962	1963	1964	1965	1966
L. Net funds obtained, capital account (I + K − G)	14.8	126.6	148.5	221.0	282.2	1,475.8	258.7	−371.7	−107.7	130.4	190.1	746.6	−832.5	1,235.3
Consolidated Account														
M. Net funds obtained, consolidated account (E + L)	−177.3	−242.8	81.8	29.9	549.3	1,258.8	1,172.4	−311.0	−650.7	−399.8	−111.6	643.3	−2,213.0	277.2

[a] Adjusted to reflect the change in trade receivables for these years. *Obshchestvennye fondy kolkhozov i raspredelenie kolkhoznykh dokhodov* (Moscow, 1961), p. 236.

Row J: Year-end balances for deferred payments for MTS assets have been estimated (in millions of rubles):

	1958	1959	1960	1961	1962	1963	1964	1965	1966
Extensions	1,150[a,b]	315[b]	0	260[c,e]	0	0	0	0	0
Retirements	0	380[g]	440[g]	440[g]	110[g]	110[g]	110[g]	100	20
Year-end balance	1,150	1,085	645[d]	465[d]	355	245	135[f]	20	0

[a] Koriunov, *Nedelimye fondy*, p. 83, and Alekseeva and Voronin, *Nakoplenie i razvitie kolkhoznoi sobstvennosti*, p. 101.
[b] Vainer (ed.), *Effektivnost' kapital'nykh vlozhenii v sel'skoi khoziaistvo*, pp. 200–201 and loan extensions in *Nar. khoz., 1962*, p. 641.
[c] M. M. Usoskin, *Organizatsiia i planirovanie kredita* (Moscow, 1961), p. 309.
[d] *Gosudarstvennyi bank SSSR*, p. 73.
[e] Ibid., p. 64.
[f] V. P. D'iachenko et al., *50-let sovetskikh finansov* (Moscow, 1967), P. 236, which indicates a balance of at least 120 million rubles on December 31, 1964.
[g] Retirement rates are arbitrarily determined to coincide with final balances for July 1, 1961, and January 1, 1965: (1) 1958 balance allotted over a three-year period; (2) 1959 and 1961 extensions allotted over five-year periods.

Sources: Row A: 1953–55: M. Atlas, *Razvitie gosudarstvennogo banka SSSR* (Moscow, 1958), pp. 141, 218, 238, 281; 1956–58: *Nar. khoz., 1958* (Moscow, 1959), p. 913; 1959: *Nar. khoz., 1959* (Moscow, 1960), p. 808; 1960–66: M. S. Atlas et al., *Kreditno-denezhnaia sistema SSSR* (Moscow, 1967), p. 151.
Row C: 1953, 1956–59: *Obshchestvennye fondy kolkhozov i raspredelenie kolkhoznykh dokhodov*, p. 188; 1954: interpolation; 1955: A.V. Bachurin and D.D. Kondrashev (eds.), *Tovarno-denezhnye otnosheniia v period perekhoda k kommunizmu* (Moscow, 1963), p. 299; 1960–62: *Nar. khoz., 1962* (Moscow, 1963), p. 639; 1963–64: *Nar. khoz., 1964* (Moscow, 1965), p. 774; 1965–66: *Nar. khoz., 1967* (Moscow, 1968), p. 891.
Row F: 1953, 1956–58: *Nar. khoz., 1958*, p. 814; 1955: Golev, *Sel'skokhoziaistvennyi kredit*, p. 53; 1959: *Nar. khoz., 1959*, p. 808; 1960–66: Atlas et al., p. 151.
Row H: 1953, 1955, 1956: Golev, p. 72; 1954: determined from long-term loan extension and retirement data and the known year-end balance for 1955, N. A. Tsagolov (ed.), *Razvitie kolkhoznoi sobstvennosti v period razvernutogo stroitel'stva kommunizma* (Moscow, 1961), p. 174; 1957–58: *Nar. khoz., 1958*, p. 909; 1959–62: *Nar. khoz., 1962*, p. 642; 1963–64: *Nar. khoz., 1964*, p. 774; 1965–66: *Nar. khoz., 1967*, p. 895.

expenses as well as the bulk of capital outlays. This opportunity has been of considerable importance, because prices on output transferred to the state ("transfer prices") were for many years, like the agricultural procurement prices received by kolkhozes, too low on most outputs to cover costs. State subsidies have absorbed for the state farm the losses kolkhozniki were obliged to absorb for the collective farm. In 1953, for example, sovkhozes (only) received a subsidy of 0.5 billion rubles, representing 48.6 percent of the sector's total outlays (*sebestoimost'*, which includes planned accumulation as well as production costs) on the products transferred to the state in that year.[31] Conditions have improved considerably since that time, for the transfer prices received by sovkhozes have been increased along with increases in the agricultural procurement prices that kolkhozes receive on their sales to state agencies, although the improvement has not been quite as substantial.[32] Meanwhile, direct budget transfers to sovkhozes (only) have increased sharply in absolute terms: 1946–50, 2.3 billion rubles; 1951–55, 4.1 billion rubles; 1956–60, 8.3 billion rubles; 1961–65, 22.0 billion rubles.[33] The relative share of budget grants in financing of all *money outlays* of sovkhozes and other state agricultural organizations has been declining in recent years, thanks to agricultural transfer price increases, but it remains surprisingly high, having fallen from 79 percent in 1959 to 64 percent in 1966.[34]

The distribution of budget grants among possible applications has also been changing in recent years. For the sovkhoz sector (only), the share devoted to financing capital investment outlays increased sharply between 1964 and 1967 (from 46.8 percent to 80.2 percent) at the expense of transfers to finance operating and working capital deficits.[35] This shift reflects an attempt by higher authorities to make sovkhozes self-sufficient on current-account operations (with the help of short-term credit).

Because of the availability of state budget transfers, sovkhozes do not appear to have suffered from the traditional stringency of bank credit policy. In any case, short-term bank credit has always been available to finance seasonal needs (including wages), expenditures on the formation of livestock herds, and other temporary shortages. Sovkhozes were, however, required to pay a higher interest charge on short-term debt than kolkhozes from 1961 until quite recently: 3 percent on outstanding notes and 5 percent on overdue notes.[36] Long-term debt has been of only marginal significance for sovkhozes, as has been the case for all state enterprises until very recent times.

Examination of table 6, in the light of our consideration of loan-fund financing for the kolkhoz sector (table 5), indicates that

TABLE 6. Loanfund and State Budget Financing on Current Account: State Farms and Other Agricultural Enterprises (in billions of rubles)

	1958	1959	1960	1961	1962	1963	1964	1965	1966	1967	1968
Assets (Dec. 31)											
A. Deposits	.295	—	.338	—	.453	.647	.697	.878	1.103	1.048	1.181
B. Increment in deposits	—	.021	.021	.057	.057	.194	.050	.181	.225	-.055	.133
C. Loanfunds receivable, n.e.c.[a]	.134	—	.221	—	.315	.345	.317	.332	.345	.339	.443
D. Increment in loanfunds receivable	—	.043	.043	.047	.047	.030	-.028	.015	.013	-.006	.104
Liabilities (Dec. 31)											
E. Bank credit	1.058	—	2.098	—	3.109	3.291	3.304	4.091	5.552	5.298	5.740
F. Increment in bank credit	—	.520	.520	.505	.505	.182	.013	.788	.461	.746	.442
G. Loanfunds payable, n.e.c.[a]	.299	—	.377	—	.561	.486	.561	.700	.759	.841	1.099
H. Increment in loanfunds payable	—	.039	.039	.092	.092	-.075	-.075	.139	.059	.082	.258
I. Net money obtained through financial channels (F + H) − (B + D)	—	.495	.495	.493	.493	-.017	.066	.731	.382	.889	.463
J. Budgetary grant to finance operating outlays	—	—	.369	.392	.409	.487	.490	.572	.718	.956	—
K. Total funds raised above (I + J)	—	—	.864	.885	.902	.470	.556	1.303	1.100	1.845	—
L. Share of state budget transfer (in percentage) (J ÷ K) × 100	—	—	43	44	45	104	88	44	65	52	—

[a] n.e.c.: not elsewhere classified.

Sources: Rows A, C, E, G (computed from absolute and percentage data): 1958, 1960, 1962–63: Nar. khoz., 1963, pp. 640, 642; 1964–65: Nar. khoz., 1965, pp. 761, 763; 1966: Nar. khoz., 1968, pp. 749, 751; row J: Atlas, Kreditno-denezhnaia sistema SSSR, p. 199.

financial policy with respect to sovkhozes and other state agricultural enterprises has been much less stringent than for kolkhozes. Net money obtained through financial channels (table 6, row I) compares very favorably not only with what kolkhozes obtained on current account, with which it is comparable, but even with net money obtained by kolkhozes on consolidated account for the relevant years. This is all the more striking because of the relatively larger volume of annual money receipts and disbursements of the kolkhoz sector during this period. It reflects, no doubt, the traditionally preferential treatment of the state enterprise sector. Short-term coverage has been broader for sovkhozes, and this, along with the assurance of state budget transfers, has also made it unnecessary for sovkhozes to accumulate and maintain large current-account special-purpose demand deposits (e.g., for money wage advances).

The data presented in table 6 on budgetary grants allocated to current account (row J) is incomplete (and not entirely comparable). Consequently, the share of state budget transfers in total funds raised from the outside on current account is probably understated for most years. However, it offers a rough idea of the relative significance of the budgetary transfer for sovkhozes and other state agricultural enterprises (row L) on current account.

Let us now turn to a consideration of the financing of money outlays on capital account for state farms and other agricultural organizations (table 7). As for all state enterprises, the state budget grant (through Stroibank) has provided the main source of funds on capital account, but it is clear that the relative share of inside-fund financing has increased substantially in recent years (rows M and O). This change reflects three different factors. First, the increased share of inside financing as of 1963 was in part a consequence of the 1962 reevaluation of the sector's capital stock and amortization schedules,[37] which resulted in a marked increase in the amortization transfer from current account (row C). Second, a 1962 decree of the Council of Ministers established a new system for the redistribution and use of sovkhoz profits, designed, among other things, to increase the amount of inside funds available to the sovkhoz for the implementation of decentralized investment projects.[38] Third, the 1966 increment reflects, at least in part, an effect of increases in agricultural transfer prices in that year.[39]

A portion of the 1966 increment in the relative share of inside funds may also reflect preliminary steps taken toward the implementation of reforms that were announced in 1965 and designed to reduce the operating dependence of sovkhozes and other state agricultural organizations on budgetary grants. The reforms were made

TABLE 7. Capital Account: State Farms and Other Agricultural Enterprises (in billions of rubles)

	1959	1960	1961	1962	1963	1964	1965	1966	
Sources of Funds									
A. Transfer from state budget	2.078	2.604	3.297	3.918	3.931	4.462	4.705	4.421	
B. Inside and equivalent funds	.556	.680	.815	1.097	1.821	2.014	2.325	2.889	
C. Amortization transfer	.490	.747	.878	1.014	1.575	1.687	1.968	2.153	
D. *Less:* Capital repair outlay	.291	.458	.553	.632	.670	.720	.831	.896	
E. *Equals:* Transfer to capital accounts	.199	.289	.325	.382	.905	.967	1.137	1.257	(C − D)
F. Other inside sources	.357	.391	.490	.715	.916	1.047	1.188	1.632	(B − E)
G. Total sources	2.634	3.284	4.112	5.015	5.752	6.476	7.030	7.310	(A + B)
Uses of Funds									
H. Formation of basic herd	.495	.713	.826	.999	1.099	1.145	1.096	1.126	
I. Capital investment	—	2.547	—	—	—	—	5.708	6.024	
J. Uses, n.e.c.[a]	—	.024	—	—	—	—	.126	.159	
K. Capital investment and uses	2.138	2.571	3.285	4.017	4.654	5.511	5.943	6.183	(G −[H + I])
L. Financed by state budget	1.855	2.227	2.897	3.446	3.513	4.242	4.455	4.212	
M. Share of state budget (in percentage)	86.8	86.6	88.0	85.8	75.5	73.9	75.0	68.1	(L ÷ K) × 100
N. Financed by inside funds	.285	.342	.389	.570	1.140	1.239	1.480	1.972	(K − L)
O. Share of inside funds (in percentage)	13.2	13.4	12.0	14.2	24.5	22.0	25.0	31.9	(N ÷ K) × 100

[a] n.e.c.: not elsewhere classified.

Sources: Row A: total budgetary grants less share earmarked for operating expenses, as given in Atlas, *Kreditno-denezhnaia sistema SSSR*, pp. 197, 199: row B: inside and equivalent funds less share earmarked for operating expenses, Atlas, pp. 197–99; row C: 1959, 1961: *Nar. khoz.*, 1962, p. 631; 1960, 1962–63: *Nar. khoz.*, *1963*, p. 635; 1964: *Nar. khoz.*, *1964*, p. 769; 1965–66: *Nar. khoz.*, *1968*, p. 771; rows H and I: Atlas, pp. 198 and 313 respectively; row L: row A less share devoted to financing formation of basic herd, Atlas, p. 198.

official in a decree of April 1967, which called for the establishment
of the principle of "full economic accounting" (*polnyi khozraschet*)
for all state farms.[40] The principle of "full economic accounting"
was developed in response to the growing disenchantment of Soviet
policymakers with the system of state budgetary grant financing,
especially in the form of interest-free capital grants.[41] The new system
has been designed to substitute inside-fund financing and access to
long-term credit for interest-free capital grants for certain specified
types of projects and to increase the sources of funds for capital
investment over which sovkhozes have independent discretion (that
is, decentralized investment).

Under the new system of "full" *khozraschet,* capital outlays are
divided into three categories for funding purposes.[42] The first includes
the acquisition of agricultural equipment, means of transportation,
nonresidential, productive construction, and certain other types of
productive investment. These capital-account uses are to be financed
primarily from retained profits and amortization fund transfer, but
long-term credit is also available on the same terms and rates as for
kolkhozes under certain circumstances—for example, if realized profit
should fall short of planned profit for reasons other than managerial
inefficiency or incompetence.[43] The second funding category is composed of all nonproductive investment and largescale meliorative
projects (construction of electric power plants, irrigation systems, and
so forth), which are to be fully funded by means of state budget
grants. The third category includes certain major productive construction projects, which are to be financed partly by state budget
grants and partly by the redistribution of state farm profits. Presumably these projects are to be identified on the basis of both scale and
multisovkhoz benefit.

These funding categories apparently apply only to centralized
investment projects. Decentralized investment projects may be devoted to both productive and nonproductive capital, the sources being
a portion of planned and overplan profits, social-cultural and other
special-purpose funds, and long-term bank credit.[44]

One effect of the reform, then, is to extend the coverage of
long-term credit for the sovkhoz sector. Sovkhozes also have access
to long-term credit now essentially on the same terms kolkhozes
receive. However, new borrowing for sovkhozes is not constrained
by overdue long-term debt outstanding, except for force-account
construction (carried out by the farm's own labor force) and equipment purchases.[45] Even so, there is no reason to expect that long-
term credit will become a major source of funds to finance investment
in the sovkhoz sector. It is clearly treated as an exceptional and

temporary source of funds under the new system. In 1969, in fact, total long-term loans extended to sovkhozes amounted only to 210 million rubles.[46] The main means by which dependence on state budgetary grants is to be reduced under the reform is increased retained income. The increase in retained earnings has been made possible, in turn, by increasing the prices sovkhozes receive for their products. When a sovkhoz is converted to "full" *khozraschet,* it thereafter transfers its output to the state at the same prices kolkhozes receive from procurement agencies, rather than at the lower transfer prices.[47]

The impetus to reform in the state-farm sector is clearly the same that prompted the Kosygin reform of 1965 for industrial enterprises: an attempt to increase enterprise efficiency. It is too early to tell very much about the success of "full" *khozraschet,* although the evidence presented above (especially tables 6 and 7) suggests that the share of inside funds has indeed increased at the expense of budgetary sources in recent years. *Polnyi khoziaistvennyi raschet* would seem to be the state farm equivalent of *samookupaemost'* for kolkhozes. Thus, contemporary reforms in the kolkhoz and sovkhoz sectors do seem to be bringing about a mutual convergence of the two in institutional structure. This is a somewhat ironic outcome of contemporary financial innovation in agricultural policy. However, our consideration of financial policy reforms for both of these sectors suggests that financial channels are not likely to become major sources of funds for either in the foreseeable future. It appears, therefore, that state financial policy toward the agricultural sector will continue to be excessively conservative in the sense that financial instruments are underused to perform the functions for which they are best adapted. Given the aims of the other general reforms that have taken place in the agricultural sector, this is an irrational financial policy, because it places an undue burden on other policy instruments. It complicates, in particular, agricultural procurement and transfer price determination, for prices must be set to finance inside-fund accumulation as well as current operating outlays.

NOTES

An earlier version of this essay was read at the Northeastern Slavic Conference, Montreal, May 5–8, 1971.

1. The scorekeeping aspect of the unit-of-account function of money has, until quite recently as a consequence of the 1965 Kosygin reforms, been much less important than the accountability aspect. Thus, for example, pecuniary performance indicators, such as the income statement, have been

considerably less significant for evaluating managerial performance than direct physical-volume success indicators. The reluctance to use pecuniary performance criteria derives, of course, mainly from ideological precon- ceptions, but the contemporary emphasis on the scorekeeping aspect of this function has encountered practical obstacles, because it requires ap- propriate (or rational) principles for price formation.

2. James R. Millar, "Financing the Modernization of Kolkhozy," in Millar (ed.), *The Soviet Rural Community: A Symposium* (Urbana, 1971), p. 286; David W. Bronson and Constance B. Krueger, "The Revolution in Soviet Farm Household Income, 1953–1967," ibid., appendix table 1, p. 41.

3. Ratios calculated from table 5, row A; *Sel'skoe khoziaistvo SSSR* (Moscow, 1960), pp. 64, 56; *Narodnoe khoziaistvo SSSR v 1962 godu* (Mos- cow, 1963), p. 342; *Narodnoe khoziaistvo SSSR v 1968 godu* (Moscow, 1969), p. 423.

4. Calculated from table 5 below; M. Z. Pizengol'ts, *Oborotnye sredstva kolkhozov* (Moscow, 1968), p. 60; *Obshchestvennye fondy kolkhozov i ras- predelenie kolkhoznykh dokhodov* (Moscow, 1961), p. 196; Millar, "Fi- nancing the Modernization of Kolkhozy," table 1, row O, p. 292; Bronson and Krueger, "Revolution in Soviet Farm Household Income," appendix table 1, p. 241.

5. Millar, "Financing the Modernization of Kolkhozy," p. 292.

6. K. S. Kartashova, *Finansy, kredit i raschety v kolkhozakh* (Moscow, 1970), p. 137. Kolkhozes were obliged, from 1956 on, to pay kolkhozniki monthly wage advances in cash equal to not less than 25 percent of actual current money receipts in all branches and 50 percent of procurement- agency advances. See K. I. Orliankin (ed.), *Sbornik reshenii po sel'skomu khoziaistvu* (Moscow, 1963), pp. 259–60.

7. Kartashova, *Finansy, kredit i raschety*, p. 136.

8. Ibid., pp. 136–38.

9. M. K. Shermenev (ed.), *Finansy i kreditovanie sel'skokhoziaistvennykh predpriiatii* (Moscow, 1963), pp. 187–94.

10. Ibid.

11. Kartashova, *Finansy, kredit i raschety*, p. 136.

12. Ibid., p. 138.

13. Pizengol'ts, *Oborotnye sredstva kolkhozov*, p. 49. In Soviet account- ing parlance, working capital is divided into two parts: productive and circulating. The former includes stocks of inputs such as fuel, seed supplies, fodder, spare parts and hand tools, young animals and cattle in feed lots, expenses under the future year's crop, and unfinished production, such as crops in the field. The sphere of circulating capital includes inventories of finished output of all productive branches, trade receivables, including money advances to kolkhozniki, and all current-account cash balances (pp. 48–49).

14. For a discussion of these reforms, see Millar, "Financing the Mod- ernization of Kolkhozy," pp. 279–81.

15. Kartashova, *Finansy, kredit i raschety*, p. 123.

16. Based on data collected and currently being processed for a Ph.D. thesis at the University of Illinois by Mrs. Christine Wollan.

17. V. N. Semenov, *Finansy i kredit v sovkhozakh* (Moscow, 1969), pp. 147–62.

18. The main exception today is the availability of long-term credit (up to a five-year term) to finance labor payments where the kolkhoz is unable otherwise to pay its wage bill at the guaranteed level. The policy was initiated in 1966, and the outstanding balance for this item on January 1, 1970, was 668 million rubles (Kartashova, *Finansy, kredit i raschety,* pp. 27, 108); total outstanding long-term loans to kolkhozes on that date exceeded 9 billion rubles (pp. 99–100).

19. I. Levchuk, *Dolgosrochnyi sel'skokhoziaistvennyi kredit* (Moscow, 1967), pp. 77–79.

20. Ibid., p. 80.

21. Kartashova, *Finansy, kredit i raschety,* p. 98; Levchuk, *Dolgosrochnyi sel'skokhoziaistvennyi kredit,* pp. 86–88.

22. Levchuk, *Dolgosrochnyi sel'skokhoziaistvennyi kredit,* pp. 93–96.

23. Kartashova, *Finansy, kredit i raschety,* p. 104.

24. Levchuk, *Dolgosrochnyi sel'skokhoziaistvennyi kredit,* p. 96.

25. Kartashova, *Finansy, kredit i raschety,* pp. 99.

26. Levchuk, *Dolgosrochnyi sel'skokhoziaistvennyi kredit,* pp. 81–83.

27. There is evidence that a number of Soviet economists remain dissatisfied, especially with long-term loan policy. See, for example, Kartashova, *Finansy, kredit i raschety,* pp. 111–15.

28. For an extended treatment, see Millar, "Financing the Modernization of Kolkhozy," pp. 279–91.

29. *Sel'skoe khoziaistvo,* pp. 64, 56; *Nar. khoz., 1967* (Moscow, 1968), p. 466.

30. This is the net flow of finance on current and capital accounts taken together.

31. V. P. D'iachenko et al., *50-let sovetskikh finansov* (Moscow, 1967), p. 217.

32. Ibid., pp. 216, 218–20.

33. Ibid., p. 211.

34. M. S. Atlas et al., *Kreditno-denezhnaia sistema SSSR* (Moscow, 1967), p. 197.

35. D'iachenko et al., *50-let sovetskikh finansov,* p. 223.

36. Semenov, *Finansy i kredit,* p. 157.

37. Kartashova, *Finansy, kredit i raschety,* p. 83.

38. D'iachenko et al., *50-let sovetskikh finansov,* pp. 218–19.

39. Ibid., p. 216.

40. Semenov, *Finansy i kredit,* p. 122.

41. D'iachenko et al., *50-let sovetskikh finansov,* pp. 223–24.

42. Semenov, *Finansy i kredit,* pp. 122–23.

43. Ibid., p. 129.

44. Ibid., pp. 124–25.
45. Ibid., p. 129.
46. Ibid., p. 6.
47. Ibid., pp. 36–37.

PART 3

Central Management and
the Emergence of Acquisitive
Socialism in the USSR

10

An Economic Overview
of the Soviet Union

Comrades, the Communist Party is advancing a great task—to achieve
in the coming 20 years a living standard higher than that of any
capitalist country and to create the necessary conditions for achieving
an abundance of material and cultural values.

—Nikita Khrushchev

In the 1980s the Soviet Union may pass through the worst period
since the death of Stalin. Growth rates will be the lowest ever, and
the population can expect a stagnating or even declining standard of
living. The very stability of the social system may be in question.

—Seweryn Bialer

Three years after announcing his heady goals (quoted above) at the
Twenty-second Party Congress,[1] Nikita Khrushchev was deposed.
The same year, 1964, the Soviet Union imported a large volume of
grain on a net basis for the first time since World War II, a policy
that was continued in ever-increasing volume throughout the Brezhnev years. The high rates of growth in gross national product and
of per capita consumption achieved during the 1950s began to decline
immediately following the congress, and they have continued in
systematic decline every since. Seweryn Bialer's prediction for the
1980s (quoted above) was based on projections to the end of the
decade of declining and/or stagnant rates of economic growth.[2]

What happened to undermine Khrushchev's confident, sunny
forecast of 1961? Is the current picture as gloomy as Bialer has
suggested? What are the leadership's economic alternatives? My purpose here is to describe and evaluate briefly the principal structural
and performance changes that have taken place in the Soviet economy
since Stalin's death in 1953. I will then examine the policy options

From *The Soviet Union Today: An Interpretive Guide,* ed. James Cracraft
(2d ed.; Chicago: University of Chicago Press, 1987), pp. 177–90. Originally
titled "An Overview." Reprinted by permission, with minor editorial changes.

currently available to Soviet policymakers and speculate about the
course of the economy in the next decade.

Soviet history is replete with abrupt, traumatic changes in social
and economic conditions. World War I, the Revolution of 1971, the
civil war, collectivization and rapid industrialization, the great purges,
World War II, and postwar reconstruction all demanded considerable
personal sacrifices and caused significant structural changes in the
economy. Change has been more gradual since Stalin's death, but
the cumulative effect of reform and policy revision during the thirty
years of Khrushchev and Leonid Brezhnev was greater than may be
generally realized. The current leadership confronts an economy that
is quite different in both structure and performance from the one
that faced Khrushchev in 1953 or Brezhnev in 1964.

Structurally, between 1928 and 1953 Soviet economic development represented a variant of the "classical" model. Growth was
achieved by mobilizing under- and unemployed labor and by shifting
labor from low- (or zero-) productivity sectors into sectors where
productivity was relatively higher (or positive) or increasing at a
relatively high rate. A large share of the resulting increase in final
product was reinvested in the growth sectors, thereby providing still
more employment opportunities in high-productivity sectors. In general, labor moved out of rural nonagricultural as well as agricultural
employment into industrial occupations. About 15 million people
migrated from the countryside between 1928 and 1940. Labor also
moved from activities not valued in the measurement of gross national product into those that are "counted." The largest single component of the latter flow was made up of women moving mainly
into the lower-productivity jobs abondoned by men — that is, into
agriculture, light industry, and retail sales.

The Soviet model differs from other classical cases of economic
development, such as that of Japan, chiefly by the degree to which
heavy industry was accorded priority. World War II and the cold war
that followed accentuated this priority in the Soviet Union, for conventional warfare requires a heavy industrial base above all else.
Autarkic development of domestic raw materials and natural resources was another response to the Soviet Union's international
situation. Thus, unlike Japan, it did not develop a comparative advantage in exportable consumer goods. It did so in energy, raw materials, and armaments.

The principal structural changes in the Soviet economy *since*
Stalin's time have been modifications designed to accommodate a
high priority for consumer goods and, perforce, a higher priority for

TABLE 1. Average Annual Growth of Soviet Gross National Product

	1956–60	1961–65	1966–70	1971–75	1976–80	1981–84
Average annual growth (percentage)	5.9	5.0	5.3	3.7	2.6	2.7

agriculture, light industry, and residential construction. This has required changes in the leadership's long-standing preferences for industry over agriculture, for the urban worker over the rural—in short, for the hammer over the sickle.

Khrushchev and Brezhnev were favored by several circumstances in seeking to revise priorities. Khrushchev obtained relatively quick, if somewhat transitory, returns by bringing 36 million hectares of virgin land under the plow and by improving incentives in agricultural production. Brezhnev benefited from the surge in employable population resulting from the country's postwar baby boom. The rural sector also provided a substantial flow of labor. Thus, although resources were gradually shifted away from previously preferred sectors, the availability of new supplies of land and labor helped to cushion both a decline in the rate of growth of total investment and the shift of an increased share of total net investment to agriculture and related industries.

Even so, the trend in the growth rate of the gross national product declined in the early 1960s (table 1).[3] The sectors into which resources were rechanneled were those of relatively lower productivity, while the increase in total factor productivity—that is, the increase in output not attributable to quantitative increases in inputs of capital and labor—also declined after 1970. Agricultural output after 1958 grew at a healthy, although slackening, rate. Unfortunately, the real resource cost of agricultural output rose continuously because productivity did not.

I do not deal here with the specific problems of the Soviet consumer and of Soviet agriculture, but a few generalizations are in order. Consumption per capita increased at an impressive rate during the post-Stalin period taken as a whole, averaging in excess of 3 percent per year for 1951–80. This performance was better than that of the United States, Canada, Sweden, Switzerland, and the United Kingdom. France, Italy, and West Germany performed somewhat better, averaging 3.9, 4.0, and 4.6 percent respectively over the same period, and Japan attained a phenomenal annual rate of 6.6 percent.

At the same time, the composition of Soviet personal consumption expenditures changed in accordance with the profile typical of industrialized countries, if at a more gradual rate than in most other developing economies. Food declined as a portion of total personal consumption, from 60 percent in 1951–55 to 45 percent in 1976–80, and durables increased from 2 to 11 percent. But services remained essentially constant at about 23 percent.

Thus, Khrushchev and then Brezhnev did succeed in raising the priority of the consumer sector in the Soviet economy. But three serious and related problems remained:

1. Attainment of a relatively high rate of growth of consumption per capita was more costly in real resources than had been anticipated.

2. The rates of growth in all consumption subseries began high but have been declining since. Although the Brezhnev government succeeded in reversing the downward trend in 1966–70, immediately after assuming power, the downward trend reasserted itself thereafter. The 1980s have been characterized by stagnation.

3. Khrushchev committed himself to policy of retail price stability, which Brezhnev followed. As agricultural production costs and money payments to farmers increased, nominal retail prices on a multitude of products, especially foodstuffs, came to bear little relationship either to cost of production or to each other. This continues to be the case.

Competition among increasingly affluent consumers for underpriced goods has perpetuated queuing as a major activity of adult Soviet citizens and fostered a wide range of illegal and quasi-legal private dealings (sometimes called the "second economy"). As rates of growth in output decline or stagnate at low levels, the hope of meeting effective demand at existing consumer prices in state retail outlets is clearly doomed. Elimination of queues and of black- and gray-market opportunities would unavoidably require price adjustments—all upward. To raise prices, however, has been considered politically risky. Scattered evidence of food riots in the Soviet Union suggests that this is not an idle consideration, as does the experience of the Polish leadership in recent years.

Irrationally low official prices create consumer expectations that are certain to be frustrated, and these frustrations are blamed on the government. Raising prices generates immediate protest. This is a dilemma no Soviet government since Stalin has been prepared to resolve. Thus, the annual state subsidy of consumer goods continued to grow, increasing from 35 billion rubles in 1981 to an estimated 50 billion in 1983.

During the rapid industrialization of the 1930s, procurement of adequate food grains to provision urban workers was the primary index of the success of Bolshevik agricultural policy. Since Stalin, the index has increasingly been the provision of animal husbandry products, particularly red meat. This was demonstrated by the Brezhnev government's willingness to expand greatly the use of hard currency to purchase large quantities of grain in the West. These purchases were not made to supply food grains for Soviet dinner tables; rather, they were needed in order to meet the goals set for livestock herd expansion, for which domestic grain and fodder production was inadequate. With the help of imports, animal husbandry expanded substantially: total meat production rose by approximately 4 percent a year between 1951 and 1979, and milk output by about 3.5 percent. Success in this endeavor may also be measured indirectly by an increasing incidence of coronary-artery disease, with attendant morbidity, among Soviet citizens.

The Brezhnev regime benefited from two windfalls that helped to finance the shift in priorities. The price of gold soared as a result of floating the dollar and other "hard" currencies in the 1970s; and the formation of OPEC drove petroleum prices up beyond any expectation. As a major producer and exporter of both gold and petroleum products, the Soviet Union enjoyed a substantially improved foreign position.

These windfalls were not sufficient, however, to offset completely a growing conflict of priorities during the 1970s and early 1980s. Sometime late in the Khrushchev period a decision was made to increase the share of gross national product devoted to defense expenditures, most probably as a response to Khrushchev's humiliation in the Cuban missile crisis of 1962. During Brezhnev's time, the Soviet Union achieved parity with the United States in military strength for the first time. This absorbed about 12–14 percent of Soviet gross national product, a proportion that rose to 15–17 percent thereafter. The implication is that an increased share of final product will continue to be required for military purposes in order to maintain parity.

The current Soviet government therefore faces direct competition between the goal of increasing per capita consumption and maintaining—let alone expanding—the Soviet military establishment. Unless a breakthrough is achieved that will accelerate technological innovation in Soviet industry and agriculture, or unless augmented supplies of labor and capital are obtained to continue the traditional pattern of growth, the regime will face a direct trade-off between producing red meat and maintaining, so to speak, the red menace. The Soviet leadership cannot determine defense policy unilaterally. It is determined by reactions to perceived external threats as well as by domestic considerations. Thus, continuation of the arms race may lead to a degree of disappointment of consumer expectation that could threaten "the very stability of the social system," as Bialer suggests. The alternative is to seek arms limitation or, better, arms reduction.

No help can be expected from the growth of employment, which has declined from 2 percent per annum during 1965–70 to about 0.05 per cent per annum currently. Projections suggest a constant labor force through the year 2000. Since labor participation rates are already high for women as well as men, when compared to those of other developed economies, there is no obvious resource to tap. Agriculture still employs a great deal of manpower, but outmigration is being discouraged for the sake of agricultural output. Only a sharp reduction of the large standing army would supply a significant new source of manpower.

Meanwhile, gross national investment has been one-third of gross national product in the 1980s, up from one-fourth in 1960. This share is already high, cross-nationally, and is unlikely to increase further. The rate of growth of investment has slowed to less than 3 percent per year, down from 7.6 percent in 1965–70. Further sources of investment capital, in short, are not likely to appear.

Imports of capital embodying new technology represent a potential source of growth, but imports have not composed a large share of total Soviet investment in machinery and equipment (only about 3 percent recently), and expansion is constrained by limits on hard-currency earnings. Recent declines in the price of oil do not help. Imports of grains, meat, and other consumer-related items compete directly for foreign exchange with imports of investment goods.

Innovation by Soviet enterprises has been slow and uncertain, and this has inhibited economic growth. Moreover, costs of most raw materials have been rising because of quality decline in mined-out regions and because of the increased cost of locating, recovering, and transporting resources from sites that are increasingly remote from traditional population centers.

To top it all off, maintaining control in Eastern Europe is increasingly costly. Intervention in Afghanistan is proving an expensive exercise, and relations with China are unlikely to improve sufficiently to permit reduction of military power designated to protect the long common border.

The economic situation looks difficult indeed for the current

Soviet leadership. A number of hard choices must be confronted, and soon.

Although the troubles and restraints enumerated above are real and serious, it does not follow that Soviet policymakers consider the situation to be as bleak as do most Western analysts. It is easy to exaggerate the long-term consequences of today's ills, and much that is completely unexpected can happen between now and the end of the century. Besides, the fundamental strength of the Soviet economy, like that of the American, resides in its size, in the skills of its population, in the extraordinary richness of its natural resources, and in the proven ability of the leadership to respond effectively to problems old and new.

The Soviet Union has experienced victory in the most ferocious and devastating war in history; a rise during the postwar years to military parity with the largest economy in the world; a doubling of the living standard of the population as a whole over that same quarter of a century; and its transformation into a modern industrial state surrounded by a large, relatively prosperous empire. Moreover, year in and year out the Soviet economy is still growing more rapidly than the U.S. economy, which means that the gap between them continues to narrow, albeit more slowly than before. Why should Soviet leaders conclude that the problems they face today are fatal?

It would be wise to discount predictions of imminent Soviet economic collapse. But how might the performance of the Soviet economy be improved over the next decade or two? Can acceptable rates of growth in the nondefense components of the gross national product be reestablished for a decade or more? The problem is at base one of stagnation, and its solution requires searching for ways to increase the supply of final products and/or to reduce final demand. Let us consider demand management first.

The most obvious solution is a reduction in the share of gross national product absorbed by defense expenditures. As we have seen, this share is currently estimated at more than 15 percent. A slowdown in the rate of increase in military expenditures from 4–5 percent per annum to, say, 1–2 percent would allow for increased rates of growth for both investment and consumption. Observers of Soviet affairs agree that the leadership is ripe for serious arms talks for this reason, but successful negotiation requires readiness on the part of the United States and its allies, which is what makes this alternative problematic from the Soviet standpoint.

There are two broad schools of thought in the West about the potential usefulness of arms limitation agreements with the Soviet

Union. One holds that fundamental change in the nature of the Soviet political system must precede any significant agreement. Otherwise, the Soviet leadership would merely exploit the agreement to its own advantage, one way or another. The other school operates on the assumption that the leadership is willing and able to conduct—and to adhere to—an arms-limiting agreement. Favorable change in the nature of the Soviet system would, in this view, be fostered by the agreement itself. Meanwhile, careful verification and vigilance would be required to ensure against cheating.

Appraisal of these two views is beyond the scope of this essay. What is significant is that from the end of 1979 or so the United States has favored the first view. In fact, some members of the Reagan administration have suggested that acceleration of the arms race by the United States would foster favorable change in Soviet domestic and foreign policies by increasing the competition for domestic resources, as defense absorbs an ever increasing share of Soviet output.

But from the Soviet point of view, as we have seen, the constraint on a policy aimed at deceleration of the arms race is its dependence on the other side. Insofar as Soviet leaders sense that U.S. disarmament policy is aimed at forcing change in Soviet domestic policies, they are certain to move slowly and with extreme caution. On the other hand, deceleration of the nuclear arms race, attractive as it must seem, does not offer them a reliable way to free resources to support a new economic policy. A more reasonable goal would be to attempt either to contain their military spending at current levels—so that the crunch does not get worse—or to reduce conventional armaments. All other economic policy options involve finding ways to increase the growth rate of the Soviet gross national product and thus the supply of final product. There remains, to be sure, the possibility of improving the way in which consumer demand is managed centrally.

There can be no doubt that demand exceeds supply for most quality commodities and services in state-operated retail outlets. This is because many of the most desirable goods and services—such as red meat, vegetables and fruits, quality apparel, and state-of-the-art durables—are underpriced by very large margins. Underpricing leads not only to queuing but to "scarcity mindedness." Runs on periodically scarce commodities in retail outlets tend to make these items scarce all the time. Underpricing must, in addition, tempt many Soviet citizens into undertaking illegal middleman activities in black and gray markets in order to collect the difference between actual and equilibrium prices. Deficit supplies of goods have a deleterious effect on total employment and on incentives to work hard and advance professionally. Time is better spent in queues or at leisure. Elimination of supply shortages would have a beneficial effect on productivity and thus on output.

Consumer demand management could be greatly improved — and illegal, petty private enterprise diminished — if flexible prices were used to a greater extent. But this would require raising prices on many goods — a process that would, in turn, redistribute income among Soviet citizens in a significant but not entirely predictable way. People with more time than money would surely lose out. And if prices were also raised in the special stores open to privileged groups, those outlets would be effectively closed. Better demand management alone, then, might do as much political harm as economic good and so is unlikely to be seen, by itself, as a way of making friends or encouraging productivity. Yet some realignment of retail prices and a consequent reduction in the huge subsidies that now support many commodities represent essential first steps toward any fundamental reform of the Soviet economy.

Soviet leaders and economists have been considering and implementing structural reforms in planning and management since the early 1960s. But if periodic reform has become institutionalized by now, thoroughgoing reform has yet to be undertaken. Nor are radical changes likely to be introduced by the leadership. The degree of centralization of the economy is unlikely ever to be reduced sufficiently to permit a significant exercise of discretion at the enterprise level. Recently the tendency to write tight plans has been curbed somewhat, but it remains a standard central management tool. The amount of detail in Soviet plans is also likely to be reduced only gradually and marginally.

A wholesale reform of Soviet central planning and of managerial incentives — a prospect that has excited the attention of many Western observers for almost two decades — does not appear to be in the making. Rather, the fundamental paradigm of central planning remains intact and, like other paradigms, will not disappear until replaced by a new conception of planning. Market socialism has, to date, been rejected by dominant Soviet economists and policymakers. And although much has been written in the West about the possible applicability of the "Hungarian model" to the Soviet economy, what is often overlooked is the fact that since its introduction in Hungary itself the rate of increase in gross national product in that country has not risen significantly. Besides, Hungary is too small and too export-oriented to serve as a model for the Soviet Union.

This does not mean that serious economic reform in the Soviet Union is out of the question; but it is more likely to happen somewhere other than the central planning and management institutions. If the reform movement of the past two decades has produced any consensus, it is that policy on consumer prices in state retail outlets must be changed before any other reforms can be expected to work properly. In short, the present price system is perceived by all concerned as capricious and inequitable and as an invitation to citizens to participate in black, gray, and other illegal marketeering.

Soviet leaders had hoped that with increased output economies of scale would eventually permit satisfaction of demand at 1953 prices. This expectation has clearly and unambiguously failed for all agricultural products. But how are anxious Soviet consumers to be persuaded, after repeated promises of stable prices, that they cannot have their cake and eat it too? Consumers complain about queues, but they complain even more loudly about price increases.

Nonetheless, Soviet authorities may seriously consider retail price reform as a component of a major economic reform program. It would not suffice by itself but would have to be part of a package that would not only make more palatable the bitter pill of income redistribution but also lead to a sustained period of improved growth performance. The appeal of price reform to Soviet leaders is obvious: it would decrease queuing and complaints about special privileges, and it would help stamp out economic crime. The danger is that consumers would not stand for it.

Price reform could be accompanied by the large-scale—but short-term—import of consumer goods. This policy would minimize the price increases required to eliminate queues in individual markets and at the same time increase total satisfaction, offsetting somewhat the impact of redistribution on the losers. Price reform would also require some wage adjustments. My guess is that the result would be greater inequality in income distribution, which might in turn have a favorable impact on incentives. Moreover, unfavorable comparison with imported consumer goods might help to improve the quality of Soviet goods. And once retail prices were better adjusted wholesale prices could be adjusted also, giving managerial incentive reform experiments a better chance of success.

A minor but potentially significant component of reform was announced in 1986. The aim was to facilitate small-scale private enterprise in urban areas, especially in services, a region that has been dominated by "second-economy" activities. The fostering of repairs of durable goods and autos, hairdressing, and similar economic activities by the private sector, accompanied by provision of the necessary tools, parts, and other supplies through state outlets, will no doubt reduce economic crime and improve the efficiency of these activities for the benefit of all—as some very limited moves in this direction in the earlier 1980s tended to show. The same holds true for permitting greater enterprise by farmers on private account. Willingness to tolerate such petty private enterprise is a victory of economic rationality over hidebound ideology.

With better management of demand and three to five years of increased imports of consumer goods, the government could buy time to focus on ways of regaining some of the dynamism of earlier growth. One possibility would be to find a way to offset the decline in the rate of growth of both manpower and capital stock. A second would be to achieve a reasonable rate of growth of total factor productivity— perhaps of 1.5–2 percent per annum.

Restructuring prices and wages ought to make material incentives work better all around, but even this would not be sufficient to achieve what is needed. Relatively unproductive labor—labor that could be shifted to better uses—does exist in the Soviet Union, but it is located far from the more industrialized regions. Restructuring of wages could be done in such a way as to attract workers from Central Asia and elsewhere to the industrial regions or to resource-rich Siberia.

Some Western specialists believe that cultural barriers limit voluntary outmigration from these areas. There is considerable countervailing evidence from elsewhere, however: in the movement of Pakistanis to England, for example, of Turks to West Germany, or of Algerians to France in the 1950s and 1960s. In the Soviet Union such a policy has never been tried with comparable incentives. The barriers may reflect racism more than cultural preference.

Internal migration is not the only possibility. The Soviet Union might decide to use foreign workers on a greater scale, adopting one of the tools of successful growth in Western Europe. There are, however, two main constraints on such a policy: (1) obtaining, or creating, currency that is "hard" enough to be an incentive; and (2) policing a large number of foreign workers. Either obstacle is probably sufficient to rule out this option.

Another possible reform would be to encourage foreign investment in the Soviet Union and to rely more heavily on foreign borrowing to finance inputs of capital. The Soviet Union has always been a very conservative debtor country, and its current debt-service ratio is relatively low. A more aggressive policy of risk taking would find lenders. Careful choice of capital imports designed to maximize desirable technological features would help generate growth of factor productivity. This option shows some promise.

Japan, for example, represents an ideal trading and venture-capital partner for the Soviet Union. Japan's technology is well developed in many of the areas where the Soviet Union is particularly weak: high technology, the production of high-quality consumer durables, and the use of robots to minimize the demand for labor in the modern industrial sector. The Soviet Union, on the other hand, has the vast natural resources that Japan lacks. There are similar possibilities with other countries, and European nations appear prepared to continue to expand economic relations with their Soviet neighbor.

Finally, if retail prices could be set at clearing levels and used flexibly to bring supply and demand into equilibrium, a solution to the food problem could be found. Because retail prices are kept artificially low to subsidize the urban dweller, producer prices also tend to be set too low to serve as adequate incentives to farmers. Besides, a wide gap between the two would cause farmers to buy at retail to deliver wholesale. Countries that subsidize farmers rather than consumers, such as the United States and France, usually face agricultural surpluses. In seeking to subsidize consumers, however, the Soviet Union perpetuates shortages. A major restructuring of retail and wholesale prices for agricultural products could break the vicious circle and go far toward generating both the resources and the incentives required to stimulate high productivity more generally.

Some combination of the policies described above could alleviate the resource crunch that the current Soviet leaders face. But there are other factors that could make these alternatives easier or harder to implement, factors over which they have no real control. A recurrence of better weather conditions for a decade or more could greatly ease things; two or three good harvests per Five-Year Plan would raise the rate of growth a percentage point or two and reduce competition for foreign exchange between investment and consumption.

Full economic recovery in the West would also be helpful. Rising world industrial production and a growth in international trade would help firm the prices of petroleum and natural gas. It would also help Eastern European economies, which depend heavily on exports to the West for prosperity. Greater prosperity in Eastern Europe might dampen political discontent there and thus reduce demands for Soviet economic assistance and for Soviet forces to cope with social unrest.

Speeches by Soviet leaders over the last several decades have often featured calls to Communist party members for a return to the ideological dedication of the halcyon days of the 1930s and to the populace as a whole for a return to the moral commitment of wartime

Russia. Thus far, they have generated little more than nostalgia. There is no evidence that the Soviet leadership or the party that it speaks for knows how to rekindle these emotions, but there is little doubt that doing so would work miracles in the economy. What seems to be needed is a "moral rearmament" movement: the creation, somehow, of born-again communists. Although it seems an unlikely prospect, we should not overlook the possibility of a rededication to Marxist goals among party members or a resurgence of long-standing populist ambitions.

The best of all possible worlds for the Soviet leadership would include a series of excellent harvests, a deceleration of the arms race, quietude in Eastern Europe, and full economic recovery in the West. Were it to adopt policies leading to an end of the war in Afghanistan, increased rationality in setting retail and wholesale prices, and the mobilization of new and/or more productive labor and capital, the Soviet gross national product could grow at a rate that would satisfy most members of society and help foster ideological and spiritual commitment to the regime and its goals.

Of course, the worst may happen instead. Climatic change may contribute to more poor harvests; the arms race may accelerate; and Eastern Europe, Afghanistan, and other parts of the Soviet Union's empire may become even more unstable and costly to discipline and police. Price reform may backfire, causing domestic unrest. Both labor and capital productivity may decline further because of the resulting economic disarray, leading to general political instability.

Usually, in history, neither the worst nor the best happens. Early indications of Soviet economic growth in 1986 are encouraging, and the prospects for success in stabilizing growth at a level tolerable to the leadership are quite good. The big question is whether the leadership has the power, the courage, and the foresight to develop and implement a well-wrought, rational policy — or whether, instead, it will hesitate before the risks that such a course of action poses and decide to follow the example set by Brezhnev at the end of his career, which was to coast, leaving the hard choices to his successors. The jury is still out on this question.

NOTES

1. *Report on the Program of the Communist Party of the Soviet Union* (Moscow: Novosti, 1961), vol. 2, p. 85.

2. Seweryn Bialer, *Time,* November 22, 1982, p. 26.

3. The performance data cited here and elsewhere in this chapter are based on the following computations and estimates: *USSR: Measures of*

Economic Growth and Development, 1950-1980. Report of the Joint Economic Committee, U.S. Congress (Washington, D.C.: Government Printing Office, 1982); *Soviet Economy in a Time of Change.* Report of the Joint Economic Committee, U.S. Congress, (Washington, D.C.: Government Printing Office, 1979); *Allocation of Resources in the Soviet Union and China in 1984.* Report of the Joint Economic Committee, U.S. Congress (Washington, D.C.: Government Printing Office, 1985); *Economic Survey of Europe in 1981* (New York: Secretariat of the U.N. Economic Commission for Europe, 1982); and *Handbook for Economic Statistics, 1985* (Washington, D.C.: Directorate of Intelligence, September 1985). See also James R. Millar, *The ABCs of Soviet Socialism* (Urbana: University of Illinois Press, 1981).

11

Soviet Macroeconomic Performance and Policy

A Methodological Note

The conception of an economy as a system is based upon empirical observation. Individual transactors and groups of transactors are linked by a number of subsystems which cause their behavior to be interdependent. For example one transactor's expenditure is, simultaneously, another's income. Because economic activity is finely divided into many different specialties, each transactor is dependent upon a network of others for its income, and each transactor's expenditures affect a large network of other transactors. Consequently, a decision by some to reduce expenditure levels is simultaneously a reduction in total income of the community—and vice versa. This is a social accounting fact of economic life with wide ramifications. A second fact is that income is an important *determinant* of expenditure for many transactors. This is a fact about behavior, and it is not true for all transactors or for all sectors of the economy. This is important because it means that a decision by one sector to change its rate of spending is likely to be amplified by others following suit. The income-and-money circuit, therefore, links government to consumers and links both to enterprises and so on—as accounting entities and behaviorally.

Changes in prices charged in state retail outlets, in tax rates, in the distribution of investment funds, or in welfare support payments produce a series of repercussions that ramify throughout the economy and rebound in some economic way to the initiator of the change. The repercussion may also be political, because such changes ordinarily affect the distribution of income to the benefit of some at the expense of others. The enormous increase that has taken place

From *The ABCs of Soviet Socialism,* James R. Millar (Urbana: University of Illinois Press, 1981), pp. 155–73. Originally titled "Macroeconomic Performance and Policy." Reprinted by permission, with minor editorial changes and omission of "selected readings."

199

in prices paid to collective and state farms for their products, for example, has been absorbed almost entirely by the Soviet state budget. The turnover tax on most agricultural products has thus been eliminated and even converted into a subsidy to keep retail prices essentially constant on important food products. Thus, increased supplies of food products have been available at highly subsidized constant prices, which has benefited those able and willing to queue for them. But this situation invites speculation and *nalevo* dealings (obtaining goods or services "on the left" or "under the counter") because there are others who have *blat* ("connections" or "string-pulling" used to advance one's own interest) or are willing to pay a price well above the state retail market price to avoid queuing. Raising official prices on meat, for example, would reduce *nalevo* dealings in meat, but it would also redistribute income significantly from those who have *blat* or the time and patience to queue to those with the ability to pay. Political repercussions are feared as a result.

The Soviet economy forms a system because it consists of a seamless web of interrelated transactions. Prices, wages, tax payments, welfare benefits, investment allocations, lending and borrowing, bonuses and plan documents tie the various transactors together; and the system is sufficiently complex to make the outcome of any particular economic policy uncertain to some degree. Freedom of calling in labor markets, open consumer goods markets, private property and freedom to buy and sell these property rights privately, and private enterprise, even though severely limited, provide room for households to maneuver, to respond with discretion to government economic activities and to central plans. Similarly, the expertise of enterprise managers and the complexity of the economy affords managers considerable room to maneuver as well. It is possible, therefore, for any given economic policy to fail its object, and that failure might make matters worse, too. Economic interdependency in the USSR is compounded by the fact that communist ideology links political and economic phenomena very closely, and Bolshevik policy and promises have reinforced the link. Thus, economic policy is highly loaded politically, and this includes even a number of quite minor economic matters.

The economic (and political) interdependence of the various sectors of the Soviet economy is a fact. Ever since the time of Adam Smith, economists have been impressed by the orderliness economic systems exhibit most of the time. Even primitive economic systems evidence complex patterned relationships among individuals. Consequently, as a matter of intellectual curiosity economists ordinarily have been fascinated by the task of understanding how economic activity is coordinated among the different individuals and specialists. Interest in how the economy works, however, leads naturally to a desire to evaluate the performance of the economic system, for the description of how it works implies making distinctions regarding how well certain subsystems work and comparisons with the way various subsystems function in other economies.

Part of an animal physiologist's job is to explain how the healthy animal, or healthy organ of the animal, works; and this involves identifying pathological symptoms. A scientific description of the physiology of a species must not be based solely upon observation of a pathological specimen. The economist has similar concerns. When it comes to describing the way an economy functions, however, evaluation is much more difficult, because one cannot so readily set up a standard of what normal physiology or behavior is on the basis of a statistical sample or in some similar objective fashion. Good performance of an economy is a prescriptive, not descriptive, matter, and it depends, therefore, upon the standard of performance adopted by the observer. Because Soviet and Western economists do not accept identical ends for economic activity, our evaluations of Soviet economic performance must also differ if each insists upon his or her own as the only standard. Unlike our characterization of the Soviet economy as a system, the purpose or end of economic activity is not a question that can be determined empirically as a general proposition. We ought, therefore, to temper our evaluation of the performance of the Soviet economy with consideration of evaluations that flow from standards held by members of the Soviet economy— consumers, managers, the military, the party, and so forth.

Our concern in what follows is, then, with presenting a more abstract picture of the important subsystems and institutions of the Soviet economy and with providing an evaluation of how well these subsystems, institutions, and the economy as a whole function.

A Macroeconomic Model of the Soviet Economy

It is an interesting exercise to begin with the kind of capitalist economic model that is presented in elementary and intermediate economics textbooks in the United States and to revise and tailor it to fit Soviet conditions. The fundamental model, as tailored to Soviet institutional arrangements, has been specified more fully elsewhere for the benefit of those who find mathematical formulation congenial.[1] Here I shall suppress the mathematical aspects as much as possible and focus primarily upon the essential features of and main inferences that can be drawn from the model. Those who find algebraic and functional notation inhibiting or disconcerting should still be able to follow the argument presented in the text, for I have made an effort to explain in words the content of each equation.

The standard macroeconomic demand submodel of a Western capitalist economy contains two statements. First, the various sectors of the economy are identified and put into a social accounting equation that expresses the fact that one sector's expenditures represent (simultaneously) the income of the other sector(s). Thus, the incomer (or product) of all sectors taken together (Y) is equal to their joint (deflated) expenditures:

$$Y = C + I + G. \tag{1}$$

We assume here that foreign trade can be neglected and exclude that sector from consideration. Our equation states, therefore, that the sum of real consumption outlays (C) by the household sector, of investment expenditures (I) of state and collective farm enterprises, and of government expenditures (G) on military and nonmilitary goods and services equals the real income of the economy (Y).

The second statement of the basic macroeconomic submodel expresses consumption (C) of the household sector as a positive function of disposable income (Y_d), which is the income that remains in the hands of members of the household sector after they have paid their taxes and/or received welfare or social security payments and other transfers from the government sector:

$$C = f(Y_d). \tag{2}$$

This basic two-equation model contains, therefore, a social accounting equation and a behavioral expression. (Technically, we have another equation which defines Y_d in terms of Y—e.g., $Y_d = Y +$ [social security benefits minus personal taxes].)

For any Western mixed economy we would go on from this basic model to attempt to explain investment expenditures (I) behaviorally, perhaps as a function of expected profits and the current rate of utilization of industrial capacity. The next step would be to attempt to explain government outlays by another behavioral equation. In the USSR, however, investment expenditure (I) is determined by Gosplan and the Council of Ministers in the planning process, and no one has yet proposed an explanation of the process that permits simple formulation, as for C in the consumption function. Government expenditure is determined similarly, although with the participation of *Gosbiudzhet* and certain political and military establishments. Because it is not clear just what the behavioral determinants might be, we are forced to treat these two components of the domestic products as fixed *exogenously,* which is a useful word behind which to screen our ignorance of the way they are in fact settled upon. Thus, we may rewrite our equation 1 to reflect this fact:

$$Y = C + I^* + G^*, \qquad (1^*)$$

in which the asterisk indicates determination outside the model.

Once we begin to reflect upon this equation in the light of central planning, however, we find ourselves in an awkward situation. The comprehensiveness and detailed character of Soviet planning means in this context that Gosplan is attempting to fix Y as well as I^* and G^* in advance of the start of the plan year. If Y is fixed as Y^*, however, then every variable in equation 1^* is determined, for consumption (C) must be equal to the difference: $Y^* - (I^* + G^*)$. That is, if consumption ($\hat{C}$) is determined as a residual, we have no need for equation 2 above, which explains C as a positive function of disposable personal income. We know that equation 1 is a true equation as a logical proposition, and empirical measurement bears it out as well.

There is no way out. If three of the variables in equation 1^* are determined by central planners, the fourth follows as a residual, and there is no need for an independent behavioral explanation of consumption expenditures.

For this reason Western scholars believed for many years that Western-type macromodels could be of no real analytic value in examining the Soviet economy. We know now, however, that this was a hasty opinion. It ought to be clear at this point that residual determination of the goods and services that are made available to households in the Soviet Union is unlikely as a general proposition. Household members in today's Soviet economy are not without direct means for influencing the division of product between investments and government expenditures, on the one hand, and personal consumption expenditures, on the other. A Politburo that is fearful of raising consumer goods prices and that is expending precious foreign exchange on fodder and meat for domestic consumption would have every reason to shun residual determination of consumption in practice, for it could only exacerbate the problem of deficit commodities.

The first obstacle that we confront in attempting to construct a basic macromodel for the Soviet economy is the possibility that the two most fundamental propositions of any macromodel, our equations 1 and 2 may contradict each other. That is

$$Y = \hat{C} + I^* + G^*, \qquad (1^*)$$

$$C + f(Y_d) \tag{2}$$

where Y_d, disposable income of households, is defined as above; the prefix f means it is dependent upon Y_d. $\hat{C}$ is residually determined consumption goods (that is, actual or planned). What happens if $\hat{C} \neq C$? Suppose, in other words, that households decide on the basis of disposable income (Y_d) to spend more than $\hat{C}$. Demand would exceed supply, and there is no obvious mechanism to assure us of equality or to set forces in motion to restore equality when demand exceeds (or is less than) supply. It would be imappropriate to introduce flexible prices to allow aggregate supply and demand for consumer goods to move toward equilibrium, because the price level is controlled and is inflexible in the USSR.

It has frequently been argued that most of the time demand does indeed exceed the supply of consumption goods in the USSR. Some analysts have argued, for example, that households taken as a group cannot spend all of their income and find themselves saving more of their disposable income than they want to save. If we let S_p represent real personal saving in any period, it is defined as $Y_d - \hat{C}$. That is, the increase in savings of households in savings accounts, bonds, and cash during the period equals the difference between disposable income and actual consumption. Unwanted, or "forced," savings (S_f) is defined by our equations, therefore, as:

$$S_f = C - \hat{C}.$$

The notion that households can be forced to save more than they want to save implies a premise of doubtful validity: that there is no way for households to evade the compulsion to save. Open labor markets and, to a limited extent only, the existence of certain *nalevo* markets and channels both represent possible avenues through which households may avoid the compulsion to save.

In order to examine the question of forced saving more closely, let us look more closely at the aggregate labor market. As indicated in our discussion above of the Soviet labor market, pressure is put on individuals, particularly upon able-bodied men and women of working age, to participate in the labor force. Labor is not conscripted, however, and there are many individuals currently engaged in economic employments who are free to withdraw from the labor market, or to withdraw efficiency from their employments, if they wish. Consequently, we may reasonably assume that the supply of labor (N_s) in the Soviet economy is, at least in large part, a positive function of the real wage (W/P), in which W is money wages and P is a price index which reduces W to real purchasing power. In order to make

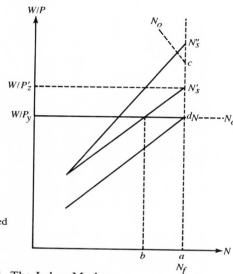

FIGURE 1. The Labor Market

where:
W/P = real wage
N = aggregate employment
N_f = administratively determined
full employment

the possible influence of forced saving explicit, let us assume that the amount of accumulated savings (M) has a negative influence on the willingness of individuals to work and/or to work intensively. That is, as unspent savings accumulate at a rate in excess of the desire of households to save, they find it convenient to reduce the family's formal work effort in order, for example, to spend more time in queues, or merely to spend time enjoying what income they have in leisure at the dacha. Our labor supply functions may be expressed, therefore, by:

$$N_s = N_s(W/P, M/P), \tag{3}$$

in which we must reduce accumulated savings to its real purchasing power by means of an appropriate price index (P).

It follows from equation 3 that a persistent discrepancy between the consumption households desire ($\hat{C}$) will cause the total amount of labor effort available to diminish, other things being equal. Labor supply curve N_s in figure 1 would shift to the left, say N_s', requiring an increase in real wages (from y to z) to maintain any current volume of employment. Otherwise employment would fall, for example, to b from a.

Representation of the aggregate demand for labor equation is complicated, but must describe it in order to determine the volume of actual employment at any given time. Doing so brings us back to the problem we found with respect to residual determination of consumption expenditures. As far as enterprise managers are concerned, their demand for labor is likely to be highly inelastic. That is, little or no penalty exists for having redundant labor. There are always times of the year, such as just before the plan period ends, when extra personnel are useful to have around. Moreover, managers cannot readily fire employees. Consequently, managers are not likely to be concerned about the real wages they must pay so long as funds are provided in the plan. But it is clear in any case that managers as a group are not in a position to determine the real wage of the aggregate labor force. If the central plan determines $\hat{C}$, then the most that any manager can do is to increase the real wages of particular employees by advancing them in rank or through bonuses. If other managers follow suit, the result will be a general advance in money wages unaccompanied by any increase in $\hat{C}$. This is why wage payments are closely monitored by Gosbank. Competition among managers for labor is regarded as primarily inflationary. (Of course, if raising wages leads to higher productivity or is taxed away elsewhere in the system, then the whole increase is not necessarily inflationary.)

Central planners face a dilemma, therefore. If they determine $\hat{C}$ as a residual, this, in turn, determines the real wage and thus employment too. If this level of the real wage is too low to maintain total employment, total output (Y) must fall, for it is clearly a direct positive function of employment N:

$$Y = Y(N, \overline{K}), \tag{4}$$

in which N is total employment and $\overline{K}$ is the capital stock (which is fixed in the short run). If Y falls, $\hat{C}$ will fall still further, unless Gosplan is prepared to reduce I and/or G in compensation.

The model shows that, given I^* and G^*, central planners can set *either Y or C, but not both.* The model reveals that "forced saving" ultimately requires "forced labor." It is obvious from figure 1, for example, that planners would set W/P, the real wage, at will if and only if they have first fixed employment. So long as workers are free to withdraw labor or efficiency from the market, it is not possible for the central plan to determine arbitrarily the consumer goods and services to be made available, because workers are in a position to retaliate by reducing total income Y. It follows that the determination of I and/or G must involve an adjustment to the real wages that workers demand to produce any given level of income Y.

The open labor market is only one avenue by which workers can influence the actual amount of consumer goods and services that they receive. In the first place, demand for additional commodities and services may call forth an additional labor effort outside of the state sector (we must exclude competition with it, or mere transfers of commodities and services between them, in this instance) that would not otherwise be forthcoming. Individuals may produce new goods and services not accounted for in $\hat{C}$, and this is one of the ways in which private legal and illegal markets supplement state economic activity. In the second place, many individuals can convert goods destined for I or G into de facto consumer goods. A hunting lodge built with military funds for the Soviet general staff may be used extensively by civilian relatives. Government cars may be used to taxi private individuals, and gasoline may be siphoned from public vehicles into private ones. Materials may be pilfered from construction sites for private construction, and so on. The actual distribution of final goods and services between government (G), enterprise capital accounts (I), and private consumers (C) may, therefore, differ significantly from official records. A discrepancy between desired consumption (C) and planned consumption ($\hat{C}$) invites this kind of illegal conversion of public property into private consumption for private gain in the USSR.

Because households do have ways to influence their own real wages, it seems reasonable to conceive of the determination of total employment as a supply and demand adjustment, but we need to add one more proposition to illustrate how this might occur. As we have seen, managers are in a position to influence only relative wages of their employees. The real wage for all workers taken together is determined elsewhere. The labor demand function must reflect the following influences. Since it has ordinarily been the primary goal of planners to maximize output (subject to certain constraints we shall here neglect), let us assume that overcommitment planning is base upon an attempt to pick an employment level that matches or overcommits full employment (N_f). Presumably, central planners are also conscious of the trade-off we have just specified between the real wage and the other components of national income. Let us write the labor demand equation as

$$N_d = N_d (W/P, N_f), \tag{5}$$

where N_f is full employment and is defined as the point at which the supply of labor becomes completely inelastic (insensitive) to further increases in the real wage (fig. 1, point c). We assume, therefore, that within a reasonably wide range (say, below point c in fig. 1), Gosplan sets the real wage to correspond to full employment (N_f). At some point, of course, as W/P increases for a given definition of N_f, state demand for labor would presumably become elastic. This point is given by c, beyond which demand is elastic and one would expect the usual type of supply and demand intersection.

Equation 4, which is a production function relating the input requirements to each level of output, and equations 3 and 5, the aggregate supply and demand for labor functions, from the aggregate supply submodel. Between them they determine the real wage, W/P; employment, N; and the level of real output, Y. Equations 1 and 2 above compose a demand submodel, but, as we have seen, we need to treat their investment or government expenditures or both as residually determined. Let us assume that investment has priority and is fixed by Gosplan, which gives us the equation:

$$I = I^*. \tag{6}$$

The model now determines the following variables: C, I, G, Y, N, and W/P. (We have another equation, of course, which determines disposable income, Y_d.)

The model also incorporates M, the sum of cash balances and savings deposits held by households at the beginning of the year. The capital stock, $\overline{K}$, in equation 4 is determined exogenously as a carryover variable determined at the beginning of the year; and full employment, N_f, is determined administratively. One more exogenous variable, the price index, P, needs to be specified, and, for simplicity of analysis, we shall assume that it is a policy variable set by the various state committees on retail and wholesale prices. We shall return to discuss the reasonableness of this assumption subsequently.

Although complex, the model yields an insight that was not previously obvious. Consumption goods and services made available by Gosplan cannot be set at just any level above subsistence. Quite apart from any political or other noneconomic retaliation that might follow from arbitrary determination of $\hat{C}$, the open labor market provides an avenue for direct economic response. It is nonsense, for example, to speak as though Soviet households cannot find enough goods and services to spend their incomes on—at least as long as any significant fraction of the labor force is free to withdraw time or efficiency from state employments. The notion of a command economy implies, ultimately, conscription of labor. This military analogy is misleading for the contemporary Soviet economy precisely because most military systems have been founded on the principle of conscription. Although the labor market is only one market, it is a large market that ramifies into all branches of the Soviet economy. Gosplan must come to terms with it or return to some brand of Stalinism.

Macroeconomic Policy in the USSR

Before the basic model can be used to analyze macroeconomic policy and to compare Soviet and Western macroeconomic tactics, one more modification is necessary. The amount of private consumption was originally made dependent solely upon real disposable income:

$$Y_d = Y - \frac{X}{P} + \frac{(U - T)}{P}.$$

In this equation, X is the proportion of total income deducted as profits and taxes from state enterprises, and $U - T$ is the net flow of transfers to and from the household sector in the way of welfare payments, pensions, and personal taxes. Exogenous variables X, U, and T are policy variables, like P, in that the *Gosbiudzhet,* the Council of Ministers, and Gosplan may set them to effect specific policy objectives. Given P, increases in U work to increase Y_d, and conversely for increases in T and X. Even with this specified we are missing an important element from our model: the role of monetary policy. The easiest way to add it is in the consumption function, so let us revise equation 2 to read:

$$C = f(Y_d, r), \tag{2*}$$

in which r is the rate of interest paid by Gosbank on private savings accounts. The question addressed by the addition is whether the rate of private saving is affected positively by the rate of interest. If so, a shortfall in the amount of consumer goods made available could be compensated by a rise in the rate of interest paid on the (extra) savings, thereby circumventing adverse effects of forced saving upon the volume of employment and the level of total output. We assume that the rate of interest, r, is set exogenously and that it is adjusted for inflation.

With this modification of the model we can now examine macroeconomic policy in the Soviet Union.

Overly ambitious planning in the Soviet Union leads to the overcommitment of all resources and to chronic supply shortages in all sectors. Excess aggregate demand appears to be as chronic a feature of the Soviet economy as is insufficient aggregate demand for most Western capitalist economies. One obvious remedy would be for Gosplan to decrease the demand of the sectors it controls directly. Investment and government expenditures could be reallocated with the aim of apportioning the potential full-employment national product in such a way that aggregate demand and supply reach equilibrium at the given aggregate supply price (P). This would be the equivalent of fiscal policy in which variations in government expenditures are used in a country like the United States to stimulate or to retard aggregate demand. Thus far, however, the Soviet government has been reluctant to reduce investment expenditures. Until quite recently the share of investment in Soviet national income has been increasing, and the declining rate of growth in national income of the last decade or so makes Gosplan understandably reluctant to reduce the share of I in GNP.

Military outlays present another kind of problem, mainly because they depend as much upon the evaluation of external factors as upon domestic ones and because, in any case, Gosplan has no expertise to evaluate them. Some Western observers have read into the Soviet Union's recent interest in détente a desire to reduce the relative significance of military expenditures and therefore the conflict with direct consumer purchases of final goods and services. Others have pointed out, on the contrary, that military expenditures are also increasing rapidly. Let us assume the reduction in the share of $I + G$ is the least desirable alternative for planners and those they serve, and let us examine the alternatives for bringing aggregate supply and demand into line with one another.

Price Policy

As we have seen, the overriding objective of state retail price policy has been to stabilize the aggregate price level. Incorrect relative price would be sufficient to explain the widespread queuing in the Soviet Union. It does not necessarily indicate that the *aggregate* price level (the weighted average of all prices) is too low. That political leaders are reluctant to change relative prices, however, is sufficient to militate against the kind of price flexibility required in a changing world to adjust aggregate supply to aggregate demand. Official price policy is not used to equate aggregate supply and demand. Unofficially, however, an excess of demand, whether originating in retail or in wholesale markets, should be reflected in an index of prices in the black market or in other *nalevo* markets. Unfortunately, we have insufficient data to construct a reliable price index of this sort. The best substitute we have is an index for the private *rynok* (any free market), which indicates relative aggregate price stability. This market carries such a small and selected volume of commodities, however, that it probably cannot be used to measure discrepancies in aggregate supply and demand.

Soviet planners are not able, or willing, to use prices to adjust aggregate supply and demand for consumer goods. Were they to do so, however, there is no reason to suppose that it could satisfactorily adjust a discrepancy between supply and demand for consumer goods. Raising all prices on consumer goods would only make apparent what most workers would already know; that the current real wage is less than the money wage. Unless they fail to think in terms of the real purchasing power of their incomes, income earners would see a general rise in prices as a decrease in unspent cash balances, but no change in what can actually be bought. There would, of course, be a redistiribution of income favoring some at the expense of others as a result of the elimination of certain black market and *nalevo* transactions, but this would only occur if relative prices are changed appropriately, and it has little to do with the aggregate price level. There is no reason to suppose that relative price adjustment would cause the labor supply function to shift one way or another, but they might cause considerable political opposition from those who lose real income in the process.

Besides the political problem of readjusting real income to a new situation of relative prices, there is another good reason why Soviet planners and politicians might be reluctant to use retail prices as a means to bring aggregate demand and supply for consumer goods into equilibrium. An increase in the general price level, P, which occasioned an expectation of further increases might very well aggravate the situation in the current period by inducing households to spend now rather than later. The general expectation of shortages is likely to be a self-fulfilling and self-perpetuating expectation, for there is no point in accumulating cash and savings accounts if inflation is expected to erode their purchasing power significantly. In the long run, therefore, it may very well be preferable policy from the standpoint of Gosplan and the Politburo to promote popular expectation of aggregate price-level stability rather than the reverse in order to validate and thus encourage private, voluntary saving. (Price increases do occur in the USSR but surreptitiously, through, for example, the introduction of new labels and/or slightly modified products at higher prices and the subsequent disappearance, or substantial reduction in output, of older lower-priced varieties and brands.)

Thus, although price policy leaves much to criticize from the vantage point of the relative prices of consumer (and other) goods and services, it is not necessarily unreasonable for policymakers to shun price-level changes when a gap in consumption $(C - \hat{C})$ is expected to persist for any considerable period. A sudden general rise in prices sufficient to equate aggregate supply and demand might well prove politically hazardous. A slow gradual rise might well prove economically counterproductive through its impact on expectations. Aggregates of markets do not ordinarily work the same way that individual markets do. The experience of simultaneously rising prices and rates of unemployment in most Western capitalist countries over the last decade offers scant ground for criticism of Soviet reluctance to use general rises in prices as an instrument of policy.

Interest Rate and Monetary Policy

Interest rates paid on private savings accounts are very low and stable in the USSR. Most accounts receive 2 to 2.67 percent per annum simple interest. This rate clearly has no bearing on investment decisions. The low and constant level of interest rates paid on household savings are good indications that they are not used to influence consumption and saving. The interest rate, r, is included in equation 2* because Western economists believe that it may have some influence on the decision to save. Confirmatory evidence is scant, even in the West, and Soviet policy certainly operates on the assumption that higher rates would not encourage additonal saving. Even if we assume that Gosplan can in fact determine $\hat{C}$ as a residual, independently of the labor market, neglect of the rate of interest would be unreasonable if some higher rate would help to provide an outlet for disposable income. Similarly, if employment and the real wage are really determined in the labor market, then an experiment with higher interest rates on private savings would seem well worthwhile. Failure to try out higher and more flexible rates of interest can only be interpreted as irrational.

Here, as in other ways, Soviet financial policy appears backward and excessively conservative to any Western economist. Interest charges on short- and long-term borrowing by state and collective enterprises are too low to encourage managers to conserve scarce capital. These charges are instead intended to defray the cost of providing and servicing loan accounts. The main function of enterprise borrowing from the standpoint of Gosbank is to provide a means of controlling their expenditures and monitoring plan performance. Interest-paying private accounts appear to have significance only as a way to monitor private saving.

Until 1957 households could buy state bonds, but over the years the purchase of state bonds had become as compulsory as personal taxes, and they were abolished for this reason. Thus, there are few instruments available for personal saving today. Consequently, interest rate policy is a particularly neglected aspect of Soviet economic policy generally, and it is therefore an area in which one should expect changes if reforms of economic policy continue. It is senseless to allow an otherwise effective instrument of policy to fall into desuetude, especially when existing instruments are inadequate to the tasks set for them. The constraint on more rational use of interest rates is doubtless ideological in origin, but inertia probably has more to do with its neglect today than ideology.

Monetary policy, in the usual Western sense of the term, simply does not exist at the aggregate level in the USSR. Monetary policy is inextricably linked to interest rate policy in Western economies, but these interest rates are not used in the USSR to influence changes in the stock of money or to allocate investment funds. Monetary policy is directed primarily to the needs of trade, and investment decisions are made without regard to raising funds. All consequential policies regarding the flow of money and other funds are micro-economic in character rather than macroeconomic. There is no reason to attempt to influence the level of output or employment through monetary policy. This is not to say that monetary policy is unimportant. On the contrary, banks directly supervise enterprise expenditures, especially outlays on wages and salaries; and this plays an essential role in preventing competition among enterprise managers for scarce skilled labor from causing an unplanned upward drift in money wages. These controls were weak during the 1930s, and wage inflation led to considerable inflation in retail prices. Gosbank also plays an important role by monitoring short-term borrowing by enterprises and thereby constraining their deficit spending to planned totals or to proportional increases (where plans are over-fulfilled).

Fiscal Policy

We have already considered the spending side of fiscal policy. Thus far the state budget, which finances most investment as well as all govenment expenditures, has not been called upon to manipulate expenditures or transfer payments (to enterprises) as a means of achieving equilibrium between aggregate supply and demand. Our simple model does not contain the state budget explicitly. We can readily add it, however, as a budget equation:

$$G + I = \frac{X + (T - U) + Z}{P}, \tag{7}$$

in which X represents tax and profit receipts, $(T - U)$ is net receipts (or payments) to the household sector, and Z is the surplus or deficit for the *Gosbiudzhet* as a whole. The budget normally runs a surplus at the present time. Deficits were common during the 1930s and 1940s, however. The main thrust of fiscal policy in recent years, therefore, has been to ensure that the various state agencies do not add unplanned demand, thereby exacerbating the chronic condition of excess demand existing in the economy.

Our macroeconomic model suggests that excess aggregate demand could be reduced by increasing personal income taxes (thereby reducing Y_d, disposable income, in equation 2*. Western economic theory holds that any kind of personal income tax, especially a progressive income tax, is bound to affect adversely incentives and thus efficiency. An increase in personal taxes, plus the application of a progressive principle, could be expected to have a negative effect on incentives to work which would be analogous to the effect produced by the accumulation of unwanted real-cash balances (M/P) in equation 2*. Thus, what is gained by reducing M/P would be lost by the decrease in employment. The conclusion is inescapable formally, but empirical experience in Western economies suggests that tax rates can be much higher than they are in the USSR and much more progressive before significant negative incentive effects come into play. Direct personal taxes are, therefore, underutilized by comparison with the West. Instead, indirect taxation and retained profits of state enterprises are relied upon for government revenue.

Examination of macroeconomic issues and policy under chronic excess demand conditions reveals several insights. The Soviet economy suffers from chronic excess of aggregate demand. In many respects the symptoms are reciprocal images of the symptoms many Western capitalist countries display as a result of a tendency to chronic deficiency of aggregate demand. Faced with persistent supply insecurity, enterprises and individuals alike seek to ensure a steady supply of deficit commodities by concentrating attention and resources on purchasing or otherwise acquiring goods. The sales effort of enterprises or individuals is of no real consequence. Persistent excess demand of this sort would generate relatively rapid and serious price and wage inflation in the absence of price and wage controls, but continous application of such controls leads to undesirable side effects in the form of black market operations, barter exchange, or privileges and special opportunities, and a general erosion in popular respect for legal restrictions on trading, prices, and individual enterprise.

Because the central plan seeks to specify all macroeconomic, as well as microeconomic, flows of goods, services, and money in the economy, macroeconomic instruments that are commonly used in Western capitalist economies are neglected in the Soviet Union. Tax rates are not systematically adjusted to constrain or to increase consumer demand in the short run. Monetary policy is not used to influence employment, investment, or the price level in any usual sense. Bank policy is important as a means of controlling enterprise expenditures and pegging them to plan targets, and it is important as a means of keeping track of household saving. These two policies have significant anti-inflationary implications. Gosbank, however, is not free to change the tightness of bank loan policy generally in order to effect any particular macroeconomic end. Interest rates play an insignificant role in determining the rate of investment or the level of economic activity.

There seems to be no reason why interest rates paid to Soviet households ought not be increased substantially to test the possibility of a favorable effect upon saving rates. Progressive taxes on personal income might also be used experimentally to ascertain the response of the public. As increases in the general level of prices are ruled out on political as well as on *reasonable* economic grounds as a way to equate aggregate supply and demand, it would appear to be irrational to neglect these other macroeconomic instruments. The alternative is to reduce the share of $(I + G)$ and/or to increase net imports to reduce the gap between desired consumption (C) at current real wage rates and available supplies $(\hat{C})$. The alternative must be persistent conflict between households and planners that can be resolved in one of two ways. Either Gosplan and the decision-makers it represents will lose and be obliged to reduce the share of $(G + I)$ in order to maintain a reasonable rate of growth of factor productivity and thus of national income and product, or controls and restrictions on labor will have to be introduced that will necessitate a return to a form of Stalinism.

NOTE

1. See James R. Millar and Joyce Pickersgill, "Aggregate Economic Problems in Soviet-Type Economies," *ACES Bulletin* 19, no. 1 (Spring 1977).

12

The Soviet Household Sector: The View from the Bottom

A Methodological Note

Most Western economists assume that the purpose of economic activity is to satisfy individual members of society, and Soviet economists are no exception to this rule. N. Ia Petrakov, a well-known Soviet economist, defined the aim recently as "maximization of the average level of satisfaction of the needs of all members of society." Placement of the individual consumer at the center of the economic universe represents a prescriptive rather than a descriptive judgment, and I concur in the desirability of this view. From a descriptive standpoint, however, several other possible ways of construing ends and means in an economic system exist, and each approach presents certain advantages and disadvantages for analysis.

If we assume that satisfaction of the wants of the individual is the sole and proper end of all economic activity, then we shall find it difficult to justify certain kinds of government expenditures that we all take for granted, such as defense expenditures, welfare outlays, and the like, where benefits and costs are not distributed according to the individual's evaluations. Moreover, our analysis cannot deal satisfactorily with a situation in which one individual's satisfaction depends upon another's fortune or misfortune. We must assume away both envy and saintliness.

Karl Marx assumed that all-round physical and intellectual fulfillment of the individual would become the goal of economic activity under socialism, at which time the creation of economic plenty would have undermined self-interest as motive to economic activity and thus the rationale for both envy and saintliness. He

From *The ABCs of Soviet Socialism,* James R. Millar (Urbana: University of Illinois Press, 1981), pp. 83–120. Originally titled "The Household Sector: The View from the Bottom." Reprinted by permission, with minor editorial changes and omission of "selected readings."

assumed that profit would be the goal of economic activity while capitalism prevailed, and he accordingly described the capitalist economy as based upon the exploitation of the many by the few in the quest for profits. The consumer is not, therefore, the end for capitalist economies in Marx's analysis. Similar assumptions have been, and are still, often made by non-Marxists as well, particularly by certain social reformers such as consumer advocates or environmental protectionists who see a conflict between the interests of ordinary people and those of giant corporation in quest of profits. Although this assumption often offers an interesting construction for thinking about the economy, it also presents problems from an analytic standpoint. Marx, for example, never did explain why capitalists were devoted to the maximization of profits, nor how they could remain blind to a growing conflict of their interests with those of workers and consumers that would, in his view, ultimately eject capitalists from the system. Marx also failed to explain what kinds of motives would ensure satisfactory production of goods and services for use rather than for profits in a system in which distribution would be according to need.

Thorstein Veblen drew a different distinction—between productive and pecuniary employments—by which he attempted to divide economic activities into those that serve matter-of-fact *real* human needs and those that serve meretricious needs derived from ignorance, gullibility, or propaganda. Hence, he adopted the assumption that individual consumers *ought* to be the goal of economic activity, but he tried to constrain their needs to a rational, scientifically based set of requirments. Veblen would have restricted economic activities to those that involve providing socially acceptable goods or services. In this respect he sought to combine the best features of both the neoclassical and Marxian approaches. The problem remains, of course, in distinguishing unambiguously between the good and bad products. Veblen thought that this distinction would be resolved by a natural process of scientific enlightenment, but it is clear some sixty years later that this was too optimistic a view.

I have reviewed these various assumptions about what the goal of economic activity ought to be in order to emphasize the evaluative and thus the relative nature of any such assumption. Many Western students of the Soviet economy have sought to describe it as an economy in which planners' preferences prevail. That is, they assume that the purpose of economic activity is to satisfy those who plan the economic system. The term "planner" is used here is what is ultimately a political and not at all an operational sense. The Politburo, not Gosplan, represents the planners in question. This assumption, like the others I have mentioned above, has certain advantages when it comes to describing central planning, especially where it is conceived as command planning. There are other advantages that make it attractive when describing the Soviet economy, where economic goals are at once also high political issues. Even so, as with any such assumption, it is not a purely descriptive concept. It was derived as the obverse of a system of consumer preferences, and no analyst has ever put it forward anywhere as a *desirable long-term basis* for organizing economic activity. Instead, it is a pejorative standard, and for good reason. Although never fully worked out, it would appear that an economy organized strictly according to the principal of planners' preferences would ultimately have to be an economy in which everyone who is not a planner would be a slave— or perhaps a mindless contributor to economic activity, like a worker bee or ant.

We shall have recourse to all of the standards I have described in considering the place of the household in the Soviet economy. We shall see that there is more than a grain of truth in the claim of contemporary Soviet economists that individual satisfaction is the aim of economic activity, and it is useful in any case to assess the discrepancies between such a standard and Soviet reality. Similarly, it will be informative to see to what extent the Soviet economy departs from the standard of planners' preferences and to try to understand how consumer and planner preferences are in fact mediated. We shall also find the standards erected by Veblen and by Marx useful alternative measures. As everywhere, it is not always easy to distinguish "goods" from "bads" when it comes to the products of the Soviet or any other economy, and the contrast that Marx drew between capitalism and socialism is helpful because it raises two fundamental and yet unresolved problems in the economics of distribution and the ethics of human conduct. If distribution of the products of economic activity is to be set according to need, how can this be reconciled with the demand that any incentive system, to be effective, must reward individuals according to their contributions? But if individuals are instead to be rewarded strictly according to their contributions to the economy, what do we do with the helpless? Moreover, do we not thereby also reinforce "lower" rather than "higher" forms of human conduct, thus sacrificing saintliness and enhancing invidious comparisons, envy, and unabashed self-interest? Are self-regard and greed the only workable bases of economic activity?

The View from the Bottom

By describing households as the bottom of the Soviet economy, I mean to contrast the perspective of a single household with that of an agency such as the Council of Ministers or Gosplan, not to indicate the ranking of the household. Individual households look out upon the economy from narrow and highly differentiated windows. The view from the bottom is a collection of views, and we shall build up a reasonably comprehensive and representative general view from the separate standpoints of various households. Although no one household has as broad a view as members of an agency such as the Council of Ministers, there are aspects of household experience that are not visible from the top. The view from the top is not better nor more complex than the view from the bottom. It is merely different.

Over 55 percent of the Soviet population now lives in regions classified as urban, but this is a recent development and a large proportion of the urban population of the USSR is first-generation urban. Approximately 25 percent of the labor force is still directly engaged in agircultural pursuits in the Soviet Union, as opposed to less than 4 percent in the United States. The exodus from the rural community has been exceedingly rapid during the last decade, averaging about 2 million persons per year. This rapid outflow from the rural sector reflects the great differential that exists between standards of living in rural and in urban areas of the USSR, and the outflow is impoverishing the rural community because the young, the energetic, the educated, and the ambitious are the ones who are leaving.

By comparison with the United States or the countries of Western Europe such as France, Italy, or Germany, the USSR is still highly rural in character and is experiencing rapid demographic change. Moreover, the gap between living conditions and professional prospects in rural and urban areas is much greater than in the West. The USSR occupies a very large area, equal to about one-sixth of the surface of the earth. By world standards it is still lightly populated. Population tends to be concentrated in European Russia, but even this is a large region and population density is low by comparison with most developed economies. The transportation network is huge when measured in total kilometers. Densities remain relatively low, however, especially in the vast reaches of Siberia and Central Asia. Consequently, the isolation of rural communities is far greater than in the West, and the absence of any significant number of private automobiles or trucks in rural areas is a contributing factor to their isolation. There is no equivalent in the USSR to the pickup truck of the American farm to take the family into town on weekends. There are some regions so remote, in fact, that there is virtually no exit for months at a time during the winter. Television reaches most of these communities, but its message is the superiority of urban life, especially urban life in the choice cities of the USSR: Moscow, Leningrad, Kiev.

Not just anyone may decide to live in a city. In order to obtain an apartment or room in a Soviet city, the individual must ordinarily be employed in the city, but it is hard to find employment unless one already lives in the city. If an individual wishes to live in Moscow, for example, he or she could sign up with the labor exchange and take a chance on being assigned to Moscow. No sane person would expect so far-fetched a hope to come true. Moscow is the most difficult city of all to move to permanently. Successful provincial administrators and party officials often are assigned to Moscow in the twilight years of their careers as a special sign of preferment and as a reward for faithful service, but ordinary folk are assigned to the regions and cities that are slated for net growth, not to Moscow. Restrictions on movement to desirable cities such as Moscow can be circumvented, but essentially only by exceptional professional success, subterfuge, or *blat*. *Blat* is probably the most important. *Blat* is used by Russians to refer to pull, connections, or string-pulling that is used to advance one's own or one's family's interests. (The polite word for *blat* is *protektsiia* [protection].)

There is a hierarchy of living conditions in the Soviet Union, with Moscow at the pinnacle and the remote villages of Siberia and Central Asia at the bottom. The upward slope measures more than access to cultural events such as the Bolshoi Ballet or the Mayakovsky Theater. Moscovites live at the center of political power, which acts as a magnet for all of the good things in Soviet life. Food supplies are more reliable and abundant in Moscow than elsewhere. Industrial commodities designed for consumers gravitate to Moscow. Housing is superior; the provision of child-care centers is more adequate; and so it goes.

Since Moscow is the political hub of a highly centralized bureaucracy, it is the best place to get things done. Moscow is the city of *blat,* an artificial city reflecting the best and the worst in the USSR. People who live elsewhere in the USSR must make periodic trips to this political and economic mecca of the Soviet system to have petitions heard, to meet with superiors, to buy commodities available nowhere else, and to vacation richly. Peasants come to Moscow from the outlying regions with their bags packed with fruit, vegetables, honey, and anything else that can be sold on the *rynok* (private market). After selling everything, they go to see Lenin's remains in Red Square. Then they spend in Moscow everything they earned at the *rynok,* buying things for themselves and their friends. They return home with their bags packed with clothing, toys, rugs, china, meat, and phonograph records. Although the details differ, a similar pattern obtains for everyone who lives outside the gates of Moscow and the other major urban centers of the USSR.

We shall begin our examination of the household sector in Moscow and work our way back along the slope down to the muddy lanes of a Siberian village. Along the way we shall need to consider differentiating factors other than urban location. National and ethnic differences, the place of women, and other factors need to be evaluated as well. Moscow is unique in many such respects, and we must bear this in mind in considering the view from the Moscovite window.

Private Enterprise and Property

The institution of private property exists in the Soviet Union, but it is circumscribed by state (public) ownership of the "means of production," which are defined to include all land, mineral wealth, and most of the reproducible capital. Private individuals may own, and are free to sell privately or through state stores that sell on commission, a wide range of items of personal property. These include not only articles of clothing, television sets, refrigerators, and other personal effects but also certain types of capital equipment such as hand tools, typewriters, gardening supplies, and the like, plus such large items of nonproductive capital as automobiles, apartments, and houses. Moreover, certain attributes of private property adhere to some forms of state property in that the right to use the property can in fact be alienated and transferred to another private party for personal gain. Families, may, for example, trade state-owned apartments with each other for mutual benefit. A newly formed family, for example, where wife and husband are legally entitled to and already hold two separate one-room apartments, may trade these for a two- or three-room apartment that houses two families. Similarly a state-owned apartment located in a desirable city such as Moscow may be traded for an apartment in a less-desirable city, plus "considerations."

Buying, selling, and trading of personal property is a perfectly legal and open activity either through state "commission" outlets or directly. Certain locations in each city have become trading centers where advertisements are posted and meetings are arranged for purposes of direct trading. The owner of the property, or the property right, is free to charge what the market will bear, without government interference. Legal marketing, of course, shades imperceptibly into illegal trading. Certain types of transactions are proscribed, such as the exchange of rubles for foreign currency. It is also illegal to serve as a middleman in private transactions. That is, one may not legally purchase goods for the purpose of reselling them for personal gain. The deciding factor is intent, because a large number of such private transactions do in fact take place at a profit to the seller. It is also illegal to purchase an apartment or an automobile for the purpose of leasing it or otherwise using it as a source of income.

Although no private individual may own land in the Soviet Union, every citizen who is in good legal standing is provided with access through one avenue or another to land for private use. Collective farm workers receive a plot of land on which to build a home and to maintain a kitchen garden as a function of satisfactory work on the collective farm. The legal situation for state farm workers is different, but actual arrangements are essentially the same as for collective farm workers. The great bulk of privately produced and privately marketed food products derives from these two types of private plot agriculture. Rural households not engaged directly in agricultural employments, such as the local schoolteacher or a clerk in a consumer cooperative (rural) outlet, are provided access to plots of land on which to build homes, to keep animals, and to tend gardens. Urban dwellers are also provided access to small plots of land on the outskirts of town, where they may build a dacha and keep a garden. Because the location is not ordinarily convenient, city dwellers rarely build substantial dwellings on the plots. They are used instead to build dachas as summer and/or winter retreats, and most of them are primitive and have few modern conveniences. Ownership of free-standing homes is, therefore, primarily a rural and primitive phenomenon. Similarly, few urban dwellers use their plots to raise substantial gardens.

The ways in which urban dwellers gain access to plots of land are complex and varied, and the size of the plot to which individuals are entitled varies by type of access. A worker may obtain a plot of land through the enterprise for which he or she works. A military officer ordinarily receives a plot through the military bureaucracy. Individuals not otherwise covered may obtain plots of land through the city administration or through a cooperative arrangement, and so forth. Over one-half of the privately held plots of land in the Soviet Union today are held by members of the nonagricultural population.

It has become increasingly popular for individuals to build, or purchase, apartments under cooperative arrangements. Many co-operatives are organized by a place of work, such as the Academy of Sciences, Moscow State University, and Gosplan; and employees sign up to purchase from their employer. The usual arrangements call for a 20 percent down payment and the remainder in installments, frequently without interest. Apartments purchased in this way are expensive, but they offer the roomiest and most comfortable living quarters available in the major cities. A group of private individuals may also arrange to build a condominium and borrow a portion of the cost from the Gosbank. In this instance an interest charge is involved, normally 2 percent per annum. Apartment ownership affords the individual in the Soviet Union the largest and probably the most lucrative investment available for private ownership and potential gain. Individuals who purchase an apartment do not pay anything for the land on which the building sits, which is a considerable private benefit in any major city.

In addition to apartments, automobiles, and other consumer durables, individuals may purchase jewelry, paintings, rare books, and similar items as forms of private savings. Individuals may also own financial assets, which include hand-to-hand currency, savings accounts with the state bank, and state 3 percent lottery bonds. A type of checking account is now available to certain Soviet citizens, but it is of little domestic use in an economy in which almost all payments are made in cash. Apart from interest receipts on savings accounts and winnings on state lottery bonds, income from property is illegal in the Soviet Union. One may lend money to a friend, but charging interest would violate the law. Under certain circumstances one may receive something in consideration for subletting one's apartment or for renting a room (a "corner") to a student, but it is not legal to go into the business of taking boarders or renting out apartments.

All private wealth may be legally inherited in the Soviet Union. Survivors ordinarily have first claim on the family apartment or dacha, and in this respect certain aspects of private ownership attach to such publicly owned items.

All other property, with the sole exception of collective farms, whose members are supposed to have indivisible (that is, inalienable) rights in the farms' capital stock, is publicly owned in the Soviet Union. Therefore, the profits of state enterprises and rental payments of the population residing in state housing are paid into the various governmental budgets. The state claims all property income in the name of the people and uses income from it to finance investment in state enterprises and construction of new housing and other outlays.

Private enterprise is not actually prohibited, but it is severely limited by prohibitions on hiring others for personal profit, on middleman activities, on private ownership of the means of production. What private enterprise does exist is necessarily small-scale. The line between legal and illegal private enterprise is not an easy one to draw. Individuals may sell newly produced items that they or their families have produced—for example, on private plots; and they may sell "secondhand" items too. A writer may hire a typist to type his or her manuscripts; families may hire housekeepers and baby-sitters; and anyone may hire work to be done or repairs to be made around the house, even though such hiring may contribute to personal income by making the hirer more efficient or by freeing him or her to earn more money elsewhere. True private enterprise is restricted in the Soviet Union to the sale of products of private agricultural plots and one-person enterprises for home repairs or to such sideline activities as taking patients or clients after work. A large proportion of the latter two categories is conducted in the penumbra of the legal. Nevertheless, private enterprise is ubiquitous and significant in almost everyone's economic life.

Most Soviet citizens work for the state in one way or another for wages or salaries, and most older members of Soviet society receive pensions from the state. Although at one time an attempt was made to maximize the share of earnings that the worker received in direct nonmonetary benefits, this is no longer the case. Education is free, including higher education in which success in entrance examinations assures all successful applicants free access plus a stipend. Medical care is free too. Prescription drugs are highly subsidized, as are public transport and even the apartments that most urban dwellers rent from the state. Meals are served very cheaply both in schools and at places of work, and child-care facilities (when available) are provided essentially free. Even so, the bulk of the typical Soviet household's income is received in money, which necessarily implies the existence of retail outlets in which households may choose the way that their incomes are distributed among the various goods, services, and financial assets that are available. Hence we see the importance of urban retail markets in the USSR.

Urban Retail Markets

Urban consumers are served by four different types of retail markets. All urban areas are served by state retail outlets. The great bulk of urban household income is expended in these shops. Soviet marketing follows the general European pattern, and most state retail outlets specialize in particular types of products, such as fish, meat and dairy products, bread and confectionary items, clothing, drugs, paper supplies, and so forth. The supermarket and the discount house are found rarely in Moscow and a few other large cities. Most families shop every day in the assortment of stores in their neighborhoods, purchasing bread in one, milk and dairy products in another, meat in a third, and beer in a fourth. Before American-style retail marketing could become widespread even in Moscow, the average household would have to buy a larger refrigerator, and automobile ownership would have to quadruple. What supermarkets do exist in Moscow work poorly because crowds are too great. One must queue to enter various departments of the store, which defeats a main function of supermarketing. Household members would also have to become accustomed to eating food that is several days old, which would require both a revolution in Soviet packaging and a deterioration in the average citizen's tastes.

Prices are fixed for state retail outlets and are not subject to bargaining. Restaurants and hotels are all state retail enterprises, and uniform pricing frequently causes anomalies. For example, most meat markets do not grade the meat that they sell by cut. Butchers (who work only with meat axes) divide the meat into portions that are equally composed of good and poor sections of the animal. The flat two-ruble charge per kilo is "justified" in this way. If one knows the butcher, the effective price for "good" cuts may be very low. Similarly, prices on similar dishes are exactly the same in good restaurants as well as bad. Consequently, a meal in a good restaurant is a great bargain, and the same meal in a poor restaurant may be indigestible.

Two kinds of subsidies therefore obtain for many state retail outlets. Many food products are substantially underpriced and are directly subsidized by the state budget (for example, most meat products, especially beef). Underpricing tends to cause queuing for the products affected, not because people go hungry or do without adequate protein, but because at state-quoted prices, which retail outlets cannot vary, these goods are a great bargain. Uniform pricing and the restricted mobility of the typical Soviet customer causes customers of poorly run shops and restaurants to subsidize the well run. Because the better-managed shops cannot expand and compete with the poorly run, these differences tend to be self-perpetuating.

An experienced and energetic Soviet shopper learns where to shop for particular items in order to take advantage of peculiarities caused by uniform prices and variations in quality. The system rewards specialized knowledge, friendship, and reciprocity. Goods do not get distributed evenly, and as we have seen, the farther one lives from a major city the less likely that any desirable commodities will ever appear. Meat, including beef, is usually relatively plentiful in Moscow, but 200 kilometers away probably none is to be found most of the time. Moreover, goods are not distributed evenly within the confines of a city such as Moscow. For complex and little-understood reasons, certain shops tend to get better and more reliable supplies than others. A certain buffet in a dormitory, for example, may almost always have beer in stock, while regular retail outlets run dry for days at a time. State retail outlets also operate "casual" stands and kiosks for "surplus" items at irregular intervals. An alert shopper learns that certain corners frequently have temporary outlets where particularly desirable goods (such as oranges and apples in winter) are sold when available. By keeping an eye on these locations, remembering which stores nearly always have milk or beer or better meat, and by staying alert to the formation of a queue anywhere, a smart shopper can maximize the opportunities to procure what Soviets call "deficit commodities." The term is used to refer to goods or services that are in short supply all or most of the time. Although there are exceptions, deficit commodities are underpriced items in the state retail network, which causes excess demand to exist for them most of the time.

It pays to make friends with sellers in the USSR, for nearly all the desirable goods that are sold in Soviet state retail outlets are in deficit supply and require the exercise of purchasemanship, the technical equivalent of salesmanship in an economy such as that of the United States. A judicious gift may get deficit commodities set aside for you. Tickets to the Bolshoi Theater ballet performances, for example, ordinarily are impossible to obtain in any normal way from a ticket window in Moscow. They are all either ordered for tourists, high officials, and special purposes, or they are distributed under the counter. Soviet shoppers worth their salt develop networks of contacts among those who sell or distribute state retail products and services which allow them to jump the queue for deficit commodities. Frequently, the recipient of such a favor is not required to pay extra for it, but he or she incurs a reciprocal obligation for the future.

Most deficit commodities and services are goods and services provided through state retail outlets, and the individuals who market them can collect what economists call the "monopoly rents" on these scarce and underpriced items. That is, the employee is in a position to capture a part, or all, of the difference between the actual price established by the state committee on retail prices and the (higher) price that would be required to clear the market (that is, exactly match the number of buyers with the number of items available). For all intents and purposes this is a property right individuals acquire by default from the state and are able to exchange for the other deficit commodities they desire.

The second type of retail outlet is the *rynok* (or collective farm market). About one-third of the value of all retail food sales in the USSR flows through the *rynok,* which is a completely unfettered market where farmers and others who have grown or produced their own products may hire a stall (and refrigeration, if necessary) to sell them. Collective farms may ship their surplus produce to the *rynok* too. Every city has one or more such markets. Many are enclosed for operation during the winter. Typical products available are carrots, potatoes, pickled cucumbers, tomatoes, peppers and apples, pickled cabbage, honey, cheese and fermented dairy products, dried mushrooms, flowers, spices, seed, and fresh meat in wintertime; and the list includes more fruits and vegetables in summer. Prices are generally much higher on the *rynok* than in state retail stores, and one is free to haggle about price. Many Soviet shoppers visit the *rynok* at least once a week, even though it is more expensive than state outlets. Quality tends to be higher, and some items sold there are unavailable in other retail outlets. Anyone planning a dinner party would be certain to visit the *rynok* to buy a delicacy or two. The role of the *rynok* is probably less significant in Moscow than it is elsewhere as a source of staples such as potatoes, milk products, meat, and vegetables because these items are more readily available in state outlets. Even so, Moscovites are relatively wealthy and able to afford the high prices charged on the *rynok*. As a general proposition, it is fair to say that the *rynok* plays a pervasive role in the supply of food products to the Soviet household, and all would be poorer without it. Thus, strange as it seems, most Soviet households deal regularly in a perfectly legal free market for day-to-day needs.

The third type of retail market available to urban dwellers is a private, informal, and legal market in homemade and secondhand commodities, in apartments, and in certain personal services such as television repair and hairdressing. The state operates secondhand stores on a commission basis. In addition, certain corners have become customary trading sites, and individuals meet there at customary times, privately, to trade apartments and sell used automobiles, clothing, records, and the like. Much of this trade is barter, and some of the items that are traded, such as state-owned apartments, are not in fact the property of those trading them. Newspapers take advertisements for certain types of goods, and both formal and informal bulletin boards are used to place advertisements. In addition, certain individuals sell their labor services informally. Any person with a skill, such as repairing electrical equipment, may work on the side on his or her own time. Whether or not the activity is legal depends upon the nature of the service, the source of spare parts used, and the social implications. Unskilled women frequently do laundry for busy single men, and they may help in shopping, child care, and cooking on a strictly private basis.

This third category of legal informal marketing is difficult to identify uniquely, for it shades off into illegal economic activities, on the one side, and into legal state-organized secondhand markets, on the other. It is worth attempting to isolate this category because of the private and legal character of these transactions. It is important to grasp the volume and diversity of private economic transactions that take place in the USSR on a perfectly legal basis. These transactions are also absolutely unavoidable if the institution of private property in personal possessions is to have operational significance. Open exchange of private property is also important as a means for redistributing durable property from those who no longer require it to those who need it. As with garage sales in the United States, in the process everyone is made better off without anyone being harmed.

Illegal market transactions comprise the fourth and final type of retail market in the Soviet Union. This market is very complex and ranges from misdemeanors to very sinister economic dealings. Because these transactions are illegal, the outside observer can obtain only a very sketchy impression of them. The evidence suggests, however, that illegal trading at the level of misdemeanor is widespread. A large proportion of the Soviet urban population is implicated — at least on a petty level. Illegal transactions are described variously by Soviet citizens. Soviets talking of obtaining goods *nalevo* (on the left), *po znakomstvu* (through a contact), *na chernom rynke* (on the black market), and *po blatu* (through pull). Each describes an important aspect of this market. Buying *po znakomstvu* is perhaps the most common and least criminal of all. In many circumstances it is more improper than illegal. Normally, in this type of purchase no direct pecuniary gain is involved for the friend, who instead merely earns a reciprocal claim upon the purchaser. Purchases on the black market are ordinarily from private entrepreneurs who operate for a profit. *Blat,* on the other hand, can be accrued either by bribing someone or by being someone important with whom others seek to curry favor. The most colorful phrase, buying *nalevo,* is the most general: its meaning encompasses the entire range of illegal and semilegal activities, both in markets and outside of them, that are encouraged by the institutional and legal structure of the Soviet economy. (Although it may offend the ears of native speakers of Russian, for convenience I shall henceforward use *nalevo* as an adjective as well as an adverb.)

The most desirable consumer goods and services are in deficit supply most of the time in the Soviet economy, and yet prices on these deficit commodities are kept constant. Consequently, queues always develop when these commodities become available, and those who deal in them for the state cannot but be tempted to take advantage of their strategic monopolistic positions to increase their own incomes, to curry favor with superiors, or to benefit their friends. Oddly enough, then, the institutional structure of the Soviet economy actually fosters a large volume of petty trading, petty middleman activities, and petty private enterprise. Today, the Soviet Union is an acquisitive society, a nation of marketeers; and an enormous amount of time is absorbed in shopping, selling, trading, scouting, and queuing for deficit commodities.

Consumption and Living Standards

By the most careful Western estimates, consumption per capita has almost doubled since Stalin's death in 1953. The fact that deficit commodities remain numerous reflects both the incredibly low standard of living at the end of postwar reconstruction and the continuation of official policies that tend to perpetuate such deficits. In planning the volume of consumer goods and services to be made available, Gosplan must consider two aspects. First, it is obvious that the total value of consumer goods and services provided by the state must have *some* relationship to the quantity of labor the state intends to employ and the average earnings of these workers. Second, and more important, the more developed the society is, the proportions in which the different consumer goods are produced (that is, how many automobiles, refrigerators, and sewing machines, and how much meat, milk, and wool cloth to produce) must bear a definite relationship to the way in which consumers wish to distribute their incomes among them. The output of consumer goods has increased very sharply in the USSR over the last twenty-five years, but changes in the composition of output have not kept pace, perpetuating the existence of deficit commodities.

Prices in state retail outlets are set by a state committee of the Council of Ministers, and they reflect many factors other than supply and demand. Prices on many items of food, such as bread, meat, and milk, have been set below cost, whereas prices on certain scarce luxury goods are set relatively high, approximating supply-demand conditions. Therefore, willingness to stand in line becomes a factor in the distribution of many goods, and the final result is a distribution of goods and services that is probably more equal than the distribution of money income. To some extent this is deliberate policy, but it also reflects a policy of stability in retail prices that Soviet leaders have promised the population ever since Stalin died. Accordingly, apart from surreptitious price changes, mainly on nonessentials, retail prices have increased only marginally in more than two decades. The Soviet population clearly appreciates this policy, for it prevents the erosion of their savings by inflation; and this is particularly important in an economy in which installment payments and other forms of credit buying are not available to consumers.

The policy of price stability has had adverse effects, however. For many food products, notably meats and products of animal husbandry, retail price stability has led to massive subsidies by the state, for the real cost of producing agricultural products has been rising rapidly since 1953. Relative prices for industrial commodities and for agricultural products are completely unrealistic, therefore, and an adjustment is long overdue. Thus far, however, the political leaders have apparently felt that trading *nalevo* (that is, under the counter) and all that it implies is more acceptable than the adverse reaction they expect to increased prices. Eventually, however, an adjustment will have to be made between agricultural products and industrial products, and among individual food products as well.

In addition to a policy that fosters the persistence of deficit commodities, the system of state retail sales outlets is inadequate to the task of supplying the Soviet consumer. Space for retail sales is inadequate. Poor service has no effect upon the incomes of retail service workers, and inventories that cannot be sold do not have a serious impact upon incomes or incentives of those who work in retail outlets. There is little incentive to provide good service, therefore; and that many commodities remain in deficit supply makes service workers surly more often than not. Retail outlets cannot respond to their customers' preferences in any case but must retail what they receive. Their only room for maneuver is on an individual basis, which means *nalevo.*

The scarcity of the more-desirable consumer goods and services has become institutionalized officially as well as privately. Whereas the private response has been to expand activities *nalevo,* the official response has been to create special shops which permit selected people to avoid queuing for deficit commodities. These special groups include foreign tourists, correspondents, and diplomats, which is understandable in a country anxious to earn foreign exchange. But these groups include individuals in Soviet society who are rewarded through special access to stores that are well stocked and do not have queues. The temptation posed by the existence of deficit commodities, which produces trading *nalevo* privately, yields special stores, with curtained windows to screen out unwelcome eyes, for high-placed Communist party and government officials and for other successful people as well. The right to purchase deficit commodities in special stores or by special order is clearly a powerful incentive in the Soviet economy, and it certainly makes sense to exempt hardworking, highly placed officials from queuing with the population. Yet the persistence of deficit commodities is having a negative effect upon the fabric of Soviet life. The closest analogy in American history is perhaps Prohibition, when keeping the right hand from knowing what the left hand was doing became a national pastime, encouraged general contempt for the law, and facilitated the widespread development of organized crime. The great expansion of trading *nalevo* and of special stores in the Soviet Union during the last decade or so is undoubtedly not only contributing to similar developments but to widespread cynicism regarding the idealistic goals the regime so often and loudly proclaims.

As I already indicated, Moscow is an artificial city in many respects, particularly when it comes to retail trade. Moscow's retail network is larger and better supplied than elsewhere in the USSR. The state also operates a large number of special stores, most of them known as *berëozki,* where foreigners, and Soviets who somehow acquire foreign currency or are given special privileges for some official reason, may purchase goods not available elsewhere or may jump the queue on generally scarce items. Naturally, there is a good deal of leakage from these special stores into private markets, and foreign visitors and dwellers offer many additional opportunities to purchase foreign-made items, such as blue jeans, Persian coats, and the like, as well as for exchanging currency. *Nalevo* markets in Moscow are, therefore, also better stocked than elsewhere.

Because of these exceptional opportunities and because of the relative wealth of the city's population, Moscovites are better dressed, better housed, better fed, better entertained, and more sophisticated than Russians in other cities, although Leningraders would be reluctant to agree on all points. Moscovites are also probably more alienated than any comparable population in the USSR. Certainly, the city is a hotbed of dissidence. Nonetheless, what is true of Moscow is true in one degree or another for other parts of the USSR. The Soviet retail distribution system is sluggish and works only in fits and starts. The farther one gets from Moscow, the less effective it is, and the smaller the community to be served, the worse the service.

Even in Moscow, for example, oranges will suddenly flood the city in the middle of winter. Oranges will be seen being vended everywhere: in regular retail outlets, in dining halls, and on street corners by state retail clerks; and for two weeks there will be an orgy of orange sales and consumption. Just as suddenly as the sale began, it will end because the entire boatload from Egypt or Sicily will have been exhausted. Wise customers, knowing that sales will soon end, will have bought as many oranges as possible. A few weeks later a similar scene will involve lemons, which have been unavailable for a month or so previously.

Moscow and other large Soviet cities are "black holes" in the Soviet system of retail distribution, which is why smaller communities rarely see deficit commodities in their stores or on their streets. That such commodities appear first in the major cities encourages villagers to visit periodically to exploit their availability, and city folks always buy extra for their relations in less-favored retailing regions. In this sense Moscow is the supermarket of the USSR, for the Soviet retail distribution system relies heavily upon private cash-and-carry distribution of deficit commodities beyond the confines of Moscow. An examination of the personal cargoes of individuals returning to Novosibirsk, Omsk, Tomsk, or Irkutsk will provide astounding confirmation of the actual volume of private distribution of deficit commodities. All major cities serve similar roles.

Rural areas are officially served by what is known as consumer cooperatives, but this network only had a separate existence years ago. Today, these outlets are indistinguishable from state retail stores (except, perhaps in being more poorly stocked), and their employees are state workers. The consumer cooperative network is, if anything, less efficient and effective than the state network, primarily for the reasons given above. In 1974 the total turnover in trade carried on in this system was less than one-half that of state retail outlets, despite the fact that it serves almost as large a population. Consequently, those people who live in the thousands and thousands of villages that compose the state and collective farms of the USSR must rely much more heavily than urban dwellers upon their own productive efforts and upon the rural *rynok,* which is a more informal market than its urban counterpart. Rural dwellers in warm agricultural regions fare quite well when it comes to certain kinds of food products, such as tomatoes, cucumbers, and fruits, which are deficit items in northern cities. Opportunities to trade these products in urban markets can offer substantial profits too. Even so, a drawback for all who live in places distant from major cities is the need both to transport their own products to market and carry back industrial products at their own expense. Having a relative or two in a major city is an essential condition for reasonable living in most rural regions. In a similar way, although cultural opportunities are provided by state agencies in remote cities and even in villages of the USSR, such appearances are sporadic and rarely include leading performers.

The difference between retail distribution systems in most Western capitalist countries and that of the USSR resembles the difference between a gravity-flow and a forced-air central heating system for a building. The latter tends to distribute heat more or less uniformly throughout the building, with only minor losses of efficiency in extreme wings. A gravity system must be properly designed to avoid uneven heating problems. The Soviet retail distribution system resembles a malfunctioning gravity-flow system, with Moscow located in such a way that deficit commodities gravitate to it at the expense of all other regions. Leningrad, Kiev, and Novosibirsk, for example, do better than Novgorod, Alma-Ata, or Irkutsk; and a hierarchy exists in the supply system that stretches all the way to the village. Moreover, the state retail system operates primarily on the basis of the tastes and cultural preferences of the great majority of the population that lives in European Russia. There are villages in Siberia and in Central Asia, for example, that are so remote culturally as well as geographically that the state retail system does not penetrate at all. The weakness of the state retail distribution system is, therefore, a powerful contributor to maintenance of the already large discrepancies that exist in the USSR today between urban and rural standards of living.

According to Western estimates, the Soviet overall standard of living has almost doubled since 1953 but this seems difficult to believe when one examines Soviet life firsthand today. It seems unreasonable, in the first place, that the standard of living in 1953 could have been as low as is implied. Our evidence indicates that the standard of living in 1953 was not materially different, overall, than it had been in 1928; and 1928 was probably not much better than 1913. For forty years, then, Soviet living standards remained at, or below, the prerevolutionary level. In the second place, it is not immediately apparent to a contemporary observer what the improvements have been.

The most striking advances in living conditions for anyone who has watched these improvements over the years are in clothing, including shoes; the supply of food, particularly in animal husbandry products, fruits, and vegetables; housing; and in ownership of consumer durables and automobiles. Ten or fifteen years ago, foreigners in Moscow stood out like a sore thumb because of the quality and cut of their clothing, and their shoes were a dead giveaway too. When women dressed their best in those years they looked inferior to women in ordinary street clothing in Moscow today; and the same holds for men's suits, overcoats, and shoes. Vegetables and fruits were simply never available in the wintertime, and the amount of meat regularly available today is striking by comparison. Housing construction has continued at a high rate for two decades now, and renovation of older dwellings has also been carried out on a large scale. The number of square feet per urban dweller has increased despite a rapid increase in the size of the urban population, and the quality of new apartments has improved because they are self-contained, not communal. Actual construction quality has probably declined, however. Some consumer durables that are commonplace today were rarities only fifteen years ago. Even the peasants have refrigerators today, although many complain that they stay empty most of the time. Sewing machines are widely owned, as are, of course, radios, television sets, and stereo systems. Finally, anyone who visited the Soviet Union in the early 1960s and returned for the first time today would be amazed by the number of private automobiles on the streets of Moscow. In the 1960s even Moscow looked like a huge construction site or a giant factory, for the streets carried mainly trucks and buses. The few automobiles were official cars or taxis.

I believe that it is possible to credit a large increase in the Soviet standard of living over the last twenty-five years, but this increase has not been evenly distributed geographically. A visit even to a large city in Siberia, for example, takes one back to the way Moscow looked ten or so years ago. Queues have diminished everywhere, and they exist in the major cities mainly for luxuries—for the best meat, for premium butter, for cucumbers or lemons in March, and so forth. The population has money and it has the habit of queuing, and it will be a long time before queuing is eliminated from Soviet shopping habits. Scarcity-mindedness causes individuals to buy large quantities of scarce items when they appear. They buy for the future, for their relatives, and for their friends. Thus, as a hedge against doing without, individuals provide the storage space for many items that are not actually scarce. Psychologically, the Soviet shopper has been traumatized by shortages and has organized his or her life in such a way that queuing, taking advantage of unexpected appearances of deficit commodities, and sharing with friends are integral aspects of everyday life. The long years of sacrifice will take an even longer time to be compensated and forgotten. Meanwhile, everyone shops with determination, a pocketful of rubles, and surprising generosity.

Labor Markets and Private Entrepreneurship

Gosplan and the various ministries plan the allocation of labor in the same way that they do other resources. Labor balances are worked out for each region and republic and compared with enterprise requirements. The allocation of labor involves markedly different problems and methods. Marxist theory, of course, distinguishes sharply between labor and commodities under socialism, for labor represents a very special kind of resource and one for which economic activity is largely intended, according to Marxian assumptions. In addition, the labor market is open. That is, although it is a regulated market in the sense that a state committee of the Council of Ministers sets wage rates, safety standards, and other conditions of work for all public employment, individual workers exercise primary discretion concerning their own participation in the economy.

Labor markets may be separated into five different categories: state, collective farm, private plot, and legal and illegal private labor service. This division emphasizes the significance of private markets. I am not suggesting that these markets operate separately. On the contrary, these various markets are intertwined in complex ways, and to an unknown degree private markets actually help to explain why the Soviet economy functions as well as it does concerning the satisfaction of consumer preferences. Products and services that would not otherwise be available are produced privately in the USSR, and private trade helps to distribute and redistribute commodities and services that would otherwise never reach those who want them most. In addition, and of particular importance, private markets tend to convert public property into private property for private gain. One result is a different distribution of final consumer goods and services than would take place in the absence of private enterprise and trade, and this means in all likelihood a distribution of goods and services that benefits higher-income classes more than the state intends. Another result is to convert what are intended as investment and government expenditures into private consumption, which tends to benefit all current consumers taken together at the expense of state nonconsumption projects. In other words, private markets, particularly illegal private markets in this instance, tend to undermine the percentage shares given in the plan for investment and for government outlays. It may, of course, be argued that current consumers are gaining at the expense of future consumption or the future military safety of the population, rather than at the expense of the state; but few citizens would be deterred by such an argument after long years of sacrificing for a future than never seems to arrive.

Immediately prior to, during, and for some years following World War II, strict controls were applied in the allocation of labor and to minimize labor shirking; and civilian labor was even at times conscripted along with military. Soviet citizens today, however, exercise considerable freedom of calling in that they may decide whether or not to work, allocate themselves among jobs, and, to a lesser extent, among locations of work; and they may determine the intensity with which they will work as well. Freedom of calling is further bolstered by the availability of employments in occupations not controlled by the state, both legal and illegal.

Most Soviet able-bodied citizens work for the state in one capacity or another. Most work for a state industrial or agricultural enterprise, but no small number is employed in the various state bureaucracies. The largest exception to state employment is the collective farm, but employment on collective farms today is not significantly different in terms and conditions than employment on state farms. For the present, we therefore shall lump together collective and state farm workers. Both in the countryside and in urban areas the rate of female participation is very high in the Soviet Union, higher than anywhere else in the world. The high rate of female participation reflects at least two factors: liberation of women by the Bolshevik philosophy and the necessity of two incomes for maintaining a satisfactory standard of living.

All able-bodied citizens are under considerable social pressure to contribute gainfully to the economy. Legal measures are also possible and have been invoked against those persons who are designated *social parasites*. The charge of social parasitism is more common these days, however, as a weapon against political dissidents than it is as a source of labor. Recently, able-bodied individuals, including those who are alienated from Soviet society, have been allowed to remain outside of regular gainful employment so long as some family member is prepared to guarantee support. If the person in question is an able-bodied woman with young children, she may withdraw from employment voluntarily to care for them and her husband, with little notice. The wives and children of well-to-do, successful members of Soviet society are not troubled by antiparasite laws either. There are many other Soviets, most of whom are beyond the age for retirement (sixty for males and fifty-five for females), who have the choice of supplementing their incomes by working as cloakroom clerks, doormen, watchmen, and so forth. A large proportion of the existing Soviet labor force is completely free to work or to withdraw from employment as it sees fit. As a result, the Soviet labor force must be regarded as a function of individual evaluation of real wages, as it is in labor markets in capitalist countries. Thus, we shall describe the labor market as open. This has an essential bearing, as we shall see, upon the central planning and management of the Soviet economy.

The labor market comprises a complex collection of markets— some public, others private; and it is a huge market because it touches the life of every Soviet household and every enterprise and organization. Because it is an open market in which individuals exercise freedom of vocation within broad limits, it is more accurate to conceive of labor as being centrally managed rather than planned, for planning under such circumstances can mean little more than extrapolation of current trends. Direct central allocation applies only to the military service, to the penal system, and to available educational slots in the USSR today. The remainder of the labor force is self-allocated by incentives provided in public and private employments, and the intensity with which individuals work in any given employment is also self-determined.

The largest and most important single labor market is employment in state and industrial enterprises. Most able-bodied men and women in the Soviet Union work with one of these economic enterprises or with the administrative, military, or police bureaucracies of the state. A large number of retired persons are also employed by state enterprises and agencies on a full- or part-time basis. Pensions are low, and not everyone of pensionable age today is entitled to a pension. Thus, many old persons work to make ends meet. Pensioners are entitled to earn up to a fixed amount per month before their pensions are docked, which is a powerful incentive to work because the upper limit is relatively high.

Employment with state enterprises and agencies is, superficially at least, not noticeably different from employment in similar occupations elsewhere in the developed world. Although there was some disagreement during the 1920s about adopting the factory system that the Bolsheviks inherited from czarist Russia and Europe, the system was adopted in all important respects. State employees work a fixed time now (averaging close to forty hours per week), are expected to appear regularly and punctually, and must work under the supervision of foremen, who are themselves directed by a single manager and his staff. In general, a casual observer from the West would see nothing peculiar about the way work goes forward on the shop floor in a Soviet enterprise.

There are, however, some distinctive features of this labor market. No Soviet enterprise or official endeavor lacks a corresponding branch of the Soviet trade-union system, known as the *profsoiuz*. But, as was pointed out earlier, trade unions have no say in the management of state enterprises or agencies. Neither do they have the legal right to strike or to order any organized withdrawal of efficiency or to protest about wages, hours of work, and so forth. Agreements are worked out periodically between the *profsoiuz* and enterprise, trust, or other administrative level, which spell out conditions of work, safety provisions, welfare benefits, and so forth, but they do not specify wage benefits. Local *profsoiuz* representatives serve as grievance boards to settle petty disputes among workers and between workers and management, and they also serve as "cheerleaders" in support of fulfilling plan targets. The Soviet *profsoiuz* is little more than an ineffectual company union, with all that implies in the way of serving the interest primarily of the bosses. Recent efforts to create independent, worker-controlled, nationally affiliated unions in Poland have no visible counterparts in the USSR, but success in Poland might very well have set a powerful example for Soviet workers. Hence the Soviet government's watchful concern.

Salary and wage scales are determined for all state enterprises, including state farms and organizations, according to schedules that are developed and maintained by the State Committee on Labor and Wages. Wage differentials are determined by considering a number of factors—such as unpleasant or dangerous conditions at work, remoteness of the region in which employment is offered, the degree of skill or educational preparation required, and seniority. Many of these factors reflect, of course, the evaluations that many individuals would make concerning the desirability of these various jobs, and to this extent centralized wage-setting indirectly reflects supply conditions. The ultimate test of a wage rate is whether too few or too many workers apply for the jobs that it governs, and in this respect the State Committee on Labor and Wages is ultimately influenced by general conditions of supply and demand as well as by the formal criteria elaborated for wage determination. The government has been trying to persuade workers to move permanently to Siberia, for example, to take part in the exploitation of the vast, almost untouched resources of the region, and wage differentials are set to make working in Siberia attractive. The differential has attracted workers, but has not been sufficient to induce them to bring their families. Consequently, workers return home to warmer, more hospitable climes after several years of concentrated saving. Given the priority that development of Siberia has had for more than two decades, this example illustrates the limits that freedom of calling places on the State Committee on Labor and Wages.

Moreover, enterprise managers compete with each other for skilled, reliable workers, which has reinforced the impact of specific shortages upon effective wages. Although managers cannot change wage rates, they can promote desirable individuals into higher pay categories in order to retain them. Or the managers can let their employees hold more than one position—so that they earn two, three, or even four salaries. In general, then, supply and demand do influence the allocation of labor in the Soviet Union both between state employment and employment in the private sector (or leisure) and among employments in the socialized sector of the Soviet economy. Wage differentials in the state sector have, however, been diminished substantially in recent years by relatively high minimum wages and by the difficulty that managers face in attempting to eliminate redundant labor. Incompetent or other unsatisfactory workers are almost impossible to fire; and wage differentials are often too weak to prevent the oversupply of some kinds of labor at the cost of undersupply for others.

Collective farms employ a large, but diminishing, number of individuals in the Soviet economy, and the conditions under which collective farm workers (kolkhozniki) work are not substantially different today from those under which state farm workers (sovkhozniki) work. Kolkhozniki are eligible for pensions; they receive the bulk of their pay in money wages rather than in kind; and they receive regular wages based upon a minimum guaranteed annual wage. Kolkhoz workers normally are given access to a larger private plot than the state farm worker, and children of kolkhozniki have a right to become a member of the kolkhoz, a right the children of sovkhozniki do not have. Most important today is the fact that members of wealthy collective farms, which usually means those that specialize in the production of certain labor-intensive and highly valuable commodities such as tea leaves, silk, or tobacco, do better on the average than state farm workers. Most collective farm workers do worse, however, although the difference has narrowed recently as a result of converting poor collectives into state farms.

The income that peasants earn from both state and collective farms has increased substantially over the last twenty-five years. Although the rate of increase has reduced the gap between industrial-urban occupations and rural employments, it has not prevented the continued migration of the most ambitious and highly skilled young people from rural occupations. Cultivation of private plots by kolkhozniki, sovkhozniki, and other rural dwellers is the third largest source of employment in the Soviet Union today, and it is the largest single private sector. At one time Soviet economists believed that private plot agriculture competed with collective farm agriculture for workers, and it may have been so. Today, however, Soviet economists are persuaded that few able-bodied workers are engaged in private plot agriculture, and the few who are able-bodied are nearly always women with young children to care for, who would not offer extensive employment to the collective in any case. Even so, the presence of the private plot serves as a powerful incentive to have one member of any rural family qualify as a full-time worker on a state or collective farm. Earnings from the plot provide an important source of consumption and of additional money income for rural families, and labor is utilized that would not otherwise be available to the farm, partiuclarly that of the very young and the old. Private plot agriculture supplies most of the products that flow through the urban *rynok* and plays an important supplemental role in both the income of farm workers and the diets of urban dwellers.

There is a fourth legal labor market in the USSR of indeterminant size. It is not possible to distinguish unambiguously between the legal market in private labor services and the illegal, but the distinction is important. Many individuals participate in both legal and illegal aspects of private employment, and some activities take place in the penumbra between the legal and illegal where the distinction is one for the courts to resolve. Among the legal occupations are those which involve a direct personal service for someone, such as caring for children, housekeeping, typing manuscripts, doing laundry, and gardening. In addition, anyone may sell the products of his or her own (or the family's) labor in the *rynok* or personally. It is also legal for a group of individuals, such as carpenters, bricklayers, or other craftsmen, to band together in a collective to build homes, do repairs, and so forth on a private, but cooperative, basis. Just how important such collectives are is not an available statistic, but they have always been more important in rural areas than in urban because there are many more private homes and dachas in the countryside. In general, individuals may exercise skills that they have acquired in order to earn, or supplement their income. But here we move into an obscure territory. A person who knows how to repair electrical equipment may freely repair his or her own or a friend's television set. That person might also repair a set belonging to a "friend of a friend" without charge but with the clear intention of collecting a reciprocal favor at a future time from the friend or the set's owner. It may even be legal for the repairer to receive a cash payment for such service, although this is not patently clear. The situation, however, is rarely so neatly defined. Any of these instances would be illegal if the repairer used spare parts taken from his or her official place of work, used stolen tools, or did the repairs on working time in the state shop without billing the customer for it.

Plumbers, carpenters, repairmen of all sorts, handymen, individuals who own private cars or who chauffeur for the state, and so forth can periodically earn a personal profit on the basis of their skills or their access to state property. Although it is technically illegal to do so, chauffeurs for state officials frequently use time that they know will otherwise be spent sitting in wait to taxi individuals for private gain, and the state pays for the gasoline. Some individuals specialize in approaching foreign tourists in hopes of buying or begging some prize item for subsequent (illegal) resale or in the expectation of obtaining foreign currency in exchange for rubles. Many individuals manufacture *samogon* (illegal drinking alcohol) in their kitchens, and those who make it well and in large quantity can exchange or sell it as a sideline. Drivers of state-owned taxis frequently take advantage of late-night fares to earn something over and above the standard fare, to sell liquor after hours, and to refer clients to ladies of the night.

In a similar vein *blat* can get one out of a difficult spot, it can help one jump a queue, and it can be used for personal advancement. For deficit commodities or services, rubles are frequently useless unless mixed with *blat,* friendship, or a contact in the black market. Where legality ends and illegality begins in these instances is hard to determine, and anyone who is involved in these kinds of transactions takes a certain risk in doing so. Interestingly enough, this implicates almost every household in the major cities of the USSR and no small number of rural folk, where producing *samogon* is the most frequently cited crime. The exceptions are likely to be officials so highly placed that *blat* works silently and unbidden for them anyway. There was a time when it was said "*blat* is higher than Stalin." Today, it is accurate to say that *blat* is the only hard Soviet currency.

To exaggerate the volume of illegal and quasi-legal economic transactions in the USSR today would be wrong. No figures and no official estimates are available about them, as there are for the collective farm markets and private plot agriculture, but no one doubts that private trading, both legal and illegal, is extremely pervasive. Whether total turnover on this market is 10 or 15 percent of total real Soviet national product, no one can say with confidence; but that it touches every household on at least a weekly basis no one could doubt. The apparent sharp increase in *nalevo* markets in recent years may serve as a measure of a growing disparity between planners' and consumers' preferences in the USSR. The lesson seems to be that planners cannot enforce their own preferences in the face of an open labor market. This would require, in all likelihood, a return to strict labor controls, a resumption of forced labor, and much more extensive policing of economic activities. No current leader has indicated willingness to pursue so drastic a solution, although one does hear nostalgic references to the public "order" that Stalin maintained.

Labor Force Participation, Mobility, and Productivity

Given existing legal restraints on working age, existing wages, and work conditions, and the social and legal pressures on the individual to contribute to economic activity, the available labor force in the USSR is determined essentially by the rate at which the overall population grows and by the way this increase is distributed geographically. The Soviet population as a whole has been growing relatively slowly over the past two decades. The rate for both the USSR and the United States has been in the neighborhood of 1.4 percent per annum, and it is declining. Like the United States, the USSR experienced a postwar baby boom. Now that this bulge in the population has been absorbed into the labor force, available labor will increase at a much slower pace than previously, and the minuscule growth of the labor force in the 1980s will adversely affect the growth of Soviet national income. Because labor participation rates of both men and women are high, little additional labor can be obtained by trying to increase participation rates. The Soviet labor participation rate for women is so high that it is much more likely to fall than to rise, and the same may be true for males, unless purchasing power increases steadily.

The main source of possible growth of the labor force for the industrial sectors of the economy would be by diminishing the labor force required by the agricultural sector. As we have seen, the proportion of labor that is currently devoted to agricultural production is large by comparison with other developed countries—about 25 percent of total employment. It is doubtful, however, that this potential pool of industrial labor can be realized in the near future because productivity is increasing very slowly and because of the priority that expansion of agricultural output occupies at present.

The distribution of the rural population poses an additional problem for Soviet planners. Population growth rates are generally lower in the cities than in rural regions; and, more important, growth rates are highest in both urban and rural regions where certain minority ethnic groups live. The populations of Central Asia, for example, are growing rapidly, especially in rural areas. Growth of the Soviet industrial labor force will require the absorption of the net increase in these populations. There are two ways to go about it. One is to encourage non-Russian nationals to move to the industrial cities outside their traditional cultural regions by creating appropriate wage differentials. Thus far Soviet planners have been reluctant to encourage members of minority groups such as those of Central Asia to move to the cities of European Russia, and it would appear also that the campaign to induce workers to move permanently to Siberia has been conducted mainly among the various European populations of the USSR. In any event, Soviet planners have not looked with favor upon the creation of ethnic outposts in the main industrial centers of the USSR. Great Russians go out to the various non-Russian republics to fill high administrative posts and skilled occupations, but no significant reverse flow of the unskilled to European Russia has taken place. Many Soviet and Western students of Soviet ethnic groups claim that these ethnic groups do not wish to move and cannot be induced to move in any case, but the argument is undermined by the presence of similar cultural and ethnic minorities—that is, Turks, Pakistanis, Indians, and Persians in the cities of Western Europe and England, which are further removed from the centers of their native cultures than are the cities of European Russia or Central Siberia.

The alternative is to distribute investment preferentially to these minority republics and regions in order to utilize the relatively rapid natural increase in their populations. But this procedure tends to reinforce "undesirable" centrifugal ethnic and national forces already underway in the USSR. Soviet planners, therefore, face a difficult dilemma, neither horn of which can be completely evaded. This is just one component of the problem that the Soviet Union's restless national minorities pose for Soviet planners and political leaders in the near future, and the underlying economic problem of labor scarcity cannot be resolved independently of official nationality policy. It is useless for Soviet leadership to proclaim, as Brezhnev has said repeatedly, that the nationality problem has been solved. The problem is yet to be addressed as a living fact, but labor scarcity and rising ethnic consciousness ensure that it will be posed, probably in dramatic fashion, in the near future.

If little industrial labor is likely to result from a diminution in the agricultural labor force during the next five years, the main source of growth must lie in the productivity of labor already in the industrial sector. When measured on an average annual basis, Soviet industry has a good record regarding increases in labor productivity since the early 1950s. The increase has, however, been erratic; and a more serious problem is an apparent downward trend over the last decade. This trend may be spurious, of course; but the evidence for stagnation in the rate of growth of labor productivity seems firm. The decline that has taken place probably reflects the fact that the largest gains from borrowing new technology from the West and from training the illiterate have already been assimilated. The decline no doubt also reflects the shift of a much larger share of investment resources to the agricultural sector in the last decade or two, for agriculture has not yielded the kind of gains in productivity that were registered in the industrial sector earlier. There is another problem that may be more fundamental—the intensity with which Soviet labor works. Increased productivity in industry, and in agriculture as well, will require the elimination of redundant labor and a renewed willingness of Soviet workers to work harder and to learn new skills.

A good deal of evidence suggests that Soviet workers could readily increase the efficiency and intensity with which they work. The problem for central planners, however, is overcoming the institutional barriers that encourage and protect redundancy and low productivity. Even casual observation reveals several different types of redundancy in the Soviet economy. In the first place, a large number of jobs exist that appear to signify little economically. For example, every public building has a doorman or doorwoman, several coatchecks, a number of janitors, and various repairmen. Moreover, every separate institute or administrative division within the building has a watchman or watchwoman who controls access to the floor or wing that the office or institute occupies. University dormitories and many apartment buildings have similar persons who ensure against unauthorized entry and therefore against theft or encroachment. Similarly, almost every office, institute, factory, and store has a fleet of automobiles and vans that are used to transport authorized people on business; and many people have chauffeured cars assigned for their exclusive use. These drivers sit idle much of the time, waiting to take someone to or from an assignment. Many of these functions are either necessary or useful, such as the ubiquitous coatchecks in a country where one wears heavy clothing over half the year, and many are sinecures that provide small incomes to retired or invalided persons. Other positions, however, such as personally assigned chauffeurs and KGB guards, are held by the able-bodied and afford good incomes.

The second type of redundancy that casual observation reveals in the USSR is in staffing services, particularly in certain types of retail sales and in offices. Oddly, this may not be true redundancy on a global basis because retail sales, for example, are understaffed in aggregate. Existing workers are badly distributed among outlets. Some hardly have enough people to serve all the customers, while others have few products to sell and nothing for half the staff to do most of the time. Judging by comments in Soviet professional magazines and newspapers, this kind of maldistribution of the existing labor force is characteristic of industrial and agricultural enterprises as well. The institutional basis for the persistence of an inefficient allocation of the labor force lies, first, in the legal difficulties that managers face in removing individuals from the work force and, second, in the fact that there is little incentive for managers to trim redundant labor. On the contrary, it is often convenient to have a certain amount of redundancy (the Soviet terminology is *reserves*) to handle peak demand, for managerial bonuses result primarily from fulfilling annual output targets, not in minimizing costs.

A third source of the inefficiency that characterizes the Soviet labor force taken as a whole is the ineffectiveness of the material incentive system. Much emphasis has always been placed in Soviet industry upon moral incentives. Moral incentives refer to nonmaterial kinds of gratification workers and managers may obtain from doing good work. They include the receiving of medals, winning competitions, having one's name or factory written up in the newspaper, and the like. Moral incentives were important sources of productivity gains in the 1930s, during World War II, and afterward, but they have apparently lost much of their effectiveness today. Unfortunately, the system of material incentives has never been thoroughly overhauled to reflect its increased significance as the prime mover in inducing efficiency and conscientiousness. Moreover, persistent shortages in retail outlets tend to undermine the effectiveness of material incentives, particularly where individuals cannot be fired for laziness or have their salary docked for lacking ambition. Obviously, a society in which acquisition of the most desirable commodities requires either queuing or *nalevo* involvement in the economy is one in which a clever worker may find advancement to a more responsible or otherwise demanding position no advantage whatever. The move up may reduce the time that he or she has available for queuing, or it may remove the individual from the strategic position he or she occupies with respect to deficit commodities of *blat*.

Increased productivity is an inviting path toward increased output in the Soviet economy, but it can only be attained in the long run by changing the institutional structure within which Soviet workers and managers operate. That the great bulk of all Soviet employed persons work for the state in one capacity or another makes the problem of eliminating redundancy and increasing productivity a political issue in the same way that the pricing of products in state retail outlets is a political problem. As an economic problem, neither issue presents any conceptual or behavioral difficulties. Socialization of the means of production has politicized economic decision-making in the USSR, as it has elsewhere following widespread nationalization. Some important problems are solved, of course, by taking them out of the economic realm; but others that are very intractable for political decision-making are often created at the same time. Although the balance depends upon one's objectives, wholesale nationalization has become less attractive to many contemporary socialists owing to this realization.

One problem that wholesale nationalization did solve in the USSR, however, involved periodic layoffs resulting from business fluctuations. The fact that Soviet enterprises do not lay off workers when sales or profits lag is, of course, the obverse side of the job security problem that managers face in trying to use labor forces efficiently. Soviet national income and industrial and agricultural output do fluctuate, but for reasons distinct from those that bring about business cycles in capitalist countries. Employment does not fluctuate systematically with output because the two are severed by job security and by the commitment of the government to provide jobs for all who seek to work. Redundancy in Soviet economic enterprises reflects these factors.

The Soviet Union has unemployment, but it tends to be one of three noncyclical types. Individuals who are in the process of voluntarily seeking different or better-located employment as well as those who have just joined the labor force through graduation from school contribute to frictional unemployment. Structural unemployment also presents problems in the Soviet Union. That is, as the economy changes under the impact of new technology and changing tastes of the population or the government (military demand, for example), certain jobs are eliminated causing skills of established workers to become obsolete. Because the USSR does not pay unemployment benefits, individuals who suffer from structural or frictional unemployment may be obliged to take much-inferior jobs— or to do without work until something suitable opens up. The third type of unemployment that individuals suffer in the USSR is seasonal, which affects primarily the rural population.

Education has always been an important means for upward mobility in the USSR. The Soviet Union adopted the American open-enrollment educational system at its inception to maximize opportunities for individuals to become educated and to learn skills. Education remains today a very important basis for successful advancement on the job, but the USSR is running into the problem of overqualified workers that afflicts many advanced countries. Individuals who find that they must accept employment in positions which are inferior to the positions for which they prepared themselves are likely to become aliented; they are *underemployed* members of society. This should perhaps be listed as a fourth type of unemployment in the Soviet Union.

In the USSR women are heavily represented in the category *overqualified workers*. Over one-half of the total Soviet labor force is female. Official doctrine calls for equal educational opportunities, equal pay for equal work, the provision of child-care services, and support for the desirability of female participation in the labor force on a full-time basis. Even so, several factors militate against the attainment of true equality with men when it comes to economic opportunities and achievements. Soviet data reveal, for example, that occupations in which women form the majority of employees, regardless of the status of these occupations outside the USSR, tend to be low-prestige, poorly paid occupations. The most flagrant example is medicine, in which women dominate the ranks of M.D.s. Yet even in occupations such as medicine or primary education, men dominate both the higher-administrative and most-specialized categories and thus the higher-paid employments. Most enterprise managers and collective farm chairpersons are men, and most high officials in the Communist party are male.

There are many reasons why women have not been able to take full advantage of the Bolsheviks' ideological commitment to equal opportunity for women. Soviet statistics make it clear that women do take advantage of early educational opportunities, but they are less likely than men to continue education to the highest levels. Accordingly, few women are surgeons, although many earn M.D.s. Second, although child-care centers exist, the spaces available are inadequate to provide care for the children of all women who wish to work, and the deficiency increases the farther one moves away from major urban areas. Third, although it seems very unlikely that there is any official support for a secondary role for women in the Soviet system, the state conducts no affirmative action programs to reverse long-standing patriarchal attitudes. These attitudes are particularly strong in certain ethnic regions, such as Central Asia, where they take the form of social prohibitions on participation by women in factory employment or the appearance of women in certain public situations. Even in European Russia, familial expectations and cultural patterns seriously handicap women. Most women do work full-time throughout the USSR, but fewer put their careers ahead of other considerations than do men.

A woman who desires to compete with men for success in a career can probably do so in the USSR more easily and with less criticism than in Europe or in the United States, but she still runs counter to cultural expectations, and this takes its toll. Women in European Russia, for example, are expected to work full-time yet do the shopping, prepare meals, keep house, and care for the children. According to reports, husbands are more willing today than in the past to assist in all of these activities, but primary responsibility remains with the woman. Should a child be ill, for example, it would almost certainly be the mother rather than the father who would stay home. Job advancement involving a change of cities would be more likely to follow the husband's opportunities than the wife's. Many women do not object, of course, to the pattern in which they, like their husbands and parents, have been inculcated. But for those women who do object the situation is no less fraught with contradictions and emotional tensions than in the West. Women comprise, therefore, the largest proportion of those who are overskilled for the positions they occupy in the Soviet labor force.

No discussion of labor in the Soviet Union would be complete that failed to take forced labor into account. Although forced labor is apparently no longer a significant source of labor in the USSR, at one time forced labor contributed significantly to national income. The total number of individuals so impressed remains secret and is thus disputed among Western scholars, and the matter will not be resolved in the near future. Everyone agrees, however, that the total was great, that it reached a peak in the years immediately following World War II, and that it began to be reduced systematically under Khrushchev, especially following his secret anti-Stalin speech in 1956. Economists generally believe that forced labor is inferior to paid labor in efficiency, and maintaining large forced labor camps is expensive. In any event, forced labor was used in the Soviet Union to perform very dangerous or particularly arduous tasks, such as construction and mining in the Arctic.

The Household Sector

The typical Soviet urban household contributes labor to the economic process and receives pecuniary and nonpecuniary benefits in return, primarily for its contributions. Nonpecuniary benefits have been declining as a share of total family income, and thus most of the family's time is spent earning and spending money income. From the family's standpoint it does not matter whether its transactions involve the private or the public sector, but when things go wrong in the public sector the state is blamed. Most households in the USSR have more than one primary wage earner, and most also receive some direct payment from a state agency. A grandparent may live with the family and draw a pension. He or she may also work at a part-time job, and in any event the grandparent would be fully occupied helping in queuing for deficit commodities, walking the baby, sitting with the children, gardening, and helping with the housework. The family may have a child in the university or in a technical school, in which case he or she would receive a stipend that would be contributed to the family's weekly income.

Spending the family income is also a collective affair, involving state retail markets, the *rynok,* private trading, and *nalevo* markets, without anyone paying much attention to the breakdown among them. Family members old enough to be responsible would normally carry a substantial sum of cash with them at all times against finding unexpected deficit commodities. Everyone in the family knows what these are and what a reasonable price would be for them. What the family does not spend is set aside for purchasing large durable goods such as automobiles, stereo sets, and so forth. Some Western observers claim that Soviet families are unable to spend as much as they like in Soviet markets and that they are therefore accumulating savings unwillingly. This is a most unlikely conclusion for the simple reason that households do not have to earn more income than they wish. The amount of income that a family earns is not determined by the state but by collective decision of the members of the household. Because queuing is so important a function in the acquisition of deficit commodities in the Soviet Union, it will always pay for one member of the family to increase his or her free time for queuing rather than to work at a job from which the income would be of little or no use.

So long as individuals are free to make their own purchases in the market, and so long as individual households may elect the total number of hours that they wish to be employed, planners are not able to determine unilaterally either the total volume of labor forthcoming in the economy or the total amount and composition of consumer goods and services that it will make available. This constraint is enhanced by the presence of private employment and private retail markets. It is further enhanced by the opportunities that individuals have to convert public property into private means to personal gain.

If the state wishes households to contribute more to economic activity, it must provide something in exchange, and that has increasingly come to mean commodities and services rather than promises of a better future or assurance against an aggressive external force. In this respect the member of a Soviet household does not experience a different economic world than does his or her counterpart in the West. A Soviet who is suddenly transposed into a capitalist economic environment is not disoriented by the difference, although the plethora of goods and of choices available might be overwhelming at first. Neither is a Western shopper disoriented in Soviet markets. The difficulties involved are irritating but not completely strange, for there are still queues in the West for certain kinds of sporting and cultural events, and queues for gasoline have reeducated an entire generation. The Soviet system of central planning and management has not yet, however, learned to accommodate independent-minded workers and equally independent-minded consumers.

The term "second economy" has become popular among certain Western specialists on the Soviet economy to describe various aspects of what I have called "open markets" and "trading *nalevo*." "Second economy" is potentially misleading because it may be taken to imply a greater degree of distinctness between the "first" economy and the "second" than exists. The concept of a dual economy was first developed in the study of developing economies to describe the difference between the advanced sector of the economy and the traditional predevelopment sector. Since the advanced sector in a primitive economy may be an exclave of Western or Soviet technology, the notion of a dual economic system is not remote for many countries, but the concept has proved troublesome even in the development literature because there are usually connections, and therefore interactions, between the two parts of the dual economy that are important to the functioning of each. Such is the case regarding economic transactions that take place *nalevo* in the USSR. As a matter of fact, neither the "first" nor the "second" economy would work as well in the absence of the other, although there are, of course, contradictions between them.

The second drawback with the notion of a "second" economy is the fact that no investigator has yet advanced a definition that everyone finds satisfactory. Every adult Soviet citizen knows the difference between the *nalevo* economy, the legal private markets, and the public economy, and it seems preferable to stick with common usage. Some Western scholars define the second economy as consisting of all free-market transactions, legal and illegal. Others define the concept as comprising all illegal economic transactions, but this bunches general criminal activities with market transactions and loses altogether the distinction between private- and public-sector transactions. Enterprise managers, for example, know how to use the *nalevo* economy to achieve state enterprise targets as well as their own creature comforts. Finally, still other Western specialists define the second economy as including only private economic activity and use it to contrast private enterprise with state planning and management. Each aspect involved in the various definitions is as important as the other in gaining an understanding of the way that Soviet planning and management of the economy interacts with the interests and behavior of the private individuals and households that compose the system. Soviet households are involved simultaneously in planned and unplanned economic transactions, in market and nonmarket economic relationships, and in private and public economic institutions. They form an undifferentiated whole in the experience of a household member, and each is an essential component of the way the Soviet economy functions for the people who live and work in the system.

13

The Little Deal:
Brezhnev's Contribution to
Acquisitive Socialism

Vera Dunham described the accommodation that emerged between regime and middle class under Stalin as the "Big Deal."[1] It represented a dilution of the idealistic, egalitarian goals of Marxian socialism by means of a tacit accommodation in practice to the materialistic, self-regarding behavior of the new Soviet middle class. For technocrats and skilled workers in preferred sectors, material incentives increasingly displaced moral incentives. For the middle class, privilege and perquisite replaced eqalitarianism and self-denial. The accumulation of private, personal property not only became acceptable, it was now protected against public encroachment, and acquisitive impulses gained relative to altruistic ones. The rehetoric of Bolshevism continued, of course, glorifying self-sacrifice, collectivism, and egalitarianism, but these goals, like a particular kind of optical illusion, retreated farther and farther into the future with each new official pronouncement. One day collective farms would be elevated to full status as socialist enterprises. Private agricultural plots would disappear. Public distribution of consumer goods and services would be entirely socialized and thus depecuniarized. "Commodity production," the "law of value," and other relics of capitalism would eventually become otiose and disappear simultaneously with the appearance of the new Soviet man (and woman).[2] Meanwhile, however, the building of heavy industry, then prosecution of World War II, then reconstruction of the postwar economy took precedence. Thus, private production, markets, differential wages, private wealth, and personal acquisitiveness had to be tolerated, and even encouraged, for the duration.

From *Slavic Review* 44, no. 4 (Winter 1985):694–706; see also *Soviet Society and Culture: Essays in Honor of Vera S. Dunham,* ed. Terry L. Thompson and Richard Sheldon (Boulder, Colo.: Westview Press, 1988), pp. 3–19. Reprinted by permission, with minor editorial changes.

The economy under Stalin relied heavily upon powerful, non-economic disincentives as well as upon material incentives. Succcess was rewarded materially *and* morally. Failure was unacceptable. Discipline and punishment provided counterpoint to privilege and perquisite, and the ensured that acquisitiveness would not jeopardize the aims of the state, however it might militate against the early appearance of the new socialist citizen.

High rates of growth and a general rise in the material standard of living of the bulk of the Soviet population during the early years of Khrushchev's rule created a strong sense of optimism.[3] Egalitarianism was taken seriously by Khrushchev and his advisers, or so it would appear. Wage differentials were reduced for managerial staff and skilled workers, and the urban-rural gap narrowed too.[4] These changes were masked in the early years by the general rise in material well-being. Everyone, or almost everyone, was experiencing real income increases, and the reduction in differentials did not appear to be at anyone else's expense.

The GNP increased at an average annual rate of about 6 percent during the 1950s, then slowed to 5 percent in the 1960s and 4 percent in 1970–78; since then growth has averaged less than 2 percent per year.[5] This decline reflected the exhaustion of postwar slack, the diversion of investment to defense and to agriculture, where marginal capital productivity was low, and social policies and demographic trends that reduced the rate of growth of the effective labor force.

Khrushchev had been inclined toward large-scale programs and reforms. The Virgin Lands program, de-Stalinization, abolition of the Machine Tractor Station (MTS) system and the old four-channel agricultural procurement system, development of sovnarkhozes, and creation of parallel rural and urban Communist party organs are principal examples. Except for the Kosygin reforms of industrial management in 1965, which had been conceived and designed in the Khrushchev years, the Brezhnev years did not witness large-scale institutional reform or further de-Stalinization. It was instead a period of institutional stability at the macrolevel.[6] Reform and change were confined to the microlevel, mainly in the forms of increased political and economic freedom within close kinship and friendship networks and greater tolerance of petty private enterprise and trade. These represented the main components of Brezhnev's "Little Deal."

The Background of the Little Deal

The overthrow of Nikita Khrushchev ushered in a new era that was more conservative in at least three respects: the new regime elected to avoid risks associated with futher de-Stalinization; it decided to avoid systemwide institutional reform; and it initiated and sustained a substantial increase in military spending.[7] The steep rise in defense spending, which became the hallmark of the Brezhnev years, jeopardized continued rapid improvement in living standards and thus progress toward Khrushchev's ambitious targets for production and consumption for 1980.

Consumerism of the Khrushchev period collided, therefore, with a new, ambitious defense policy, and the collision was all the greater because of the general slowdown in growth rates. This slowdown was partly a consequence of demographic changes that reduced the rate of growth of the labor force. It was also caused by an inefficient managerial system. Poor weather conditions and a failure of agriculture to respond to large investments with substantial total factor productivity increases were also important. The success of Khrushchev's egalitarianism, that is, the reduction in differentials within industry and between industry and agriculture, may have also had an unfavorable influence upon work incentives. Moreover, shortages of the most desirable consumer goods and the continued need for queuing reduced the effectiveness of material incentives. Absent illegal middleman activity or privileged access, chronic disequilibrium in consumer goods markets has the effect of reducing the effectiveness of income differentials. Purchase requires queuing time as well as cash. Each household must, therefore, optimize in allocating members' time between remunerable work and queuing, and individuals with pent-up demands are wise to slight their jobs in favor of slipping off to queue.

The Brezhnev regime did not repudiate consumerism as a principal goal, as increasingly heavy agricultural imports during the period testify. It did, however, halt and begin to reverse the egalitarian results of Khrushchev's wage reform.[8] It also chose not to reverse the policy of retail price stability that had been established and repeatedly promised ever since Stalin's death. Thus, the resource crunch could not but be reflected in lengthened queues for desirable consumer goods and/or in decreased incentives to work hard or to work at all.

The problem of "deficit commodities" could not be resolved by 1980, as Khrushchev had hoped, by increasing output to absorb excess demand. Raising prices to equilibrium levels was ruled out too, apparently for political reasons. Under these circumstances, the temptation to individuals who were favorably situated with respect to deficit commodities (and services) to profit themselves and their families would certainly be overwhelming in the absence of severe, swift, and certain punishment for doing so. Ideological commitment to the collective, and to socialist goals in general, was no longer sufficient to avert favoritism, nepotism, or even outright corruption. Stalin's system of discipline and punishment apparently could not be reestablished. Consequently, the very structure and functioning of the Soviet socialist economy, and the policies Soviet leadership believed could be invoked successfully, created the cracks, crevices, and other interstices within which private economic activity could flourish to redistribute, and in some cases to augment, Soviet national product.

As the Brezhnev regime matured, existent, but little-noted, private nonagricultural enterprise gained new significance and augmented the flow of private goods and services partly through the *rynok* but mainly through direct, unlicensed, floating free markets. Stalin's compromise with the peasantry in the 1930s had been forced by violence and the threat of destabilization, and it led to the retention of at least one free market in the Soviet economy, the collective farm market (CFM). Khrushchev was made to accept private plots and the CFM too, despite several attempts to drive it out of existence.[9] His government also accepted an increased flow of consumer goods through regulated state retail markets, at the expense, proportionately speaking, of direct, nonmarket distribution.

The Brehnev leadership struck a new but implicit bargain with the urban population: to tolerate the expansion of a wide variety of petty private economic activities, some legal, some in the penumbra of the legal, and some clearly and obviously illegal, the primary aim of which was the reallocation by private means of a significant fraction of Soviet national income according to private preferences. A new institutional mix was tacitly approved at the microlevel, one that elevated the importance of private markets, of which the officially sanctioned *rynok* was only one, of private enterprise, and of kinship and friendship reciprocity networks relative to official state retail outlets. Ironically, the Little Deal afforded the individual increased freedom to wheel and deal at the microlevel of Soviet society, while at the macrolevel managerial discretion was restrained, overt political dissent was persecuted and generally repressed, and a gray, conservative pallor overspread the regime. Freedom of petty private economic transactions was accompanied by greater freedom of association and of private conversation (and criticism).

Western economists have long agreed that free exchange among marketeers who start out each with different initial resource endowments and with different preference functions can achieve an increase in total welfare of all marketeers taken together—without anyone losing in the process.[10] There is little doubt that this was one outcome

of the Little Deal, although we cannot know whether it was anticipated or an aim of the leadership. The advantages to potential participants, which would have included a very large proportion of the
population, may have seemed so patent and so harmless to households that the regime elected not to stand in their way. Tolerance of
petty marketeering and of petty private enterprise was the obverse
side of the decision to set aside, for the duration, managerial and
other reforms for state enterprises.

Gur Ofer described the Soviet consumer economy as a cash-
and-carry system in which consumers are obliged to pay cash and
to transport goods from points to their homes.[11] Expansion of petty
marketeering represents a means to offset to some degree the inefficiency and maldistributions caused by the cumbersome Soviet retail
distribution system. In any event, the Little Deal included tolerance
of an expansion of private enterprise, especially in service activities
such as hairdressing, auto and electrical appliance repair, and the
like, of illegal middleman activity, of nepotism, and of the conversion
of public property for personal use or for private pecuniary gain.

Obtaining Goods and Services Nalevo

The Little Deal tolerated an expansion of private nonmarket
as well as private market activities. The second of these has been
widely described as the "second," the "parallel," or the "underground" economy and represents straightforward market transactions. The former is composed primarily of reciprocity exchanges,
which have not been dealt with extensively thus far in the literature.
Both types of exchange have had legal existence in the Soviet Union
at least from the beginning of the New Economic Policy. Both shade
from the legal and overt into the illegal and covert, passing through
a region in which legality is a matter of judicial discretion. Our
primary concern is with the illegal and the questionably legal in both
cases, that is, with transactions in which ultimate consumers receive
valued goods and services *nalevo* and with the producers and marketeers of these goods and services. (Subsequently, I shall use *nalevo*
as both an adjective and an adverb. My apologies to the tender ears
of native speakers.)

Private Enterprise and Marketeering

Let me take up *nalevo* market activities first.[12] I have defined
the accommodation of the Brezhnev government to *nalevo* marketeering as a component of the Little Deal because scale appears to

have been a very important constraint on it as far as regime tolerance was concerned. Petty trade, petty middleman activities, petty private enterprise, even petty theft or personal (illegal) use of government property have, for the most part, been winked at by the regime. This represents a "deal" in the sense that these activities frequently take place in plain view of police, citizens, bureaucrats, and high officials. What is striking is not so much the total magnitude of petty enterprise and marketeering, which in any case would be difficult if not impossible to measure, but the pervasiveness of these activities that proves that a deal, albeit tacit, was struck between the regime and an acquisitive population.

Anyone who has spent an extended period living and working in the USSR will have witnessed and/or participated in a wide variety of *nalevo* transactions. Recent emigrants from the USSR have told endless tales of these illegal and quasi-legal transactions. Although anecdotal evidence cannot yield a reliable estimate of the total volume of such transactions, expressed as a percentage of national income or of urban household budgets, it does put two observations beyond doubt: (1) almost everyone, including party members, has obtained some goods *nalevo;* and (2) discretion is usually expercised by those engaging in *nalevo* transactions, but not to the extent that their pervasive character is disguised.

Let me give a few examples. Anyone seeking a taxi in Moscow will from time to time be offered a ride by a chauffeur in a state limousine. The driver will, of course, expect a gratuity for the transportation provided, even though he or she is using the state's gasoline and is being paid by the state to wait for his or her boss or, say, for a delegate to a congress in Moscow. Such experiences are so common as to cause no remark. Similarly, taxi drivers expect special gratuities for certain services, such as driving to an out-of-the-way hotel or residence after public transport has shut down for the night. They also frequently have vodka that they will sell to partying citizens, after hours, for a premium price. Again, from any apartment overlooking a collection of garages for private automobiles one periodically witnesses the arrival of official cars and trucks from which gasoline is siphoned into private vehicles. I witnessed such activities from my kitchen window in 1979, and, as the number of chauffeured limousines arriving each morning before my building clearly indicated, so could many high Soviet officials, including academics, party members, and high-ranking police and military officers who also lived in the building. It would, in fact, have been impossible to miss these sorts of activities, which became so common and obvious during the last years of the Brezhnev era that one can only suppose that punishments for such infractions were too mild or improbable to make reporting them worthwhile.

The case appears to have been similar for the resale of one's own "special distributions," such as the special packages of cold cuts and other delicacies that widows of former high-ranking officials and officers receive, or the occasional buying and reselling of items purchased through privileged access to special state stores or from foreign colleagues. Once again, scale appears to have determined risk. Large-scale middleman dealings are clearly illegal and severely punished. Not so petty, infrequent transactions conducted in modest volume with discretion. The degree of risk associated with most of these sorts of transactions would appear to have been less during the later Brezhnev years than buying a joint or two on any urban high school or university campus in the United States today.

When one sees state retail clerks selling special cuts of meat or chocolate or other deficit commodities at hastily improvised outdoor stands, one cannot but wonder about how far petty profit-seeking has penetrated the state retail network itself. Willingness to pay a slightly higher price, or a rebate, allows the customer to jump the queue. The question is, however, who pockets the premium? Is the individual the profiteer, or is the state mimicking private trade as a way of charging a price more nearly at an equilibrium level?

It is certainly common for individuals who occupy state-owned apartments to barter them and to pocket, in the process, the "rent of location" that technically should accrue to the state. A three-room apartment, well located in Moscow, for example, can readily be traded for an apartment elsewhere, in Moscow or in another city, *plus* a consideration reflecting the locational or other desirable features. Dachas are also sold at prices that reflect the value of the location as well as of the structure, even though the individual does not have title to the land. And so it goes. As a general proposition, true for the Brezhnev years at a minimum, Soviet citizens have been able to collect these kinds of economic "rents," attributable to scarcity of desirable properties, because the state does not. Only fear of swift, certain, and severe penalties could prevent their doing so. This, too, is an aspect of the Little Deal.

One could relate anecdotes about private marketeering indefinitely. Let me confine myself, however, to a third and very important category: the provision of services by private entrepreneurs. Contrary to the belief of many outside the USSR, private enterprise is not illegal there. It is illegal to put money out at interest or to rent out land or housing professionally. It is also illegal to hire others for profit or to engage in middleman activities. What you sell and profit from must be of your own (or your family's or cooperative's) making; it cannot embody the labor of others. People do rent out "corners," of course, and they do legally hire typists, housekeepers, launderers, and the like. But it is the prohibition upon hiring others for profit, upon middleman activities, upon putting out money at interest, and upon the purchase or rental of land that ensure that legal private enterprise will be small both in scale of production and in distribution.

Apart from the production and marketing of agricultural products from private plots of kolkhozes and sovkhozes, legal private enterprise in the USSR during the Brezhnev years has been composed primarily of individuals offering services in a service-starved economy. The repair of automobiles, of television, radio, and stereo systems, and of other consumer durables represents a large class of such activities. Hairdressing, tutoring, clerical help, housekeeping, and other similar direct services to the individual, including private medical care, represent a second large class of petty private enterprise. The variety is endless. Some individuals, for example, make a substantial living queuing for others. In an economy where the most desirable goods, and at times even some necessities, are in deficit supply, it can pay to shop for others.

The activities described above are characterized by being small-scale individual or family enterprises and by a dubious legal standing. That they persist and are so pervasive is evidence that the Little Deal was a conscious, if implied, contract between Brezhnev's leadership and the population of the USSR's urban centers.

Let me give one example to indicate some of the ambiguities that characterize the legal status of petty, private service enterprises. My typewriter broke down during a recent extended stay in Moscow, and I was anxious to have it repaired promptly. Friends put me onto a private repairman, who appeared a day later at 5:15 P.M. with an apprentice in tow. The master's coat was lined with tools and spare parts, and he soon "manufactured" a workable spare part for my German-made machine. The charge was high but reasonable, given my haste. The question is: Was the transaction legal? In general, the answer is yes. He was free to charge what the traffic would bear, and I paid in rubles. The repairman was off duty, working on his own time. But what about the apprentice? Is it legal to take someone other than a family member for an apprentice? What about the tools he used? Were they borrowed from his place of state employment? It is unlikely that such tools are sold retail anywhere in the USSR. The spare part he adapted had probably the same dubious provenance. And this enterprising repairman also offered to buy my typewriter when I was ready to leave the country. The probability is, therefore, considering all factors, that the transaction was illegal and that criminal sanctions could have been invoked against the repairman, and perhaps against his customer too. This kind of complex interdependency between private and public transactions is what makes most private transactions (outside the CFM) *nalevo* transactions, that is, transactions that are either illegal or in the penumbra of the legal only.

These types of questionably legal and illegal private enterprises, and private marketeering in general, have been studied in some detail by Western scholars. Gregory Grossman and Vlad Treml call them part of the "second economy." Others describe them as composing the "parallel" or "underground" economy of the USSR. These studies suggest that such activities compose a significant fraction of total final product transactions in the Soviet economy, and they cover large-scale, Mafia-type black market activities as well as petty private marketeering and enterprise. To my mind, the term "second (or "parallel") economy" implies a degree of separateness that is misleading, especially where the focus is upon the small-scale transactions covered by what I have called the "Little Deal." These transactions do not necessarily operate outside the system; nor do they operate parallel to it. They stand, instead, in a symbiotic relationship with state enterprise and marketing, serving to make the total system more flexible and more responsive to Soviet household demand. They also produce some products and services that would otherwise not be available.

For my purpose, which is to make a case for the existence of the Little Deal, that is, an accommodation between political leaders and an increasingly acquisitive society, I need to show that: (1) petty private marketeering and enterprise are ubiquitous; (2) government officials are well aware of their existence; and (3) both sides stand to gain something from the deal. As I have pointed out earlier, there can be little question about the first two. The symbiotic character of the bulk of *nalevo* transactions and enterprises is sufficient evidence that both state and marketeer stand to gain from the deal. The final distribution of consumer goods and services would be less satisfactory from a welfare standpoint than would be the case should *nalevo* activity be halted by strict police action—unless the state is prepared to reform the systems by which consumer goods and services are produced, priced, and distributed by the state. This is the sense in which the Little Deal represents an alternative to serious, thoroughgoing, large-scale economic reform. The Brezhnev regime elected instead to temporize, and the Little Deal was thereby contracted.

Kinship and Friendship: Private Reciprocity Systems

Nalevo economic transactions in the USSR comprise more than market transactions. A large volume of nonmarket transactions takes place by means of reciprocity. This aspect of private economic activity in the USSR has been examined hardly at all by Western scholars. Reciprocity systems for the distribution and redistribution of goods and services were first discovered by anthropologists. The most systematic analysis of such systems was produced by Karl Polanyi.[13] All economies we know of have relied upon reciprocity to distribute certain valued goods and services; it represents a nonmarket distributional system. In Polanyi's words, the distributional function is "embedded in social relations" and driven by them, as, for example, by kinship and/or friendship relations.

As a principal for organizing economic activity, reciprocity is familiar to us all. Take, for example, the mutual dependence relationship of parents and children. As is typical of many such reciprocal systems, the relationship is temporal. Tradition calls for parents to care for children when they are young and helpless and, in turn, for them to be cared for by their children when old age, misfortune, or illness has undermined their ability to support and care for themselves. Reciprocal economic obligations are still quite obvious, even in highly industrial, pecuniary societies, within the family and within friendship networks. Blood is, of course, thicker than water, as mutual obligation among siblings testifies even in today's atomized Western economies. But friendship reciprocity systems remain strong too.

The important point about reciprocity systems is that the initial contribution of a valued good or service does not thereby establish a contractual or legally negotiable claim on the recipient. The obligation of parents to children may be codified in law, but the child is not required by any enforceable claim to render a quid pro quo. The claim is enforceable only by custom and tradition, by the shame attached to an ungrateful child. It is defined and socialized as a kinship obligation, not as an economic exchange of "equivalents." In many, if not most, reciprocal relationships the initial contributor does not receive a quid pro quo even from those who benefited initially—as may be seen, for example, when friends help each other move, or when neighbors get together to harvest the crops of an ill or widowed acquaintance. Current fraternity and sorority members benefit from alumni, and they will contribute themselves to a completely different membership generation.

Benefits that parents provide their children may appear to be comparable to an investment on which a return is expected, but this is misleading because the children's performance cannot be enforced as an economic contract or alienated to a third party. A reciprocal obligation is not comparable to a debt or other market transaction. It is an IOU enforceable only by custom and tradition, and it may be collected, if at all, from *any* member of the kinship or friendship circle when it falls due, whether or not he or she was a member at the time the obligation was undertaken. The result of failure to meet a reciprocal obligation is not bankruptcy but the destruction of that particular reciprocal relationship. Parents disown children. Siblings cease to communicate. Friendships end. Blood feuds begin.

Reciprocity relationships may permeate the economy, but they are confined to specific kinship and friendship networks. They are thus atomized and necessarily small-scale. They cannot link all households in the economy the way open markets do or the way nationwide taxation benefit systems do. Reciprocity is distinctly personal and attached to the person or family. As a principle for organizing economic activity, reciprocity is nonmarket *and* nonstate, and it has flourished under all sorts of economic systems. It has represented for centuries the main way that families and friends have traditionally protected the individual against both the vagaries of economic fortune and the arbitrary exercise of economic power by the state.

The Little Deal of the Brezhnev years extended to reciprocal economic relationships as well as to petty marketeering. The ever-present condition of excess demand in the Soviet economy not only creates opportunities for personal gain to individuals willing to act as middlemen or to intercept rents the state declines to gather from deficit goods and services but enhances the benefits that flow from membership in kinship and friendship networks. It pays to have a relative or friend located strategically with respect to deficit commodities: someone in Moscow to buy scare goods when they appear and to store them for your arrival from Omsk; someone employed by a retail fur outlet to set aside a *real* fur coat from the next shipment, before the store opens; someone in admissions at the university to shepherd your child's papers. The very structure and functioning of the Soviet economy, with its deficit commodities and services and its faltering, uneven retail distribution system, reinforces the benefits of reciprocity systems and therefore reinforces kinship and friendship ties.

Brezhnev's Little Deal included a tacit accommodation with private reciprocity systems as well as with petty private marketeering and enterprise. Soviet citizens have been openly allowed to obtain goods and services not merely *nalevo* but also *po druzhbe* (through friends), *po znakomstvu* (through acquaintances), *po sviazi* (through connections), and *po protektsii* (through protection). In its most attractive form reciprocity reflects the concern of family and friends for one another. In its least attractive form it is nepotism, favoritism, and cronyism. Reciprocity has the advantage of not being a straight economic exchange, and thus the risk of a penalty for setting a deficit commodity aside, for using state enterprise tools and/or spare parts for private advantage, for allowing someone to jump the queue for tickets to the Bolshoi or Taganka theater, and so forth, is much less.

Although participation in reciprocity networks is less risky in general than petty marketeering or enterprise, many reciprocity transactions violate either the letter or the spirit of the law. Every adult member of society is in a position to do some kind of favor for someone else. The main function of reciprocity systems in the USSR has been to allow individuals access to deficit commodities or services that would otherwise be impossible or uncertain. A few examples will be sufficient to illustrate this point.

With reciprocity systems it is difficult to know where friendship or kinship feeling ends and pure economic calculation begins. A friend or relative on the admissions committee to Moscow State University is of incalculable value if one has university-age children. A friend or relative with access to tickets to the Bolshoi or the Taganka theater is essential if an ordinary Moskovite wants to attend performances. Friendly relations with the neighborhood butcher pay dividends in an economy in which all cuts of *any* red meat are two rubles a kilo. Having relatives or friends who know you are "in the market" for a special type of boot, fur coat, or rare book will maximize your chance of satisfying this desire. If you live outside the main cash-and-carry supermarkets of the USSR, that is, outside Moscow, Leningrad, Kiev, and a few other major state retail markets, kin or friends are essential to a reasonable style of life, regardless of income level. The payoff of reciprocal relationships is so great that young people find it difficult to survive independently of their families, for the family is the nexus of reciprocity networks. Kin and friends are thus both more desirable and more burdensome in the USSR.

As in the case of petty marketeering and private enterprise, any given reciprocal transaction may involve illegal or questionable elements. Privately repairing a friend's TV set may involve company time, company tools, and/or illegally acquired spare parts. Setting aside a fur coat for kin or friend to buy later, even without a private markup, could bring the law down upon one's head. Giving a regular customer better than average cuts of meat at no extra cost, but in return for a future possible gift of American-made cigarettes or an occasional "single" to the Bolshoi, could mean trouble. And it is not difficult to imagine much more gross violations of law in the realm of nepotism, expensive durables, or contacts with foreigners from hard-currency countries.

The Future of the Little Deal

I have argued that the Brezhnev regime contracted a deal with the Soviet population, especially with the urban population, tacitly agreeing to overlook and thus condone petty private marketeering and enterprise as well as instances of petty reciprocal advantage. The critical element has been the state's willingness to permit an expansion throughout Soviet society of the quest for the individual's, but especially the individual household's, gain, as opposed to collectivist and traditionalist socialist aims. This implicit contract has tended not only to increase the rewards for petty materialism and self- or family-centered acquisitiveness but to strengthen the family as *the* fundamental societal unit of authority, employment, and distribution.

The Little Deal has also had an important impact upon the distribution of real income in the USSR. There can be little doubt that the distribution of real product (and services) in the USSR more nearly corresponded with the diverse preferences of the population as a result of the Little Deal than would have been the case otherwise, absent thoroughgoing reform of the production, pricing, and distribution of consumer goods and services. Because time—especially queuing time, but even time to negotiate, plan, and scout—has been so important a requisite for acquisition of deficit commodities in the USSR, the Little Deal has tended, in all likelihood, to produce a more equal distribution of real consumption than would otherwise have been the case, for time is distributed essentially equally on a per capita basis.

Ironically, the Brezhnev government was not prepared to accept fully this implication of the Little Deal. As a result, and as testimony to the effectiveness of petty private marketeering and private reciprocity systems, Brezhnev expanded "special-access" stores for the state's own reciprocity "partners." Where scarcity of the most desirable consumer goods and services is a chronic feature of the economic landscape, the privilege of jumping the queue is potentially so powerful an incentive to work and so gratifying a reward for loyalty that it would be surprising had the Brezhnev regime denied itself use of these techniques. Thus, special-access stores, "closed medical clinics," and similar special distribution systems multiplied during the later Brezhnev years, for party members, high officials, successful scientists, artists, workers in priority industries, and others of importance to the state.

The growth of special distribution and of limited-access outlets highlights a chronic dilemma for Soviet leadership. The thrust of Marxism is toward equity in the distribution of (real) income, regardless of "rents" of ability, location, special training, and so forth. But "equity" seems to fly in the face of the need to reward those who are prepared to make a special effort to become skilled, to accept extra responsibilities, to work efficiently, or to render a full day's work.

The tension between the desire to ensure that each citizen has his or her needs met and the need to motivate each to contribute his or her best is not new. The tension between "moral," or spiritual, incentives and material incentives antedates Marxism by many centuries, and no clear resolution has been achieved anywhere, whether sought by religious, secular, or revolutionary organizations. Acceptance of the imperative of material incentives pushes Soviet leadership toward increased use of markets, money, and other pecuniary institutions, that is, toward accepting operation of the "law of value" and of "commodity production" under socialism. Aspiration of the leaders for a society governed by "moral" incentives pushes Soviet leadership toward a completely different model, one in which a small, but *pure,* minority imposes its spiritual aims on the majority. The Soviet government is not the first institution in the history of Western civilization to be faced with this choice; nor is it the first to try first one and then the other, and then to reconsider.

What is the future of the Little Deal now that Brezhnev's regime has been replaced? The most fundamental issue, as I suggested earlier, is that of systemwide reform versus the Little Deal. Because of his background with the secret police (KGB), there was speculation that Andropov was not happy with what I have described as Brezhnev's Little Deal. It implicitly sanctioned petty illegal activities and implicitly decriminalized a wide range of petty economic crimes. And it probably also contributed to a widespread contempt for the law. Andropov's reported distaste for the Little Deal would therefore have been quite understandable. Chernenko gave mixed signals about continuation of the Little Deal during his brief rule, and it is much too early to anticipate what Gorbachev will do.

There are, however, some constants that any policy will have to confront. One way to eliminate petty marketeering and enterprise and the most blatant and undesirable forms of reciprocity is to initiate systemwide macroreforms designed to eliminate the rewards that the system now affords those activities. This would require increasing the prices of deficit commodities and services to equilibrium levels, which would eliminate the "scarcity rents" that so tempt individuals today. It would require increased powers by which enterprise managers could reward good, efficient workers and penalize the poor, inefficient workers. Reform would be required also to ensure that goods and services produced in state enterprises are distributed solely according to ability to pay, regardless of the location of the customer. This would require a complete overhaul of the retail distribution system to reflect consumer preferences and to overcome geographical obstacles. In the end, reform would have to include improvements in product and service quality and, in all likelihood, an increased share of resources flowing to the household sector.

This is a tall order, and it is not surprising that Brezhnev and his government were intimidated by the prospect. Hence, the Little Deal was an accommodation that required neither major reform nor a significant reallocation of resources, only ideological retrenchment.

There is every reason to expect that the new leadership under Mikhail Gorbachev will also be intimidated by what the abrogation of the Little Deal would entail. The establishment of equilibrium, or market-clearing, prices in state retail outlets would have to be accomplished in one fell swoop. Prices would have to be raised to or above equilibrium levels at once, or things would in fact get worse. A general popular expectation of a sequence of price rises over time would only make matters worse by encouraging spending now rather than later when prices will be higher.

The problem presented by the system of prices that now exists in the Soviet economy is as much one of incorrect relative prices as it is underpricing in general. The reluctance of the state to revise prices periodically over the last twenty-five to thirty years has caused prices of most food products, for example, to be underpriced relative to manufactures. But the problem is even more complex than this because the costs of producing various food products and the various consumer manufactures and services have changed over time at different rates. And wholesale prices are similarly out of alignment. Merely setting "correct" prices would itself, therefore, be a horrendous task.

Assuming that the regime is successful in establishing market-clearing prices, the result on the day they became effective would be a massive redistribution of real income. The precise impacts would be difficult to specify. In general, however, real purchasing power would be redistributed more unequally than before the reform because the ability and willingness of marketeers to spend time queuing would no longer count. Those with money income as well as those with money savings would benefit differentially. This answer must be qualified, however, by the fact of kinship and friendship networks. Marketeers who were "rich" in well-placed and numerous kin and friends would lose relative to those who were poor in such relationships at the time of the reform. Similarly, citizens who had access to special stores, special distributions, and other similar queue-jumping perquisites would lose real purchasing power.

It appears, therefore, that the privileged, the poor, and the gregarious would all stand to lose real purchasing power as a result of the establishment of market-clearing prices, and that is potentially a powerful alliance. Price reforms would, of necessity, have to be accompanied by an income policy designed to cushion the impact of the reform, and, once again, piecemeal reforms would be worse than no reform at all.

The Soviet experience with socialism has produced several important lessons. Among the most important is that socialization of production and distribution politicizes even the pettiest economic problem. Thus, whether or not to change a given price must be taken on political rather than economic grounds.

Political wisdom would argue for gradual adjustments of prices toward equilibrium levels. Economic wisdom argues decisively for a once-and-for-all adjustment. The outcome is a deadlock that no regime since Stalin has been able to break. It will be interesting to see whether the new administration will be able to deal more effectively with the economy than Brezhnev's did. When all is said and done, there is much to be said for continuation of the Little Deal.

NOTES

1. Vera S. Dunham, *In Stalin's Time: Middle-class Values in Soviet Fiction* (New York: Cambridge University Press, 1976), esp. pp. 3–5.

2. See, for example, the pronouncements in J. V. Stalin, *Economic Problems of Socialism in the U.S.S.R.* (Peking: Foreign Languages Press, 1972).

3. Consider, for example, Khrushchev's prediction: "In the coming 10 years *all Soviet People will be able to obtain consumer goods in sufficiency, and in the following 10 years the consumer demand will be met in full.*" *Documents of the 22nd Congress of the CPSU,* vol 2: "Report on the Program of the Communist Party of the Soviet Union," October 17, 1961 (New York: Crosscurrents Press, 1961), p. 85.

4. See Alastair McAuley, *Economic Welfare in the Soviet Union: Poverty, Living Standards, and Inequality* (Madison: University of Wisconsin Press, 1979); Michael Ellman, "A Note on the Distribution of Earning in the USSR under Brezhnev," *Slavic Review* 39, no. 4 (December 1980); Basile

Kerblay, "Social Inequality in the USSR," *Problems of Communism* (January-February 1982); Alec Nove, *An Economic History of the USSR* (New York: Penguin Books, 1982), esp. pp. 347–49.

5. Statement of the Honorable Henry Rowen, Chairman, National Intelligence Council, CIA, Before the Joint Economic Committee, Congress of the United States, December 1, 1982 (mimeo), pp. 5–6.

6. For a discussion, see James R. Millar, *The ABCs of Soviet Socialism* (Urbana: University of Illinois Press, 1981), esp. pp. 182–87.

7. The magnitude and burden of military expenditures remains a matter of dispute. See, for example, Franklin D. Holzman, *The Soviet Economy: Past, Present, and Future* (New York: Foreign Policy Association, 1982), pp. 28–31.

8. See n.6; see also the preliminary findings of the Soviet Interview Project.

9. Nove, *An Economics History,* p. 368.

10. See, for example, Kenneth E. Boulding, *Economic Analysis* (3d ed., New York: Harper & Brothers, 1955), chap. 37.

11. Gur Ofer, *The Service Sector in Soviet Economic Growth: A Comparative Study* (Cambridge: Harvard University Press, 1973).

12. For a good, concise description, see Gregory Grossman, "The 'Second Economy' of the USSR," *Problems of Communism* 26 (September-October 1977):25–40.

13. See, for example, Karl Polanyi, *The Great Transformation* (Boston: Beacon Press, 1957), esp. chap. 4.

14

Perestroika and Glasnost':
Gorbachev's Gamble on
Youth and Truth

Between 1970 and 1984, more than 125,000 Soviet citizens emigrated from the Soviet Union to the United States. The presence of this large and diverse living archive in the West offers a rare opportunity for Western students of Soviet society to learn about everyday life in the USSR using survey techniques that are commonly applied in the West but are almost nonexistent in socialist countries. I have directed large-scale, systematic interviews with thousands of these former Soviet citizens, and the data thus obtained form the basis of my evaluation of Mikhail Gorbachev's political gamble. My purpose is to analyze the sources of support for and resistance to Gorbachev's policies.

Gorbachev has labeled one plank of his political platform *perestroika* (reconstruction), which deals with the renovation of the Soviet economy. Anyone who has visited the USSR and done any shopping has come across signs that indicate a particular store is closed *na remont* (for repairs or renovation). *Perestroika* carries a similar meaning: namely, the economy has lost its dynamism and needs to be brought up-to-date and/or put into efficient working order. The other plank is called *glasnost'* (transparency) and describes the conditions under which future policy and political actions generally are to take place. The closest analogue in the United States is probably the so-called sunshine laws, which require that certain kinds of decisions undertaken by political entities be made in public forums and therefore subject to public scrutiny. *Glasnost'* is supposed to accomplish the same thing in the Soviet Union; that is, it is a way to enforce accountability of governmental bodies to the public.

A revised version of this essay was presented at the Fourth Annual Lawrence Jepson Symposium, "Soviet-American Economic Relations: Implications for the Midwest," at the University of Northern Iowa, April 5–6, 1988.

Why *perestroika?* Since the 1960s, when I first started teaching students about the Soviet socialist economy, rates of growth have systematically declined—for example, from a 10 percent rate of growth of industrial production in 1951–55 to 2 percent per year for 1985–88. Labor productivity, technical innovation, and standard of living increases have all shown similar declines over time in the USSR. Meanwhile, Western capitalist economies have picked up some momentum, making the relative comparison even more bleak for a Soviet leadership committed to proving that socialism is the superior system. *Perestroika* is supposed to correct this imbalance by generating new energy, higher productivity, more innovation, and, in general, a more efficient economic system. Success will depend upon the ability of Gorbachev to capture the imagination and support of the new generation of Soviet citizens, notably of youth.

Why *glasnost'?* The policy of *glasnost'* is designed to restore the credibility of Soviet leadership. For years Soviet leaders have actually ignored the truth as much as they have distorted it deliberately. Airplane crashes have not been reported unless foreign citizens were aboard. Serious malfunctions of citywide heating or electric power systems were simply ignored in the press. When infant mortality statistics took a turn for the worse in recent years, the solution was to stop publishing the figures, and the same was done with grain harvest data when output failed dramatically. Failure to publish or to discuss in public the country's social problems or economic short-comings did not—indeed, could not—disguise the fact of failure. It was a form of lying by omission, and as such it helped to undermine the reputation of Soviet leadership and the government for honesty and concern. *Glasnost'* is, then, a means to achieve *perestroika;* it represents a commitment by the leadership to be accountable for failures as well as successes, a commitment to operate and make decisions in the open sunlight. As you might imagine, many established Soviet bureaucrats find this new policy completely wrong-headed and perhaps even foolhardy. However, the important thing to remember in our context is that *glasnost'* is being offered as a token in good faith by the Communist party and the political leadership to Soviet citizens in return for a commitment by them to *perestroika.* Without *glasnost', perestroika* has no chance of success.

Sources of Support and Alienation in Gorbachev's USSR

The data upon which the analysis presented below is based were collected by the Soviet Interview Project (SIP) and are part of a larger project designed to discover from recent emigrants from the USSR how the Soviet system really works and how Soviet citizens work the system for their own benefit. The data analyzed here were gathered in 1983–84 by a general survey (G1) in which 2,793 individuals, or 79 percent of the sample, were interviewed in person for approximately three hours by means of a structured, Russian-language questionnaire. The sampling frame consisted of 33,624 individuals who arrived in the United States between January 1, 1979, and March 30, 1983, and who were between twenty-one and seventy years of age at the time of arrival. The sample was stratified by ethnic origin, educational attainment, region of origin, and city size. Stratification was designed to maximize heterogeneity. The referent population is defined operationally as the "adult, European population of large and medium-sized cities in the USSR."[1]

Although the overall assessment of most former Soviet citizens who have immigrated to the United States regarding life in the USSR is not in doubt, SIP respondents were able to differentiate between those aspects of the Soviet social system they repudiated and those about which they remained positive. Attitudes of SIP respondents might, of course, have been affected negatively by any difficulties they encountered in leaving the USSR and by their experiences in the West. We sought to minimize these latter influences by asking survey respondents to base their answers on their experiences, attitudes, and beliefs during what we called the "last normal period of life" (LNP) in the Soviet Union, which was defined as the five-year period ending at the time the respondent's life changed because of the decision to emigrate. The LNP ended for most respondents at the time they applied for permission to leave; and for the vast majority of the G1 sample, the LNP ended in 1978 or 1979. Interviewers were trained to remind respondents to focus on their LNP, and thus on a period in their lives before the decision was made to leave the USSR, in formulating their answers.

Westerners tend to think that Soviet citizens are thoroughly discontented with their lives and with all aspects of the Soviet economy and politics. The SIP survey shows that this is not the case. The questionnaire called, for example for self-evaluations by respondents of the quality of life during the LNP. Respondents were asked whether they had been "very satisfied," "somewhat satisfied," "somewhat dissatisfied," or "very dissatisfied" with their standard of living during their LNP in the Soviet Union (see table 1). Approximately 11 percent, or 310 respondents, reported that they had been "very satisfied"; 60.1 percent, or 1,653 individuals, were either "very satisfied" or "somewhat satisfied"; and only 14.7 percent claimed to

TABLE 1. Self-assessed Satisfaction

		Standard of living	Housing	Goods	Job	Health care
		"How satisfied were you with":				
Very satisfied	N	310	645	139	711	518
	%	11.3	23.3	5.1	31.8	19.3
Somewhat satisfied	N	1,343	1,213	488	1,054	1,142
	%	48.8	43.8	17.8	47.1	42.6
Somewhat dissatisfied	N	694	379	634	303	570
	%	25.2	13.7	23.2	13.5	21.3
Very dissatisfied	N	403	533	1,477	170	450
	%	14.7	19.2	53.9	7.6	16.8
Total	N	2,750	2,770	2,738	2,238	2,680
	%	100	100	100	100	100
Missing values	N	43	23	55	555	113

Source: SIP General Survey Codebook, release 3.1

have been "very dissatisfied" with their standard of living in the USSR before deciding to leave. The remaining 25.2 percent were "somewhat dissatisfied."

Even though our respondents had voted with their feet about whether to live in the Soviet Union, they nonetheless represent a heterogeneous group with respect to self-evaluations of their standard of living while they were Soviet citizens. This suggests that they can tell us something about the ultimate sources of both support for and alienation from various aspects of Soviet life. What is more, variation among our respondents may be used to analyze the characteristics that predispose Soviet citizens toward alienation or support with respect to specific Soviet institutions and conditions of life.

Most Western observers of Soviet life have indicated surprise at the high proportion of former citizens who reported some degree of satisfaction with their standard of living. It is interesting to note in this connection that length of time since departure from the USSR had no significant impact upon reported satisfaction or dissatisfaction while in the Soviet Union.[2] We also know that the majority of respondents were satisfied with their incomes in the United States, which suggests that the LNP concept was in fact successful in minimizing contamination subsequent to the decision to leave the USSR. Moreover, the response on standard of living is consistent with the proportion of respondents who reported an economic reason for leaving the USSR. We coded up to three answers for each respondent to the open-ended question "What were your reasons for leaving the Soviet Union?" Only 27 percent gave an economic motive as either the first, second, or third reason, as opposed, for example, to totals of 46 percent who cited a religious/ethnic reason and 43 percent who gave a political reason.[3] Economic discontent was clearly not the prime motive for emigration by SIP respondents.

In considering determinants of reported satisfaction with standard of living in the USSR, the degree of satisfaction with housing in the LNP was the single most important factor. About 23 percent of respondents (see table 1) reported themselves to have been "very satisfied" with their housing when they were living in the Soviet Union; a total of 67.1 percent, or 1,858 resopndents in all, reported themselves to have been either "very satisfied" or "somewhat satisfied"; and only 19.2 percent were "very dissatisfied."

Most knowledgeable students of Soviet society have found these statistics difficult to believe. Soviet living space per capita is sparse even by European standards, not to mention comparison with space available per household member in the United States, and the quality of much housing in the USSR is also visibly poor in terms of both maintenance and amenities. Yet it is possible to test the credibility of our respondents' subjective evaluations of their USSR housing with objective data collected from each respondent. One expects on a priori grounds for satisfaction with housing to vary directly with square meters available per member of the family, and our respondents are not exceptional. Living space per capita is the single most significant determinant of reported satisfaction with housing. Moreover, it is known on the basis of studies throughout the world that dwellers who own their own homes normally report themselves as more satisfied with their housing than do renters, and this is true for the SIP resondents also. About one-third of them owned their own homes or apartments in the USSR, and they were significantly more satisfied than those who rented.

In the Soviet case, there is a more important determinant of satifaction or dissatisfaction with housing than ownership and that is the extent to which the respondent (and family) had been obliged to share facilities with members of other households. Soviet citizens have unambiguously rejected communal housing. The more they had to share, such as kitchens, toilets, and the like, the less likely they were to report satisfaction with their housing in the Soviet Union. The least satisfied were students living in dormitories or individuals living in "corners" of other peoples' homes—those who were obliged to share everything: kitchen, bath, living space, hallway, entrance, and exit. These results confirm the political wisdom of both the extraordinary home-building and home-renovation program that has been underway for more than three decades in major Soviet cities and the arrangements by state, local, and economic enterprise authorities for the development and expansion of private condominium ownership.

As is clear from several independent sections of the questionnaire, housing is a highly salient factor in the lives of Soviet citizens. We asked, for example, whether the respondents had ever contacted a Soviet official or an official agency about any matter (other than emigration) during their LNP. Nineteen percent had done so, more than half of them with regard to housing. Interestingly, a majority of these respondents reported that their complaints (or requests) had ultimately been satisfied to some degree.[4] Another indication of the salience of housing is the fact that some 192 couples in the SIP sample who had lived together during their LNP and who were still living together in the United States at the time of the interview reported essentially identical totals for square meters of living space in the USSR, even though members of each pair were interviewed separately (either simultaneously or sequentially) and could not have known the other's answer.[5]

Additional confirmation is provided by the results of a parallel interview project among former Soviet citizens of German extraction, modeled on SIP, that was conducted in West Germany by the Oesteuropa Institute of Munich.[6] The German-Russian sample differs substantially in composition from the SIP sample in that it had a significant representation of rural and small-city population and was mainly Protestant, blue-collar, and less well educated. Despite these differences, answers to the satisfaction questions correspond very closely to those received by SIP. Sixty-nine percent of the German-Russian sample reported that they had been either "very satisfied" or "somewhat satisfied" with their housing in the USSR, and 60.7 percent reported that they had been either "very satisfied" or "somewhat satisfied" with their standard of living, percentages that are essentially identical to SIP responses for the same categories (see table 1).

The former Soviet citizens who responded to the SIP general survey were, of course, far from satisfied with all aspects of Soviet economic life. Only 5 percent reported that they had been "very satisfied" with the availability of goods during their last normal period of life in the Soviet Union (see table 1), compared to an overwhelming 77.1 percent who had been either "very dissatisfied" or "somewhat

TABLE 2. Dietary Frequencies

		"How often did you eat/drink":				
		Meat	Cheese	Kefir	Milk	Eggs
Daily	N	575	738	635	672	514
	%	62.4	80.0	68.9	72.9	55.7
Several times per week	N	265	144	220	155	319
	%	28.7	15.6	23.9	16.8	34.6
Several times per month	N	16	14	21	25	40
	%	1.7	1.5	2.3	2.7	4.3
Never	N	56	19	35	63	32
	%	6.1	2.1	3.8	6.8	3.5
Total	N	918	919	917	919	916
	%	99.00	99.00	99.00	99.00	99.00
Missing values	N	4	3	5	3	5
	%	0.4	0.3	0.5	0.3	0.5

Source: SIP General Survey Codebook, release 3.1.

dissatisfied." This result is not surprising to anyone who has done any shopping in the Soviet Union. Queues are still ubiquitous for fresh foodstuffs and for quality merchandise of all types. In fact, the smart Soviet shopper will join a queue before looking at or even learning what is being sold, because delay could cost several places in line. One can always check out the merchandise after establishing a place in the queue.

Somewhat surprising in the SIP findings is the fact that many goods that are scarce in state stores (according to our respondents) are nonetheless consumed frequently. Meat, for example, was reported as "usually" scarce by over 80 percent of SIP respondents—in fact, the phrase "There is no meat" is common even in major cities—but 62.4 percent claimed that they ate meat every day, and 28.7 percent said they ate it several times per week (see table 2). Only 7.8 percent reported eating meat several times a month or not at all. Similar high weekly consumption rates were reported for cheese, kefir (yogurt), milk, and eggs. This suggests that Soviet consumers are obtaining a significant portion of these products outside of the official state retail network. Special distribution of food products—for example, by place of work or as part of one's social, political, or economic status—is more important than the unofficial *nalevo,* or the black market, as an alternative to the official retail network.

The dissatisfaction consumers felt about the availability of goods did not arise, therefore, from malnutrition or serious deprivation but from frustration with the system of production and distribution as a whole, based in part upon thwarted expectations. Indeed, better-off consumers were more dissatisfied. Contrary to what has been believed in the West, however, the dissatisfaction of the better-off citizens did not stem from an inability to spend their income, for they had lower saving rates than those who reported lesser degrees of dissatisfaction. Dissatisfaction for these citizens stemmed instead from an inability to purchase the assortment they preferred for their market baskets. The picture one obtains of better-off consumers is of individuals who spent a disproportionate amount of working time on personal shopping. They also tended to spend disproportionately more time on the legal private market (*rynok*) and on unofficial markets (*nalevo*), yet they still failed to satisfy their preferences in an optimal way with respect to the composition and quality of their market baskets.[7]

It is important to note that our respondents differed in degree of satisfaction on demographic variables other than income. Older respondents, for example, tended to be less critical of shortages, presumably because of a longer reference period extending back into the years of extreme privation caused by the industrialization drive of the 1930s, World War II, and postwar reconstruction. Citizens from the largest cities and the better educated tended to be the most critical of the availability of goods, even though they were relatively better off according to objective measures and by self-evaluation of their economic status. Their reference groups were perhaps outside the country for they were the most likely to have been informed about life beyond the borders of the USSR via foreign and domestic media.

Buying goods and services in the Soviet Union requires a time budget as well as a money budget. Those with proportionally more time than money benefit differentially from the fact that the best goods inevitably require queuing; those with more money than time are likely to become angry and frustrated because they may be required to steal time from work to spend their incomes. The latter also are obliged to spend a disproportionate share of their incomes in private markets, where prices are higher than in state retail stores, or on quasi-legal and even outright illegal channels, which puts them at a certain personal risk in addition to paying higher prices.

Interestingly, these better-off customers did not prefer shopping in private markets when they were living in the USSR, and very few SIP respondents felt that higher prices ought to have been charged in state stores. What they seem to have wanted was supplies of goods as plentiful as existed in private markets but at low official state retail prices—prices that have required over a 50 billion ruble annual state subsidy in recent years. The shortages met with in the state stores were blamed on poor production, not subsidized prices, while high prices on private goods were considered gouging by the peasantry. The most fortunate consumers would appear to have been those with relatively high household income and with several nonworking "shoppers" in the form of grandparents or other senior relatives.

All of this suggests that reform of the retail distribution network will prove difficult for Mikhail Gorbachev. SIP respondents did not agree that a policy of higher prices in state retail outlets would be acceptable as a solution to the problem of queues. What is more, although a very large majority indicated a preference for private agricultural production, there was no indication of a similar preference for privatization of the economy in general. The preferred solution—increased quantities of products at existing subsidized prices—represents a desire to eat one's cake and have it too, which is not an encouraging outlook for Soviet leadership seeking to rationalize the economy. Things will not get better with the passage of time, according to SIP findings, because the most supportive group will diminish over the years as the population becomes better educated, more urban, and more cosmopolitan, for each characteristic yields less-satisfied citizens. Moreover, a significant majority of SIP respondents indicated that supply conditions had deteriorated during their LNP, that is, toward the end of the 1970s and in the early 1980s.

Jobs represented a very different domain of satisfaction. In fact, SIP respondents recalled their jobs as the single most satisfying aspect of economic life in the USSR. Fully 78.9 percent reported themselves to have been either "very satisfied" or "somewhat satisfied" with their jobs during their last normal period of life in the Soviet Union (the figure for the German survey is 76.7 percent); only 7.6 percent of SIP respondents represented themselves as having been "very dissatisfied" (see table 1). For all but professional workers, job satisfaction depended only marginally upon satisfaction with income earned on the job. When asked, for example, about low productivity in the workplace, over 60 percent of those who had been employed in their LNP put the blame on inadequate material incentives, and this included especially those who had been occupied on the workshop floor, that is, the regular workers and their foremen.[8] This has an obvious positive implication for Gorbachev's desire to rationalize production through *perestroika*.

Despite poor or poorly designed material incentives, however, people evidently still found a great deal of satisfaction with their work. The single most significant determinant of satisfaction or dissatisfaction was whether one was able to work in the specialty for which he or she was trained.[9] Overall satisfaction or dissatisfaction with one's job was also associated with job security, listed by 37 percent of blue-collar workers as a main source of job satisfaction (compared to less than 1 percent who listed income as the key). Job conditions proved important also, especially whether one had the equipment and information required to do the job well, and being able to work in the specialty for which one was trained was of particular importance to white-collar workers. Poor working conditions, in fact, were mentioned by only about 1 percent of the respondents as a significant cause of low productivity. It is ironic that workers who are considered unproductive actually appear to enjoy their jobs.[10] These conditions would seem to suggest that improving incentives—and, in the end, that means consumer satisfaction—would provide considerable leverage with respect to productivity increases.

It is striking to note in the SIP results that women reported even higher levels of satisfaction with their jobs than did men, despite the fact that women earned considerably less. On average for the sample, women earned only about 71 percent as much as men,[11] which is slightly better than the situation in the United States. Of particular interest in this comparison is the fact that Soviet gender differential in earnings derived predominantly from differential pay for similar jobs, whereas in the United States job segregation has been the main factor, with jobs dominated by women paying significantly less than other types of employment. Only about 10 percent, or one-third, of the differential in the USSR could be attributed to occupational segregation. Despite this large earnings differential, women reported greater job satisfaction than did men, and they registered one of the highest rates of labor-force participation in the world: 80 percent.

With the exception of dissatisfaction with goods availability, women in the SIP sample generally reported higher levels of satisfaction, or lower levels of dissatisfaction, along all dimensions than did men when recalling life during their last normal years in the Soviet Union. It is not at all clear what this signifies, especially in the light of answers to the question "Who has it better in the Soviet Union?" Three percent of the men and 2 percent of the women in the sample reported that "women have it better." This response no doubt reflects general awareness among men and women of the "double burden" Soviet women carry for family as well as work responsibilities, a burden that can be measured in part by its impact on leisure time. Women, for example, spent much more time shopping, on average, per day than did the men, and women participated in leisure activities only half as much, on average, per day as men. The relatively greater sense of satisfaction female members of the sample expressed about their lives in the Soviet Union does not appear to be supported by the objective data collected about their experiences. It derives perhaps from subjective evaluations rooted in the very significant role women play in family life in Soviet society.

In any event, evidence on job satifaction is somewhat ambiguous with respect to Gorbachev's reforms. Workers place a high value on job security, and they seem to value egalitarianism too. Therefore, attempts to raise incentives generally will be appreciated, but attemps to differentiate incentives to reward better workers or to lessen job security for those who do not work well will meet serious worker resistance.

Health care in the contemporary Soviet Union has been the subject of considerable study and concern in the West in recent years, yet SIP data suggest widespread *satisfaction.* Over 19 percent of the sample stated that they had been "very satisfied" with free public health care during their last normal period of life in the Soviet Union, and 61.9 percent reported having been either "very satisfied" or "somewhat satisfied" (see table 1). Consequently, if there is a health care crisis in the USSR, our respondents were unaware of it. Of course, they are not experts, but it remains significant that they did not perceive a crisis in health services.[12]

The answers to several of the survey questions provide indirect support for the conclusion that there is genuine and wide acceptance of socialized medicine among citizens in the USSR. We asked respondents, for example, "In what ways do you think that the United States could learn from the Soviet Union?" This was a completely open-ended question, and we coded up to three answers per respondent. Less than 17 percent said that there was "nothing" that could be learned (see table 3). Among the more positive responses, control of crime was number one and was mentioned as a first, second, or third lesson by a total of 50.9 percent of the sample. The educational system was number two, at 47.5 percent, and health care ranked third (27.8 percent). A random one-third of the sample was also asked what, if anything, they would keep if they had an opportunity to "create a system of government in the Soviet Union that is different from the one which currently exists." The Soviet medical care system was mentioned first, second, or third by 68.9 percent of those who

TABLE 3: What the United States Could Learn from the Soviet Union

| | "In what ways do you think that the United States could learn from the Soviet Union?" | | | |
	1st answer (%)	2nd answer (%)	3rd answer (%)	Total (%)
Crime; legal system	21.8	16.0	13.1	50.9
System of education; access to education	15.9	18.0	13.6	47.5
Health care	6.6	11.5	9.7	27.8
Military readiness	5.7	6.7	6.0	18.4
Child rearing/discipline	2.4	7.1	5.6	15.1
Upkeep of cities	2.6	5.2	6.4	14.3
Public transportation	1.7	3.0	5.6	10.3
Limit liberalism/freedom	3.4	2.1	1.9	7.4
Housing: price and quantity	1.4	2.1	2.9	6.4
Can learn nothing	16.8	0.1	—	16.9
Other	21.7	28.2	35.2	85.1
N =	2,545	1,344	662	4,551
Missing values	248	1,449	2,131	3,828

Source: SIP General Survey Codebook, release 3.1

agreed that something might be kept (see table 4). Overall, the survey establishes that there is substantial citizen support for free public medical care in the Soviet Union.

These findings regarding Soviet medical care support data gathered by the Harvard Refugee Project of the 1950s. Respondents to that survey also listed medical care, along with the educational system, as institutions worth preserving in any post-Bolshevik government.[13] The former Soviet citizens who have been interviewed in West Germany have also given a high ranking to both public health care and education.

General Patterns of Support and Alienation

As was indicated earlier, SIP results do suggest the existence of significant gender differences. Women report themselves as having been either "more satisfied" or "less dissatisfied" in general than men in every area tested except with respect to goods availability. Of particular salience is job satisfaction, where women report relatively high levels of satisfaction despite the fact that they earn less, are

TABLE 4. What to Keep from the Soviet System

	"Think for a moment about the Soviet system with its good and bad points. Suppose you could create a system of government in the Soviet Union that is different from the one which currently exists. What things in the present Soviet system would you want to keep in the new one?"			
	1st answer (%)	2nd answer (%)	3rd answer (%)	Total (%)
Health care	26.5	24.7	17.7	68.9
Free public education	12.2	29.5	5.4	47.1
Crime control	6.3	4.0	10.5	20.8
Job security	3.1	3.1	11.2	17.4
Inexpensive housing	1.1	1.5	10.2	12.8
Keep nothing	19.4	0.2	—	19.6

Source: SIP General Survey Codebook, release 3.1.

obliged to bear a disproportionate double burden represented by family responsibilities, and agree with the statement that "men have it better" in Soviet society. Women are also less likely to have participated in unconventional political activity, and they are less likely to have initiated the decision to leave the USSR. Relatively speaking, therefore, women represent a conservative force in Soviet society and thus a potential source of regime support.

The most striking demographic finding of SIP thus far, however, is the strength and pervasiveness of generational differences. Older respondents reported themselves as "more satisfied" or "less dissatisfied" along all dimensions of measurement, and this holds for almost any pair of aged-differentiated segments. It is widely believed that older members of any society are likely to report higher levels of satisfaction, but this is not the case cross-nationally. In recent years in Western Europe, for example, it is the young who have reported higher levels of satisfaction. The older generations therefore represent another conservative force in Soviet society, one that must be regarded as a "wasting asset." Gorbachev's policies thus appear to be responsive to the growing share of the population represented by postwar and post-Stalin generations.

There is other evidence to support the conclusion that the differences we have found are true generational differences, not merely life-cycle effects. Donna Bahry has pointed out, for example, the contrast with the Harvard Refugee Project of the 1950s, where it was the young who reported greater relative satisfaction with their earlier lives as Soviet citizens than did members of the older generations.[14] In fact, what one finds is that the current older SIP respondents were more satisfied as youths than are today's youth. This is supported further by the fact that when asked about brushes with the law and participation in unconventional activities, members of the older generations report such activities, if at all, as having occurred relatively recently in their lives, and thus at a later stage than for younger former citizens. According to Bahry: "The Soviet generation gap is indeed political. . . . In each case, the postwar and post-Stalin generations prove to be the most active: the most interested in public affairs, the most heavily engaged in 'mobilized participation,' but at the same time taking a greater part in unsanctioned study groups, protests, strikes, and other unconventional activities. Official Soviet ambivalence about the young would thus appear to be well founded."[15]

The dissatisfaction of youth with the economic, political, and cultural stagnation of the late Brezhnev years is, presumably, offset for the senior members of Soviet society by still-vivid memories of industrialization and the purges, World War II, and postwar reconstruction, and Stalinism in general. The enormous gains since Stalin seem to have made them more tolerant of flattening trends, or even trend reversals, in the quality of economic, political, and cultural life in the late 1970s and early 1980s.

There is more than a little evidence for this view. We asked our respondents a series of questions that required them to compare the Stalin, Khrushchev, and Brezhnev eras. These questions sought to elicit, for example, in which era censorship was the most instrusive and when it was the least. Similar questions were asked about economic inequality and privilege, nationality policy, and the role of the KGB. Let us divide the respondents according to those who were born in 1940 or earlier (the Stalin generation) and those born in 1941 or after (the post-Stalin generation), on the assumption that the younger group would not have reached political and historical consciousness before Stalin died in 1953. What we find is that a majority of the older group rated the Khrushchev era as the best and Stalin's as the worst. The younger group agreed upon the Khrushchev period as a kind of "golden age" but in most cases voted Brezhnev's the worst. Even with respect to the power of the KGB a significant minority of the post-Stalin generation voted Brezhnev's era as the worst.

We also asked our respondents to review a set of statements

about Soviet history during Stalin's time with the purpose of identifying those who were prepared to say something positive, however
mild, about Stalin. The majority of our respondents were unwilling
to do so; and the only significant minority that would do so was
found again among the youngest generations. Thus, if there is any
significant neo-Stalinism in the USSR today, it would be found among
the young. This says something about the teaching, or nonteaching,
of history in the Soviet Union, where leaders can become "unper-
sons" for entire generations of the population and where the past is
controlled and manipulated officially for contemporary political purposes. Indeed, young people from families that had suffered from
repression under Stalin were indistinguishable in their responses from
older generations. The family, presumably, was the teacher of true
Soviet history in these cases.[16]

As Donna Bahry and Brian Silver have shown,[17] additional
differences by age group may be seen in their evaluations of the
competence and honesty of regime leaders of eight key Soviet bureaucracies. Members of the older generations were less likely to
provide positive evaluations of either the competence or the honesty
of middle-elite regime leaders. Fifty-seven percent of all respondents,
for example, reported that "all" or "almost all" KGB leaders were
competent (as opposed to 66 percent for the best-regarded institution,
the Academy of Sciences). With respect to honesty (or integrity),
only 14 percent of all respondents said that most or all leaders of
the KGB were honest (as opposed to 35 percent for the Academy
of Sciences). The case for *glasnost'* could not be clearer. Unless the
honesty and competence of Soviet elite groups can be reestablished,
perestroika is doomed. World War II can no longer serve as a source
of leadership legitimacy. The cover-up must end, and corruption
must be rooted out. Otherwise, no one will pay attention to any
reform movement.

Educational differences among SIP respondents are almost as
striking as generational differences. The less well educated respondents were more likely to report satisfaction with housing, jobs,
medical care, and standard of living than were the better educated,
and they were less dissatisfied with the availability of goods. These
differences persist even when other differences such as age and region
of origin are controlled. This finding stands in contrast to the results
of the Harvard Refugee Project, wherein those who had advanced
their educational attainments under Soviet power tended to have
been more satisfied and accepting of basic Soviet institutions such
as public ownership of industry and limitations on the right to strike.
In fact, the strength of the positive relationship that was found by

the Harvard Refugee Project investigators between education and regime support led many contemporary observers to conclude that education could and was being used to shore up the regime. The frightening long-run prospect was of a nation of educated, but brainwashed, regime supporters.

SIP results show just the opposite for the effect of education upon regime support. Holding material reward constant, every increase in educational attainment, even at the lowest levels of education, decreases regime support and also relative satisfaction with life conditions. As educational attainment increases, so, normally, do material rewards in the Soviet system, but the subjective satisfaction SIP respondents extracted from material improvements did not keep pace.[18] Thus, former Soviet citizens in skilled blue-collar or white-collar and other middle-elite positions requiring relatively higher educational levels were more likely to report themselves as dissatisfied and to question regime values and its policies despite the fact that they represent, today, the principal beneficiaries of the social system created by the Bolshevik revolution. There is also the need for party and governmental agencies to establish moral as well as practical credibility. To continue to deny or ignore unpleasant reality is to alienate completely the most essential ingredient of reform: educated youth.

Conclusion

Analysis of the first general survey conducted by the Soviet Interview Project reveals some striking patterns that no Soviet specialist has previously had an opportunity to observe. The first, and probably the most significant in the short run for policies being proposed or implemented by Gorbachev, is the strength and character of generational differences within the urban population. Whether for reasons of educational silence about the harsh, turbulent years under Stalin or merely from present-mindedness and sheer impatience with the relative backwardness of Soviet consumer and citizen comforts, the young are highly involved and highly critical and thus reform-minded. The young and well educated are more likely than other groups to participate in both conventional and unconventional social and political activities.[19] The older generation is, on the contrary, more cautious, cynical, and conservative in its evaluation of the system and its prospects, and it is more likely to be passive as well. Educational influences reinforce this generational divergence, for the young are, in general, the better-educated members of Soviet society. Similarly, women tend to be less critical than men, and they also are

TABLE 5: What to Change in the Soviet System

	"What things in the present Soviet system would you be sure to change?"			
	1st answer (%)	2nd answer (%)	3rd answer (%)	Total (%)
Political system	27.0	6.6	6.5	40.1
Allow private enterprise	9.3	10.5	9.8	29.6
Control of speech	3.5	8.8	13.6	25.9
Collective-farm system	9.4	9.3	7.1	25.8
Enforce rights	3.5	11.1	10.2	24.8
One-party system	6.3	6.0	4.4	16.7
Economic planning	2.4	3.3	3.8	9.5
Internal passports	1.3	3.6	3.1	8.0
Everything	6.5	0.5	—	7.0

Source: SIP General Survey Codebook, release 3.1.

less well represented at the highest levels of attainment in the Soviet educational system as well as in top jobs. Gorbachev's gamble, then, is to win over educated Soviet youth to a rejuvenated party and political leadership.

Respondents were asked an open-ended question designed to elicit the nature and strengths of their retrospective criticisms of Soviet society as of the date of the SIP interview: "Think for a moment about the Soviet system with its good and bad points. Suppose you could create a system of government in the Soviet Union that is different from the one which currently exists. What things would you want to keep in the new one?" The answers reinforced those given earlier in response to the questions about what the United States could learn from the Soviet Union (see table 4). Public health care, free public education, crime control, job security, and inexpensive housing top the list. Note that all of these represent activities of the Soviet state that subsidize the welfare of the individual household member of the Soviet society.

Respondents were also asked "What things in the present Soviet system would you be sure to change?" A list of these responses is presented in table 5. Note that 40.1 percent would change the political system, as a first, second, or third answer, and 16.7 percent recommended changing the one-party system. The overall responses point to a desire for more political and economic diversity and for broader civil rights; but it is clear also that even after several years (on average) of life in the United States, only a few SIP respondents were prepared to repudiate entirely the Soviet political, economic, and social system. This suggests that, although difficult, the task Gorbachev has assumed is not a hopeless one. A certain amount of common ground exists between Soviet educated youth and the official elite.

Although many SIP respondents were critical of specific aspects of American life, for the most part they had succeeded in establishing themselves in the United States at the time of their interview. Almost 61 percent were employed and 6 percent (of adult immigrants) were attending school. Only 5.7 percent were truly unemployed; the rest were either keeping house, on pension, or otherwise occupied.

The criticism of the Soviet regime and dissatisfaction with Soviet economic and political life in general during the LNP as found among SIP respondents, hardly merits the label "dissent." These former Soviet citizens definitely were not revolutionaries; nor were they demonstrators. Over half of them (1,401) were defined by Rasma Karklins as "noncritical passives," for they offered neither criticism nor overt acts of any sort that might have been construed as hostile to the regime during their LNP. "Critical passives," who numbered 718 (26 percent of the sample), had held critical views but had not expressed them in even the mildest form, such as participating in an unofficial study group. Only 16 percent (445) of the respondents were both critical and activist in any degree during their last normal period of life in the Soviet Union and of these, no more than 2 percent might be considered active enough to warrant the label "dissident." The implication is that the regime is under pressure from reformists, not revolutionists; from individuals, not from any sort of organized opposition, whether loyal or not.[20] Once again, this is an encouraging sign for Gorbachev's reforms.

Insofar as we can project SIP findings upon the Soviet urban population, we may conclude that Soviet citizens who live in the most desirable cities (such as Moscow, Leningrad, and Kiev), have achieved the highest educational attainments, hold the most highly skilled jobs, earn the highest incomes, occupy the most comfortable housing, and dominate consumption in all markets, private as well as public — in short, the best and the brightest of Soviet society — are the least-satisfied members of that society and also the most ambiguous supporters of regime goals. This suggests that Gorbachev's pursuit of political reform and economic reconstruction is well founded in the desires and expectations of this critical mass of the young and the educated. However, SIP findings about specific attitudes, beliefs, and behaviors toward the essential ingredients of any such reforms —

such as the negative relationship between education and regime support, the gradual diminution to be anticipated in the ranks of the more supportive older and less-urbanized populations, the distaste for price adjustments in state stores, and the high premium workers place on job security — suggest that Gorbachev may find success for his reform program elusive. It also follows that the failure of Gorbachev's reforms would entail continued economic stagnation *and* continued calls for reform, not political unrest. SIP results suggest that it is not regime stability that is at stake but the image the Communist party has cultivated for itself as a force for progress and modernity and for successful competition with the advanced noncommunist world.

The results of the SIP survey suggest that Mikhail Gorbachev's gamble on youth and truth is well placed. The question remains, of course, whether the regime as a whole is willing to gamble heavily enough on truth to succeed in winning over Soviet youth. Failure to do so will further alienate youth and isolate the party of Lenin, dooming *perestroika* as a reform and creating conditions under which Gorbachev would be removed after the fashion of Khrushchev, as a "harebrained" reformer.

NOTES

1. Its is obvious even to people with little statistical sophistication that a survey of former Soviet citizens about their lives in the Soviet Union must suffer from a number of potential biases. The respondents are emigrants, which ipso facto makes them different from their former compatriots who did not, or could not, leave and who therefore also have not experienced life outside the USSR. For a full description of the project design and of the technical details regarding sampling frame, sample, and questionnaire, see James R. Millar (ed.), *Politics, Work and Daily Life in the USSR: A Survey of Former Soviet Citizens* (New York: Cambridge University Press, 1987), esp. chap. 1 and app. A.

2. Michael Swafford, Carol A. Zeiss, Carolyn S. Breda, and Bradley P. Bullock, "Response Efforts in SIP's General Survey of Soviet Emigrants," in Millar, *Politics, Work, and Daily Life in the USSR*, app. B, pp. 372–405.

3. The most frequently cited reason for leaving was to accompany family and/or friends (48 percent).

4. James R. Millar and Elizabeth Clayton, "Quality of Life: Subjective Measures of Relative Satisfaction," in Millar, *Politics, Work, and Daily Life in the USSR*, pp. 31–57.

5. Barbara Anderson and Brian D. Silver, "The Validity of Survey Responses: Insights from Interviews of Married Couples in a Survey of Soviet Emigrants," *Social Forces* 66 (December 1987):537–54.

6. For a description of this project, see Barbara Dietz, "Interviews with

Soviet German Emigrants as a Source of Information for Soviet Studies," SIP Working Paper #G4, University of Illinois, 1987.

7. Millar and Clayton, "Quality of Life."

8. Paul R. Gregory, "Productivity, Slack and Time Theft in the Soviet Economy," in Millar, *Politics, Work, and Daily Life in the USSR*, pp. 241–75.

9. Millar and Clayton, "Quality of Life."

10. It should be noted that only 20 percent of SIP work-force respondents attributed low productivity to poor worker behavior in the form of alcoholism, apathy, or laziness; and only 8 percent cited poor management. See Gregory, "Productivity, Slack and Time Theft in the Soviet Economy."

11. Paul Gregory and Janet Kohlhase, "The Earnings of Soviet Workers: Human Capital, Loyalty and Privilege (Evidence from the Soviet Interview Project)," SIP Working Paper #13, University of Illinois, 1986.

12. The health care area, along with goods availability, is an area in which SIP respondents perceived a significant decline in quality in recent years.

13. Alex Inkeles and Raymond A. Bauer, *The Soviet Citizen: Daily Life in a Totalitarian Society* (Cambridge, Mass.: Harvard University Press, 1959), esp. chap. 10.

14. Donna Bahry, "Politics, Generations and Change in the USSR," in Millar, *Politics, Work, and Daily Life in the USSR*, pp. 91–94.

15. Ibid., pp. 85–86.

16. Rasma Karklins, "The Dissent/Coercion Nexus in the USSR," SIP Working Paper #36, University of Illinois, 1987.

17. Donna Bahry and Brian D. Silver, "The Intimidation Factor in Soviet Politics: The Symbolic Uses of Terror," SIP Working Paper #31, University of Illinois, 1987.

18. Brian D. Silver, "Political Beliefs of the Soviet Citizen: Sources of Support for Regime Norms," in Millar, *Politics, Work, and Daily Life in the USSR*, pp. 100–141.

19. William Zimmerman, "Mobilized Participation and the Nature of the Soviet Dictatorship," in Millar *Politics, Work, and Daily Life in the USSR*, pp. 332–53. Bahry, "Politics, Generations and Change in the USSR."

20. Karklins, "The Dissent/Coercion Nexus in the USSR."

Index

Aggregate demand: chronic excess, 209, 214; during WWII, 152
Agrarian colonialism, 54
Agricultural surplus, xi, 27, 37, 40n, 41n, 53; differing conceptions of, xi–xii; extraction of, 93; formulation of, 41n; marketed surplus defined, 31; measurement of, 30–34; net surplus defined, 32; and nonempirical standards of appraisal, 34; in physical-volume measures, 29; role in rapid industrialization, xii; unconsumed surplus defined, 31
Agriculture (*see also* Collectivization; Kolkhoz; Sovkhoz; Family labor farm), 18, 96–101, 107–8; as Achilles' heel, x; American, 88n; capital stock of, 57; climatic differences in, 98; composition of labor force in, 101; contemporary model of Soviet, 91; decision-making authority in, 104; depecuniarization of, 93; diminishing returns to scale in, 104; education facilities in, 101; grain marketing, 71; as high priority in planning, 106; history of reforms in, 90–97; imports, 91; increased priority of, 161; infrastructure of, 101; large-scale, Marxist view of, 74–75; marketed surplus of, 43n; marketing during 1924, 13; mobilization of, 78; net material contribution to industry, 43, 46–47; net material trade surplus of,

47–48; pecuniarization of, 92, 94, 103; policies of Stalin, 34; policy during NEP, 46; prerequisites for modernization of, 97; private sector, 104; productivity, of, 75, 76, 104; returns to scale, 95; scale of enterprises, 104; sectoring criteria of, 60n; Stalinist model of, 91, 94; standard story of contribution to rapid development, 61n; structure of post-Stalinist, 106; subsidies to, 97, 109n; substitution of pecuniary, for in-kind payments, 94; unconsumed surplus, 42n; undercapitalization of, 101
—output: comparative growth, 94, 98, 100–106; gross, 31, 42n, 43n; during 1930s, 35, 58; after 1958, 187; poor performance of, x
—procurement: during collectivization, 33; compulsory, 78; four-channel system, 94, 253; system of, 39, 47, 57–59, 161
Anderson, Barbara, 287n
Andropov, Yuri, 265
Arms race, 190–92

Baby boom, postwar, 187, 252
Bahry, Donna L., 132n, 154n, 282, 283, 288n
Balance of trade, 63n
Bank policy, 215
Baran, Paul, 40n, 60n
Barsov, A. A, xii, 45–59, 60n, 61n, 63n, 70, 77, 82, 89n
Bauer, Raymond A., 288n
Belugin, Yu. M., 132n

James R. Millar, professor of international affairs and director of the Institute for Sino-Soviet Studies at George Washington University, is the author of *The ABCs of Soviet Socialism* and the editor of *The Soviet Rural Community* and *Politics, Work, and Daily Life in the USSR*. He spent 1988–89 as a fellow at the Kennan Institute for Advanced Russian Studies.

Susan J. Linz, associate professor of economics at Michigan State University, is the editor of *The Impact of World War II on the Soviet Union* and the co-editor of *Reorganization and Reform in the Soviet Economy*.